# BUILDING
# WINDOWS 95
# APPLICATIONS

KEVIN J. GOODMAN

M&T BOOKS

**M&T Books**
A Division of MIS:Press, Inc.
A Subsidiary of Henry Holt and Company, Inc.
115 West 18th Street
New York, New York 10011

© 1995 Kevin J. Goodman

Printed in the United States of America

**Library of Congress Cataloging-in-Publication Data**

```
Goodman, Kevin J.
    Building Windows 95 applications / Kevin Goodman.
        p.   cm.
    Indludes index.
    ISBN 1-55851-425-2
    1. Operating systems (Computers)  2. Microsoft Windows 95.
    I. Title.
    QA76.76.063G66344      1994                        94-43538
    005.265--dc20                                      CIP
```

98 97 96 95      4 3 2 1

| **Editor in Chief:** | Paul Farrell | **Managing Editor:** | Cary Sullivan |
|---|---|---|---|
| **Technical Editor:** | Alex Leavens | **Production Editor:** | Maya Riddick |

**Development Editor**   Michael Sprague

The programming information in this book is based on information for developing applications for Windows 95 made public by Microsoft as of February of 1995. Since this information was made public before the final release of the product, there may have been changes to some of the programming interfaces by the time the product is finally released. We encourage you to check the updated development information that should be part of your development system for resolving issues that might arise.

The end user information in this book is based on information on Windows 95 made public by Microsoft as of February of 1995. Since this information was made public before the release of the product, we encourage you to visit you local bookstore at that time for update books on Windows 95.

If you have a modem or access to the Internet, you can always get up-to-the-minute information on Windows 95 direct from Microsoft on WinNews:

| | |
|---|---|
| On CompuServe: | GO WINNEWS |
| On the Internet: | ftp://ftp.microsoft.com/PerOpSys/Win_News/Chicago |
| | http://www.microsoft.com |
| On AOL: | keyword WINNEWS |
| On Prodigy: | jumpword WINNEWS |
| On Genie: | WINNEWS file area on Windows RTC |

You can also subscribe to Microsoft's WinNews electronic Newsletter by sending Internet email to enews@microsoft.nwnet.com and putting the words SUBSCRIBE WINNEWS in the text of the email.

**DEDICATION**

*To my family*

# TABLE OF CONTENTS

# CHAPTER 1

# INTRODUCING 32-BIT WINDOWS

It may seem to some people that the introduction of Windows 95 is arriving just as thousands of programmers (and millions of users) are getting comfortable with Windows 3.1. But, in the software industry, innovation means developing something that your customers need *before* they know they need it. If you are one of the many Windows 3.1 developers, you know that Windows 95 is long overdue. If you are not a Windows 3.1 developer, perhaps it is because you already are aware of Windows 3.1's limitations! However, to demonstrate that a 32-bit operating system is not just an exercise in computer science, this chapter details the limitations of 16-bit computing and explains how 32-bit computing overcomes these limitations. This chapter also explains some of the nuances of programming for 32-bit operating systems in general and Windows 95 and Windows NT in particular.

Since writing the code that runs on a 32-bit operating system is just a small piece of the picture, this chapter also explains a little bit about Intel and RISC platforms so you can debug your code when things go wrong.

1

# THE ADVANTAGES OF 32-BIT COMPUTING

There are many reasons why 32-bit processors and operating systems are better than 16-bit processors. The tangible benefits can be drawn into four categories:

- ■■ The linear instead of segmented programming model
- ■■ More data and address space is available
- ■■ Complicated compiler support is not necessary
- ■■ Processors are optimized for 32-bit mode

We'll look at these advantages one a time.

## THE LINEAR PROGRAMMING MODEL

One of the major benefits of a 32-bit processor is the availability of the linear programming model. The memory model associated with the *linear* programming model is sometimes referred to as *Flat model*. Flat model is analogous to Tiny model in the segmented world. The Flat model is not new to Intel class machines, it is just one of the benefits of moving from 16-bit to 32-bit mode (Windows 3.1 provides Flat model when writing device drivers). To access a memory location in Flat model, you use only the offset. Because registers are 32 bits wide, Flat model can address up to 4GB of memory. In Flat model, the segment registers become insignificant to the developer. Often you will hear that in Flat model the SS, DS, and CS registers are always equal (SS==DS==CS) in an Intel system. For all intents and purposes, this is true because they all point somewhere into the same physical address space. However, when debugging, you will see that the SS, DS, and ES registers are always equal, and CS is always a different value. RISC-based machines only support 32-bit modes and some support 4-bit modes.

What makes these registers insignificant is the fact that none of these values can be changed by an application that runs in user-mode. (In NT, processes are separated into two types: *unprivileged user-mode* and *privileged kernel-mode*. The examples in this book are all user-mode processes.) Even though Windows 95 is not a true client-server type operating system, the term user mode still applies. The values of CS, DS, ES, and SS are determined by the kernel (which runs in kernel-mode) when it creates a user-mode process. This is how Windows

**2**

95 and NT separate address spaces. An offset in process A has a different physical memory location from the same offset in process B. As a developer, you can completely ignore the segment registers. This is especially true on MIPS, PowerPC, and Alpha processors, which have no segment registers!

## MORE DATA AND ADDRESS SPACE AVAILABLE

Flat model provides another advantage—it eliminates the need for the compiler to support memory models. Most 16-bit compilers normally support four or five different memory models:

- ▪ Tiny: In this model, both code and static data (including the stack) must fit in a 64KB segment. Most protected-mode programs cannot support this mode. Therefore, many compilers do not provide support for this model. If a compiler does support Tiny model, the resultant program is known as a *COM program* (from the .COM extension).

- ▪ Small: Small model programs contain a one code segment and a separate data segment, both of which must be less than 64KB.

- ▪ Medium: Medium model programs can contain multiple code segments, each of which must be less than 64KB, and one data segment.

- ▪ Compact: Compact model programs are just the opposite of Medium model programs. In Compact model programs, there is only one code segment and multiple data segments

- ▪ Large: Large model programs can have multiple code segments and multiple data segments.

- ▪ Huge: Huge model programs are the same as Large model with the added capability of creating data objects, such as arrays, larger than 64KB.

Thankfully, all of these memory models go away in Win32. However, one of the vestiges of multiple model programming that still exists in Win32 is the use of the FAR and NEAR keywords. (NEAR and FAR are actually typedefs. The ANSI standard requires _near and _far.) In 16-bit computing, FAR and NEAR help you to traverse memory models. For example, in a Medium model program you can still access data outside the default data segment by using the FAR keyword. Instead of using just a 16-bit offset, FAR instructs the compiler to de-reference a variable using both the selector and offset.

In Large, Compact, and Huge model, data is FAR by default. To access data within the default data segment in Large, Compact, and Huge programs, 16-bit programmers use the NEAR keyword. The same holds true for code segments: NEAR is the default for Tiny, Small, and Compact models; FAR is the default for Medium, Large, and Huge models. For compatibility's sake, they are still supported in Win32. However they are completely meaningless. So, if you look at someone else's code and it contains FAR pointers and FAR functions, don't panic. The person who wrote the code either is trying to maintain source level compatibility with Win16 or is just an old Win16 programmer who hasn't shaken the habit of programming for a segmented operating system.

Everything in Windows 95 and NT is NEAR by default (the equivalent of Tiny model) because only an offset is used to de-reference objects and call functions.

Eliminating the 64KB barrier imposed by 16-bit computing is another significant advantage of 32-bit systems. With 2GB available per process for code and data, NT and Windows 95 can much more efficiently support data objects, such as arrays greater than 64KB, coordinate spaces for graphics greater than 64KB, as well as code. In Huge model programs,16-bit compilers are able to support these items. However, this next section shows why it is so slow in doing so.

## COMPLICATED COMPILER SUPPORT NOT NECESSARY

In his article, "The Case for 32 Bits" in *Microsoft Systems Journal*, July 1992, Charles Petzold demonstrates how the 16-bit version of a program runs up to five times slower than an equivalent 32-bit version. The reason for this performance degradation is the extra work required for a 16-bit compiler to perform 32-bit operations. In 32-bit mode, the compiler (or the user) need not generate extra code to manage objects distributed across multiple segments. Take a look at the following code sample that performs the addition of two numbers, and then calls a fictitious averaging function, *avg*:

```
void avg(int *, int *, int *);
int a,b,c;
void main(void)

c=a+b;
avg(&a,&b,&c);
```

When compiled as a Small model program, the 16-bit assembly language generated by Microsoft C 8.00 looks like this:

```
_main       PROC NEAR
    mov     ax,WORD PTR _b
    add     ax,WORD PTR _a
    mov     WORD PTR _c,ax
    push    OFFSET DGROUP:_c
    push    OFFSET DGROUP:_b
    push    OFFSET DGROUP:_a
    call    _avg
    add     sp,6
    ret

_main       ENDP
```

However, when compiled for Large model, 16-bit assembly code balloons to this:

```
_main       PROC FAR
; Line 4
; Line 5
    mov     es,WORD PTR $T106
    mov     ax,WORD PTR es:_b
    mov     es,WORD PTR $T107
    add     ax,WORD PTR es:_a
    mov     es,WORD PTR $T108
    mov     WORD PTR es:_c,ax
; Line 6
    push    es
    push    OFFSET _c
    push    SEG _b
    push    OFFSET _b
    push    SEG _a
    push    OFFSET _a
    call    FAR PTR _avg
    add     sp,12       ;000cH
; Line 7
    ret
```

If you never looked at the assembly language output, you might never know that the Large model version of this program is about 15 percent larger. Because the variables a, b, and c are located in separate data segments, the 16-bit compiler must generate additional code to manipulate these segments. The same is true for the call to *avg*. As far as the compiler knows, *avg* is in a separate code segment and the compiler must make accommodations for it. If we actually compiled and linked this simple program we would see this difference in the size of the programs on disk as well, as Listing 1–1 shows. In Win32, since there is only one model, the compiler doesn't require this extra support.

**Listing 1–1**   16-bit programs vary in size because of memory models.

```
TEST     EXE        2875 9-29-94  9:44a
TESTFAR  EXE        3257 9-29-94  9:44a
         2 file(s)  6132 bytes
```

## PROCESSORS OPTIMIZED FOR 32-BIT MODE

The original rallying cry of OS/2 was "A Better Windows than Windows." IBM designed this marketing slogan to lure operating system buyers away from Windows 3.1. This may have misled some developers, however, because a better depiction of reality would be that a 32-bit solution is better than a 16-bit solution. In other words, don't talk developers into developing 16-bit applications for your 32-bit operating system. Convince them to develop native 32-bit applications instead

This same scenario holds true for Windows 95 and Windows NT. The processors that they supports are faster when running in 32-bit mode than when running in 16-bit mode. Moreover, on processors such as the MIPS R4x00 and Alpha AXP, native applications have an incredible advantage over 16-bit applications because these processors must run 16-bit software via an emulation mode. If it is performance you seek, then a 32-bit version of your Windows application will run faster on NT than a 16-bit version will.

This is especially true if the 16-bit version requires Large model. What particularly bothers me is when I see someone using Large model in 16-bit Windows when it is not necessary. Many times an inexperienced programmer will not realize the damage that is taking place when Large model is used. After all, the C code looks the same as any other model. If you have less than 64KB of static data, then Large model is unnecessary in Windows 3.1. In NT this is just one less thing the developer has to worry about.

Unfortunately for Windows 3.1 programmers, in some cases Large model is unavoidable. In Windows 3.1, all Microsoft Foundation Class (MFC) classes that reside in a DLL must be compiled as Large model. Again, this is because of the complicated programming model of 16-bit systems, which decrees that the stack segment and the data segment (SS!=DS) are not equal in a DLL.

Even if you manage to escape Large model in Windows 3.1, FAR calls and FAR data items still degrade performance. Selector loads are particularly expensive. *Selector loads* occur when calling routines in other segments or manipulating data in multiple segments. Selector loads are expensive. Compare the time differential between a 16-bit NEAR call and a 16-bit FAR call on an Intel *x*86 system:

| Call | Time |
|------|------|
| NEAR Call | 7 clock cycles |
| FAR Call to segment in memory | 28 clock cycles |

This is a common occurrence in Windows 3.1, where most programs are Medium model. In order to avoid unnecessary loads of selectors in Windows 3.1, developers sometimes hand-optimize code so that functions that call each other frequently wind up in the same segment, becoming a quasi-NEAR call.

In the Standard mode of Windows 3.1, programmers have the added responsibility of making sure that segments do not grow too large. Unlike 386 Enhanced mode, which can page memory out to a swap device in 4KB chunks, standard mode can only swap out entire segments. This has led to a whole cottage industry of Windows 3.1 third-party programs that unify code segments for you. The idea is: if all your segments are the same size, the Memory Manager in Standard mode can swap segments in and out at will, without having to search to find a space wide enough to place the segment.

The 64KB barrier in 16-bit mode does not apply to just code and data segments. Arithmetic suffers as well in 16-bit mode. By moving to 32-bits, the performance of integer arithmetic is improved because the compiler no longer has to emulate 32-bit mode using several temporary 16-bit registers.

None of this is necessary in Win32, however. In Win32, if you are writing brand-new code you can forget about NEAR and FAR and 64KB limits. If you are porting from 16-bit Windows, the NEARs and FARs are benign.

There is one slight benefit to Large model, however. Since pointers in Large model programs are 32-bits by default, the effort to port Large model code to 32-bit is not as great as a Medium model program (where you must ensure that all pointers are converted from 16 bit to 32 bits).

# KNOWING YOUR TARGET PLATFORM

Many of the inherent deficiencies of 16-bit computing do not appear at the programmer's level. If you don't take the time to see what your 16-bit compiler produces, you might develop a program that performs very poorly and not know the reason why. This fact carries over to Win32. Just because Windows 95 and Windows NT use 32-bit mode and 32-bit mode solves some of problems of 16-bit computing is no excuse for ignoring the underlying levels. Especially these days, when it seems that each new release of a development tool takes you farther and farther from the actual machine you are running on. With programs like Windbg or Visual C++ 2.0 (see Figure 1–1 and Figure 1–2) it is easy to get separated from the underlying machine.

This is particularly true when programming for a graphical environment like Windows. Imagine a scenario in which a bright person new to Windows 95 learns "Power Objects" (a fictitious programming environment that builds code for you) while not bothering to learn anything else about the environment. Within a matter of days that person will be able to deliver a prototype displaying some pretty snazzy graphics. Unfortunately, weeks later that person has probably not been able to deliver much more than the prototype. Why? Well, it is certainly not Power Object's fault. In the hands of an accomplished DOS/Windows programmer, Power Objects can deliver. But a high-level tool can take you only so far. When you reach the limitations of your tool, unless you know how the tool works, your will be incapable of going further. In other words, in the hands of a novice, every tool has severe limitations.

**8**

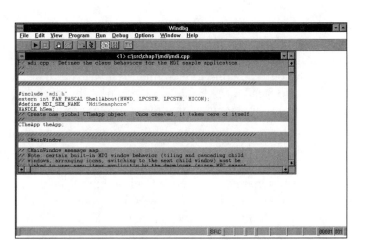

**Figure 1–1** Windbg, a GUI source level debugger

Many successful Windows 3.1 developers will tell you that part of the reason they have been so successful is because they know the underlying hardware so well. The same will be true for Win32 developers.

Don't get me wrong. I am not knocking the "Power" type languages. In fact, the examples in this book have been created with Visual C++. However, there is a big difference. Once you know the Win32 API and once you become familiar with the underlying architecture of both Windows 95 and NT, you will be able to debug a problem or get past a limitation of Visual C++.

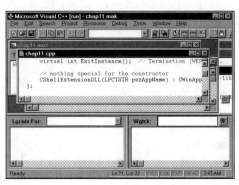

**Figure 1–2** Visual C++ 2.0≠GENERIC

If you do not know what the compiler is doing to your code, you have no hope of writing an efficient program. If you do not know what your machine expects to see, you are at the mercy of your compiler. One way to discover what the compiler does with your source is to examine the MAP file that the compiler produces (see "How to Read a MAP File" at the end of this chapter). The other way is to know the assembly language that the compiler produces.

That's right—the assembly language. With so much discussion about how NT is itself almost written entirely C/C++, one tool you may be tempted to dispense with is your assembler. (Windows 95 is written in C and assembly) Since most compilers generate and understand assembly language (with the _inline keyword), it is a good idea to throw away your assembler, not your assembly knowledge. I understand the temptation to forget your assembly skills. After all, unless you code to Win32, your code will not be portable to other platforms. And portability is achieved by writing C/C++ code, not assembly language. The temptation increases with debuggers like the one in Visual C++ that allow you to debug in source level. For this reason, I rarely debug my own programs at the source level. If I wrote the source I should know what it is doing! I want to know what the compiler thinks my source should be doing. So the perfect balance is to write C/C++ code but understand the assembly language of the underlying hardware.

Windows NT enables you to have programs that are source-code-compatible with MIPS, Intel, PowerPC and Alpha platforms (and other platforms as they become available). At the time of this writing, no cross-compilers are available for the NT environment. This means that if you want to ship an Alpha version, you must have an Alpha and be prepared to debug on the Alpha. If you want to ship a MIPS version, you will eventually have to debug on a MIPS machine. If you want to ship an Intel version—well, I think you get the idea.

## SIZING UP BASIC TYPES

On any operating system you intend to develop for, it is important to know the size of basics types, because the size of many basic types are implementation-dependent. Table 1–1 lists the basic types in Win32 and their sizes.

**Table 1–1** Size of basic types on Win32 platforms

| Type | Size |
| --- | --- |
| char | 8 bits (one byte) |
| short | 16 bits |
| int | 32 bit |
| long | 32 bit |
| float | 32 bit (IEEE) |
| double | 64 bit (IEEE) |
| ULONG; | 32 bits |
| USHORT; | 16 bits |
| UCHAR; | 8 bits |
| DWORD; | 32 bits |
| BOOL; | 32 bits |
| BYTE | 8 bits |
| WORD | 16 bits |
| LONGLONG | 64 bits |
| DWORDLONG | 64 bits |
| LARGE_INTEGER | 64-bits* |

Since integers target the register size, the most significant change from the 16-bit world is to the size of an integer (from 16 to 32-bits). Another important point to note is that a WORD is 16-bits in Win32. In Windows 3.*x*, many developers associate a WORD with an unsigned integer. As we shall see in Chapter 2, "Porting Applications to Win32," this mistake can and will be costly in Win32.

Currently, the three most popular platforms for developers that Windows NT supports are the 32-bit Intel *x*86, MIPS, and DEC Alpha AXP platforms. By the time you read this, there may be other platforms available (PowerPC), but these three are the only platforms consistently mentioned in the SDK header files. If you are going to develop for any of these platforms, the next section will get you started by introducing the underlying architectures. (You would be foolish not to develop for all of these platforms. Because, using the techniques described in this and subsequent chapters, you can ensure your code will run on all platforms that NT supports—as long as you have the platform to create the executable.)

## THE INTEL 386/486 REGISTER SET

In 32-bit mode of the Intel 386 and 486 (*x*86), all of the registers are 32 bits wide (as opposed to 16 bits in 16-bit mode), with the exception of the segment registers, which stay 16 bits. Two additional segment registers, the FS and GS, are also available. The total registers are:

**Segment Registers:** CS, DS, SS, ES, FS, GS

**32-bit Registers:** EAX, EBX, ECX, EDX, ESI, EDI EBP, EIP, EFLAGS

To show you what goes on behind the scenes, I have compiled the GENERIC.C example from the SDK with the /Fa (produce assembly listing option).

The first thing you should notice is the .model FLAT directive. It appears instead of the all the segment listings:

```
TITLE       GENERIC.c
.386P
include listing.inc
if @Version gt 510 ; If in NT use the FLAT keyword
.model FLAT
else        ; use the old style
_TEXT       SEGMENT PARA USE32 PUBLIC 'CODE'
_TEXT       ENDS
_DATA       SEGMENT DWORD USE32 PUBLIC 'DATA'
_DATA       ENDS
CONST       SEGMENT DWORD USE32 PUBLIC 'CONST'
CONST       ENDS
_BSS        SEGMENT DWORD USE32 PUBLIC 'BSS'
_BSS        ENDS
$$SYMBOLS   SEGMENT BYTE USE32 'DEBSYM'
$$SYMBOLS   ENDS
$$TYPES     SEGMENT BYTE USE32 'DEBTYP'
$$TYPES     ENDS
_TLS        SEGMENT DWORD USE32 PUBLIC 'TLS'
_TLS        ENDS
FLAT        GROUP _DATA, CONST, _BSS
     ASSUME  CS: FLAT, DS: FLAT, SS: FLAT
endif
```

The next important item is the declaration of external functions:

```
EXTRN    _LoadAcceleratorA@8:NEAR
EXTRN    _GetMessageA@16:NEAR
EXTRN    _TranslateMessage@4:NEAR
EXTRN    _DispatchMessageA@4:NEAR
```

Compare this to the excerpt for the 16-bit version of GENERIC and you will notice there is a new calling convention:

```
EXTRN    LOADACCELERATOR:FAR
EXTRN    GETMESSAGE:FAR
EXTRN    TRANSLATEMESSAGE:FAR
EXTRN    DISPATCHMESSAGE:FAR
```

This new convention is the Standard calling convention and its keyword is:

```
__stdcall
```

The NT C/C++ compiler supports two other calling conventions in addition to StdCall: C _(_cdecl) and Fastcall (__fastcall). The Standard convention is the default convention. The Pascal calling convention, which is the default convention for Windows 3.1, is no longer supported by the NT C/C++ compiler.

It is easy to recognize __stdcall when debugging. The compiler prepends an underscore and appends an @ sign and the number of bytes to be pushed on the stack (in decimal). Consequently, the prototype for *LoadAccelerators* looks like this:

```
HACCEL WINAPI LoadAccelerators(hinst, lpTableName)

HINSTANCE hinst;     // handle of application instance      */
LPCTSTR lpTableName; // address of table-name string
LoadAccelerators looks like this when viewed through a debugger:
push    OFFSET FLAT:_szAppName
mov     eax, DWORD PTR _hInstance$[ebp]
push    eax
call    _LoadAcceleratorsA@8
```

Since *LoadAccelerators* takes two parameters, each four bytes long, you would think that the actual function name would be *_LoadAccelerators@8*. But instead it is *_LoadAcceleratorsA@8*. Where did the *A* come from? To get the answer you must look in WINUSER.H:

```
HACCEL WINAPI
LoadAcceleratorsA(HINSTANCE hInstance,
                  LPCSTR lpTableName);
HACCEL WINAPI
LoadAcceleratorsW(HINSTANCE hInstance,
                  LPCWSTR lpTableName);
#ifdef UNICODE
#define LoadAccelerators   LoadAcceleratorsW
#else
#define LoadAccelerators   LoadAcceleratorsA
#endif // !UNICODE
```

To differentiate between UNICODE and ANSI functions, Win32 defines two functions, one for UNICODE and one for ANSI. The UNICODE function ends with a *W,* and the ANSI function ends with an *A*. Since the compiler handles UNICODE for you at compile time, the only time you will see the appended *W* or *A* is when debugging.

```
Wading through the calling parameters
Now the question is, where is __stdcall? It's not in the prototype.
For this answer, you must look in WINDEF.H:
#if (_MSC_VER >= 800)
#define CALLBACK     __stdcall
#define WINAPI       __stdcall
#define WINAPIV      __cdecl
#define APIENTRY     WINAPI
#define APIPRIVATE   __stdcall
#define PASCAL       __stdcall
#else
#define CALLBACK
#define WINAPI
#define WINAPIV
#define APIENTRY     WINAPI
```

```
#define APIPRIVATE
#define PASCAL       pascal
#endif
```

If the compiler version is greater than or equal to 8.00, WINAPI is equal to __stdcall. The other #defines are for compatibility. For example, *CALLBACK* is a vestige of Win16 and is not necessary in an Win32 program. The same is true for PASCAL, which now is also defunct. *APIENTRY* is a type I first saw in OS/2. Unfortunately many of the Win32 SDK samples have adopted *APIENTRY*, thereby introducing a subtle bug. Since the latest version of the 16-bit Microsoft C/C++ compiler doesn't define *APIENTRY*, the samples are not portable between Win16 and Win32. (As of this writing, the compiler that ships with Visual C++ Version 2.0 is the most current.)

The one sample, Generic, which does define *APIENTRY*, defines it as:

```
#if !defined (APIENTRY) // Win32 defines APIENTRY, but
                        // Win16 doesn't
#define APIENTRY far pascal
#endif
```

Herein lies the subtle bug. *WinMain*, which is prototyped as:

```
int PASCAL WinMain(HINSTANCE, HINSTANCE, LPSTR, int);
```

It will fail in Small model if you call it with *APIENTRY* the way the Win32 SDK Generic does:

```
// In a Small Model program WinMain does not return far.
//
int APIENTRY WinMain(HINSTANCE hInstance,
                     HINSTANCE hPrevInstance,
                     LPSTR lpCmdLine,
                     int nCmdShow)
```

Getting back to __stdcall, notice that the arguments are passed from right to left, but the called function cleans up the stack. This means that all __stdcall functions take a fixed number of arguments. If your function requires a variable number of parameters (or if you are calling an existing function that takes a variable number of parameters), use the __cdecl calling convention. In the __cdecl calling convention, the arguments are pushed from right to left, and the calling process is responsible for cleaning up the stack.

The third calling convention is called the __fastcall convention, and its parameters are passed in registers. Registers are faster than using the stack, hence the name. However, since an Intel *x*86 has only so many registers, once the ECX and EDX registers are full, the rest of the parameters are placed on the stack.

Returning to our GENERIC example, let's take a look a another function:

```
hWnd = CreateWindow("GenericWClass",
                    "Generic Sample Application",
                    WS_OVERLAPPEDWINDOW,
                    CW_USEDEFAULT
                    CW_USEDEFAULT,
                    CW_USEDEFAULT,
                    CW_USEDEFAULT,
                    NULL,
                    NULL,
                    hInstance,
                    NULL);
```

In Win16, the assembly language looks like this:

```
push    ds
push    OFFSET DGROUP:$SG3258
push    ds
push    OFFSET DGROUP:$SG3257
push    207     ;00cfH
push    0
push    -32768  ;8000H
push    -32768  ;8000H
push    -32768  ;8000H
push    -32768  ;8000H
push    0
push    0
push    cx
push    0
```

```
push    0
call    FAR PTR CREATEWINDOW
mov     si,ax
```

In Win32, the assembly language looks like this:

```
push    0
mov     eax, DWORD PTR _hInstance$[ebp]
push    eax
push    0
push    0
push    -2147483648    ;80000000H
push    -2147483648    ;80000000H
push    -2147483648    ;80000000H
push    -2147483648    ;80000000H
push    13565952       ;00cf0000H WS_OVERLAPPEDWINDOW
push    OFFSET FLAT:$SG9245
push    OFFSET FLAT:$SG9246
push    0
call    _CreateWindowExA@48
mov     DWORD PTR _hWnd$[ebp], eax
```

In the 16-bit version of *CreateWindow*, the calling convention is FAR PASCAL, so the parameters are pushed in the opposite order of *CreateWindow* for Win32. Notice how the 16-bit version of *CreateWindow* must push both the DS and the offset for the *ClassName* and *WindowName* parameters. In the Win32 version, only the offset is passed. This fact alone accounts for much of the performance improvement in 32-bit programs.

The other thing to notice is that the Win32 version actually calls *CreateWindowEx* instead of *CreateWindow*. A quick look at the following code, excerpted from WINUSER.H, explains why:

```
#ifdef UNICODE
#define CreateWindowEx   CreateWindowExW
#else
#define CreateWindowEx   CreateWindowExA
#endif // !UNICODE
```

```
#define CreateWindowA(lpClassName, lpWindowName, dwStyle,
                    x, y,nWidth, nHeight, hWndParent,
                    hMenu, hInstance, lpParam) \
par CreateWindowExA(OL, lpClassName, lpWindowName, dwStyle,
                    x,y, nWidth, nHeight, hWndParent, hMenu,
                    hInstance, lpParam)

#define CreateWindowW(lpClassName, lpWindowName, dwStyle, \par
                    x, y, nWidth, nHeight, hWndParent, \par
                    hMenu, hInstance, lpParam)\par
CreateWindowExW(OL, lpClassName, lpWindowName, dwStyle, \par
                    x, y, nWidth, nHeight, hWndParent, hMenu, \par
                    hInstance, lpParam)
#ifdef UNICODE
#define CreateWindow   CreateWindowW
#else
#define CreateWindow   CreateWindowA
#endif // !UNICODE
```

*CreateWindow* is just a macro for *CreateWindowEx*. That's why the 32-bit version pushes an extra zero for the first parameter. Armed with this knowledge, you can avoid using the *CreateWindow* function entirely. However, this is information you might never learn unless you drop down into assembly language (or read Chapter 2, "Porting to Win32").

## MIPS R4000 AND R4400 PROCESSORS

The MIPS architecture uses a somewhat different approach from the Intel *x*86 approach. The MIPS R4000 and R4400 processors are known as *RISC chips*. RISC stands for reduced instruction set computer. The goal of RISC processors is to increase performance by increasing the number of CPU instructions per machine cycle. Complex instruction set processors (CISC), such as the *x*86 chips, take multiple cycles to execute one instruction.

The R4*x*00 chips strive to execute an average of one instruction per CPU cycle. To do this, the R4*x*00s use the concept of a *pipeline*. In a pipeline, multiple instructions are stacked so that various pieces of several instructions are executed simultaneously. There are eight distinct operations that take place when an Rx400 instruction executes, and each R4$x$00 instruction takes eight clock cycles to execute. At the end of eight CPU cycles, eight instructions will have executed for an average of one per CPU cycle. Keeping the CPU "load-balanced" is potentially more efficient than the CISC way of doing things. I say "potentially" because circumstances can arise that can impede an instruction from executing. For example, when you execute an instruction that loads a register from memory, the next instruction cannot access that register (a load or store operation takes longer than one CPU cycle). Instead, a deliberate delay (a NOP instruction) must be inserted. This is why an optimizing compiler plays such an important role for a RISC-based processor. At compile time, it is the compiler's job to recognize and eliminate delay instructions by shuffling instructions around so that useful work takes place during the delay.

Take a look at the next two instructions produced by the NT C Compiler for MIPS with the options /Od (disable optimizations) and /Fa (produce assembly listing):

```
.livereg    0x0C00000E,0x00000000    jal    LoadAcceleratorsA
```

On Intel-based machines, it is customary to turn off optimization during the development of a project. This facilitates source-level debugging because the generated code follows the actual source. However, for a MIPS compile this won't always be true. The .livereg pseudo-op is produced by the code generation phase of the compiler. It instructs the optimization phase of the compile that there are registers that contain "live" data. The optimization phase of the compile will use this information in its attempt to produce code that doesn't contain NOPs. This even takes place during an /Od compile. Therefore, if you develop for MIPS, you must be aware of this phenomenon during debugging, or else you'll think your compiler is playing tricks on you.

To walk you through a typical debugging session, I have compiled the Generic application from the SDK. Listing 1–2 contains the source of the Generic application's function CenterWindow and listing 1–3 contains the output of a /Fa compile of the CenterWindow function. This should get you used to dealing with the MIPS op codes and its register set. However, it is no substitute for fully understanding the MIPS architecture. For that, I recommend reading *MIPS RISC Architecture*, by Kane and Heinrich (published by Prentice Hall).

The first thing you notice when you look at the assembly language output is the pseudo op-codes. Pseudo op-codes begin with a period and are actually commands for the compiler.

The next thing to notice is the registers. MIPS chips have 32 general purpose 32-bit registers. Sixty-four-bit arithmetic is achieved by two additional multiply and divide registers. The location of the next instruction to execute is stored in the program counter (PC). There are no op codes to access memory, besides loading or storing. So these extra registers come in handy. In Listing 1–1, the registers are named $0 through $31. MIPS chips follow a frame-based architecture, meaning they have the concept of a stack. The stack pointer is referenced as $SP in listing 1–3.

Unlike the *x86*, MIPS supports only one calling convention and it is equivalent of Fastcall. Actually, all calling conventions are supported. They just equate to the same calling convention. In the call to *GetWindowRect*, you can see that the parameters are stored in the $4 and $5 registers:

```
# The pound sign signifies a comment
# lw is the load word instruction
lw   $4, 140($sp)

# addu means add unsigned
addu $5, $sp, 136
addu $5, $5, -40
#
.livereg    0x0C00000E,0x00000000
#

# jal is Jump and Link
jal     GetWindowRect
```

Return values are normally stored in the $2 register. Here we see a break not equal (bne) if *InitApplication* returns a value other than zero. The $32 stands for a label in this case, not a register:

```
        jal     InitApplication
        bne     $2, 0, $32
    .
    .
    .
$32
```

When a *jal* instruction is issued, the $31 register is used for the return address. Here's the code for *CenterDialog*, which retrieves the return address off the stack, cleans up the stack, and returns:

```
lw    $31, 44($sp)
$73:
    addu
    $sp, 136   j    $31   .end
```

**Listing I–2** The CenterWindow function from the SDK application Generic

```
/***********************************************************

        FUNCTION: CenterWindow (HWND, HWND)

        PURPOSE:  Center one window over another

        COMMENTS:

Dialog boxes take on the screen position that they were designed at,
which is not always appropriate. Centering the dialog over a
particular window usually results in a better position.

***********************************************************/

BOOL CenterWindow (HWND hwndChild, HWND hwndParent)

        RECT    rChild, rParent;
        int     wChild, hChild, wParent, hParent;
        int     wScreen, hScreen, xNew, yNew;
        HDC     hdc;
        // Get the Height and Width of the child window
        GetWindowRect (hwndChild, &rChild);
        wChild = rChild.right - rChild.left;
        hChild = rChild.bottom - rChild.top;

        // Get the Height and Width of the parent window
        GetWindowRect (hwndParent, &rParent);
```

**21**

```
    wParent = rParent.right - rParent.left;
    hParent = rParent.bottom - rParent.top;

    // Get the display limits
    hdc = GetDC (hwndChild);
    wScreen = GetDeviceCaps (hdc, HORZRES);
    hScreen = GetDeviceCaps (hdc, VERTRES);
    ReleaseDC (hwndChild, hdc);

    // Calculate new X position, then adjust for screen
    xNew = rParent.left + ((wParent - wChild) /2);
    if (xNew < 0)
        xNew = 0;
     else if ((xNew+wChild) > wScreen)
        xNew = wScreen - wChild;


    // Calculate new Y position, then adjust for screen
    yNew = rParent.top  + ((hParent - hChild) /2);
    if (yNew < 0)
        yNew = 0;
     else if ((yNew+hChild) > hScreen)
        yNew = hScreen - hChild;


    // Set it, and return
    return SetWindowPos (hwndChild, NULL,
            xNew, yNew, 0, 0, SWP_NOSIZE | SWP_NOZORDER);
```

**Listing 1–3** CenterWindow compiled with the /Fa switch

```
        .text
        .align    2
        .globl    CenterWindow
        .loc      0 339
        .ent      CenterWindow 2
CenterWindow:
        .option   O1
```

```
subu       $sp, 136
sw         $31, 44($sp)
sw         $4, 136($sp)
sw         $5, 140($sp)
.mask      0x80000000, -92
.frame     $sp, 136, $31
.prologue 0
.file      0 "generic.c"
.bgnb      12637
.loc       0 340
.loc       0 341
.loc       0 342
.loc       0 343
.loc       0 346
lw         $4, 136($sp)
addu       $5, $sp, 136
addu       $5, $5, -16
.livereg 0x0C00000E,0x00000000
jal        GetWindowRect
.loc       0 347
lw         $14, 128($sp)
lw         $15, 120($sp)
subu       $24, $14, $15
sw         $24, 116($sp)
.loc       0 348
lw         $25, 132($sp)
lw         $8, 124($sp)
subu       $9, $25, $8
sw         $9, 112($sp)
.loc       0 351
lw         $4, 140($sp)
addu       $5, $sp, 136
addu       $5, $5, -40
.livereg 0x0C00000E,0x00000000
jal        GetWindowRect
.loc       0 352
lw         $10, 104($sp)
lw         $11, 96($sp)
```

```
subu       $12, $10, $11
sw         $12, 92($sp)
.loc       0 353
lw         $13, 108($sp)
lw         $14, 100($sp)
subu       $15, $13, $14
sw         $15, 88($sp)
.loc       0 356
lw         $4, 136($sp)
.livereg   0x0800000E,0x00000000
jal        GetDC
sw         $2, 84($sp)
.loc       0 357
lw         $4, 84($sp)
li         $5, 8
.livereg   0x0C00000E,0x00000000
jal        GetDeviceCaps
sw         $2, 80($sp)
.loc       0 358
lw         $4, 84($sp)
li         $5, 10
.livereg   0x0C00000E,0x00000000
jal        GetDeviceCaps
sw         $2, 76($sp)
.loc       0 359
lw         $4, 136($sp)
lw         $5, 84($sp)
.livereg   0x0C00000E,0x00000000
jal        ReleaseDC
.loc       0 362
lw         $24, 92($sp)
lw         $25, 116($sp)
subu       $8, $24, $25
div        $9, $8, 2
lw         $10, 96($sp)
addu       $11, $10, $9
sw         $11, 72($sp)
.loc       0 363
bge        $11, 0, $66
```

```
        .loc    0 364
        sw      $0, 72($sp)
        .loc    0 365
        b       $68
$66:
        .lab    $$12583
        .loc    0 365
        lw      $12, 72($sp)
        lw      $13, 116($sp)
        addu    $14, $12, $13
        lw      $15, 80($sp)
        ble     $14, $15,
$68
        .loc    0 366
        subu    $24, $15, $13
        sw      $24, 72($sp)
        .loc    0 367
        .loc    0 370
$67:
        .lab    $$12585
$68:
        .lab    $$12584
        lw      $25, 88($sp)
        lw      $8, 112($sp)
        subu    $10, $25, $8
        div     $9, $10, 2
        lw      $11, 100($sp)
        addu    $12, $11, $9
        sw      $12, 68($sp)
        .loc    0 371
        bge     $12, 0, $69
        .loc    0 372
        sw      $0, 68($sp)
        .loc    0 373
        b       $71
$69:
        .lab    $$12586
        .loc    0 373
        lw      $14, 68($sp)
```

```
        lw        $15, 112($sp)
        addu      $13, $14, $15
        lw        $24, 76($sp)
        ble       $13, $24,
  $71
        .loc      0 374
        subu      $25, $24, $15
        sw        $25, 68($sp)
        .loc      0 375
        .loc      0 378
$70:
        .lab      $$12588$71:
        .lab      $$12587
        .loc      0 379
        lw        $4, 136($sp)
        move      $5, $0
        lw        $6, 72($sp)
        lw        $7, 68($sp)
        sw        $0, 16($sp)
        sw        $0, 20($sp)
        li        $8, 5
        sw        $8, 24($sp)
        .livereg  0x0F00000E,0x00000000
        jal       SetWindowPos
  $72:
        .lab      $$12571
        .endb     12638
        .livereg  0x2000FF0E,0x00000FFF
        lw        $31, 44($sp)
  $73:
        addu      $sp, 136  j   $31   .end
```

## DEC ALPHA AXP

The Alpha is a 64-bit RISC processor that also uses the concept of a pipeline. However, the goal of the Alpha is to average two instructions per CPU cycle. The Alpha AXP has 32 integer registers that are 64 bits wide, 32 floating point registers, each 64-bits wide, and a register to hold the address of the next instruction to execute (called the program counter or PC). Like the MIPS, the Alpha has a load-and-store architecture and is also frame-based.

When I was at the Alpha Porting lab, the folks in charge there were quick to point out that there is a difference between an architecture and an implementation. For example, the number of registers is the architecture; their use is the implementation. To illustrate how NT implements the Alpha, Listing 1–4 contains the partial assembly language output of GENERIC.C. As you can see, the integer registers are named $0 through $31. NT uses $30 as the stack pointer. In assembly language listings, the stack pointer is referred to as *$sp*. Register $29 is used as a global pointer (*$gp*) and $31 is used as the return value. Listing 1–4 shows their usage.

**Listing 1–4** Partial listing of GENERIC.C

```
 #    88            if (!InitInstance(hInstance, nCmdShow))
      ldl    $16, 64($sp)
      ldl    $17, 88($sp)
      .livereg    0x0001C002,0x00000000
      jsr    $26, InitInstance
      ldgp   $gp, 0($26)
      bne    $0, $33
      .loc   2 88

      .loc   2 89
 #    89            return (FALSE);
      bis    $31, $31, $0
      br     $31, $37
 $33:
```

The *ldl* instruction loads a *LONGWORD* (32-bit value) into a register. In this case, $16 and $17 are loaded with the values for *hInstance* and *nCmdShow*. As with MIPS processors, the .livereg pseudo op informs the compiler of registers that cannot be optimized. The *jsr* instruction jumps to the subroutine, *InitInstance*. Upon return, the *ldgp* instruction loads *$gp* to retrieve the return value. If the value is not zero, the *bne* instruction (break not equal) sends control to the $33 label. If the result is not equal, the *bis* instruction ORs the value from $0 into $31 and the function returns.

**27**

## SUMMARY

I hope this chapter has impressed upon you the need to understand the underlying architectures of the machines for which you plan to develop products. As I said earlier, I think it would be foolish to ignore any one particular platform. If it comes down to your application versus a competitor's and only your application has versions for all the platforms that Win32 supports, your application will probably sell more copies.

## HOW TO READ A MAP FILE

Knowing how to read the output of a compile is essential for fully understanding program flow and debugging. I'll describe what's contained in a typical MAP file by describing each section. The listing at the end of this chapter shows HELLO.MAP, which is the output from the link of HELLO.EXE.

At the beginning of the MAP file is the name of the executable and the timestamp showing when the linker generated the executable. Following the timestamp is the preferred load address. If HELLO is loaded at this address, there will be no need to perform fixups.

The next part lists all of the sections in the executable. You can think of sections as a rough equivalent to DOS's segments. For example, the .text section contains code, the .bss section contains uninitialized data, the .debug$ sections contain debug information, the CRT*** sections contain startup code information, and so on. From left to right, the columns describe the beginning and ending of each section, the length of each section, the name, and then the class. As you can see by what is in the Length column, there are 0x80DC hex bytes in the .text section and 0x70CC hex bytes in the .data section. Next column over is the "class" of each segment. Section classes just indicate the type of section and should not be confused with C++ classes. Section classes fall into one of two categories, code or data.

After the sections, all of the public variables are sorted by section, then offsets in the section are listed. For example, one of the first public variables in HELLO is the ??0CMainWindow@@QAE@XZ variable. This is the decorated name for the CMainWindow constructor. Now you know why they call it name "mangling." There is no way a programmer can accidentally define a function with the same name. Known as *type-safe linking*, this technique gives a new "mangled" name for each overloaded function. The rva+base column lists the relative virtual address plus the base address. The next column over lists the library that the function or variable was extracted from.

After the variables is the entry point of the program. For HELLO the entry point is 0x00000C50. If you scan the variables section, you will see that 0x00000C50 corresponds to _WinMainCRTStartup, the starting point for the program.

After the entry point are the static symbols followed by the fixups. The fixups describe how the variables are to be relocated at runtime.

By examining a MAP file, you can get a good look at what a compiler does to your code. Many times looking at the MAP file will prove more valuable than running your debugger. If you come across a situation where you change one piece of code and another totally unrelated function starts failing, look in the MAP file to see if the variable you changed is located next to a variable in the unrelated function. If it is, there's a good chance that you have exceeded the bounds of your first variable. Problems such as these don't always show themselves very clearly in the debugger.

```
HELLO

Timestamp is 2ca5e2bf (Sun Sep 26 11:43:11 1993)

Preferred load address is 00010000

Start          Length      Name        Class
0001:00000000  000080dcH   .text       CODE
0002:00000000  00005c99H   AFX_COR2    CODE
0003:00000000  0000b5f9H   AFX_COR1    CODE
0005:00000000  000046abH   AFX_DBG1    CODE
0006:00000000  0000460eH   AFX_AUX_    CODE
0007:00000000  0000220dH   AFX_INIT    CODE
000a:00000000  000059c6H   AFX_COL1    CODE
000b:00000000  000024a8H   .bss        DATA
000c:00000000  000000a8H   .rdata      DATA
000d:00000000  000070ccH   .data       DATA
000d:000070d0  00000004H   .CRT$XCA    DATA
000d:000070d4  00000004H   .CRT$XCL    DATA
000d:000070d8  000000a0H   .CRT$XCU    DATA
```

```
000d:00007178 00000004H  .CRT$XCZ              DATA
000d:00007180 00000004H  .CRT$XIA              DATA
000d:00007184 00000004H  .CRT$XIC              DATA
000d:00007188 00000004H  .CRT$XIZ              DATA
000d:00007190 00000004H  .CRT$XPA              DATA
000d:00007194 00000004H  .CRT$XPX              DATA
000d:00007198 00000004H  .CRT$XPZ              DATA
000e:00000000 000001bcH  .rsrc$01              DATA
000f:00000000 00000078H  .idata$2              DATA
0011:00000000 000a4351H  .debug$C              DATA
0011:00145c6b 00005238H  .debug$T              DATA


  Address              Publics by Value              Rva+Base    Lib:Object


 0000:00000000         ___drectve_user32             00010000
LIBC:WINCRT0.OBJ
 0001:0000001a         ??0CMainWindow@@QAE@XZ      0001101a f HELLO.OBJ
 0001:00000075         ?OnPaint@CMainWindow@@QAEXXZ 00011075 f
HELLO.OBJ
 0001:0000088b         _GetClipboardFormatNameA@12 0001188b
user32:user32.def
 0001:0000093f         _SetWindowExtEx@16            0001193f
gdi32:gdi32.def
 0001:00000c15         _GetFileTitleA@12             00011c15
comdlg32:comdlg32.def
 0001:00000c33         _RegQueryValueA@16            00011c33
advapi32:advapi32.def
 0001:00000c39         _DragFinish@4                 00011c39
shell32:shell32.def
 0001:00000c50         _WinMainCRTStartup            00011c50 f
LIBC:WINCRT0.OBJ
 0001:00000e00         __onexit                      00011e00 f
LIBC:ONEXIT.OBJ
 0001:00000e80         _atexit                       00011e80 f
LIBC:ONEXIT.OBJ
 0001:00001530         __msize                       00012530 f
LIBC:MSIZE.OBJ
 0001:00001550         _strncmp                      00012550
LIBC:STRNCMP.OBJ
 0001:0000158c         __memicmp                     0001258c
```

```
LIBC:MEMICMP.OBJ
  0001:000015e0      _realloc                000125e0 f
LIBC:REALLOC.OBJ
  0001:00001910      __c_exit                00012910 f
LIBC:CRT0DAT.OBJ
  0001:000019d0      _mktime                 000129d0 f
LIBC:MKTIME.OBJ
  0001:00001c50      _time                   00012c50 f
LIBC:TIME.OBJ
  0001:00002ccc      _strcspn                00013ccc
LIBC:STRCSPN.OBJ
  0001:00002d08      _strrchr                00013d08
LIBC:STRRCHR.OBJ
  0001:00002d30      _strstr                 00013d30
LIBC:STRSTR.OBJ
  0001:00002d90      __purecall               00013d90 f
LIBC:PUREVIRT.OBJ
  0001:00002da0      _abort                  00013da0 f
LIBC:ABORT.OBJ
  0001:00002dc0      _calloc                 00013dc0 f
LIBC:CALLOC.OBJ
  0001:00002e00      __access                00013e00 f
LIBC:ACCESS.OBJ
  0001:00002e54      __except_handler2        00013e54
LIBC:EXSUP.OBJ
  0002:000000f4      ??0CFrameWnd@@QAE@XZ    0001a0f4 f
nafxcwd:winfrm.obj
  000f:00000b6c      __imp__EnableScrollBar@12 0005eb6c
user32:user32.def
  000f:00000dd0      77USER32__imp__NULL     0005edd0
user32:user32.def


  entry point at     0001:00000c50


Static symbols


  0001:00000000      __adm                   00011000 f HELLO.OBJ
  0001:000001fb      __adn                   000111fb f HELLO.OBJ
  0001:000019a0      __initterm              000129a0 f
LIBC:CRT0DAT.OBJ
  0001:00001820      __heap_expand_block     00012820 f
```

```
LIBC:REALLOC.OBJ

FIXUPS: 1f72 ffffe95 1e 12 4f 20 13 ffffdce a a 3a 5 5 5 5 53 1e 6 6
FIXUPS: 1d83 15 2e 19 947 73 13 14 f 2a f fffffd06 fffffff4 fffffff8
fffffb6
FIXUPS: 1207 1a 18 5 24.
```

**CHAPTER 2**

# PORTING TO WIN32

Many developers feel that the term porting has negative connotations. When non developers use the term "port," normally they do it in a conversation that begins "This shouldn't take too long… it's just a port." But developing an application for a new operating system is not an easy task, no matter what state the existing code base is in—even if it is just a port. Throw in the fact that the existing code base could be spaghetti, and fantasies about winning the lottery and quitting work start creeping into your dreams. Moreover, some developers feel that there is little glamour in porting. Try to improve the code along the way, and it appears the port is taking too long. But if you perform a straight port from one operating system to another without taking advantage of the new operating system's features, you'll hear those nondevelopers complain about performance, usability, and so on.

This chapter deals with all of the ramifications of porting applications to Win32. You'll also learn the difference between "porting" and "portable." Moving your existing code to Win32 is porting. Source code that is compatible with both Win16 and Win32 is portable. Due to Windows 95's strict requirement upon compatiblity you'll see that Windows NT and Windows 95 require different levels of effort.

Depending upon what you decide, you will end up with several different maintenance scenarios:

- ■■ Two code bases: One for Win16 and one for Win32 (supports Windows 95 and NT)

- ■■ Three code bases: One for Win16 and two for Win32 (one for each Windows 95 and NT)

- ■■ One code base: both Win16- and Win32-compatible (Windows 3.1, Windows 95 and NT)

- ■■ One code base: Win32 only (Win32s for 16-bit Windows)

This last scenario takes place if you port, but write your code in such a way that it can run as a Win32s application. The idea of doing this is so intriguing, two chapters are dedicated to the subject. Chapter 14 discusses all the possibilities of creating a Win32s application—when it is appropriate and when it is inappropriate. The next chapter discusses thunking, which is the ability to have 16- and 32-bit code in one application. So I won't go into detail here.

Note that this chapter also leaves it up to other chapters to explain how to take advantage of specific NT or Win32 features. For instance, Chapter 4 explains how to use CreateProcess instead of WinExec, and Chapter 5 explains how to take advantage of the Win32 memory management APIs.

No matter what you decide, start thinking about NT-specific features now. As we go through each of the following scenarios, you can be thinking about how and when to implement them.

# TWO CODE BASES: ONE FOR WIN16 AND ONE FOR WIN32

Two code bases are generated when you make a copy of your entire code base, save the original somewhere (either literally or by using a version control system), and then start making changes to the copy. When you complete the port, you will have two separate code bases, two makefiles, two separate executables, and so on. The benefit of this method is that it is usually the quickest way to complete a port. This method also frees you from worrying whether you have done anything to your original base to stop it from working.

The following sections describe the specific items you need to be aware of to complete your port.

## HANDLING MAKEFILE PROBLEMS

First, make sure that you are using a valid makefile. If you try to compile the Win16 version of GENERIC in NT you will receive the following error messages:

```
C:\msvc\samples\generic>cl  generic.c
Microsoft (R) 32-bit C/C++ Optimizing Compiler Version 9.00 for 80x86
Copyright (c) Microsoft Corp 1984-1994. All rights reserved.


generic.c
generic.h(6) : error C4226: nonstandard extension used : '__export'
is an obsolete keyword
generic.h(7) : error C4226: nonstandard extension used : '__export'
is an obsolete keyword
generic.c(71) : warning C4047: 'argument' : 'unsigned int ' differs
in levels of indirection from 'void *'
generic.c(71) : warning C4024: 'GetMessageA' : different types for
formal and actual parameter 3
generic.c(72) : warning C4047: 'argument' : 'unsigned int ' differs
in levels of indirection from 'void *'
generic.c(72) : warning C4024: 'GetMessageA' : different types for
formal and actual parameter 4
generic.c(110) : warning C4047: '=' : 'unsigned int ' differs in
levels of indirection from 'void *'
generic.c(207) : error C4226: nonstandard extension used : '__export'
is an obsolete keyword
generic.c(236) : warning C4047: 'return' : 'long ' differs in levels
of indirection from 'void *'
generic.c(260) : error C4226: nonstandard extension used : '__export'
is an obsolete keyword
```

This happens because the makefile for the 16-bit version of GENERIC is meant for the 16-bit compiler. I cannot emphasize this enough: take care of your makefile first. It will save you tons of headaches later on. I suggest finding a makefile in the SDK and cannibalizing it for your project. Make the changes for EXEs, DLLs, RESs, and LIBs. All compile and link differently in NT. If you have a 16-bit version of a third-party make program, either convert to NMAKE (the 32-bit make executable that ships with Visual C++) or upgrade to your third-party's 32-bit version if one is available. Another method (the one I think is the easiest) is to use Visual C++ 2.0 and have Visual C++ convert your makefile for you. If you are porting from the 16-bit version of Visual C++ 1.5 the process is a breeze.

Once you have a working makefile, it's time to compile. The Microsoft Porting Lab staff recommends commenting out troublesome spots and concentrating on getting a minimal port working first. By troublesome spots, they mean items that don't port easily, such as DOS assembly language calls. This is good advice because it's encouraging to have the shell of your 16-bit Windows program up and running as a native 32-bit process. It's also the easiest part of the port. That's because resources—cursors, icons, bitmaps and dialogs—are unchanged between Win16 and Win32 (except for the makefile stuff I talked about). However, eventually you will have to deal with the following issues, each of which is discussed in the following pages:

- The change in the size of data types
- Changes to Window messages
- Changes to API calls
- Segmented architecture issues
- Direct access of WIN.INI and SYSTEM.INI
- Use of undocumented functions and internals
- Virtual Device Drivers
- Dependence upon hPrevinstance
- Changes in input state
- Dependendencies upon DOS

## THE CHANGE IN THE SIZE OF DATA TYPES

As we discussed in Chapter 1, the size of an integer (32 bits) is the most significant change from 16- to 32-bits. This change will affect limits, counters, masks, array indexing, and structures. The size of a structure will grow if one of the members is an integer, and this change in size may affect the alignment of your structure. Alignment rules on 32-bit machines dictate that you naturally align characters (8 bits) on byte boundaries; shorts (16 bits) on two-byte boundaries; and integers and longs (32 bits) on 32-bit boundaries. Accessing a misaligned structure member degrades performance on an x86 machine. The MIPS, POWERPC, or Alpha AXP architectures actually generate an exception when an instruction attempts to read or write data to or from an address that is not naturally aligned. However, you won't see this exception in a user-mode program because the developers of the Win32 subsystem code used structured exception handling to trap it. This was necessary for compatibility reasons. Take the BITMAPFILEHEADER structure from WINGDI.H as an example:

```
#pragma pack(2)
typedef struct tagBITMAPFILEHEADER {
        WORD    bfType;
        DWORD   bfSize;  // is misaligned in a 32-bit
                         // environment
        WORD    bfReserved1;
        WORD    bfReserved2;
        DWORD   bfOffBits;
} BITMAPFILEHEADER, FAR *LPBITMAPFILEHEADER, *PBITMAPFILEHEADER;
#pragma pack()
```

The BITMAPFILEHEADER data structure contains information about the type, size, and layout of a file that contains a device-independent bitmap. This structure dates back to Windows 3.0 and, if changed, would render the new 32-bit bitmaps incompatible with Windows 3.0 and 3.1 bitmaps. The developer who created this structure probably had no clue that one day the bfSize field would be considered misaligned data when running on a 32-bit processor. To counteract this problem, the Win32 subsystem on a MIPS, POWERPC, or Alpha AXP uses structured exception handling to trap this exception and automatically pad the data. Unfortunately, this process is very slow because it takes over one thousand instructions to do this! If it's any consolation, it's also slow on an x86. So, if you are creating your own structures, make sure they are aligned properly.

To give you an idea how important this is, I've created a small program that accesses the bfFile variable (see Listing 2–1). Using the profiler from Visual C++, you can see that to access bfFile 64KB times takes 25.384 milliseconds (see Listing 2–2).

**Listing 2–1** Accessing misaligned data

```
BOOL CTheApp::InitInstance()
{

BOOL CTestApp::InitInstance()
{
     volatile BITMAPFILEHEADER bf;
for (int        i=0; i <0xffff; i++)
          bf.bfSize = 10;

  return FALSE;
}
```

**Listing 2–2** Profile output of misaligned data

```
Program Statistics
_____

    Command line at 1994 Oct 30 23:09: C:\test\WinDebug\test
    Total time: 217.934 millisecond
    Time outside of functions: 5.230 millisecond
    Call depth: 5
    Total functions: 76
    Total hits: 19
    Function coverage: 25.0%
    Overhead Calculated 27
    Overhead Average 27
```

Module Statistics for test.exe
————————————

    Time in module: 212.704 millisecond
    Percent of time in module: 100.0%
    Functions in module: 76
    Hits in module: 19
    Module function coverage: 25.0%

| Func Time | % | Func+Child Time | % | Hit Count | Function |
|---|---|---|---|---|---|
| 89.281 | 42.0 | 114.666 | 53.9 | 1 | _WinMain@16 (mfc30d.dll) |
| 48.922 (test.obj) | 23.0 | 48.922 | 23.0 | 1 | CTestApp::CTestApp(void) |
| 28.033 (test.obj) | 13.2 | 28.033 | 13.2 | 1 | CTestApp::~CTestApp(void) |
| 25.384 (test.obj) | 11.9 | 25.384 | 11.9 | 1 | CTestApp::InitInstance(void) |
| 20.217 (crtexew.obj) | 9.5 | 212.704 | 100.0 | 1 | _WinMainCRTStartup |
| 0.522 | 0.2 | 0.522 | 0.2 | 1 | __onexit (atonexit.obj) |
| 0.189 | 0.1 | 49.658 | 23.3 | 1 | _$$0a00 (test.obj) |
| 0.042 (fp8.obj) | 0.0 | 0.042 | 0.0 | 1 | __setdefaultprecision |
| 0.023 | 0.0 | 0.023 | 0.0 | 1 | _$$5900 (mainfrm.obj) |
| 0.013 | 0.0 | 0.013 | 0.0 | 1 | _$$5900 (testdoc.obj) |
| 0.013 | 0.0 | 0.013 | 0.0 | 1 | _$$8900 (testview.obj) |
| 0.011 | 0.0 | 28.044 | 13.2 | 1 | _$$e900 (test.obj) |
| 0.010 | 0.0 | 0.033 | 0.0 | 1 | _$$6900 (mainfrm.obj) |
| 0.010 | 0.0 | 48.932 | 23.0 | 1 | _$$b900 (test.obj) |
| 0.008 | 0.0 | 0.536 | 0.3 | 1 | _$$f900 (test.obj) |
| 0.008 | 0.0 | 0.021 | 0.0 | 1 | _$$6900 (testdoc.obj) |
| 0.007 | 0.0 | 0.019 | 0.0 | 1 | _$$9900 (testview.obj) |
| 0.006 | 0.0 | 0.528 | 0.2 | 1 | _atexit (atonexit.obj) |
| 0.005 | 0.0 | 0.005 | 0.0 | 1 | __setargv (dllargv.obj) |

In comparison, Listing 2–3 contains the same program, except I've replaced the BITMAPFILEHEADER with a naturally aligned structure, MYBITMAPFILEHEADER. The difference in times is astonishing (see Listing 2–4). For the naturally aligned version, InitInstance requires only 17.172 milliseconds—a significant decrease just for aligning a structure!

**Listing 2–3** The naturally aligned version

```
typedef struct tagmyBITMAPFILEHEADER {
        WORD     bfType;
        DWORD    bfSize;
        WORD     bfReserved1;
        WORD     bfReserved2;
        DWORD    bfOffBits;

} MYBITMAPFILEHEADER;

BOOL CTestApp::InitInstance()
{
    // Standard initialization
    // If you are not using these features and wish to reduce the size
    //  of your final executable, you should remove from the following
    //  the specific initialization routines you do not need.

      volatile MYBITMAPFILEHEADER bf;
    TRACE( "HELLO WORLD\n" );
    for (int      i=0; i <0xffff; i++)
        bf.bfSize = 10;

  return FALSE;
}
```

**Listing 2–4** Profile for the naturally aligned version

| Func Time | % | Func+Child Time | % | Hit Count | Function |
|---|---|---|---|---|---|

| | | | |
|---|---|---|---|
| 148.936 | 53.1 | 166.108 | 59.2 | 1 _WinMain@16 (mfc30d.dll) |
| 53.622 | 19.1 | 53.622 | 19.1 | 1 CTestApp::CTestApp(void) |
| (test.obj) | | | | |
| 37.625 | 13.4 | 280.688 | 100.0 | 1 _WinMainCRTStartup |
| (crtexew.obj) | | | | |
| 22.065 | 7.9 | 22.065 | 7.9 | 1 CTestApp::~CTestApp(void) |
| (test.obj) | | | | |
| 17.172 | 6.1 | 17.172 | 6.1 | 1 CTestApp::InitInstance(void) |
| (test.obj) | | | | |
| 0.655 | 0.2 | 0.655 | 0.2 | 1 __onexit (atonexit.obj) |
| 0.246 | 0.1 | 54.593 | 19.4 | 1 _$$0a00 (test.obj) |
| 0.216 | 0.1 | 0.216 | 0.1 | 1 __setdefaultprecision |
| (fp8.obj) | | | | |
| 0.057 | 0.0 | 0.716 | 0.3 | 1 _$$f900 (test.obj) |
| 0.023 | 0.0 | 0.023 | 0.0 | 1 _$$5900 (mainfrm.obj) |
| 0.013 | 0.0 | 0.013 | 0.0 | 1 _$$8900 (testview.obj) |
| 0.012 | 0.0 | 0.012 | 0.0 | 1 _$$5900 (testdoc.obj) |
| 0.009 | 0.0 | 0.032 | 0.0 | 1 _$$6900 (mainfrm.obj) |
| 0.009 | 0.0 | 53.631 | 19.1 | 1 _$$b900 (test.obj) |
| 0.009 | 0.0 | 22.074 | 7.9 | 1 _$$e900 (test.obj) |
| 0.007 | 0.0 | 0.018 | 0.0 | 1 _$$6900 (testdoc.obj) |
| 0.007 | 0.0 | 0.019 | 0.0 | 1 _$$9900 (testview.obj) |
| 0.003 | 0.0 | 0.003 | 0.0 | 1 __setargv (dllargv.obj) |
| 0.003 | 0.0 | 0.659 | 0.2 | 1 _atexit (atonexit.obj) |

If compatibility reasons force you to have unaligned structures (perhaps you also have a file format that must be shared with an existing Windows 3.1 application), remember that the C/C++ compiler for Windows NT aligns data on 4-byte boundaries by default. That's what the #pragma directives before and after the BITMAPFILEHEADER structure are for.

The pragma

```
#pragma pack(2)
```

causes packing on 2-byte boundaries, and the

```
#pragma pack()
```

resets the default.

Without the proper packing, your offsets would be wrong when you read in a bitmap. Instead of reading the bfSize field, you would read 2 bytes of padding and only 2 bytes of bfSize, which would really throw things off.

## CHANGES TO WINDOW MESSAGES

The good news is that WORD, DWORD, and LONG are the same size between NT and 16-bit Windows. The bad news is the Win16 API has lulled programmers into using WORDs and DWORDs improperly. In Win16, it is acceptable to interchange a WORD for a HANDLE or a WORD for an integer. It Win32, where both integers and HANDLES (and HMODULEs, HWNDs, and so on) are 32-bits, it is not acceptable. The majority of your porting labor will be fixing problems associated with the WORD type. If you were lulled into using WORD when your shouldn't have been lulled, you are not the only one. For example, take functions that have wParam and a lParam parameters, such as a WindowProc:

```
LRESULT CALLBACK WindowProc(hwnd, uMsg, wParam, lParam)
```

In Windows versions prior to 3.1, wParam was a WORD and lParam was a LONG. When Windows 3.1 was released, these parameters changed to a WPARAM and a LPARAM. WPARAM and LPARAM are typedefs:

```
typedef UINT WPARAM;
typedef LONG LPARAM;
```

In Win32, wParam grows to 32 bits. If you use Hungarian notation, then you may be confused to find a variable named wParam that is not a WORD. Oh well, so much for Hungarian notation. Maybe one day compilers will be smart enough to flag Hungarian notation violations. Until then, expect to see wParam as a 32-bit variable. I've seen some folks recommend that you change the name of wParam to uParam or iParam. I don't recommend it, but point it out in case you see sample code like this. The reason I don't recommend it is because the Win32 help files and the prototypes in the headers in the SDK still have references to wParam and WPARAM.

I mentioned the fact that handles grow to 32 bits. This fact causes an upheaval in the way many Window messages arrive to your window procedure.

Window message order stays the same. For example, PostNCClientDestroy is the last message to arrive. But, handles are only 16 bits in Win16, and some Window messages pack both a handle and another 16-bit variable into lParam. In Win32, there is not enough room in the 32-bit lParam to hold both a 32 bit handle and another variable, so some juggling had to take place. The WM_COMMAND message is a good example. Table 3–1 lists all of the affected messages. When you receive a WM_COMMAND message, the wNotifyCode indicates that the message is from a control, accelerator, or menu. In Win16, wNotifyCode arrived in the HIWORD (upper 16 bits) of lParam. In Win32, the window handle takes up all of lParam, so wNotifyCode moves to the HIWORD of wParam.

**Table 2–1** List of messages where parameters differ

| Window Message | Win16 Parameters | Win32 Parameters |
| --- | --- | --- |
| WM_ACTIVATE | wParam =fActive<br>lParam =<br>fMinimized, hwnd | wParam = fActive,<br>fMinimized<br>lParam = hwnd |
| WM_CHARTOITEM | wParam =nKey<br>nCaretPos<br>=hwndListBox,<br>iCaretPos | wParam =nKey, lParam<br><br>lParam<br>=hwndListBox |
| WM_COMMAND | wParam =idItem<br>wNotifyCode<br>wNotifyCode | wParam =wId, lParam =hwndCtl,<br><br>lParam =hwndCtl |
| WM_CTLCOLOR | wParam =hdcChild<br>lParam =hwndChild,<br>nCtlType | Obsolete (replaced with<br>individual messages for<br>each control) |
| WM_MENUSELECT | wParam =wIDItem<br>lParam =fwMenu, | wParam =uItem,<br>fuFlagshmenu       lParam =hmenu |
| WM_MDIACTIVATE | wParam =fActivate<br><br>lParam =hwndChildAct<br>hwndDeact | wParam =hwndDeactlParam =<br>hwndAct, |

**43**

**Table 2–1** continued

| Window Message | Win16 Parameters | Win32 Parameters |
|---|---|---|
| WM_MDISETMENU | wParam =fRefresh <br><br> hmenuWindow | wParam =hmenuFramelParam = lParam =hmenuFrame, hmenuWindow |
| WM_MENUCHAR | wParam =chUser fuFlaghmenu | wParam =chUser, lParam =fMenu, lParam =hmenu |
| WM_PARENTNOTIFY | wParam =fwEvent idChildwValue2 | wParam =fwEvent, lParam =wValue1, lParam =lValue |
| WM_VKEYTOITEM | wParam =wVkey nCaretPosnCaretPos | wParam =vkey,lParam =hwndLB, lParam =hwndLB |
| WM_HSCROLL | wParam = nScrollCode, nPoslParam = nPos, | wParam =wScrollCode lParam = hwndCtl hwndScrollBar |
| WM_VSCROLL | wParam = nScrollCode, nPoslParam = nPos, | wParam =wScrollCode lParam = hwndCtl hwndScrollBar |
| EM_LINESCROLL | wParam =0 lParam =cyScrollcyScroll | wParam =cxScrolllParam =cxScroll, |
| EM_GETSEL | wParam =0 lParam =lpdwEnd | wParam =lpdwStartlParam =0l |
| EM_SETSEL | wParam = lParam =nEnd | wParam =nStartlParam = |

Some messages don't have enough room to expand. Take for instance the Win16 WM_CTLCOLOR message. WM_CTLCOLOR is sent to the parent of a system-defined control class or a message box when the control or message box is about to be drawn. By responding to this message, the parent window can set the control's text and background colors. In Win16, wParam is equal to the hDC, the LOWORD (lower 16-bits) of lParam is equal to the window handle, and the HIWORD is equal to a constant specifing the type of control.

In Win32, there is not enough room to hold a 32-bit hDC, 32-bit hWnd, and a control constant. So, in Win32, you no longer receive a WM_CTLCOLOR message. Instead you receive one of the following messages:

- WM_CTLCOLORBTN
- WM_CTLCOLORDLG
- WM_CTLCOLORLISTBOX
- WM_CTLCOLORMSGBOX
- WM_CTLCOLORSCROLLBAR
- WM_CTLCOLORSTATIC
- WM_CTLCOLOREDIT

In each of these messages, the wParam contains the hDC and the entire lParam contains the window handle.

Another message that ran out of room is WM_MDIACTIVATE. An MDI child receives a WM_MDIACTIVATE when it is being activated or deactivated. In Win 16, wParam contains a flag that tells the MDI child if it is the window being activated or deactivated. The lParam contains both the hWnd of the child being activated and the hWnd of the child being deactivated. The Win32 WM_MDIACTIVATE dispenses with the activate flag and justs sends the two window handles. If you have a MDI child window sitting on WM_MDIACTIVATE, you may have to adjust your code to accommodate this change.

If your Win16 code looks like this:

```
if (wParam) // use fActivate to
            // determine if this is my window
```

Then change it to look like this:

```
if (wParam == myhWnd) // if this is your window
                      // then wParam will equal
                      // your window handle
```

## CHANGES TO API CALLS

The primary goal of the Win32 API is to be upwardly compatible with Win16 API. However, besides widening many parameters from 16 to 32 bits, there are some instances where the API calls have changed. These changes were necessary for the two reasons: modifications due to changes in return values and modifications to manipulate system information.

The first change is to Win32 APIs that have had their return values modified. One of the advancements to Win32 API is the requirement that all functions return an error status. If you call a function and it fails, call GetLastError to retrieve the error. Unfortunately, this requirement forced some APIs to change from Win16. The changes are worth it though. If your code checks the return status it is impossible to use an invalid handle. One of the functions that required changing is the MoveTo function. MoveTo moves the current position to the specified coordinates. The return value is x and y coordinates of the previous position. Since there is no room for a return value, the MoveTo function has been dropped from the Win32 API. Use the MoveToEx function instead. MoveToEx has another parameter, a point structure in which the previous position will be returned.

If your Win16 code looks like this:

```
HDC hdc;
MoveTo(hdc, 10, 20);
```

then change it to look like this:

```
#define MoveTo(hdc, x, y) MoveToEx(hdc, x, y, NULL)
HDC hdc;
MoveTo(hdc, 10, 20);
```

Most developers never check the return value of MoveTo in 16-bit Windows (I know I never do), so this change isn't a big deal. As a matter of fact, Windows 3.1 introduced MoveToEx (the Windows 3.1 team knew Win32 was coming), so you may have this function already ported.

The second major change is to the Win32 APIs that modify the window and class extra words. Since handles such as a Window handle are now 32 bits, you cannot use functions such as GetWindowWord(hWnd, GWW_HWNDPARENT), or GetClassWord(hWnd, GCW_HICON). To remedy this, the already existing GetClassLong and GetWindowLong have been extended to include all of the

GWW_* and GCW_* constants (with one exception, as GCW_ATOM remains 16-bits in Win32 and still exists). Therefore, if you used GCW_HICON, rename it to GCL_HICON. GWW_HWNDPARENT becomes GWL_HWNDPARENT, and so on.

## SEGMENTED ARCHITECTURE ISSUES

If you are a DOS or 16-bit Windows programmer, a significant part of your porting labor will be spent removing assumptions about segmented architectures.

The following commonly used "tricks" in segmented-land must be migrated to the Flat model world of Windows 95 and NT:

- Assumptions about address wrap: In 16-bit operating systems, addresses can be made to wrap when they are incremented past 0xFFFF. In Windows 95 and NT, the address after 0xFFFF is 0x10000. Anywhere you have assumptions about address wraps will have to be changed.

- Segment arithmetic: Adding segments is how most compilers implement HUGE arrays. Since there are no segments in Windows 95 or NT, all those sophisticated techniques used to get around the 64KB limit are no longer needed.

- Pointer manipulation: Breaking up pointers and separately storing selector and offset is commonplace in Win16. You will have to examine all your occurrences of pointers and port accordingly.

- GlobalLock (and malloc) do not return 64KB aligned pointers: In Win16, you can always count upon GlobalLock returning a pointer with an offset of zero. This isn't the case in Win32, so anywhere you depend upon this type of behavior will have to be changed to work under Windows 95 or NT.

## DIRECT HARDWARE ACCESSES

Windows 95 allows you to access hardware, but directly accessing hardware from a user-mode program in NT is a security violation. This includes reading or writing to ports (including comm ports), BIOS, DMA, or hardware devices.

If it's your own hardware device that you are trying to access, you will have to write a device driver. Although writing a device driver is beyond the scope of this book, here's how to open a device under Windows NT(and also Windows 95):

```
sprintf(Drive, "\\\\.\\%s",driveName);
hdrive = CreateFile(Drive,
GENERIC_READ | GENERIC_WRITE,
0,
NULL,
OPEN_EXISTING,
0,
NULL);
if hDrive == INVALID_HANDLE_VALU)
{
MessageBox(NULL, "Open Failed","Open Device", MB_OK);
return
}
```

## DIRECT ACCESS OF WIN.INI AND SYSTEM.INI

In 16-bit Windows, many developers felt the need to open WIN.INI via OpenFile and directly access the sections. Perhaps for their applications it was faster than using the documented WriteProfileString and GetProfileString. Nevertheless, NT interfaces with INI files differently. You can't read or write directly to WIN.INI anymore because calls to the profile functions may be mapped to the Registry database instead. You can tell if a particular INI file section will be mapped by looking in the Registry under the following:

```
HKEY_LOCAL_MACHINE\Software\Microsoft\
        Windows NT\CurrentVersion\IniFileMapping.
```

Check out Chapter 6, "The Registry Database," for all the details on INI files and Registry access.

In Windows 95 you can access INI files via OpenFile (or CreateFile (...OPEN_EXISTING) for that matter), but it is still not a good idea. Go ahead and port .

## USE OF UNDOCUMENTED FUNCTIONS AND INTERNALS

Undocumented Windows states,

The future Windows NT is causing much excitement right now and curiosity about whether Windows applications with undocumented calls will run under NT...Using undocumented functions certainly isn't safe all by itself...Undocumented functions really are different: they could be removed or altered in some fundamental way, in the next release of Windows.

Well, the next releases of Windows are here. This is one area in particular that Windows 95 and NT differ. Following its theme of strict compatibility, Windows 95 supports most undocumented functions. Windows 95 even goes so far as to validate the parameters passed to all the undocumented functions. (It makes you wonder why they don't just document them). Following is a look at some of the "undocumenteds" in Windows applications.

Some of the undocumented functions have become documented in Win32. For example, ShellAbout, which the samples in this book use extensively (one less dialog box to create) is now documented. Here's how ShellAbout is called for the sample program in the book:

```
ShellAbout(m_hWnd, "Multithreaded MFC App",
        "From Windows NT: A Developer's Guide"
        "\r\nby Kevin Goodman",
        LoadIcon(AfxGetInstanceHandle(), "threads")));
```

Many undocumented functions are no longer necessary. All of the functions that deal with selectors and real-mode are now obsolete.

If your application relies on undocumented messages, the following are now documented in Win32. I won't bother describing what these messages do because if you are using them in Win16, you know what they are for. However, I will point out any Win32 messages that perform differently than their undocumented cousins.

▪▪   WM_ENTERMENULOOP, WM_EXITMENULOOP: Instead of always returning 0 as documented (or should I say undocumented) by Schulman, wParam is a boolean that describes whether the menu is a popupmenu.

**49**

- ■■ WM_GETHOTKEY, WM_HOTKEY, WM_SETHOTKEY
- ■■ WM_PAINTICON: wParam is always equal to 1.
- ■■ LB_ADDFILE
- ■■ EM_SCROLL
- ■■ LB_SETANCHORINDEX, LBGETANCHORINDEX

As far as I can tell, no undocumented structure became documented in Win32. You will have to examine each case indivdually. In many cases, you will find the need to use an undocumented structure no longer necessary. For instance, one Windows 3.1 program that I wrote took advantage of the undocumented WaitEvent and PostEvent functions to simulate suspending a thread and then resuming the thread. (WaitEvent and PostEvent change a boolean field in the undocumented Windows 3.1 Task Database.) Well, Win32 has SuspendThread and ResumeThread functions, so hammering the Task Database is no longer necessary.

## VIRTUAL DEVICE DRIVERS (VXDS)

VxDs are very powerful system-level extensions to 16-bit Windows that run at ring 0. They are not supported in NT. However, they are very much alive in Windows 95. Some of the reasons for writing a VxD in Windows NT have gone away (like interfacing with real mode DOS), but other valid reasons still exist. Windows NT supports the concept of Virtual Device Drivers (VDD). To write a VDD you will have to buy the Device Driver Development Kit.

## DEPENDENCE UPON HPREVINSTANCE

In 16-bit Windows, the second and subsequent instances of an application share code segments and read-only data with the first instance and subsequent instances. This is not the case in NT, so hPrevInstance will always equal NULL. If your code uses hPrevInstance as a flag to determine if another instance is running, it will have to be changed. First, do all the initialization that you would normally perform if you were the first instance (such as registering a wndclass.) Second, if you want to prevent your application from running multiple copies, you have a couple of choices. One method that is portable between Win16 and Win32 is to use a registered message. Another method is to use FindWindow. However, FindWindow is difficult to use when working with MDI programs or programs in which an application framework defines the window class for you.

A method that will work in Win32 only is to create a named semaphore:

```
hSem = CreateSemaphore(NULL,1,1, MDI_SEM_NAME);
    if (hSem == NULL )
        {
        CloseHandle(hSem);
        hSem = NULL;
//Error out couldn't get a semaphore
        MessageBox("Couldn't get a semaphore");
        return 1;
        }
    if (GetLastError() == ERROR_ALREADY_EXISTS)
        TRACE("Already Exists");
```

## CHANGES TO INPUT STATE

The desynchronized message queue in Win32 may cause you to change the way you call functions such as GetFocus and GetActiveWindow. In Win16, the GetFocus function obtains the handle of the window that currently has the input focus. In Win32, if the calling thread doesn't have the focus, then GetFocus returns NULL. If your code always depends upon functions such as GetFocus returning something other than NULL, your logic will have to change.

## DEPENDENCIES UPON DOS

The assembly language interface of MS-DOS (INT 21H calls) is not supported in either Windows 95 or Windows NT. To port to Win32 you will have to migrate all of your DOS calls. Fortunately, the meaningful DOS functions have Win32 equivalents. It is important to note that other forms of DOS calls are supported. For instance, the assembly language INT 21H function 3DH method of opening a file is not supported in Win32, but the standard library call fopen (which, in DOS, is just a shell around the INT 21h 3DH) is supported. That's because in Win32, fopen is just a shell around CreateFile.

This next sections lists the assembly language DOS functions and their Win32 replacements. Instead of listing the DOS calls numerically, I've grouped them functionally.

## File management services

File names are no longer limited to 8.3 and path names can now grow longer than 128 bytes. Use the constant variable MAX_PATH (which equals 260) to define your maximum buffer sizes.

| Description | DOS Call | Win32 Function |
| --- | --- | --- |
| Create File | 3CH | CreateFile |
| Open a file | 3DH | CreateFile |
| Close a File | 3EH | CloseHandle |
| Read a File | 3FH | ReadFile |
| Write a File | 40H | WriteFile |
| Delete a File | 41H | DeleteFile |
| Move File Pointer | 42H | SetFilePointer |
| File Attributes | 4300H | Get/SetFileAttributes |
| Duplicate File Handle | 45H | DuplicateHandle |
| Rename File | 56H | MoveFile |
| File Date and Time | 5700H | Get/SetFileTime |
| Create Temporary File | 5AH | GetTempFileName, CreateFile |
| Create a new File | 5BH | CreateFile |
| Set maximum handle count | 67H | SetHandleCount (only necessary in Win32s) |
| Commit a file | 68H | FlushFileBuffers |
| Extended open/create | 6CH | CreateFile |

## Directory management services

| Description | DOS Call | Win32 Function |
| --- | --- | --- |
| Create Directory | 39H | CreateDirectory |
| Remove Directory | 3AH | RemoveDirectory |

| Change Current Directory | 3BH | SetCurrentDirectory |
|---|---|---|
| Get Current Directory | 47H | GetCurrentDirectory |
| Find First File | 4EH | FindFirstFile |
| Find Next File | 4FH | FindNextFile |
| Rename File | 56H | MoveFile(Ex) |
| Lock - Unlock File | 5CH | LockFile, UnlockFile |

## Drive management

| Description | DOS Call | Win32 Function |
|---|---|---|
| Reset Drive | 0DH | FlushFileBuffers |
| Default Drive | 0EH, 19H | Get/SetCurrentDirectory |
| Set Disk Transfer Address | 1AH, 2FH | no correlation |
| Get Startup Drive | 3305H | no correlation |
| Get Disk Free Space | 36H | GetDiskFreeSpace |

## Input/output control (IOCTL)

Win32 supports an arbitrary device control API. By using the DeviceIoControl function, you can gain specific information about a device. All of the public IO controls are in winioctl.h.

| Description | DOS Call | Win32 Function |
|---|---|---|
| Device Data | 44H | GetFileType |
| Control Data from Character Device | 44H | no correlation |
| Control Data From Block Device | 44H | DeviceIoControl |
| Check Device Status | 44H | no correlation |
| Removable Media | 44H | GetDriveType |
| Is Drive Remote | 44H | GetDriveType |
| Is File or Device Remote | 44H | GetDriveType |

| Description | DOS Call | Win32 Function |
|---|---|---|
| Generic IOCTL | 44H | no correlation |
| Get Logical Drive Map | 44H | no correlation |

| | | |
|---|---|---|
| Set Logical Drive Map | 44H | no correlation |
| Query IOCTL Handle | 44H | DeviceIoControl |
| Query IOCTL Device | 44H | DeviceIoControl |

## Character I/O

Much of the DOS character I/O interface is duplicated with the console APIs. Note that directly reading or writing to a screen buffer is not supported. Chapter 9, "Console Programming," discusses the console interface.

| Description | DOS Call | Win32 Function |
|---|---|---|
| Direct Console I/O | 06H | ReadConsoleCharacter |
| Direct Console Input | 07H | ReadConsoleCharacter |
| Read Keyboard /w Echo | 08H | PeekConsoleInput |
| Check Keyboard Status | 0BH | PeekConsoleInput |
| Flush Buffer | 0CH | FlushConsoleInputBuffer |

## Memory management

There is no correlation between the DOS memory management routines and the rich set of memory management functions provided by Win32. Check out Chapter 5, "Memory Management."

| Description | DOS Call | Win32 Function |
|---|---|---|
| Allocate Memory | 48H | no correlation |
| Free Allocated Memory | 49H | no correlation |
| Set Memory Block Size | 4AH | no correlation |
| Get Allocation Stategy | 58H | no correlation |
| Set Allocation Strategy | 58H | no correlation |
| Get Upper Memory Link | 58H | no correlation |
| Set Upper Memory Link | 58H | no correlation |

## Program management

| Description | DOS Call | Win32 Function |
|---|---|---|
| Terminate Program | 4CH | TerminateProcess, ExitProcess |

| | | |
|---|---|---|
| PSP (Program Segment Prefix) functions | | No correlation |
| Keep Program | 31H | No correlation |
| Get InDos Flag Address | 34H | No correlation |
| Load and Execute Program | 4BH | CreateProcess |
| Get Child Program Return Value | 4DH | WaitForSingleObject |
| Get Extended Error | 59H | GetLastError |
| Set Extended Error | 5DH | SetLastError |

## System management

| Description | DOS Call | Win32 Function |
|---|---|---|
| Set Interrupt Vector | 25H | No correlation |
| Get Time,Date | 2AH | GetSystemTime |
| Set Time,Date | 2BH | SetSystemTime (privilege required) |
| Get Version Number | 30H | GetVersion |
| CTRL-C Check Flag | 33H | SetConsoleMode |
| Get Interrupt Vector | 35H | No correlation |

## PORTING ASSEMBLY LANGUAGE

As I stated earlier, assembly language ties you to a specific platform and should be avoided. I know that is an easy thing to say. The truth is, selling an x86-only version is better than not selling anything. So, if I can't talk you out of porting your assembly to C or C++, following are a few pointers.

Make liberal use of the Version 6.x .Model PROTO and INVOKE macros. Using these macros will enable you to conditionally assemble your code, like so:

```
IFDEF WIN32
.586
.MODEL flat, stdcall
ELSE
.386
.MODEL medium, pascal
ENDIF
  .
```

**55**

```
        .
        .
INVOKE MessageBox, ;;Will work in either OS
        hWnd,
        msg,
        title,
        MB_OK
```

Use 386 instructions even in 16-bit mode. You'll have to check, but it is possible that a 386 system is the low end system for your customers. If so, start assembling your code with the .386 switch. This will help you in porting because you can start using the eax register for returns (even though your 16-bit version will only access ax). This will help your performance on both the 16-bit side and the 32-bit side. Another added bonus will be the ability to index from registers like eax (which can only be done when you use the .386 switch).

# ONE CODE BASE: BOTH WIN16- AND WIN32-COMPATIBLE

With one code base that is both Win16- and Win32 compatible, you can use the C way or the easy way, which involves using an application framework. Both are discussed here, with the C way first.

## THE C WAY

To write C code that is portable between Win16 and Win32 you have two options, conditionally compiling or use the SDK-provided macros.

Most of the sample C functions in the SDK use the first method, which is to conditionally compile the source for either Win16 or Win32 functionality. Conditionally compiling simply means you define a constant at compile-time to let the compiler know to compile one statement or another. Take this excerpt from GENERIC.C for example:

```
switch (message) {
        // message: command from application menu
```

```
case WM_COMMAND:
#if defined (_WIN32) || defined(WIN32)
                wmId    = LOWORD(uParam);
                wmEvent = HIWORD(uParam);
#else
                wmId    = uParam;
                wmEvent = HIWORD(lParam);
#endif
```

Depending upon which environment you build, Generic determines the value of the wmEvent. (Either the upper 16 bits of wParam or the upper 16 bits of lParam.) By conditionally determining the value of wmEvent at compile-time, you can make the WM_COMMAND message portable between operating systems. Going about this procedure is known as cracking the message.Cracking the message at the very beginning of a CASE statement enables you to concentrate all of your conditional code in one small area. This improves readability and maintainability. In the Generic example, the wmId variable now contains the proper value in either operating system. It is much easier to look at code like this:

```
switch (wmID) {
```

Instead of this:

```
#if defined (_WIN32) || defined(WIN32)
            switch (LOWORD(uParam)) {
#else

            switch (uParam) {
#endif
      case IDM_ABOUT:
```

Having too many #ifdefs in your code is the equivalent of having two code bases—in the same file!

One way to write portable C code that allows you to avoid directly using #ifdefs is to use the SDK-provided message cracking macros. The message cracking macros are included in the WINDOWSX.H header file. (If you are compiling a Win16 version of your code, make sure you use the lataest Win16 version of Windowsx.h. You can find it on the Win32 SDK as Windowsx.h16.) Make sure that windowsx.h is the last file to be included. If you don't, some macros will not get defined. The Cls_OnDropFiles and FORWARD_WM_DROPFILES macros depend upon _INC_SHELLAPI being defined, but _INC_SHELLAPI doesn't get defined unless SHELLAPI.H is included, as Listing 2–5 demonstrates.

**Listing 2–5** Excerpts from WINDOWSX.H and SHELLAPI.H

```
// shellapi.h must be included first or the following
// won't evaluate to TRUE
#ifdef _INC_SHELLAPI
/* void Cls_OnDropFiles(HWND hwnd, HDROP hdrop) */
#define HANDLE_WM_DROPFILES(hwnd, wParam, lParam, fn) \
    ((fn)((hwnd), (HDROP)(wParam)), OL)
#define FORWARD_WM_DROPFILES(hwnd, hdrop, fn) \
    (void)(fn)((hwnd), WM_DROPFILES, (WPARAM)(HDROP)(hdrop), OL)
#endif   /* _INC_SHELLAPI */


/*
 *   shellapi.h
 *
 *   Header file for shell association database management functions
 */

#ifndef _INC_SHELLAPI
#define _INC_SHELLAPI
```

The message-cracking macros encapsulate the wParam and lParam so you don't have to worry how the parameters are packed. If you use the WM_COMMAND message as an example, you can see the difference between the Win16 and the Win32 version of Windowsx.h in Listings 2–6 and 2–7.

**Listing 2–6** Windowsx.h Win32 version

```
// void Cls_OnCommand(HWND hwnd, int id, HWND hwndCtl, UINT codeNotify)
#define HANDLE_WM_COMMAND(hwnd, wParam, lParam, fn) \
    ((fn)((hwnd), (int)(LOWORD(wParam)), (HWND)(lParam),\
    (UINT)HIWORD(wParam)), OL)
```

```
#define FORWARD_WM_COMMAND(hwnd, id, hwndCtl, codeNotify, fn) \
    (void)(fn)((hwnd), WM_COMMAND, MAKEWPARAM(UINT)(id),\
    (UINT)(codeNotify)), (LPARAM)(HWND)(hwndCtl))
```

**Listing 2–7** Windowsx.h Win16 version

```
// void Cls_OnCommand(HWND hwnd, int id, HWND hwndCtl, UINT codeNotify)
#define HANDLE_WM_COMMAND(hwnd, wParam, lParam, fn) \
    ((fn)((hwnd), (int)(wParam), (HWND)LOWORD(lParam), \
    (UINT)HIWORD(lParam)), 0L)
#define FORWARD_WM_COMMAND(hwnd, id, hwndCtl, codeNotify, fn) \
    (void)(fn)((hwnd), WM_COMMAND, (WPARAM)(int)(id), \
    MAKELPARAM((UINT)(hwndCtl), (codeNotify)))
```

To use the message crackers, you must create a function for each message you want to crack. You can find the prototype for each function in Windowsx.h (there's one right before each macro, commented out). For example, WM_COMMAND is

```
// void Cls_OnCommand(HWND hwnd,
//                    int id,
//                    HWND hwndCtl,
//                    UINT codeNotify)
```

The Cls part of the function name is just a placeholder (it stands for class). Make a copy of this prototype (strip off the comment) and change the Cls to the name of the class you want to crack messages. To give you a real-life example, let's convert Generic from the conditional compilation example to one that uses message cracking macros. The Cls_OnCommand prototype turns into:

```
void Generic_OnCommand(HWND hwnd,
                       int id,
                       HWND hwndCtl,
                       UINT CodeNotify);
```

In the place where you need to crack the message, use the HANDLE_MSG macro. For WM_COMMAND, it looks like this:

```
switch (message) {
```

**59**

```
        // message: command from application menu
        HANDLE_MSG(hWnd, WM_COMMAND, Generic_OnCommand)
```

When expanded, HANDLE_MSG looks like this:

```
switch (message) {
        // message: command from application menu
        case WM_COMMAND:
          HANDLE_WM_COMMAND(hWnd,
                                wParam,
                                lParam,
                                Generic_OnCommand);
```

Then create a Generic_OnCommand function to perform the work that was in the WM_COMMAND body. (see Listing 2–8). Inside Generic_OnCommand, use the FORWARD_WM_COMMAND macro to send any unused messages to DefWindowProc.

**Listing 2–8** Generic_OnCommand

```
    FORWARD_WM_COMMAND(hwnd,
                        id,
                        hwndCtl,
                        codeNotify,
                        DefWindowProc);


    void Generic_OnCommand(HWND hwnd,
                        int id,
                        HWND hwndCtl,
                        UINT CodeNotify)
    {
    FARPROC lpProcAbout;  // pointer to the "About" function


        switch (id)
        {
        case IDM_ABOUT:
```

```
        lpProcAbout = MakeProcInstance((FARPROC)About,hInst);

        DialogBox(hInst,        // current instance
                "AboutBox",     // dlg resource to use
                hWnd,           // parent handle
                (DLGPROC)lpProcAbout);    // About()

    FreeProcInstance(lpProcAbout);
    break;

    case IDM_EXIT:
        DestroyWindow (hwnd);
        break;
.
.// other messages
.
.

    default:
        return FORWARD_WM_COMMAND(hwnd,
                        id,
                        hwndCtl,
                        codeNotify,
                        DefWindowProc);
    }
return;
}
```

Windowsx.h provides macros for all messages, but it's not an either all or nothing situation. You can mix code that uses message crackers for some messages with code that responds to other messages directly. However, it doesn't require a considerable amount of labor to convert. If you are going to use the message-cracking macros you should convert everything. This will keep your code base neat and maintainable.

## GET PORTING MACROS

There is one case where the HANDLE_xxx macros are inconvenient.

The basic problem is that there are messages whose return values are ignored by Windows, but may be used by applications. Again, WM_COMMAND is a good example. When used inside a dialog proc, its return value is a signal to the dialog window proc. Unfortunately, the standard HANDLE_WM_COMMAND throws away the return.

In this case you can use the GET_xxx macros. Following are GET_WM_COMMAND macros. First, the Win32 version:

```
#define GET_WM_COMMAND_ID(wp, lp)      LOWORD(wp)
#define GET_WM_COMMAND_HWND(wp, lp)    (HWND)(lp)
#define GET_WM_COMMAND_CMD(wp, lp)     HIWORD(wp)
```

Here's the Win16 version:

```
#define GET_WM_COMMAND_ID(wp, lp)      (wp)
#define GET_WM_COMMAND_HWND(wp, lp)    (HWND)LOWORD(lp)
#define GET_WM_COMMAND_CMD(wp, lp)     HIWORD(lp)
```

## PORTING MACROS FOR CONTROLS

The control macros allow you to abstract message passing when sending a message to a control. One message that needs this is the EM_SETSEL message. An application sends an EM_SETSEL message to select a range of characters in an edit control. Since a 16-bit edit control holds less than 64KB, the range can be expressed in two-byte variables. Win32 edit controls, however, have a range that requires 4 bytes. To write portable code that sends a EM_SETSEL to an edit control use the Edit_SetSel macro. Here's the Win32 version:

```
//Win32
#define Edit_SetSel(hwndCtl, ichStart, ichEnd)  \
        ((void)SendMessage((hwndCtl), EM_SETSEL, \
                (ichStart), (ichEnd)))
```

Here's the Win16 verson:

```
// Win16
#define Edit_SetSel(hwndCtl, ichStart, ichEnd)  \
```

```
((void)SendMessage((hwndCtl), EM_SETSEL, 0, \
                MAKELPARAM((ichStart), (ichEnd))))
```

Although very few messages to controls had their parameters changed from Win16 to Win32, Windowsx.h has control macros for every possible control message. You may consider replacing all of your SendMessage statements to controls with the control macros. Not only will it insulate you from Win16 to Win32 differences, it will make your code look cleaner and easier to maintain.

Of course, up until now we have just been talking about porting C code. This next section will show you how easy it is to port code using C++.

## THE EASY WAY: USING AN APPLICATION FRAMEWORK

Once you have an idea of what it will take to port your code, you'll be better prepared to give an estimate of how long it will take. Does it compile cleanly with the STRICT constant defined in warning level /W3? Microsoft introduced STRICT with the release of Windows 3.1. In early versions, Windows attempted to achieve encapsulation by decaring all pointers to internal data structures as HANDLEs. In versions prior to 3.1, and when STRICT is not defined, a HANDLE is typedef'd as a UINT. Unfortunately, this means that you can erroneously pass any HANDLE (HTASK, HWND, HPEN, and so on) when an SDK function requires a specific one. Many times this caused Windows 3.0 to corrupt its internal structures, which resulted in a general-protection violation. STRICT is designed to combat this. When you define STRICT (either in your makefile or on the compiler command line) each HANDLE is declared as an individual pointer to a structure. Any attempt in your code to pass an invalid pointer will be flagged as an error by the compiler. (Windows 3.1 also has other safeguards, such as parameter validation, to protect itself from corrupting internal structures.)

Another question to ask is why is your code in C instead of C++? Either will port to Win32, but if it's worth porting, now may be the time to move your C code to C++. Why? Well, J.D. Hildebrand said it best in his editorial in the April 1993 issue of Windows Tech Journal:

C is not an appropriate primary tool for the creation of Windows applications. I have never heard of a Windows application written in C being delivered on time. Windows is a whole new ball game, and it requires new tools. You can choose object-oriented programming or you can choose visual programming, but choose you must.

If you do decide to migrate your C to C++, there are three steps that are necessary in the migration from C to C++:

1.  Upgrade the code base to an acceptable level to prepare it for migration.

2.  Compile the C source as a C++ program.

3.  Introduce objects such as the Microsoft Foundation Class Libraries into the program.

Following is a look at each step.

## UPGRADING YOUR C CODE BASE TO AN ACCEPTABLE LEVEL

Since the rules for C++ are much stricter than C, the easiest way to improve the existing code base is to get the code to compile cleanly at warning level /W4 and to use the #define STRICT option. In the compiler that ships with Visual C++ 2.0 there are over 700 possible warnings that the compiler can generate. Although C code will compile and still produce an .EXE when it compiles with warnings, allowing warnings in your code is courting disaster. Many hidden or subtle bugs are the result of unheeded warnings. When you convert your program to C++, many of these warnings turn into errors. This is one of the reasons so many industry folks are saying that C++ is a better C than C. Unfortunately, many of these warnings are cryptic. Some warnings show up in in odd places in your code and the rest are just plain confusing. If you have been ignoring warnings all along, the thought of turning on the /W4 switch must be overwhelming.

Fortunately, there is a technique that will break down these 700 plus warnings into manageable pieces. Known as walking up the warning level ladder, this process gets you to compile clean under warning level /W1, then /W2 all the way up to /W4, which is the strictest. Because some errors in your code will cause several warnings, all of them at different levels, the quickest way to remove all warnings is to start at the bottom.

The first rung of the ladder is /W0. This warning actually suppresses all warnings and should be avoided.

The next warning, warning level /W1, is the least strict and generates warnings that normally indicate flaws in your coding logic, an oversight, or some type of typographical error. A typical example of a logic error is "function declared with a void parameter list.". This warning is generated when a parameter is passed to a function that is expecting a void parameter list. In most cases, level /W1 warnings require you to reexamine your code to see what your intentions are. Now you may be saying, "If I pass a parameter and the function doesn't use it, big deal?". Well, if the calling convention of your function is _stdcall, your program will not clean the stack properly and return to who-knows-where. At this point your application and probably your boss (when he or she finds out you've added three weeks to the porting schedule) will go non-linear. If the calling convention is cdecl, the program will return correctly and the stack will stay intact, but you may end up with a debugging nightmare depending on what you expected to happen with that parameter you passed. Suffice it to say, if your programs consistently work with these types of level /W1 warnings it is just a coincidence. Level-one warnings of this nature produce errors in C++ and must be corrected before you can migrate. The other type of level-one warning is probably a typographical error. An example of this is "expected a comma; found token." This warning happens when you forget to put a comma between arguments to a pragma. What will happen is the whole pragma will be ignored. Even though these type of warnings are also just warnings in C++, they should still be corrected before migrating.

At this point, continue through the cycle of removing warnings and recompiling. When you can compile, clean-change the command line option to /W2.

Warning level /W2 displays intermediate level messages. The best example of a level /W2 warning is the warning "no function prototype given." Function prototypes tell the compiler important details about the size of the parameters. Without a prototype, the compiler assumes that the variables passed are the correct size. Do not make your compiler guess. If you don't have prototypes in your code, you have no hope of migrating to C++. Fortunately, the command line parameter /Zg will generate function prototypes for all of your existing functions. I normally route the output of a /Zg compile to a file using indirection:

```
cl /c /Zg foo.c >proto.h
```

I then #include "proto.h" into foo.c to take care of all of my functions. This leaves all external functions which must be taken care of separately.

Level /W2 also has its typographical-related errors. A typical warning is "No symbols were declared." This happens when you enter something like the following line:

```
int ;
```

The compiler will not generate any instructions by this statement, so it is tempting to ignore, but mistakes like this clutter up your source and make it harder for others who follow you to maintain your programs. Another reason to eliminate this kind of warning is that if enough benign warnings appear during your compile, you may become insensitive to them and not notice when another type of warning occurs.

Warning level /W3 will catch even more mistakes and will also flag dead code. Many level-three warnings occur during unwanted conversions or comparisons. For example, the following code will generate a "conversion between different integral types" :

```
WORD w;
UINT ui;
w = ui;
```

It may be tempting to use a cast such as

```
w = (WORD)ui;
```

I'm not suggesting even for a minute that you should never cast. On the contrary, casting is a normal, everyday occurrence. But be careful. What is it that you are casting? Your shoe size? The number of sightings of Elvis? Make sure that you are not introducing a subtle bug. By casting an integer to a WORD, two bytes of information are lost. If those two bytes are not needed—fine. But if, down the road, you change the code to use the upper 16 bits of UI you have silenced the only means the compiler has to warn you. (There goes that schedule again.) When you use a cast, you tell the compiler to shut up because you know what you are doing. So don't just cast to make the warning go away. You must heed warnings such as this one if you want your code to be portable between Win16 and Win32. In Win16 an integer is 16 bits, but in Win32 an integer is 32 bits. What this warning really does is tell you that you have a logic error in your program.

Several warnings are generated as the result of possible dead or unused code, including "unreferenced formal parameters," "unreferenced local variables," and "unreferenced labels." Unlike functions that use the _cdecl calling convention, _stdcall requires a fixed number of parameters whether you use them or not. In an effort to quiet the compiler, many programmers who were not processing parameters from the command line resorted to action such as this:

```
int WINAPI WinMain( HINSTANCE hInstance,
                HINSTANCE PrevInstance,
                LPSTR lpszCmdLine,
                int nCmdShow)
{
lpszCmdLine;     //Force compiler to be quiet about
                 //not using the command line parameters
.
.
.
}
```

While this appeases warning level /W3, it causes a "statement has no effect" in /W4. In Win32, these same developers will use #pragma warning(disable:4100) to turn off the warning or use the UNREFERENCED_PARAMETER macro. Neither of these gyrations is really necessary in C++, however. If the function is your own function and it is generating this warning, then perhaps you need to look at your logic to determine whether you need parameters in your function or not. If it is not your function, then C++ allows you to not name the uneeded parameter, as in this example:

```
int WINAPI WinMain(HINSTANCE hInstance,
                HINSTANCE PrevInstance,
                LPSTR,  //do not give parameter a name if you
                    //are not using it.
                int nCmdShow)
```

Warning level /W4 displays additional messages that provide warnings of ANSI violations and also provide very detailed lint-like messages. You would probably be able to convert your code at level /W3 if it weren't for one particular message to be aware of. The warning "uses old-style declarator" occurs when your code contains an old-style declaration such as:

```
int main(argc,argv)
int argc;
char **argv;
{}
```

If your code contains these old-style declarators, you must convert them to the new-style:

```
int main(int argc, char **argv)
{}
```

because the old-style declarations are unacceptable in C++.

In previous versions of the Microsoft compiler, level /W4 wasn't as useful because it was impossible to turn off unwanted warnings, including the warning for double slash comments. A double slash comment is not part of the ANSI standard in C, but I use it quite frequently. The current version makes it possible to instruct the compiler to ignore a particular warning message with #pragma warning. The following line turns off warnings for #4001:

```
#pragma warning(disable: 4001)     // nonstandard extension
                                   // double slash comment
                                   // used
```

My only suggestion is: if you choose to suppress any warning, not just ANSI violation warnings, remember to turn them back on once you've passed the affected piece of code. You do this with the same #pragma warning, but with "default" keyword instead of "disable":

```
// warn for double slash comments
#pragma warning(default: 4001)
```

While I am on the subject of ANSI compatiblity, all non-ANSI runtime library calls now need an underbar in front of the function call name so they can link. Therefore, for your non-ANSI runtime library functions to become ANSI-compliant, cputs becomes _cputs, cprintf becomes _cprintf, and so on.

Once you can compile-clean at /W4, add the /WX option. This will force the compiler to treat the first warning it encounters as an error, causing your build to fail. This way warnings will not creep back into your program.

Once you can compile successfully at /W4, compile with the constant STRICT defined.

## COMPILING THE C PROGRAM AS A C++ PROGRAM

The next step will be to compile the C program as a C++ program. To do this, rename your files with a .CPP extension. This will tell the compiler that the you are compiling C++ code. This automatically enables the program to take advantage of type-safe linking. Type-safe linking is the process that makes it impossible to call a function with parameter mismatch. By using a method called "decorating," the compiler places prefixes and suffixes around the function name based on what parameters the function takes. Another term for decorating is "name-mangling." (See "How to Read a .MAP File" in Chapter 1 to see how variables are decorated).

Type-safe linking is necessary due to the function overloading feature of C++. Function overloading eliminates situations where you have multiple functions that do very similiar operations. This phenomenon is known as "code-cloning," and the best example I can think of is in Win16 where you have strlen for near-string-length functions and lstrlen for far operations. In the early days of C++ you had to physically declare a function with the overloaded keyword, but today this is no longer a requirement. That means that every function, whether it is overloaded or not, is "decorated." Because the C runtime library functions are not stored in decorated format, you must let the compiler know not to mangle their names. You do this with the following linkage specifier:

```
extern "C"
{

}
```

Use extern "C"' on any variable, function, or header file that has been compiled as C source, even if its calling convention is something other than _cdecl (like _stdcall or _fastcall). This includes all prototypes for assembly functions. As of this writing, the current version of the 32-bit version of MASM (Version 6.11) doesn't support decorated names. Therefore, any assembly functions will also have to be declared with "C" linkage (assuming you haven't already converted them to C++). The predefined variable __cplusplus gives you the capability to have one header file for both C and C++ files—just #ifdef __cplusplus around all of your extern "C" specifiers. Every header file from the SDK uses this technique. Here's an example:

```
#ifdef __cplusplus
extern "C" {   // Assume C declarations for C++
#endif // __cplusplus

// C style declarations go here
.
.
.

#ifdef __cplusplus
}          // End of extern "C"
#endif        // __cplusplus
```

## INTRODUCING MFC OBJECTS

If we quit right here and didn't migrate any further, the C++ Compiler would still have earned its purchase price because of its improved warnings and stricter type checking. Now that the code is ready to be migrated, the real value in C++ lies in its ability to be extended with class libraries. This is where the Microsoft Foundation Class Libraries come in.

MFC encapsulates everything necessary to move from Win16 to Win32. This includes message cracking, as well as replacing Win16 calls with their Win32 equivalents. Since this book concentrates on Win32 instead of MFC, I won't go too deep into how to program in MFC. But if you use the message-cracking macros in C, you will have no trouble adjusting to the message map of MFC.

## MFC 2.X VS MFC 3.0.

There are several versions of MFC kicking around— Version 2.*x* that ships with Visual C++ 1.51, and Version 3.0 that ships with Visual C++ 2.0. Visual C++ 1.51 generates 16-bit applications and version 2.*x* generates 32-bit applications.

If you are converting your 16-bit MFC Version 2.*x* code, your porting efforts should be trivial. Occasionally you will receive a warning in the 32-bit version that the 16-bit version doesn't complain. To port, simply recompile. Fix any warnings as they arise. Otherwise, the port will be a snap. There are some differences between 2.0 and 3.0 when porting. These differences are all minor. Most of them deal with additional parameters of the Version 3.0 member functions. The easiest way to port is to recompile. If your application has no errors, you're ready to go. If your code receives errors related to the conversion it will probably be one of six error messages. These errors are all listed in TechNote 19, which ships with Visual C++.

## SOME NOTES ABOUT MFC

Just because MFC makes porting a snap doesn't mean it's a panacea. Portability is only a small piece of the puzzle. In order to have a successful, money-making application in Windows 95 and NT, you will have to do more than just port your Win16 application. If that is all you are planning, you might as well have your customers run your Win16 application in the WOW layer. To fully take advantage of Windows 95 and NT, you must fully take advantage of Win32. A good example of this is MFC 2.1. In MFC 2.1, which is the version that shipped with Visual C++ 1.0 for NT the MFC libraries were just a straight port of the 3.1 libraries; they lacked classes to fully support Win32. For example, there are no classes to do the following:

■ Access the registry

■ Use remote procedure calls (RPCs)

■ Take advantage of UNICODE

■ Use the security APIs

■ Access the new IPC APIs (mapped files)

■ Use the console APIs

▪   Take advantage of multiple threads

And that was by no means a comprehensive list. In Windows NT: A Developer's Guide I griped about the lack of support in MFC. Version 3.0 has addressed some, but not all of these problems.

# UNICODE SUPPORT

All of the Microsoft Foundation class libraries are now UNICODE enabled.

## MFC AND MULTIPLE THREADS

MFC 3.0 now contains a CWinThread class that you can use to develop multi-threaded applications. Chapter 4, "Processes" takes you through all the steps necessary to create a multithreaded application using the Microsoft Foundation class libraries.

## BENEFITS OF MFC

The Microsoft Foundation class libraries significantly reduce the amount of visible code or "surface area" your application has. If you are a C programmer, herein lies the difference between class libraries and any third-party C runtime libraries you may be familiar with. C runtime libraries are extensible to the point that if you buy the source you are free to go in and change it. If the vendor of the third-party library makes a change to the original source code, you either have to forego the changes or reincorporate them in your code. On the other hand, the MFC can change its internal workings and the interface will stay the same. This is why MFC makes porting to Win32 almost trivial.

   This doesn't mean that the MFC class libraries are unique in this ability. On the contrary, OWL from Borland and zAPP from [help, what's their name!!]have 32-bit versions of their Windows 3.x application frameworks. I'll bet that, when finished, they will port just as easily. I've concentrated on MFC here because it shipped with the BETA of NT and Windows 95.

Before you decide to convert everything in the house to MFC, there are some caveats. While absolutely everything qualifies to become better C than C, the same cannot be said about the MFC. For some very small projects there may be too much overhead in adding the MFC.

No matter which method you choose to create your Win32 code, you might consider attending a porting lab.

# ATTENDING A PORTING LAB

The Microsoft porting lab is located in Redmond, Washington on the Microsoft campus. If the building the porting lab is in did not contain the porting lab, it would probably house Microsoft developers. Every office is the same size and has the same furniture as a real Microsoft developer would have.

I had the opportunity to use the porting lab for a week in November, 1992. The most impressive thing about the porting lab is the direct access you have to Microsoft support personnel. While out there, I was porting a Program Manager replacement program from Windows 3.1. When a question came up that one of the support personnel couldn't answer, he sent an e-mail message to the one of the developers who wrote Program Manager. When a question came up about the Lan Manager for NT (that's what is was called back then), the support person located the source to LanMan on the network and answered my question. The lab's kitchen has a cooler stocked with every type of soft drink imaginable—all complimentary. The cabinets are stocked with teas, coffee, and instant soups. To tell you the truth, I didn't want to leave.

I saw hardware developers writing drivers, UNIX developers, DOS developers, and other Windows developers all porting with varying degrees of success. If Microsoft makes a porting lab available to you. (They seem to come and go depending on the what the next major release is) here are a few pointers:

▟ Since you only have a week to port your application and the porting lab is open 24 hours a day, you will probably be working long hours. Rent the cheapest hotel you can find. You won't be using it much. The Porting Lab has a shower, but I don't recommend trying to live at the porting lab. Its one couch normally has someone cat-napping on it. Rest before you get there.

▪▪ Don't worry too much about the security of your source code. You are assigned an office that locks, and you will be given the only key. The building has security-badge access, and I'm told that only other porters and the porting lab staff have access. I heard of other developers who backed up their machine every night, then deleted the source before they left. They then restored their source every morning. You can do this if you want to, but it will waste precious time. I am not sure anyone at Microsoft would even want something I wrote.

▪▪ Come prepared. It's a good idea to follow the steps in this chapter before you arrive. If you get to the porting lab and you have never even booted the operating system you are porting to, you won't get much accomplished. When we arrived (I went with another developer), we came with our code already built under the October BETA. I also had a list of about fifteen questions and reported about four "bugs" for the porting lab folks. As it turned out, most of the bugs were user-error bugs and all my questions were answered. When we left, we had a working port. It was demo'd at the 1992 Comdex Convention.

## THE DIGITAL EQUIPMENT CORPORATION'S ALPHA MIGRATION LAB

DEC has Alpha migration labs all over the country, but lucky for me there was one right around the corner from where I live. The Alpha migration lab was founded to field-test the Alpha before it went into production (and before they changed the name to AXP). I was there in the Spring of 1993. At the time, NT was still in Beta and the Alpha C++ compiler wasn't soup yet. The week-long trip was still profitable, however. I ported all of the working x86 C samples that I had.

If DEC decides to reopen their Alpha Migration Lab (perhaps for that 100,000 mhz version), here are a couple of pointers.

▪▪ Have your application running on an x86 or MIPS platform machine before you arrive. The purpose of the Alpha Migration Lab is to port your working windows NT Program to the Alpha. It is not there to help you write Windows NT code from scratch. Remember, Windows 95 only runs on Intel class machines so until there is a Windows NT 95, Alpha won't support it.

▣ Have alternative means of technical support available. The Alpha Migration folks know their hardware extremely well, but most cannot answer SDK questions. If you are having SDK type trouble, it is best to have your Microsoft support line handy.

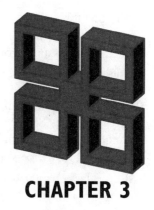

## CHAPTER 3

# THUNKING

When developing for Win32, the term *thunking* simply refers to any code that allows 16-bit code to call 32-bit code or 32-bit code to call 16-bit code. This is different from porting which we covered last chapter. In porting, you convert the code from 16-bits to 32-bits and hopefully you are done. Thunking is what you do when for some reason you can't port everything to 32-bits. This chapter delves into all the nuances of thunking, and it does so for Windows 95, NT, and Windows 3.1 running Win32s.

Thunks solve the problem of trying to get 32-bit code and 16-bit to coexist in the same operating system or in the same executable. So what's the problem? Why can't 16-bit code call 32-bit code and vice-versa? Well, as pointed out in Chapter 1, "32-bit Programming Rules," Win16 combines a 16-bit selector with a 16-bit offset to produce a pointer to memory (referred to as 16:16 pointers). In Win32, the selector remains static and the offset is 32-bits (referred to as 0:32). This means that translating 16:16 pointers to 0:32 requires determing the segment base for the selector portion of the pointer and adding the offset to it. Translating a 0:32 pointer to a 16:16 pointer involves allocating a selector and calculating the offset from the base of the corresponding segment.

Not that this is impossible to do. On the contrary, it is quite easy. The problem lies with the fact that 16-bit compilers assume you are calling 16-bit code and 32-bit compilers assume you're calling 32-bit code. Therefore, when you make a function call there is no code placed in your function to automatically check to see if the call requires a step down or step up. This also causes problems for the stack. C and Pascal calling conventions use the stack to pass parameters. In 16-bit mode that means SS:SP and 32-bit mode means ESP. Therefore, since compilers are ignorant of switching modes (thunk-challenged, to be politically correct), a 16- to 32-bit (and vice-versa) transition will corrupt the stack.

In the last chapter, I mentioned that one of the most significant changes in moving from 16- to 32- bits is the fact that the an *int* doubles in size. This fact is significant when passing parameters on the stack, but also when passing parameters via registers. If the 16-bit side places variables in the AX:DX register and the 32-bit side expects the variable in EAX, you can imagine what will happen.

In Windows 3.1 with Win32s, many of the Win32 calls thunk down to their 16-bit equivalents as shown in Figure 3–1. In Windows NT, Win16 applications make 16-bit calls that thunk up to the 32-bit equivalent.(see Figure 3–2). Windows 95 has situations where it does both. (Figure 3–3).

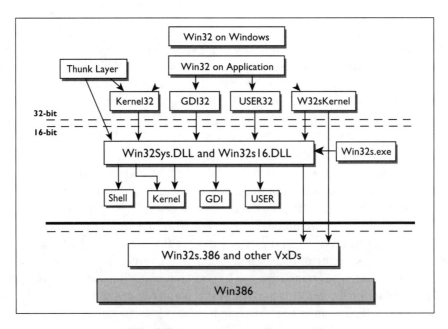

**FIGURE 3–1** Thunks under Win32s

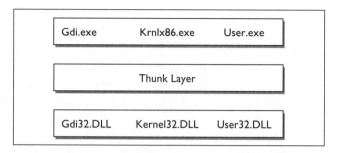

**FIGURE 3–2** Thunks under Windows NT

**Table 3–I** Thunks under Windows 95

| | |
|---|---|
| Universal Thunks (from Win32s) | not supported. |
| Generic Thunk (from Win NT) 16-bit to 32-bit | supported in M7 |
| Generic Thunk (from Win NT) 32-bit to 16-bit | not supported |
| Compiled Thunks (from Win95) | supported in M6 |
| Compiled Thunks (from Win95) | not supported in Win32s or WinNT |

In all of these situations, thunking takes place without your knowledge. It's just part of the normal occurrence of making operating systems that support both 16- and 32-bit executables load and execute. But what about your programs? What if you want to take advantage of these thunking mechanisms?

Well, it is possible to do so on each platform, but not without consequences. This chapter details each type of thunk and explains when they are appropriate. Of course, the Microsoft marketing machine never lets much go by without catchy titles and thunks are no exception. In Win32s, thunks are called Universal Thunks; Windows NT has Generic Thunks, and Windows 95 (which also supports Generic Thunks) has Compiled Thunks.

All these catchy titles may make you decide to run out and start thunking. But, before you decide to ship the next version of your application as a set of 16- and 32-bit components, here are some reasons not to.

▐ It may take as long to write the thunk code as it would to port your 16-bit components to 32-bits. Thunking in Windows 95 requires knowledge of assembly language. Although, the thunk compiler provided with the Windows 95 SDK generates the assembly for you, it is by no means a completely automated process.

▚ Debugging the other side of the thunk (that is the 32-bit side in Windows 3.1 and the 16-bit side in Windows 95 and NT) is a royal pain. It's possible, however, and I'll give you some tips on how to do it, but it slows the development process.

▚ The overall performance may not meet your expectations. There is overhead involved in implementing thunks. Obviously the thunk code requires clock ticks, but selector loads on the 16-bit side also takes time. (9 ticks each on a 486). While most programs may not suffer, if you need speed, thunking is not the way to go. Microsoft estimates that the Windows 95 thunks within the operating system take anywhere from 63 to 100 clocks. If your 16-bit function accesses data using a lot of far pointers, the function makes more than 7 selector loads.

▚ Win32s supports only Universal Thunks while Windows 95 does not. Windows NT does not support thunking to 16-bit DLLs. Thus, you will need different thunking mechanisms depending on which platform your application is currently executing. That means you'll need a pair of 'thunking' DLL's for each operating system (Windows 95, Win32s, and NT) to provide whatever thunking may be required.

▚ The only truly portable way to get 16-32 interoperability is to use OLE automation. With OLE, you can run the same binaries on all Win32 implementations. The 16-bit code becomes the OLE server, the 32-bit code the OLE client. Microsoft has never promised that thunking will work the same way on all platforms. Microsoft has, however, stated that OLE is the proper method to communicate between 16 and 32-bits.

Before I completely scare you off thunks let me say that there are several compelling reasons to implement thunks:

1. If you can't port your application easily, thunking could be a working solution. If your applications written in a language in which no known 32-bit version exists, or perhaps it was written by someone who no longer works at your company (probably because that person wrote such horrible code) then you may decide it will take too long to port.

2. You want a stop-gap measure. Suppose you have a group of developers working on the 32-bit port, but one guy is behind on his DLL and you promised the marketing geeks you'd be ready by COMDEX. (Or, more realistically, you promised code by Fall COMDEX, but marketing promised your customers that it would be ready by Spring).

3.  You want to port your Win16 application piece by piece to 32-bits. Many developer's like to ease into Win32 programming by porting the main application and leaving some 16-bit DLLs for later. There is no anxiety like being four months into a project and not even being able to show your main window to your boss. Porting in pieces enables you to show accomplishments, even if only temporary.

4.  Or, perhaps just the opposite. You may want to just take advantage of an existing 32-bit DLL but still use your 16-bit executable to call the 32-bit DLL. Marketing wants to know how much faster 32-bits will be before they commit to a year long project. One way to tell them is to port a small piece and then extrapolate. "Well we converted XYZ.DLL and speed went way up (or down)."

5.  Your 16-bit application or DLL doesn't support OLE2. We all know that OLE2 is the way to go even for 16- to 32-bit communication. But, what if your 16-bit application doesn't support OLE2. Why spend the time to implement OLE2 into an application your trying to get rid of?

6.  Thunking is better than not shipping. I once spent about ten minutes explaining to a police officer why I didn't have my license on me when I was driving. It was a perfectly valid explanation. What he said to me as he handed me the ticket was, "I don't care, you gotta have a license." The same goes for your application. Perfectly good reasons why you can't ship a 32-bit solution won't wash with your customers. They'll buy your competition's product. It happened to great DOS products that didn't convert to Windows in time. It will happen to greate 16-bit Windows applications if they don't port to Windows 95 in time. Even if a 16- 32-bit combined solution isn't as great as an all 32-bit solution, perhaps it will buy you time to develop a 32-bit solution.

The rest of this chapter goes over each type of thunk—Compiled, Generic, and Univeral.

## COMPILED THUNKS

Compiled thunks are specific to Windows 95. As the name implies, you use a compiler to create these thunks. Compiled thunks support both 16->32-bit and 32->16-bit. If you use the thunk compiler to create your thunks, it generates code that automatically grabs the Win16Mutex when thunking from 32 to 16 bits, so you don't have to use your own mutexes. This is better than using your own mutex because all 16-bit components are protected against other Win32 processes you don't know about (and thus won't use your mutexes).

The are six steps you must take to create compiled thunks.

1   Create thunk scripts for the compiler

2   Compile the thunk script to produce an assembly (.ASM) file.

3   Assemble the .ASM file with the (/DIS_32 ) switch to create a 32-bit (.OBJ) object file.

4   Assemble the .ASM file with the (/DIS_16 ) switch to create a 16-bit (.OBJ) object file.

5   Link your 32-bit OBJ into your 32-bit DLL.

6   Link your 16-bit OBJ into your 16-bit DLL.

I'll go over each step and walk you through a typical process of creating both 16->32-bit and 32->16-bit thunks. For illustrative purposes, let's say that we have functions that we want to thunk that is in a third-party DLL. ThirdParty16 is a 16-bit, third party DLL that we must have for our application. Following my own rules for determining when and when not to thunk we see that ThirdParty Corporation (the provider of ThirdParty16) has been slow in providing a 32-bit beta version of their DLL, but they have stated that 32-bits is their company's direction. Oh well, it looks like they have hung us out to dry. Since we are not in the ThirdParty16 business we can't (or don't want to) write our own 32-bit version of ThirdParty Corporation's 16-bit DLL, so we decide to thunk to their 16-bit DLL.

## CREATE SCRIPTS FOR THE THUNK COMPILER

The first step in creating compiled thunks is to create thunk scripts for the thunk compiler. A thunk script is a file that contains typedef's and declarations for any functions you wish to thunk. Script files usually have the extension .THK. The best way to create a THK file is by starting with the prototypes of the functions you want to thunk. For example, one of the functions in ThirdParty16 that we need is prototyped as:

```
BOOL ThirdFunc(int n);
```

So in the script file enter the typedefs for BOOL and INT. Like this:

```
typedef int BOOL;
typedef int INT;
```

Then prototype the function this way:

```
BOOL ThirdFunc(INT n)
{
}
```

You'll see why the braces are necessary in the next example. It is an example of a function that takes pointers in its parameter list. But before I show it to you let me review the difference between regular pointers and pointers that are const. A const pointer is a pointer that will not be updated by the called function. The second and third parameters to MessageBox are examples of const pointers:

```
int MessageBox(

    HWND  hwndOwner,      // handle of owner window
    LPCTSTR lpszText,     // address of text in message box
    LPCTSTR lpszTitle,    // address of title of message box
    UINT  fuStyle   // style of message box
    );
```

When you call MessageBox you know that the second and third parameters will not be modified by the MessageBox function. The thunk compiler calls const pointers *input* pointers.

The opposite of a const pointer really doesn't have a name (other than pointer), but the thunk script divides it into two categories: output only pointers and input/output pointers.

An example of an output only pointer is in the GetWindowsDirectory function:

```
UINT GetWindowsDirectory(
    LPTSTR lpszWinPath,     // address of buffer for Windows directory
    UINT  cchWinPath);      // size of directory buffer
```

It doesn't matter what is contained in the data that lpszWinPath points to when you call GetWindowsDirectory. That because GetWindowsDirectory overwrites what is contained their with the path of the Windows directory.

An example of an input and output pointer is in the function *lstrcat*

```
LPTSTR lstrcat(
    LPTSTR lpszString1,    // address of buffer for concatenated strings
    LPCTSTR lpszString2);  // address of string to add to string1
```

The first parameter, lpszString1, is an input-ouput pointer. The value passed in lpszString2 (an input only parameter) is concatenated with the value passed in lpszString1 (the input part) and returned to the called in lpszString1 (the output part).

Now, conveniently for us, ThirdParty16 has a function that we need to thunk that has all three types of pointers. ThirdFunc2 is a function that takes a pointer to an input string, updates the inputted second string, and outputs a third string:

```
BOOL ThirdFunc2(LPSTR lpstrInput, LPSTR lpstrInOut, LPSTR Output);
```

The corresponding THK declaration for this function is:

```
typedef char *LPSTR;

BOOL ThirdFunc2(LPSTR lpstrInput, LPSTR lpstrInOut, LPSTR Output)
    {
        pstrInput = input;      // Optional since pointers are input
                                // by default.
        lpstrInOut = inout;     // Pointer taken in and updated
        lpstrOutput = output;   // Pointer returned.
    }
```

The direction of the thunk, that is whether your are thunking down to 16-bits or up to 32-bits is controlled by the *enablemapdirect* THK command:

To create 32->16 thunks use:

```
enablemapdirect3216 = true;      // Creates 32->16 thunks
```

or to create 16->32 thunks use

```
enablemapdirect1632 = true;      // Creates 16->32 thunks
```

A couple of warnings about the thunk compiler. The thunk compiler does not recognize the functions that return a pointer to a structure. The thunk compiler has no place to put a packed structure on return and no way to free anything allocated at this point. In general, thunking a function that returns a pointer to something either requires reformatting in place, or managing and synchronizing shadow structures. The appropriate solution depends how the service provider and user allocate responsibility for creating, modifying and freeing the structure. The thunk compiler doesn't have the information needed to decide this tradeoff. There a limit of 56 bytes for all the parameters a function can pass. If you need more, one alternative is to pass a pointer to the arguments and push them back on to the stack at the receiving end.

## COMPILE THE SCRIPT TO PRODUCE AN ASSEMBLY (.ASM) FILE

Once you create your THK file you compile it with the Thunk Compiler. The thunk compiler is a console application so you run it from the command line or from your make file. Here's the syntax:

```
thunk.exe <inputfile> [-o <outputfile>]
```

The following output lists all the options available to override the default behavior.

```
Microsoft (R) Thunk Compiler Version 1.01  Aug 23 1994 16:35:46
Copyright (c) Microsoft Corp 1988-1995. All rights reserved.


Thunk compiler usage
```

**85**

```
thunk [{-|/}options] infile[.ext]
```

```
where options include:
        ?                Display this help screen
        h                Display this help screen
        o <name>         Override default output filename
        p<n>             Change 16-bit structure alignment (default = 2)
        P<n>             Change 32-bit structure alignment (default = 4)
        t <name>         Override default stem name

        Nx <name>        Name segment or class where x is
              C32        32-bit code segment name
              C16        16-bit code segment name
```

Listing 3–1 is the completed thunk script file, THIRD.THK, and Listing 3–2, THIRD.ASM, is the assembly language output from the thunk compiler.

### Listing 3–1 THIRD.THK

```
//
// Thunk Script file for Third-party DLL
//
//
//


        enablemapdirect3216 = true;     // Creates 32->16 thunks


        typedef char *LPSTR;

          typedef int BOOL;
          typedef int INT;


BOOL ThirdFunc(INT n)
          {
          }
```

```
BOOL ThirdFunc2(LPSTR lpstrInput, LPSTR lpstrInOut, LPSTR
lpstrOutput)
    {
        lpstrInput = input;       // Optional since pointers are
input
                                  // by default.
        lpstrInOut = inout;       // Pointer taken in and updated
        lpstrOutput = output;     // Pointer returned.
    }
```

**Listing 3–2** THIRD.ASM

```
      page    ,132

;Thunk Compiler Version 1.01  Aug 23 1994 16:35:46
;File Compiled Sat Jan 28 16:04:38 1995

;Command Line: thunk third

      TITLE   $third.asm

      .386
      OPTION READONLY
      OPTION OLDSTRUCTS

IFNDEF IS_16
IFNDEF IS_32
%out command line error: specify one of -DIS_16, -DIS_32
.err
ENDIF  ;IS_32
ENDIF  ;IS_16



IFDEF IS_32
IFDEF IS_16
%out command line error: you can't specify both -DIS_16 and -DIS_32
.err
```

```
ENDIF ;IS_16
;*********************** START OF 32-BIT CODE ***********************


        .model FLAT,STDCALL


;-- Import common flat thunk routines (in k32)

externDef AllocMappedBuffer:near32
externDef FreeMappedBuffer          :near32
externDef MapHInstLS        :near32
externDef MapHInstLS_PN     :near32
externDef MapHInstSL        :near32
externDef MapHInstSL_PN     :near32
externDef FT_PrologPrime    :near32
externDef FT_Prolog :near32
externDef FT_Thunk  :near32
externDef QT_Thunk  :near32
externDef QT_ThunkPrime     :near32
externDef FT_Exit0  :near32
externDef FT_Exit4  :near32
externDef FT_Exit8  :near32
externDef FT_Exit12 :near32
externDef FT_Exit16 :near32
externDef FT_Exit20 :near32
externDef FT_Exit24 :near32
externDef FT_Exit28 :near32
externDef FT_Exit32 :near32
externDef FT_Exit36 :near32
externDef FT_Exit40 :near32
externDef FT_Exit44 :near32
externDef FT_Exit48 :near32
externDef FT_Exit52 :near32
externDef FT_Exit56 :near32
externDef SMapLS    :near32
externDef SUnMapLS  :near32
externDef SMapLS_IP_EBP_8   :near32
```

```
externDef SUnMapLS_IP_EBP_8:near32
externDef SMapLS_IP_EBP_12 :near32
externDef SUnMapLS_IP_EBP_12        :near32
externDef SMapLS_IP_EBP_16 :near32
externDef SUnMapLS_IP_EBP_16        :near32
externDef SMapLS_IP_EBP_20 :near32
externDef SUnMapLS_IP_EBP_20        :near32
externDef SMapLS_IP_EBP_24 :near32
externDef SUnMapLS_IP_EBP_24        :near32
externDef SMapLS_IP_EBP_28 :near32
externDef SUnMapLS_IP_EBP_28        :near32
externDef SMapLS_IP_EBP_32 :near32
externDef SUnMapLS_IP_EBP_32        :near32
externDef SMapLS_IP_EBP_36 :near32
externDef SUnMapLS_IP_EBP_36        :near32
externDef SMapLS_IP_EBP_40 :near32
externDef SUnMapLS_IP_EBP_40        :near32


MapSL        PROTO NEAR STDCALL p32:DWORD



    .code


;******************** COMMON PER-MODULE ROUTINES ********************


    .data


public third_ThunkData32    ;This symbol must be exported.
third_ThunkData32 label dword
    dd      3130534ch       ;Protocol 'LS01'
    dd      0827h   ;Checksum
    dd      0       ;Jump table address.
    dd      3130424ch       ;'LB01'
    dd      0       ;Flags
    dd      0       ;Reserved (MUST BE 0)
    dd      0       ;Reserved (MUST BE 0)
    dd      offset QT_Thunk_third - offset third_ThunkData32
```

```
        dd      offset FT_Prolog_third - offset third_ThunkData32



        .code


externDef ThunkConnect32@24:near32

public third_ThunkConnect32@16
third_ThunkConnect32@16:
        pop     edx
        push    offset third_ThkData16
        push    offset third_ThunkData32
        push    edx
        jmp     ThunkConnect32@24
third_ThkData16 label byte
        db      "third_ThunkData16",0




pfnQT_Thunk_third   dd offset QT_Thunk_third
pfnFT_Prolog_third  dd offset FT_Prolog_third
        .data
;; Initialized for BETA-1 compatibility only.
QT_Thunk_third label byte
        db      0ebh, 30
        db      30 dup(0cch)    ;Patch space.
        db      0e8h,0,0,0,0    ;CALL NEAR32 $
        db      58h      ;POP EAX
        db      2dh,32+5,0,0,0 ;SUB EAX, IMM32
        db      0bah     ;MOV EDX, IMM32
        dd      offset third_ThunkData32 + 8 - offset QT_Thunk_third
        db      068h     ;PUSH IMM32
        dd      offset QT_ThunkPrime
        db      0c3h     ;RETN
```

```
;; Initialized for BETA-1 compatibility only.
FT_Prolog_third label byte
      db      0ebh, 30
      db      30 dup(0cch)    ;Patch space.
      db      0e8h,0,0,0,0    ;CALL NEAR32 $
      db      5ah      ;POP EDX
      db      81h,0eah, 32+5,0,0,0   ;SUB EDX, IMM32
      db      52h      ;PUSH EDX
      db      068h     ;PUSH IMM32
      dd      offset third_ThunkData32 + 8 - offset FT_Prolog_third
      db      068h     ;PUSH IMM32
      dd      offset FT_PrologPrime
      db      0c3h     ;RETN


      .code




;*********************** START OF THUNK BODIES***********************




;
public ThirdFunc@4
ThirdFunc@4:
      mov     cl,1
; ThirdFunc(16) = ThirdFunc(32) {}
;
; dword ptr [ebp+8]:  n
;
public IIThirdFunc@4
IIThirdFunc@4:
      push    ebp
      mov     ebp,esp
```

```
        push    ecx
        sub     esp,60
        push    word ptr [ebp+8]        ;n: dword->word
        call    dword ptr [pfnQT_Thunk_third]
        cwde
        leave
        retn    4




;
public ThirdFunc2@12
ThirdFunc2@12:
        mov     cl,0
; ThirdFunc2(16) = ThirdFunc2(32) {}
;
; dword ptr [ebp+8]:   lpstrInput
; dword ptr [ebp+12]:  lpstrInOut
; dword ptr [ebp+16]:  lpstrOutput
;
public IIThirdFunc2@12
IIThirdFunc2@12:
        push    ebp
        mov     ebp,esp
        push    ecx
        sub     esp,60
        call    SMapLS_IP_EBP_8
        push    eax
        call    SMapLS_IP_EBP_12
        push    eax
        call    SMapLS_IP_EBP_16
        push    eax
        call    dword ptr [pfnQT_Thunk_third]
        cwde
        call    SUnMapLS_IP_EBP_8
        call    SUnMapLS_IP_EBP_12
```

```
        call    SUnMapLS_IP_EBP_16
        leave
        retn    12




ELSE
;********************* START OF 16-BIT CODE *********************




        OPTION SEGMENT:USE16
        .model LARGE,PASCAL



        .code



externDef ThirdFunc2:far16
externDef ThirdFunc:far16



FT_thirdTargetTable label word
        dw      offset ThirdFunc2
        dw         seg ThirdFunc2
        dw      offset ThirdFunc
        dw         seg ThirdFunc




        .data

public third_ThunkData16    ;This symbol must be exported.
third_ThunkData16    dd     3130534ch       ;Protocol 'LS01'
```

```
        dd      0827h   ;Checksum
        dw      offset FT_thirdTargetTable
        dw      seg    FT_thirdTargetTable
        dd      0       ;First-time flag.



    .code


externDef ThunkConnect16:far16

public third_ThunkConnect16
third_ThunkConnect16:
    pop     ax
    pop     dx
    push    seg     third_ThunkData16
    push    offset third_ThunkData16
    push    seg     third_ThkData32
    push    offset third_ThkData32
    push    cs
    push    dx
    push    ax
    jmp     ThunkConnect16
third_ThkData32 label byte
    db      "third_ThunkData32",0



    ENDIF
    END
```

Assemble the .ASM file with (/DIS_16) switch to create a 32-bit .OBJ

To create the 16-bit side of the thunk, assemble the resulting .ASM with IS_16 defined. For example, I use Microsoft Macro Assembler Version 6.11 and the syntax looks like this:

```
ml /DIS_16 /c /W3 /nologo /Fo third16.obj third.asm
```

Assemble the .ASM file with (/DIS_32) switch to create a 32-bit .OBJ

Here's the syntax for the 32-bit side:

```
ml /DIS_32 /c /W3 /nologo /Fo third32.obj third.asm
```

Link your 32-bit OBJ to create a 32-bit DLL.

Once you have successfully created the object files, the next step is to build the DLLs. You need to add the calls to import *CTHKSL_ThunkConnect16* and *CTHKSL_ThunkConnect32* into the DLLEntryPoint routines of both DLLs and export the required symbols.

You need to recompile the generated ASM file with /DIS_16 and link with a 16-bit DLL. This 16-bit DLL should have the following function added:

```
BOOL FAR PASCAL __export DllEntryPoint (DWORD dwReason,
                            WORD  hInst,
                            WORD  wDS,
                            WORD  wHeapSize,
                            DWORD dwReserved1,
                            WORD  wReserved2)
{
    OutputDebugString("In 16bit DllEntryPoint: Calling thkThunkConnect16");
    if (!thk_ThunkConnect16("DLL16.DLL",
                        "DLL32.DLL",
                        hInst,
                        dwReason))
    {
        OutputDebugString("\n\rIn 16bit DllEntryPoint: thkThunkConnect16 ret
FALSE");
        return FALSE;
    }

    OutputDebugString("\n\rIn 16bit DllEntryPoint: thkThunkConnect16 ret
TRUE");
    return TRUE;
}
```

ThunkConnect16 needs to be called in the 16-bit DllEntryPoint, which is a new feature for 4.0 dll's. This is not the same thing as LibMain, which is only called when the library is first retrieved from the disk. The 16-bit DllEntryPoint is called each time the module's usage count is incremented or decremented. If its incrementing dwReason will be 1 and if its decrementing than it will be 0. One thing to remember is that the GetModuleUsage() function is undefined inside DllEntryPoint. You must maintain your own counter if you need to know the current usage.

Also, don't make any calls to thunked routines inside DllEntryPoint. You must wait until both DLLs are initialized before calling any thunked routines.

Don't forget to link the 16-Bit DLL with THIRDPARTY16.LIB to get to the original functions.

Make sure that the following is in the 16-Bit thunk DLL's Def File:

```
EXPORT
    DllEntryPoint  @1 ResidentName
    ....

IMPORTS
    C16ThkSL01      = KERNEL.631
    YThunkConnect16     = KERNEL.651
    .....
```

Your 32-bit DLL's entry point (DLLMain by default), include the call (the names of the DLL's are provide for illustrative purposes):

```
        BOOL WINAPI FOO_ThunkConnect32(LPSTR pszDll16,
                                       LPSTR pszDll32,
                                       DWORD hIinst,
                                       DWORD dwReason);

        BOOL _stdcall DllMain(DWORD hInst, DWORD dwReason, DWORD dwReserved)
        {
            if (!(FOO_ThunkConnect32("THIRD16.DLL",   // Name of 16-bit DLL
                                     "THIRD32.DLL",   // Name of 32-bit DLL
                                     hInst,
                                     dwReason)))
            {
                return FALSE;
            }
```

```
        // Process dwReason
    }
```

To your 32-bit dll's def file, add

```
    EXPORT
        THIRD_ThunkData32
```

Listing 3–3, THIRD16.DEF, is the DEF file definitions for the 16-bit side of the thunk and Listing 3–4, Third32.DEF, lists the 32-bit side.

### Listing 3–3 THIRD16.DEF

```
    EXPORTS
        DllEntryPoint          @1  RESIDENTNAME
        third_ThunkData16      @2
        ThirdFunc              @3
        ThirdFunc2             @4


    IMPORTS
        C16ThkSL01      = KERNEL.631
        ThunkConnect16 = KERNEL.651
```

### Listing 3–4 THIRD32.DEF

```
    EXPORTS
      CTHKSL_ThunkData32
```

When building the 16-bit DLL, be sure to mark it so it is compatible with Windows 95. You do this with the Windows 4.0 Resource Compiler on the DLL:

```
    \sdk\binw16\rc -40 <.DLL output file>
```

If your 16-bit DLL is not marked as a 4.0 DLL, then Windows 95 will not call the DLLEntryPoint function upon startup. This is especially important for 16-32-bit thunks because if Windows 95 doesn't call your DllEntryPoint function, your 32-bit DLL will not load.

# HOW COMPILED THUNKS WORK.

Let's review what we have so far. We have a 16-bit DLL from ThirdParty Corporation, called 3rdParty.DLL. In it are two functions: ThirdFunc and ThirdFunc2. We now have two thunk DLLs: Third16.DLL and Third32.DLL. Our goal is to take a 32-bit Windows 95 application (let's call it TestThunk.EXE) and eventually call the two functions in 3RDPARTY.DLL.

On the 16-bit side there is a jump table containing the 16:16 address of both ThirdFunc and ThirdFunc2. In your case, there will be a addresses for each function named in the THK file. In our example, they correspond exactly to the functions in 3rdParty.DLL. In either case, they correspond to the functions that need to be thunked.

On the 16-bit side, the thunk compiler creates a jump table:

```
externDef ThirdFunc2:far16
externDef ThirdFunc:far16


FT_thirdTargetTable label word
     dw       offset ThirdFunc2
     dw          seg ThirdFunc2
     dw       offset ThirdFunc
     dw          seg ThirdFunc
```

On the 32-bit side, the thunk compiler creates a STDCALL function for each thunk. These functions convert their parameters to 16-bits and then calls the 16-bit target named in the jump table. Your 32-bit application calls these compiler-generated STDCALL functions directly.

Here's the 32-bit half containing the parameter conversion code:

```
public ThirdFunc@4
ThirdFunc@4:
     mov    cl,1
; ThirdFunc(16) = ThirdFunc(32) {}
;
; dword ptr [ebp+8]:  n
;
```

```
;
public IIThirdFunc2@12
IIThirdFunc2@12:
    push    ebp
    mov     ebp,esp
    push    ecx
    sub     esp,60
    call    SMapLS_IP_EBP_8
    push    eax
    call    SMapLS_IP_EBP_12
    push    eax
    call    SMapLS_IP_EBP_16
    push    eax
    call    dword ptr [pfnQT_Thunk_third]
    cwde
    call    SUnMapLS_IP_EBP_8
    call    SUnMapLS_IP_EBP_12
    call    SUnMapLS_IP_EBP_16
    leave
    retn    12
```

When TESTTHUNK.EXE calls the ThirdFunc, it transfers directly to the above routine, which builds the 16-bit call frame and calls a local routine asking it to please invoke table and sign-extend the return value (each component gets its own set of QT_ routines which knows what jump table to use.)

# DEBUGGING

In order to debug, I manually edit the assembly file produced by the thunk compiler and place an int 3 instruction in the thunk connect routine. Then I start codeview under VC1.51 and point it at the source for the 16 bit dll. Then I start my 32 bit application. Codeview assumes it owns int 3 and breaks on the thunk connect routine.

# GENERIC THUNKS

Whenever the subject of 16-bit applications in 32-bit operating systems arises, the two most common tasks requested are the ability to pass data from 16 to 32-bit and to call 32-bit functions from a 16-bit application. Both Windows 95 and Windows NT make provisions for 16-bit applications to transmit data and make 32-bit calls(see sidebar WOW - Win16 on Win32). This is to be expected since most of the 16-bit support in both operating systems is layered on top of 32-bit DLLs. To perform this feat, both operating systems use a facility known as *generic thunks*. This next section explains how you can take advantage generic thunks to create your own 16-bit to 32-bit communication.

In the example for compiled thunks we used a fictitious company, ThirdParty Corporation to demostrate how to thunk our 32-bit application to their 16-bit DLL. In this section let's suppose that ThirdParty is an agressive corporation who already has a 32-bit version of their DLL shipping. However, in this example it's our application that is still 16-bits. Of course we're on the way to 32-bits. but in the mean time we want to see what happens if we take our 16-bit application and call a function in ThirdParty's DLL call MongoCalc. Supposedly, MongoCalc is much faster in 32-bits and we would like to time it. And, because this is a totally contrived situation to show you generic thunks, we'll have to assume that it will be quicker to call MongoCalc from out 16-bit application rather than writing a test 32-bit executable.

There are a total of four 16-bit functions that we will use to implement generic thunks. This next section goes over each.

```
HINSTANCE FAR PASCAL
LoadLibraryEx32W(LPCTSTR  lpLibFileName,  // points to name of
                                          // executable module
                  HANDLE  hFile,   // reserved, must be NULL
                  DWORD   dwFlags); // entry-point execution flag
```

This function is just a 16-bit version of the Win32 *LoadLibraryEx* function. Use this function to load the 32-bit DLL from your 16-bit code. Like this:

```
HINSTANCE hInstance = LoadLibraryEx32W("THIRD32.DLL",
                                        NULL
                                        0);
```

**100**

The next generic thunk function you need is

```
LPVOID FAR PASCAL
GetProcAddress32W(HMODULE  hModule,       // handle to DLL module
                  LPCSTR  lpszProc);     // name of function
```

Once you have the 32-bit DLL loaded into your 16-bit process space. call *GetProcAddress32W* to get the entry point of the function you want to call. This allows your 16-bit application to get the entry point of a 32-bit thunk routine. The address that you get back from GetProcAddress32W is a 32-bit address that you do not call directly (like you would with a return from *GetProcAddress*). Instead, use this address as a parameter to the function *CallProc32W.*

```
DWORD FAR PASCAL CallProc32W( DWORD dwParam1, DWORD dwParam2,..,
                             LPVOID lpProcAddress32,
                             DWORD fAddressConvert,
                             DWORD nParams);
```

As you can tell from the prototype, *CallProc32W,* takes a variable number of parameters. This makes it an easy function to mess up since there are no compiler checks made on the number of parameters. Therefore, I'll go over the parameters one by one.

```
DWORD   param1      /* All parameters must be DWORDS and match the type
                       that the 32 bit thunk DLL is expecting, no
                       conversion (appart from 16:16 address to 32 bit
                       addresses ) is performed.   There can be a
                       variable number of parameters which MUST match
                       that for the 32 bit Thunk DLL being called. */

LPVOID  lpProcAddress32 /* 32 bit linear Address of procedure to be called
                           as returned by GetProcAddress32 (see above) */

DWORD   fAddressConvert /* If any bit is set ( 1 ) then the corresponding
                           param(32....1) is assumed to be a 16:16 pointer
                           and will be converted to a 32 bit flat linear
                           pointer before the 32 bit proceedure is called.
```

**101**

```
                              No checking is performed - if the address is
                              invalid a NULL will be passed to the routine. */

        DWORD    nParams      /* Number of DWORD params passed.    For functions
                              that take no parameters this will be Zero. */
```

The minimum amount of parameters is three (lpProcAddress32, fAddressConvert and nParams). The maximum is 32 optional parameters.

When you are done, call *FreeLibrary32W*.

```
        BOOL   FAR PASCAL FreeLibrary32W(HINSTANCE hLibModule);
```

This routine allows your 16-bit DLL to free the 32 bit DLL. Since WOW doesn't perform cleanup, you must call this function to avoid the loss of resources in the 16-bit subsystem.

Listing 3–2 (shown previously) contains all the code for our 16-bit DLL to call ThirdParty's 32-bit DLL. However, you'll notice that our example oversimplified things. In many cases, in order to get the parameters to match up correctly, you will have to write your own 32-bit DLL to interface with the original 32-bit DLL.

## UNIVERSAL THUNKS

Win32s provides a mechanism to accomplish this called Universal Thunks. Universal Thunks enable Win32s applications to call functions from 16-bit DLLs.

The Universal Thunk API consists of four functions, as shown in Table 3–2. You can do anything a Win16 application can do on the 16-bit side of the thunk. This includes making DOS calls (Int 21h), DPMI calls, or calling virtual device drivers (VxDs).

**Table 3–2** Universal Thunk API Functions

| Function | Description |
|---|---|
| UTRegister | Creates the thunk and loads the 16-bit DLL according to Windows 3.1 DLL loading rules. |
| UTUnRegister | Destroys the thunk created by UTRegister and performs the equivalent of FreeLibrary on the 16-bit DLL. |

| UTSelectorOffsetToLinear | Translates a selector:offset combination to flat address. Available to 16-bit processes only. |
| UTLinearToSelectorOffset | Translates a flat address to selector:offset. Available to 16-bit processes only. |

## REGISTERING THE THUNK

Before making a call into a 16-bit DLL, you must register the thunk with the UTRegister call. Unfortunately, you must confine all Universal Thunk API calls to 32-bit DLLs because the NT version of KERNEL32.DLL does not export the UT API calls. By restricting UT calls to a DLL, you can avoid an "unresolved call" error by using LoadLibrary, as in this example code:

```
#define WIN32S 0x800000001

if ( (GetVersion() & WIN32S) )    // Are we a Win32s app as opposed to NT?
{
hModule = LoadLibrary("KERNEL32.DLL");

  // Use GetProcAddress for each UT function you need

pfnUTRegister=GetProcAddress(hModule,"UTRegister");
pfnUTUnRegister=GetProcAddress(hModule,"UTUnRegister");
.
.
return pfnUTRegister(hInst        // instance handle of 32-bit DLL
          "My16BIT.DLL",    // name of "MY16BIT DLL"
          "DllInit16",      // init routine exported
                            // from "MY16BIT.DLL"
          "UTProc",         // name of 16-bit routine also exported
                            // from "MY16BIT.DLL"
                            //
          &pfnUTProc,       // Global variable to
                            // receive thunk address
          NULL,             // call back functions go here
          NULL              // shared memory can go here
          );
```

```
}
else      // We must be in NT, and NT doesn't support UT
```

UTRegister creates the thunk and loads the 16-bit DLL into memory. If you place this code within the DLL Initialization function (DllInit) of your DLL, you can set up the thunk once, upon DLL_PROCESS_ATTACH. (The DllInit function of a Win32 DLL is called each time a process attaches or detaches with the fdwReason flag set to DLL_PROCESS_ATTACH or DLL_PROCESS_DETACH). If UTRegister is not within your DLL initialization function, be sure to check the error return for ERROR_SERVICE_EXISTS. This means that the Universal Thunk is already registered.

The third parameter to UTRegister is a pointer to a 16-bit initialization function. This allows you to place the address of any exported, 16-bit function from thunk DLL that you want called when the thunk is registered. The initialization function must have the following prototype:

```
DWORD FAR PASCAL UT16INIT(UT16CBPROC pfnUT16Callback,
                          LPVOID lpBuff);
```

The UT16CBPROC is a callback to a function in your 32-bit DLL, and lpBuff is a void pointer to any data that you want to share between the 16-bit and 32-bit sides. (These are the sixth and seventh parameters to UTRegister, respectively.) If you don't require 16-bit initialization, you pass a NULL for the third parameter to UTRegister.

The fourth parameter (UTProc) contains the name of the exported function within the 16-bit DLL that will serve as the thunk.

The fifth parameter (pfnUTProc) receives the address of a pointer to a 32-bit function. You call your 16-bit function indirectly through this pointer.

If you take advantage of the 16-bit initialization function, the sixth parameter is a pointer to your 32-bit callback routine that gets passed to the 16-bit initialization function. The seventh parameter is a void pointer to any 32-bit memory that you want to share with the initialization function. If you do not have an initialization function, the sixth and seventh parameters are ignored. If you don't require a callback or shared memory, you pass NULLs in these parameters.

## UNREGISTERING THE THUNK

The UTUnRegister function unregisters the thunk. You must unregister the thunk before your process terminates or you will orphan resources. If you placed the UTRegister function in the DLLInit section, call UTUnRegister upon DLL_PROCESS_DETACH. Otherwise, you should call UTUnRegister sometime before you terminate your application:

```
UTUnRegister(hModule);
```

## TRANSLATING POINTERS

A Win32 application cannot receive a handle from a Win16 application and then GlobalLock it and use the pointer. Since 16-bit applications live in a segmented world and Win32 applications live in a flat model world, the pointers do not translate. In Chapter 9, "Memory Management," I show you how to pass handles around in NT by using the magical ReadProcessMemory and WriteProcessMemory functions. Unfortunately, ReadProcessMemory and WriteProcessMemory are not supported in Win32s. It may be possible to write an assembly language function that uses 16:32 pointers to move data back and forth. However, I do not recommend doing this. This will not work on Windows NT, and it is not portable to other platforms. Besides, there is an easier way. Universal Thunks provide what is known as a translation list. If you call back from the 32-bit DLL to the 16-bit DLL, the translation list translates the x:32 pointers (flat pointers) to 16:16 (FAR pointers) in place. For the 16-bit to 32-bit callbacks, the FAR pointers are translated to FLAT pointers. So any place that you have pointers in your data, use the translation list.

The sending side of the callback has three parameters, but the receiving side only has two parameter (you'll see why in a minute).

The sending side looks like this:

```
UTSendDataProc(LPVOID lpBuffer,
        DWORD dwUserDefined,
        LPVOID *lpTranslationList);
```

The lpBuffer parameter points to a general-purpose memory buffer. Win32s translates this pointer automatically to the proper format (from segmented to flat if you are calling from 16-bit, or from flat to segmented if you are calling from 32-bit).

If you have several pointers that you wish to pass, package them into an array, make the last entry a NULL to indicate the end of the list, and pass the address of the structure to the third parameter of the callback procedure, lpTranslationList. Win32s will scan the translation list and translate the pointers to the proper format.

In this following example, gpfnUT16Callback is a pointer to a 32-bit callback located in the 32-bit DLL.

```
LPVOID    TransList[4];      // Three pointers need translation:
DWORD     Args[3];           // function has three arguments

  Args[0] = (DWORD) lpPtr1;    // FAR pointer
  Args[1] = (DWORD) lpPtr2;    // FAR pointer
  Args[2] = (DWORD) lpPtr3;    // FAR pointer

//
// build translation list for all the far pointers that need to
// be translated to flat pointers.
//

  TransList[0] = (LPDWORD)&Args[0];
  TransList[1] = (LPDWORD)&Args[1];
  TransList[2] = (LPDWORD)&Args[2];
  TransList[3] = 0;

//
// The following shows how to call the 32-bit DLL thru the
// 16-bit thunk. Exit32s doesn't use the callback, so it is
// ifdef'd out.
//
// Remember, this is 16-bit Windows, use the IsBadxx functions
// liberally.
//
```

```
if (!IsBadCodePtr((FARPROC)gpfnUT16Callback))
{
gpfnUT16Callback((LPDWORD)Args,dwFunc,(LPVOID)TransList);
}
```

The receiving side looks like this:

```
DWORD FAR PASCAL UTReceiveData(LPVOID lpBuff
                              DWORD dwUserDefined);
```

During the translation process, the lpTranslationList parameter gets dropped and all of the pointers in lpBuff are translated to their proper format.

The second parameter, dwUserDefined, is a DWORD that is available for user-defined data.

One of the limitations of Universal Thunks is that Win32s allows only one Universal Thunk per Win32 DLL. Perhaps there is some design issue I'm unaware of that the designers of Win32s faced (it may have been a time-to-market issue).

# SAMPLE PROGRAM: EXITWINDOWS32S

Universal Thunks are also useful when your Win32s application must take advantage of system features that aren't available in NT, but are in Windows 3.1 (such as VxDs or Win16-specific KERNEL, USER, or GDI API calls). The ExitWindows sample program in Chapter 5, "Security," provides three ways to exit NT: log off, shut down, or reboot. To exit Windows in Windows 3.1, you can log off (return to DOS) and reboot (the same as pressing Ctrl-Alt-Delete twice), but there is no function to correspond to shutting down. Instead, 3.1 allows you to restart windows (it's as if you logged off, then entered win at the DOS prompt).

To provide this restart capability, ExitWindows32s registers a Universal Thunk that calls the 16-bit ExitWindows(EW_RESTARTWINDOWS) function. Listing 3–5 is the source for exit.cpp, and Listing 3–6 for the Universal Thunk sections of ExitWindows32s. The major difference between ExitWindows and ExitWindows32s is the fact that ExitWindows32s is aware of Win32s. One of the first things ExitWindows32s does is check which operating system is running:

```
BOOL
CMainWindow::IsWin32s()
{
 return  (GetVersion() & 0x80000000) ? TRUE: FALSE;
}
```

Actually, ExitWindows32s is a complete replacement for Chapter 5's ExitWindows. Once it knows which operating system is running, ExitWindows32s makes some operating-system-dependent decisions. For example, if Win32s is running, ExitWindows32s appends "Restart Windows" to the system menu. Otherwise it appends "Shutdown System", as shown here:

```
if (CMainWindow::IsWin32s())
    {
    m_pMainWnd->GetSystemMenu(FALSE)->AppendMenu(MF_STRING |
                MF_ENABLED,
                IDM_RESTART,
                "Restart Windows");
}
```

**Listing 3–5** ExitWindows32s

```
//**********************************************************
//
// exit.cpp : Defines the class behaviors for ExitWindows
// KJG
//
//
//**********************************************************

#include <afxwin.h>
#include "resource.h"

#include "exit.h"


/////////////////////////////////////////////////////////////////
```

```
// theApp:
// Just creating this application object runs the whole application.
//
CTheApp theApp;


//////////////////////////////////////////////////////////////////////
// CMainWindow constructor:
// Create the window with the appropriate style, size, menu, etc.
//

CMainWindow::CMainWindow()
{
    Create("ExitWindows");
  fStatus = Logoff;



}

BOOL CMainWindow::Create(LPCSTR szTitle,
    LONG style /* = WS_OVERLAPPEDWINDOW */,
    const RECT& rect /* = rectDefault */,
    CWnd* parent /* = NULL */)
{
    const char* pszWndClass =
    AfxRegisterWndClass(CS_HREDRAW | CS_VREDRAW,
                NULL,
                    (HBRUSH)(COLOR_WINDOW+1),
                    LoadIcon(AfxGetInstanceHandle(),
                    TEXT("exiticon")));

    return CFrameWnd::Create(pszWndClass, szTitle, style,
                    rect, parent, NULL);
}

//
// This function gets control upon a WM_SYSCOMMAND msg.
//
```

```
void CMainWindow::OnSysCommand(UINT nID, LONG lParam)
{
    switch (nID)
    {
//
// Sets the default to Shutdown
//
   case IDM_SHUTDOWN:
     GetSystemMenu(FALSE)->CheckMenuItem(IDM_SHUTDOWN,
                                   MF_CHECKED);
     GetSystemMenu(FALSE)->CheckMenuItem(IDM_LOGOFF,
                                   MF_UNCHECKED);
     GetSystemMenu(FALSE)->CheckMenuItem(IDM_REBOOT,
                                   MF_UNCHECKED);
     if (IsWin32s())
     GetSystemMenu(FALSE)->CheckMenuItem(IDM_RESTART,
                                   MF_UNCHECKED);

     fStatus = Shutdown;
     break;

//
// Sets the default to Restart
//

   case IDM_RESTART:
     GetSystemMenu(FALSE)->CheckMenuItem(IDM_RESTART,
                                   MF_CHECKED);
     GetSystemMenu(FALSE)->CheckMenuItem(IDM_LOGOFF,
                                   MF_UNCHECKED);
     GetSystemMenu(FALSE)->CheckMenuItem(IDM_REBOOT,
                                   MF_UNCHECKED);
     if (!IsWin32s())
     GetSystemMenu(FALSE)->CheckMenuItem(IDM_SHUTDOWN,
                                   MF_UNCHECKED);

     fStatus = Restart;
     break;
```

```
//
// Sets the default to logoff
//

   case IDM_LOGOFF:
      GetSystemMenu(FALSE)->CheckMenuItem(IDM_LOGOFF,MF_CHECKED);
      GetSystemMenu(FALSE)->CheckMenuItem(IDM_SHUTDOWN,MF_UNCHECKED);
      GetSystemMenu(FALSE)->CheckMenuItem(IDM_REBOOT,MF_UNCHECKED);
      fStatus = Logoff;
      break;


   case IDM_REBOOT:
       GetSystemMenu(FALSE)->CheckMenuItem(IDM_REBOOT,MF_CHECKED);
       GetSystemMenu(FALSE)->CheckMenuItem(IDM_LOGOFF,MF_UNCHECKED);
       GetSystemMenu(FALSE)->CheckMenuItem(IDM_SHUTDOWN,MF_UNCHECKED);
          if (IsWin32s())
          GetSystemMenu(FALSE)-
>CheckMenuItem(IDM_RESTART,MF_UNCHECKED);
         fStatus = Reboot;
      break;

//
// Displays the About Box
//
   case IDM_ABOUT:
       ShellAbout(m_hWnd, "Exit Windows", "Developing Windows 95
Applications \r\nby Kevin Goodman",
                 LoadIcon(AfxGetInstanceHandle(),TEXT("exiticon")));
       break;
   default:
       Default();
   };
}

BOOL
CMainWindow::GetPrivilege()
```

```
{

HANDLE hToken;
TOKEN_PRIVILEGES tkp;
//
// SeShutdownPrivilege must be enabled
//
   if (!OpenProcessToken(GetCurrentProcess(),
              TOKEN_ADJUST_PRIVILEGES |
              TOKEN_QUERY, &hToken))
      {
      return FALSE;
      }
//
// Get a LUID for SeShutdownPrivilege
//
   LookupPrivilegeValue(NULL, TEXT("SeShutdownPrivilege"),
      &tkp.Privileges[0].Luid);

//
// PrivilegeCount enables more than one privilege to be set
// at a time.
//
   tkp.PrivilegeCount = 1;
   tkp.Privileges[0].Attributes = SE_PRIVILEGE_ENABLED;

//
// Some privileges are initially disable. So each process must adjust the
// privilege by calling AdjustTokenPrivilege
//
   if (!AdjustTokenPrivileges(hToken, FALSE, &tkp, 0,
                  (PTOKEN_PRIVILEGES)NULL, 0))
      return FALSE;
   return TRUE;
}

void CMainWindow::OnShutDown()
{
//
```

```
//  Shutdown the system
//


        ExitWindowsEx( EWX_SHUTDOWN, 0 );
//      ExitWindowsEx( EWX_SHUTDOWN | EWX_FORCE, 0 );
}




void CMainWindow::OnReboot()
{

//
// Reboot
//
    if (IsWin32s())
        {
        ExitUT(EXIT_SRV_REBOOT);
        }
    else
        ExitWindowsEx(EWX_REBOOT | EWX_FORCE, 0);


}

void CMainWindow::OnLogOff()
{
//
// Logoff
//

    ExitWindowsEx( EWX_LOGOFF | EWX_FORCE, 0 );

}

void
CMainWindow::OnRestart()
{
```

```
        ExitUT(EXIT_SRV_RESTART);
}



BOOL
CMainWindow::OnQueryOpen()
{

    switch (fStatus)
    {
    case Shutdown:
        OnShutDown();
        break;
    case Logoff:
        OnLogOff();
        break;
    case Reboot:
        OnReboot();
        break;
    case Restart:
        OnRestart();
        break;
    }

 return FALSE;
}

BOOL
CMainWindow::IsWin32s()
{
 return  (GetVersion() & 0x80000000) ? TRUE: FALSE;
}



// CMainWindow message map:
// Associate messages with member functions.
//
```

```
// It is implied that members connected with the ON_COMMAND macro
// receive no arguments and are void of return type, e.g., "void
// OnAbout()".
BEGIN_MESSAGE_MAP( CMainWindow, CFrameWnd )
    ON_WM_QUERYOPEN()
    ON_WM_SYSCOMMAND()
END_MESSAGE_MAP()


/////////////////////////////////////////////////////////////////////
CTheApp

// InitInstance:
// When any CTheApp object is created, this member function is
// automatically called. Any data may be set up at this point.
//
// Also, the main window of the application should be created and shown
// here. Return TRUE if the initialization is successful.
//
BOOL CTheApp::InitInstance()
{
    TRACE( "Exit Windows\n" );

    m_pMainWnd = new CMainWindow();
      m_pMainWnd->GetSystemMenu(FALSE)->AppendMenu(MF_SEPARATOR);

      m_pMainWnd->GetSystemMenu(FALSE)->DeleteMenu(4,MF_BYPOSITION);
      m_pMainWnd->GetSystemMenu(FALSE)->DeleteMenu(3,MF_BYPOSITION);
      m_pMainWnd->GetSystemMenu(FALSE)->DeleteMenu(2,MF_BYPOSITION);
      m_pMainWnd->GetSystemMenu(FALSE)->DeleteMenu(0,MF_BYPOSITION);
      if (CMainWindow::IsWin32s())
        {
        m_pMainWnd->GetSystemMenu(FALSE)->AppendMenu(MF_STRING |
                    MF_ENABLED,
                    DM_RESTART,
                    "Restart Windows");

        m_pMainWnd->GetSystemMenu(FALSE)->AppendMenu(MF_STRING |
                    MF_ENABLED,
```

```
                        IDM_REBOOT, "Reboot");


        }
    else
        {
//
// If the user has the SE_SHUTDOWN_PRIVILEGE append the menu items
//

        if (CMainWindow::GetPrivilege())
          {
            m_pMainWnd->GetSystemMenu(FALSE)->AppendMenu(MF_STRING |
                        MF_ENABLED,
                        IDM_SHUTDOWN, "Shutdown System");

            m_pMainWnd->GetSystemMenu(FALSE)->AppendMenu(MF_STRING |
                        MF_ENABLED,
                        IDM_REBOOT, "Reboot");
          }
        }
        m_pMainWnd->GetSystemMenu(FALSE)->AppendMenu(MF_STRING |
                        MF_ENABLED,
                        IDM_LOGOFF,
                        CMainWindow::IsWin32s() ?
                           "Return to DOS...":"Logoff");

        m_pMainWnd->GetSystemMenu(FALSE)->AppendMenu(MF_SEPARATOR);

        m_pMainWnd->GetSystemMenu(FALSE)->AppendMenu(MF_STRING |
                        MF_ENABLED,
                        IDM_ABOUT, "About...");


//
// Make Logoff the default
//
    m_pMainWnd->GetSystemMenu(FALSE)->CheckMenuItem(IDM_LOGOFF,
                                        MF_CHECKED);
```

```
        m_pMainWnd->ShowWindow(SW_MINIMIZE);
        m_pMainWnd->UpdateWindow();

    return TRUE;
    }
    /////////////////////////////////////////////////////////////////////
```

**Listing 3–6** Universal Thunk section of ExitWindows32s

```
    // KJG

    #define W32SUT_16

    #include <windows.h>
    #include "w32sut.h"
    #include "exitut16.h"


    /*
     * constants for dispatcher in 16bit side
     */

    #define EXIT_SRV_GETVERSION   0
    #define EXIT_SRV_REBOOT       1
    #define EXIT_SRV_RESTART      2
    UT16CBPROC gpfnUT16Callback = NULL;

    typedef struct
    {
    LPSTR FirstName;
    LPSTR LastName;
    LPSTR Address;
    LPSTR Zip;
    }NAME, FAR *LPNAME;

    NAME x;
    LPNAME n=&x;
```

**117**

```
LPSTR lpszFirst= "First";
LPSTR lpszSecond="Second";
LPSTR lpszThird=NULL;

BOOL CALLBACK
LibMain(HINSTANCE hinst, UINT wDS, UINT cbHeap, DWORD unused)
{

//
// This is the Win16 method of initializing a DLL.
// Return TRUE for success. Just return here because all initialization
// is performed in the DllInit16 function called by UTRegister.

return TRUE;

}

DWORD FAR PASCAL _export
DllInit16(UT16CBPROC pfnUT16Callback, LPVOID lpBuff)
{


//
// Save off the Callback Address into a global
//

gpfnUT16Callback = pfnUT16Callback;


//
// Return 1 for success, 0 for failure
//

return 1;

}

DWORD WINAPI test(LPVOID lpBuff,
```

CHAPTER 3: THUNKING ■■

```
                    DWORD dwUserDefined,
                    LPVOID *lpTranslationList);

DWORD FAR PASCAL _export _loadds
UTProc(LPVOID lpBuf, DWORD dwFunc)
{
LPVOID    TransList[4];    // Three pointers need translation:
DWORD     Args[3];         // function has three arguments
  Args[0] = (DWORD) lpszFirst;
  Args[1] = (DWORD) lpszSecond;
  Args[2] = (DWORD) lpszThird;

//
// build translation list for all the flat pointers that need to
// be translated to segmented form.
//
  TransList[0] = (LPDWORD)&Args[0];
  TransList[1] = (LPDWORD)&Args[1];
  TransList[2] = (LPDWORD)&Args[2];
  TransList[3] = 0;


//
// The following shows how to call the 32-bit DLL thru the
// 16-bit thunk. Exit32s doesn't use the callback, so it is
// ifdef'd out.
//
// Remember, this is 16-bit Windows, use the IsBadxx functions
// liberally.
//

#ifdef LATER

    if (!IsBadCodePtr((FARPROC)gpfnUT16Callback))
    {

    gpfnUT16Callback((LPDWORD)Args,dwFunc,(LPVOID)TransList);
    }
```

**I I9**

```
#endif


//
// Call 16-bit functions based on the dwFunc
//
    switch (dwFunc) {

    case EXIT_SRV_GETVERSION:
        return( (DWORD) 0x100 );

    case EXIT_SRV_REBOOT:
        ExitWindows(EW_REBOOTSYSTEM,0);
        return(0);

    case EXIT_SRV_RESTART:
        ExitWindows(EW_RESTARTWINDOWS,0);
        return(0);

    }

    return( 0 );
}



DWORD
WINAPI test(LPVOID lpBuff,
        DWORD dwUserDefined,
        LPVOID *lpTranslationList)
{
char ach[80];
LPNAME x=(LPNAME)*lpTranslationList;
wsprintf(ach,"Name =%s ",x->FirstName);
MessageBox(NULL,ach,"16-bit Test",MB_OK);
return TRUE;
}


// File EXIT.H
```

```
#define W32SUT_16

#include <windows.h>
#include "w32sut.h"
#include "exitut16.h"


/*
 * constants for dispatcher in 16-bit side
 */


#define EXIT_SRV_GETVERSION    0
#define EXIT_SRV_REBOOT        1
#define EXIT_SRV_RESTART       2

UT16CBPROC gpfnUT16Callback =NULL;

BOOL CALLBACK
LibMain(HINSTANCE hinst, UINT wDS, UINT cbHeap, DWORD unused)
{

//
// This is the Win16 method of initializing a DLL.
// Return TRUE for success. Just return here because all
// initialization is performed in the DllInit16 function called
// by UTRegister.
//

return TRUE;

}

DWORD FAR PASCAL _export
DllInit16(UT16CBPROC pfnUT16Callback, LPVOID lpBuff)
{
char ach[80];
```

```
wsprintf(ach,"pfnUT16Callback = %x",pfnUT16Callback);
MessageBox(NULL,ach,"UT16INIT",MB_OK);

//
// Save off the Callback Address into a global
//
gpfnUT16Callback = pfnUT16Callback;


//
// Return 1 for success, 0 for failure
//

return 1;

}

DWORD FAR PASCAL _export _loadds
UTProc(LPVOID lpBuf, DWORD dwFunc, LPVOID lpTranslationList)
{
static char achMsg[80];
        wsprintf(achMsg,"dwFunc = %x\nlpBuf = %x",dwFunc,lpBuf);
        MessageBox(NULL,achMsg,"UTProc", MB_OK);
_asm{int 3};


//
// Remember, this is 16-bit Windows, use the IsBadxx functions
// liberally.
//

        if (!IsBadCodePtr(*gpfnUT16Callback))
            {
        MessageBox(NULL, "About to call 32-bit dll thru 16-bit thunk",
                "UTPROC",MB_OK);
          gpfnUT16Callback(NULL,dwFunc,NULL);
            }
```

```
dwFunc = EXIT_SRV_REBOOT;
//
// Call 16-bit functions based on the function Id.
//
    switch (dwFunc) {

    case EXIT_SRV_GETVERSION:
        return( (DWORD) 0x100 );

    case EXIT_SRV_REBOOT:
        MessageBox(NULL,"Reboot","UT TEST", MB_OK);
        ExitWindows(EW_REBOOTSYSTEM,0);
        MessageBox(NULL,"Reboot","UT TEST", MB_OK);
        return(0);

    case EXIT_SRV_RESTART:
        MessageBox(NULL,"Restart","UT TEST", MB_OK);
        ExitWindows(EW_RESTARTWINDOWS,0);
        MessageBox(NULL,"Restart","UT TEST", MB_OK);
        return(0);


    }

    return( 0 );
}
```

# DEVELOPING FOR WIN16

If you have never programmed for Win16, there are some anomalies you should be aware of. This section describes them.

Compile with the option to explicitly set DS register on entry on 16-bit side. If you don't do this, all your statics and quoted strings will be inaccessible. Remember, in a Win16 DLL, the stack segment and the data segment are not equal (SS!=DS).

Use the TranslationList for const pointers only. It modifies pointers in place when you thunk, but does not modify them back when you return. In other words, if your receive side modifies the pointers passed to it, they become garbage upon return. If you must modify the pointers in the receive side, save them off before making the callback. From the 16-bit side you can use the either UTSelectorOffsetToLinear or UTLinearToSelectorOffset to manually translate pointers. If you used GlobalAlloc to allocate memory from the 16-bit side, you must GlobalFix the memory before calling UTSelectorOffsetToLinear, like so:

```
HGLOBAL hGlobal = GlobalAlloc(GMEM_SHARE, 1024);
GlobalFix(hGlobal);
```

Be aware of how your compiler pads structures. If you pass data structures from 32-bit to 16-bit (or vice versa), ensure that your 16-bit compiler pads structures in the same was as your Win32 compiler. You can avoid this by following the advice from Chapter 2 about ensuring that every short has an even byte offset, every long a 4-byte offset, and so on.

## COEXISTING WITH WIN16 APPLICATIONS

If you develop your application under NT and initially run it in NT, it is easy to forget that the underlying operating system for a Win32s application is not NT. Therefore, the following suggestions will help your Win32s application coexist with other Win16 applications and Windows 3.1:

Remember to yield. Windows 3.1 is non-preemptive. You must voluntarily give up your time slice or other applications will freeze (remember the Terminator from the Introduction.)

Don't depend upon specific memory locations. One of the parameters to the VirtualAlloc function allows you to specify a virtual address. In NT, the virtual addresses of all user mode processes are in the lower 2GB of memory. WIN32s runs on top of the Windows 3.1 memory manager and virtual memory system and relies on Windows 3.1 for memory management. Windows 3.1 allocates memory where the resulting linear addresses can be either above or below the 2GB boundary. WIN32s simply asks Windows 3.1 for memory and WIN32s returns the address to your application. Win16 applications are ignorant of the linear address because Win16 applications reference memory via selectors.

Therefore, the ability to specify an initial address from VirtualAlloc is not conducive to portable programs.

SetHandleCount increases file handles. In Windows 3.1, a Win32 program has only 15 file handles free. Originally there are 20 minus stdin, out, err, prn, and aux. The SetHandleCount function sets the number of available file handles for the calling process. The range is from 20 to 255. When using CreateFile under NT, you are only limited by available memory, thus SetHandleCount is unnecessary.

Determining a Win32s application from a Win16 program. According to Undocumented Windows, offset 0x16 in a Windows 3.1 task database is a word containing the task flags. A Win32s App will have a value of 0x10 in this field. The following function, IsWin32sApp, accesses the undocumented task structure and returns the value at offset 0x16. Of course, this function is not portable to NT.

```
WORD WINAPI IsWin32sAPP(HANDLE hTask)
{
  ASSERT(IsTask(hTask));
  if ((*((WORD far *) MK_FP(hTask, 0x16))) == 0x10)
      return TRUE;
  else return FALSE;
}
```

## NOTIFYREGISTER AND WIN32S

NotifyRegister is a function exported from the Win16 TOOLHELP.DLL. NotifyRegister installs what is known as a "notification handler" that will call your callback based on certain events. One of these events is the starting of tasks (NFY_STARTTASK). Because Win32s requires the PE loader for Win32 executables, the results of NotifyRegister can get confusing. Instead of passing the name of the Win32 executable that is starting, NotifyRegister gives you the name of the PE loader, Win32s.exe.

Suppose you wanted to keep a record of all programs executed by Windows 3.1. The following code snippet shows how to modify a NotifyRegister callback to report Win32 executables correctly. This callback is 16-bit code that is meant to be incorporated into a Win16 program. I will show you ways to duplicate NotifyRegister functionality in Win32 next. This callback makes use of the Win16 API function, GetCurrentPDB. This is the method used to retrieve a Win16 executable's command line parameters. In Win32, this function is obsolete. To retrieve the command line in a Win32 program you would call GetCommandLine:

```
BOOL CALLBACK _export
NotifyHandler(WORD wID, DWORD dwData)
{
GLOBALENTRY ge;
MODULEENTRY me;
  if (wID == NFY_STARTTASK)
    {

  ge.dwSize=sizeof(ge);
  if (GlobalEntryHandle(&ge,HIWORD(dwData)) == 0)
      return 01;
    me.dwSize = sizeof(me);
    if (ModuleFindHandle(&me,ge.hOwner) == 0)
      return 01;


    if (_fstrstr((LPSTR)me.szExePath,"WIN32S.EXE") != NULL)
  {
  static char szApp[256];

//
// Get the command line from the Program Segment Prefix,
// same as you would in DOS. Then copy to the global gszAppName
//
    LPSP lpsp = (LPSP) MAKELP(GetCurrentPDB(), 0);
    lstrcpy((LPSTR)gszAppName,
          (LPSTR)lpsp->pspCommandTail+1);
    }
```

# SUMMARY

The term *thunk* has got to be one of the most overused phrases in Windows programming. I have heard it used as a verb, a noun, a the name of a product-- and everything in between. It seems to me that the only portable yet efficient way to get 16/32 interoperability is to use OLE automation. Now that Win32s 1.2 is close to be released, you can run the same binaries on all Win32 implementations. The 16bit code becomes the OLE server, the 32 bit code the OLE client. Microsoft never promised that thunking will work the same way on all platforms, if it works at all. They do, however, promise that OLE2 will work between 16/32.

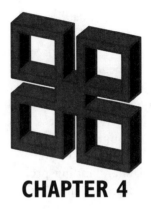

**CHAPTER 4**

# THE LIFE OF A PROCESS

Every operating system must provide a way to run programs and Windows 95 and Windows NT are no exceptions. Examining how an operating system loads a program into memory and begins execution provides valuable insight as to how the operating system functions. To explain how programs, called processes these days, load and execute, this chapter takes you through the life of a typical process. It also shows you the techniques necessary to develop your own programs that load and execute processes.

A process is loaded into memory when another process, called the parent process, invokes the CreateProcess API. When you double-click on an icon in the Explorer window, the shell program SHELL.EXE is activated and becomes the parent process that calls the CreateProcess function. The same is true at the command line prompt or in the File Manager, except in those cases CMD.EXE or WINFILE.EXE calls CreateProcess. Unlike Windows 3.1, both Windows 95 and NT load each new 32-bit process into its own separate address space (NT has the added capability to load 16-bit processes into their own separate address space). Unlike OS/2, this address space can be as large as 2GB for your code and data. In addition to the 2GB for your process, NT reserves 2GB for system DLLs, synchronization objects, pipes, and handles. Windows 95 reserves 1GB for system DLLs and such and 1GB for shared memory. From the beginning, you can see that processes are completely different in these new operating systems. If you examine the life of a typical process under Windows 95 or NT you will see that processes are also coded differently. Beginning with the CreateProcess function call, I'll chronicle a process from its inception through its termination in this chapter. This chapter also explains the differences between a process in Win32 and processes in Win16 or OS/2. Understanding processes and what makes them tick is the foundation to understanding all of Win32.

# A CLOSE LOOK AT CREATEPROCESS

The CreateProcess function replaces the Win16 WinExec and LoadModule functions. WinExec and LoadModule still exist, but they are now just stubs for CreateProcess. ShellExecute, which is in SHELL32.DLL, is another example of a function that now calls CreateProcess. Many developers of "shell" programs designed to replace the Program Manager find ShellExecute valuable because it can execute programs by association. For example, ShellExecute("README.TXT"...) executes NOTEPAD.EXE. However, by looking at the third and fourth arguments to CreateProcess, you can see why WinExec and LoadModule are now obsolete. The following code shows the arguments for CreateProcess:

```
BOOL CreateProcess(lpszImageName,
                   lpszCommandLine,
                   lpsaProcess,
                   lpsaThread,
                   fInheritHandles,
                   fdwCreate,
                   lpvEnvironment,
                   lpszCurDir,
                   lpsiStartInfo,
                   lppiProcInfo)
```

```
LPCTSTR lpszImageName;                  // image file name
LPCTSTR lpszCommandLine;                // command line
LPSECURITY_ATTRIBUTES lpsaProcess;      // process security
                                        // attributes
LPSECURITY_ATTRIBUTES lpsaThread;       // thread security
                                        // attributes

BOOL fInheritHandles;                   // indicates whether new process
                                        // inheritshandles or not
DWORD fdwCreate;                        // creation flags
LPVOID lpvEnvironment;                  // new environment block
LPTSTR lpszCurDir;                      // name of new current
                                        // directory
LPSTARTUPINFO lpsiStartInfo;            // points to STARTUPINFO
LPPROCESS_INFORMATION lppiProcInfo;     // points to
                                        // PROCESS_INFORMATION
```

The first two parameters to CreateProcess are not new; they describe the name of the file (or image as it is called in Win32) and its command line arguments. In the introduction, I wrote briefly about the security features of NT; you use the third and fourth parameters to establish the security for the process. Use the third parameter, lpsaProcess, to describe the security attributes for the process, and the fourth parameter, lpsaThreads, to set the security attributes for the initial thread of the process. Chapter 12, "The Windows NT Security Architecture," discusses all the nuances of the security attributes, so I will skip the details. Even though Windows 95 doesn't support security the call is the same for compatibility's sake. Suffice it to say that you can restrict the rights of a child process and its initial thread in NT. I'll delve into threads a little deeper in the following sections. For now, let's finish creating our process. Because NT is designed to be C2-secure, and because C2 security means discretionary access control, the fifth parameter, fInheritHandles, is a Boolean flag that allows the parent process to specify whether the child inherits the parent's handles. However, it is not an all or nothing situation. Limitations are imposed as to what can and cannot be inherited by a child process. By examining these limitations, you get a better understanding of how processes and NT work. First, let's look at which attributes can be inherited.

## WHAT CAN BE INHERITED BY A CHILD PROCESS

I am going to preface what can be inherited with a comment. All Win32 functions that return an inheritable handle take a security descriptor as an argument. Anytime a NULL is passed as the security descriptor, the handle returned by the function cannot be inherited. For example, look at the CreateFile function call in Listing 4–1.

**Listing 4–1** Using a NULL security descriptor

```
hReadWriteInput = CreateFile("FILE.DAT",
                   GENERIC_READ | GENERIC_WRITE,
                   FILE_SHARE_READ | FILE_SHARE_WRITE,
                   NULL,   /* This NULL means that
                        hreadWriteInput is
                        not inheritable*/
                   OPEN_EXISTING,
                   0,
                   NULL);
```

Okay, having said that, what can be inherited? Handles to threads, named and anonymous pipes, mail slots, mutexes, events, semaphores, mapped files, regular files, as well as communications ports, such as COM1, COM2, and so on. If the parent process is a console process, the console input and output buffers, CONIN$ and CONOUT$, can also be inherited. The current directory and the environment block round out the list.

## WHAT CANNOT BE INHERITED

Since processes are in separate address spaces, you know immediately that handles to memory objects can't be inherited. Since DLLs are loaded and unloaded based on a usage count, handles to DLLs (hINSTANCEs) cannot be inherited. You also cannot inherit handles to GDI objects. Also, handles to USER objects are not inheritable.

For the child process to use the inherited handles, the parent must collaborate with the child to actually get the handles. Win32 just gives the parent permission to pass the handles on to the child; it doesn't actually pass the handle between processes. A couple of crude but effective methods are to pass the handles on the command line or to create an entry in the environment for the handle. For example, to create an entry in the environment for the handle hFile, this code could be used:

```
TCHAR s[10];
wsprintf(s, "%d",hFile);
if (! SetEnvironmentVariable("HFILE=", s)
    ErrorExit("SetEnvironmentVariable failed");
/* Create a child process. */



fSuccess = CreateProcess(NULL, "childenv", NULL, NULL, TRUE, 0,
    NULL,    // inherit parent's environment
    NULL, &siStartInfo, &piProcInfo);
if (! fSuccess)
    ErrorExit("CreateProcess failed");
```

The child process would then call the GetEnvironmentVariable function to retrieve the handle:

```
TCHAR s[10];
GetEnvironmentVariable("HFILE", s, BUFSIZE);
sscanf(s,"%d",hFile);
```

The other method is to use one of the many interprocess communication (IPC) APIs available to you. I discuss these APIs in Chapter 5, "Memory Management."

At times, you may need for a child process to inherit some, but not all, of your handles. Even though fInheritHandles can only be TRUE or FALSE, you are not stuck. One solution is to use a NULL security descriptor on all of the objects you do not want the child to inherit. In the case where the parent process inherited its handles from its parent, you can use the DuplicateHandle function:

```
hReadWriteInput = CreateFile("FILE.DAT",
                GENERIC_READ | GENERIC_WRITE,
                FILE_SHARE_READ | FILE_SHARE_WRITE,
                lpsa,   // lpsa is a pointer to a
                    // Security Attribute
```

**133**

```
                    // which allows this handle to
                    // be inherited.
                OPEN_EXISTING,
                0,
                NULL);

    hCurrentProcess = GetCurrentProcess();
    DuplicateHandle(hCurrentProcess,
            hReadWriteInput,
            hCurrentProcess(),
            hNewHandle,
            0,
            FALSE,
            DUPLICATE_SAME_ACCESS);
    CloseHandle(hReadWriteInput);
```

The reverse is also true. For example, back in Listing 1–1 the handle to hReadWriteInput cannot be inherited because I passed in a NULL security descriptor. If I create a child process that needs to inherit hReadWriteInput, I can duplicate the handle by using DuplicateHandle with the fInherit flag set to TRUE, as shown in the following example:

```
    BOOL DuplicateHandle(hSourceProcess,
                hSource,
                hTargetProcess,
                lphTarget,
                fdwAccess,
                fInherit,
                fdwOptions)
```

## CREATION FLAGS FOR DETERMINING PRIORITY CLASS AND PROCESS TYPE

The sixth parameter to CreateProcess, fdwCreate, is for the creation flags. The creation flags determine the priority class for the process and control the type of process being created. The following list defines each creation flag.

**134**

| Creation Flag | Explanation |
|---|---|
| CREATE_NEW_CONSOLE | A process created with CREATE_NEW_ CONSOLE will gain a new console (one separate from the parent) to run in. |
| CREATE_SUSPENDED | When the process is created, its initial thread is suspended and won't start executing until another thread calls ResumeThread. In other words, WinMain or main will not execute until ResumeThread is called. Debuggers use this parameter to create the process as a suspended process, gain control, and then allow the user to step through line by line. In the sample application, CREATE_SUSPENDED is used to get control of the thread and change its priority before it runs. |
| DEBUG_PROCESS | This flag is normally set by debuggers. Processes created with DEBUG_PROCESS can call the WaitForDebugEvent function to receive debug events. This flag also enables notifications of debug events for child processes. |
| DEBUG_ONLY_THIS_PROCESS | Same as DEBUG_PROCESS only there are no notifications for child processes. |
| DETACHED_PROCESS | Used only by console processes. When a process is detached, it initially is in the background and has no way of communicating with the user. If the process needs user input or needs to display a message, it can call AllocConsole. For example, suppose you have a process that performs backup. Normally it is in the background, but when it requires user intervention to switch a tape or a diskette, the process calls AllocConsole and puts up a message box. |

The fdwCreate parameter can also control the priority class for the new process. Since Windows 95 and NT are preemptive multitasking systems, they needs to know which thread (or threads in the case of a multiprocessing, or MP, system in NT) to run next. This piece of the operating system is called the scheduler. If you are originally from the Win16 world, the whole priority system may seem complicated, but it really is quite slick. There are four classes of priorities: Idle, Normal, High, and Real-time. The class you assign to a priority is solely dependent upon the requirements of the process.

If your process has no special needs, assign it to the Normal priority class. Most processes have threads in the Normal class. Threads running in the Normal priority class will be preempted by everything except threads running in the Idle priority class.

Idle priority is for processes that need to run only when no other activity is taking place. In other words, if the processor has nothing better to do, it executes Idle priority threads. An example of an Idle priority is the thread that does background repagination in a word processor. Background printing is another example. Basically, most compute-bound tasks are candidates for Idle priority.

High priority is reserved for processes that require the immediate attention of the processor. The threads of High priority processes preempt the threads of Normal and Idle processes. Any application that uses a hot-key sequence is a candidate for High priority. One example of a High priority process is the Windows Task Manager. When you press Ctrl-Esc or double-click on the desktop in Windows 3.x, Windows spawns the program TASKMAN.EXE. In NT, the TASKMAN.EXE process is always running and waiting for the hot-key sequence as a HIGH_PRIORITY_CLASS thread. If the TASKMAN process had just a Normal, or worse yet, an Idle priority thread, there could be a delay between the hot-key sequence and the appearance of the TASKMAN window. Any thread that is I/O bound is a candidate for High priority. It is inefficient for the disk drive to remain Idle because a thread is Normal priority. In this case you want the disk to be in use as much as possible.

Next on the list is the Real-time priority class. In the introduction I wrote that all PC operating systems have an Achilles heel. Well, the Real-time priority class is an Achilles heels. The threads of a Real-time process run at a higher priority than the raw input thread (the thread that collects input from the user). If a Real-time priority thread dawdles, the mouse and keyboard become sluggish. The REALTIME_PRIORITY_CLASS flag wasn't documented in the preliminary release of the Win32 specification. If there is only one Real-time priority thread in the system and it gets stuck in a loop, both NT and Windows 95 can hang. Not even Ctrl-Alt-Del will get you out. I'm still searching for a good definition of a Real-time process that runs in User mode. Communicating with hardware is a good candidate except that User mode programs cannot communicate directly with the hardware in NT (it would be a security violation). Even for the inp or outp functions, you must write a device driver.

If you are writing a device driver, I can think of plenty of examples that would need REALTIME_PRIORITY_CLASS. If you have an idea of why to use Real-time and you don't want your program to be the one that freezes, here's a way to implement it:

▪▪    Block on a certain event.

▪▪    When the event happens, handle the critical stuff.

▪▪    Hand the rest of the stuff off to lower priority threads or reduce your priority class.

▪▪    Block on the event again.

One reason not to use REALTIME_PRIORITY_CLASS is to gain more CPU Cycles! Making your thread a High or Real-time priority class just because you think it will make your program seem to run faster is wrong. Instead of saying "Gee, your product really blazes," users will say, "Every time I run your product my mouse and keyboard become unresponsive. That's why I deleted it from my system. Please send me my money back." If every process ran at REALTIME_PRIORITY_CLASS it would be the same as if everything was running at NORMAL_PRIORITY_CLASS.

# THREADS

When a new process is created, its main thread must be set to one of these priority classes. The default is NORMAL_PRIORITY_CLASS, and this is the class that processes spawned by CMD.EXE, PROGMAN.EXE, or WINFILE.EXE run in. The Win32 documentation defines a thread as the basic entity to which the operating system allocates CPU time. That's a technical way of saying that a process doesn't really execute. Instead, one or more of its threads execute. So, this parameter really controls how threads will be created in the new process. When you reach WinMain, main (or if you are using a DLL, whatever you set DLLEntrypoint to), you are running on the initial thread. Under normal circumstances, each subsequent thread you create is in the same priority class. If you have code you want to run in a priority class other than the default, you have two choices. You can use the GetPriorityClass or SetPriorityClass calls to determine and then set your priority level. The following code shows how to use the calls:

```
if (GetPriorityClass(hProcess) != IDLE_PRIORITY_CLASS)
    SetPriorityClass(hProcess,IDLE_PRIORITY_CLASS);
```

Or, you can create a new process with the desired priority class. The following code shows how to create a new process with the correct priority class:

```
CreateProcess("PROCESS_WITH_REAL_TIME_THREAD.EXE",
              lpszCommandLine,
              lpsaProcess,
              lpsaThread,
              fInheritHandles,
              HIGH_PRIORITY_CLASS,
              lpvEnvironment,
              lpszCurDir,
              lpsiStartInfo,
              lppiProcInfo);
```

Each priority class has several levels. as shown in Figure 4–1. This facilitates the ordering of threads within your process.

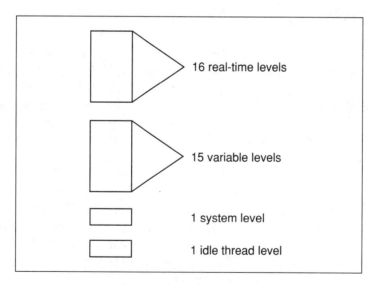

**Figure 4–1** Priority levels

Each additional thread is capable of accessing all global and system variables. These threads can create windows if they want to. Any window created by one of these threads will receive messages in that thread.

## WHEN TO USE ADDITIONAL THREADS

If you are from the UNIX or OS/2 world, you are probably familiar with threads. But if you are from the Win16 world, you may wonder when exactly to use threads. Threads should be used in the following situations.

To distinguish between disparate tasks. Because Windows 3.x is single-threaded, applications that need to perform simultaneous tasks sometimes spawn additional processes. Programs such as Lotus 1–2-3 for Windows are really several executables rolled into one application. These separate processes all work together to accomplish the goal of the application. In Win32 the answer would be to have separate threads. In the classic example, one thread handles user interaction, and a separate thread processes the time of day. A process should have multiple threads in situations where the application has to run several tasks concurrently. For example, an application that opens more than one window can use a separate thread to perform the work of the application in each window.

To discern between tasks with different priorities. For example, a High priority thread handles time-critical tasks and a Low priority thread performs other tasks. This is known as scheduling.

To achieve an alternate method to polling. Anywhere you use a Timer in Win16 is a candidate for a separate thread in Win32.

As an effective means of load balancing (also known as CPU tuning). Tasks that take a long time to complete can run in a separate thread from the thread that interacts with the user, resulting in overlapping tasks, such as filling a list box or recalculating a spreadsheet.

To divide the execution of parallel tasks. For example,  a server application could start an identical thread for each client that made requests to the server.

Each thread that is created has its own stack and machine state. Therefore, use the stack (local variables) and avoid using static (global) data. If you use static data, use CONST to make it read-only. If you use read/write global variables, you must synchronize the execution of your threads. Otherwise, you could have two threads both trying to write to the same location at the same time. Fortunately, synchronizing threads isn't hard because Win32 provides a complete set of synchronizing functions, which are described at the end of the chapter.

## CREATING THREADS

The code in Listing 4–2, found later in this chapter, is an example of a multithreaded application. Figure 4–2 shows the About box for this sample application. A new thread is created for each new MDI child window that is created. Figure 4–3 shows what the application looks like when it's running. The listing demonstrates how to create a new thread with the C++ member function, CThreadWnd::ThreadFunc.

```
this->m_hThrd=CreateThread(NULL,
          0,
          this->Threadfunc,
          this,
          CREATE_SUSPENDED,
          &this->threadid);
```

My example program uses the MFC, but it's easy to do in C:

```
hThread = CreateThread(
          NULL,         // no security attributes
          0,            // use default stack size
          (LPTHREAD_START_ROUTINE) ThreadFunc, // thread
                        // function
          0,            // no parameter
          0,            // use default creation flags
          &dwThreadId); // returns thread id
```

Thread functions have the prototype:

```
LONG WINAPI threadfunc(LPVOID);
```

If you want your thread function to be a C++ member function, the parameter passed to it must be the this pointer. All C++ member functions have the this pointer as a hidden first parameter. Otherwise, it can be any 32-bit value you want. However, don't pass the address of a local variable as the parameter unless you are sure the calling function will not return before the thread function becomes active. If the calling function does return, the stack will be garbage and the address will be of no use.

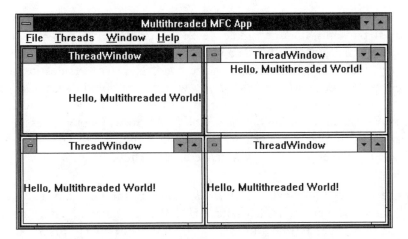

**Figure 4–2** The Multithreaded MFC application

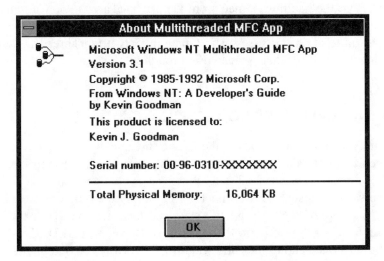

**Figure 4–3** The About box for Multithreaded MFC

Use the CreateThread function to create the thread. There is no practical limit to the number of threads that can execute a thread function. Just remember that each thread will have its own stack. When you pass the this pointer, you get access to all of the class. You always have access to global variables, but if you use global variables you will have to synchronize to make sure your threads don't trip over each other when accessing these variables.

The CreateThread function allows you to set the initial stack size of the new thread (if you want). In our example we set this parameter to zero, which is the default. I normally choose the default during development and then determine the exact stack size when optimizing the code. The stack resides in the data segment of the process (it has to, or you wouldn't be able to access it). If the default size is too small, it will grow automatically. When the thread terminates, the stack will automatically be freed. So why bother messing with the parameter at all? Why not always leave it at the default? Because, as we shall see in Chapter 5, "Memory Management," there is a performance penalty for doing so.

If CreateThread succeeds, it returns a handle to the thread. You'll use this handle in subsequent calls that take a HTHREAD parameter. An important thing to remember is that this handle is valid until it is closed. Use the CloseHandle function to close a handle. When an object's handle count goes to zero (when the last handle is closed), the object is deleted. This handle is different from the handle returned from GetCurrentThread. GetCurrentThread returns a pseudo handle that can only be used in the current process and cannot be passed on to child processes. The function, GetCurrentThreadID, returns a unique identifier (ID #) that you can use throughout the system.

## SUSPENDING THREAD EXECUTION

One thing you should notice about the CreateThread call is that there is no way to set the new thread's priority. Instead there is a creation flag that enables you to create the thread in a suspended state. When suspended, the thread does not run until you call the ResumeThread function. In the sample program, we create all threads in a CREATE_SUSPENDED state and then use the SetThreadPriority call to set the thread's priority to PRIORITY_BELOW_NORMAL. This ensures that the thread that handles the child windows will always be of a higher priority than the worker threads and will allow the child window thread to be responsive to the user.

Threads can also be suspended by using the SuspendThread call. The sample contains menu options that suspend and resume any window. Actually it just appears that way. The only part that is suspended is the code that moves the string on the screen and calls InvalidateRect. The scheduler skips over all threads that are in a suspended state—they simply do not get any CPU time. Since the suspended thread is no longer calling InvalidateRect, the associated child window won't receive any WM_PAINT messages. This makes it appear as if the entire window is suspended. Here is the big difference: In the Multithreaded MFC Application (see Listing 1–2), the child window can be cascaded or tiled. If you suspend the window, it won't be able to repaint and will spoil the UI. (Nothing looks more like a bug than a window that doesn't repaint its frame.) Call ResumeThread when you want the thread to start running again. However, don't use SuspendThread as a method of synchronization, since you cannot determine where in the thread the suspension will take place.

If you want to suspend yourself for a certain period of time, call Sleep or SleepEx. Both functions take a timeout variable that is measurable in milliseconds. The sample has Sleep(500) in each thread to put a delay before each call to InvalidateRect. This keeps the output from flickering.

## SETTING THREAD PRIORITIES

In theory, if every thread in your system is the same priority, and the scheduler will "round-robin" each thread. If there are ten threads in the system, the scheduler splits available CPU time ten ways. Thread number 10 will have to wait until threads 1 through 9 run before it gets its chance. In practice this makes for a very inefficient system. Suppose thread 10 is the thread of the window that has the input focus. When a user types or uses the mouse, thread 10 has to wait for threads 1 through 9 to complete before it can process its window messages. To combat this problem, you can make thread 10 a HIGH_PRIORITY thread. That way, thread 10 is assured of being responsive to the user. Don't bet on it! If you make this mistake and threads 1 though 9 stay as NORMAL_PRIORITY when the user clicks in another window, you have the same problem all over again.

Clearly this is not the answer, which is why Win32 provides the concept of priority levels. Each priority class has five priority levels: Lowest, Below Normal, Normal, Above Normal, Highest. When created, a thread is automatically given a Normal priority. The scheduler determines which thread (or threads in an MP system) to run next based on one of the 33 priority levels.

Win32 introduces a few new terms when discussing the priority levels of threads. The current priority is the level at which the thread is currently executing. The GetThreadPriority function is used to get the current priority level of a thread. The base priority is either NORMAL or whatever priority is set by the SetThreadPriority function. The dynamic priority is the result of the scheduler either raising or lowering the priority based upon some significant event. There are a couple of ways that either you or the scheduler can adjust these levels.

Even though you cannot alter the dynamic priority of a thread, it's important to understand what is going on. (Later on in this chapter, when we go over Synchronization, understanding dynamic priority will help you eliminate a couple of bugs called deadlocks and race conditions from your code.) The dynamic priority changes when the scheduler needs to bump a particular thread's place in the queue. For example, in our previous example, thread 10 receives a dynamic boost when its window receives the focus. This dynamic boost automatically moves thread 10 to the front of the queue. Once a thread's dynamic priority is raised, the thread experiences a phenomenon known as quantum decay. Each time the thread completes a time slice, the scheduler lowers (decays) the dynamic priority by one until it reaches its base priority.

Although there is nothing you can do programmatically about the dynamic priority, you can change the base priority of the thread by calling the SetThreadPriority function. Consider the following example:

```
// get current priority level. Not necessarily the base
// priority
if (GetThreadPriority(hThread) =< NORMAL)
    SetThreadPriority(hThread,ABOVE_NORMAL); //set new base
                                             //priority
```

## USING THREAD LOCAL STORAGE

In our example, only constant data variables are in ThreadFunc. In some cases each thread must have a private copy of read/write data. You have several options if you want to create the data outside of the function and pass an address to it via ThreadParam. In our example, we pass the this pointer. In C programs, you can pass a pointer to a data structure. But what if we want each thread to have its own private copy of data variables that the thread itself created? One answer is to have stack (local) variables. That way, each thread can have separate variables. However, these variables go in and out of scope each time you call Threadfunc. The answer is to use thread local storage (TLS).

With TLS, Threadfunc can allocate an index that points to static data on a per-thread basis each time it is called. This way multiple threads can have their own copy of data to manipulate at will. TLS is extremely effective when used in a DLL. In the Introduction, I talked about the new DLLEntryPoint in Win32 DLLs. In your entry-point function, place the calls to allocate a TLS index when the .DLL is attaching to a new thread. Then place the free function when the thread is detaching. When the DLL attaches to a new process, the entry-point function calls TlsAlloc to allocate a TLS index for that process. When the DLL attaches to a new thread of that process, the function you designate as the entry point allocates dynamic memory for that thread and uses TlsSetValue to save private data to the index.

The only catch is that only threads of the same process can participate. In other words, a thread from one process cannot access data from a thread in a different process using the first thread's index value. Listing 4–2 contains the code to modify our Multithreaded MFC application to one that uses thread local storage.

**Listing 4–2** Code to use thread local storage

```
// Threadfunc:
//
DWORD CThreadWnd::Threadfunc(void *)
{
static const COLORREF clrTextArray[] = { RGB (0, 0, 0), RGB (255, 0,
0),
                    RGB (0, 255, 0), RGB (0, 0, 255),
                    RGB (255, 255, 255) };

LPVOID lpvData;

    /* Initialize the TLS index for this thread */

lpvData = (LPVOID) LocalAlloc(LPTR, 256);

if (! TlsSetValue(dwTlsIndex, lpvData))
        ErrorExit("TlsSetValue error");
```

```
while(1)
{
CommonFunc();

if (m_nColor < IDM_WHITE)
    m_nColor++;
else
    m_nColor=IDM_BLACK;
if (m_bKillme)
    {
    lpvData = TlsGetValue(dwTlsIndex);
    if (lpvData != 0)
        LocalFree((HLOCAL) lpvData);
    return(0); //could ExitThread() here, also.
    }
else
    m_clrText = clrTextArray[m_nColor - IDM_BLACK];
Sleep(500);
Invalidate();
    }

}


VOID
CommonFunc(VOID)
{

LPVOID lpvData;
TCHAR s[64];

  // Retrieve data pointer for current thread
  lpvData = TlsGetValue(dwTlsIndex);
  if ((lpvData == 0) && (GetLastError() != 0))
    ErrorExit("TlsGetValue error");

  /*
   *    Use data stored for current thread
```

```
    */



}

VOID
ErrorExit (LPTSTR lpszMessage)
{

    MessageBox(NULL,lpszMessage,"Error",MB_OK);
    ExitProcess(0);
}
```

Take the following steps to implement TLS:

- Call TlsAlloc to allocate a TLS index. If our example were a DLL, then you call TlsAlloc during an attach. In regular processes, make the call before calling CreateThread.

- Associate the pointer to your thread's dynamic storage.

- The storage returned from any call you make to allocate memory is considered dynamic. Use TlsSetValue to associate the index with the pointer.

- Call TlsGetValue

- Pass in the index to retrieve the pointer.

- Make sure to free memory.

- When all threads are finished processing, call TlsFree.


## TERMINATING A THREAD

Use one of the following methods to terminate a thread:

- Call ExitThread. Pass in a exit code if you want. Although this seems to be the preferred method, I rarely use it. If I call ExitThread, I don't need to call return. If I don't return I get a warning from the compiler.

- ▚ Call return. If your thread function returns, the runtime library code calls ExitThread. The runtime library code passes the parameter to the return function to ExitThread. If this thread is the only thread, the runtime library calls ExitProcess instead of ExitThread.

- ▚ Call ExitProcess. However, there seems to be a time delay between the point when your process appears to terminate and when the last thread dies. You can try this with the MDI example by running it from a DOS box and then executing a sysmenu..close. The DOS box from which you started the process will be suspended pending termination of the last thread.

- ▚ Some other thread calls TerminateThread with a handle to your thread. This method can leave your thread in an unstable state because you will have no chance to perform any clean up. You will not be notified, and therefore you won't be able to release objects. Obviously, this method should be used only as a last resort to get rid of a thread that has stopped responding to the system.

- ▚ Someone calls TerminateProcess with a handle to your thread's process. Again, this is a last resort option because resources may not be freed.

## WHEN THREADS AREN'T NECESSARY

The good news about Windows 95 and Windows NT is that it supports threads. The bad news is that it supports threads. Just because you have the capability to create threads whenever you want doesn't mean you should rush out and do so. Threads are not salt. They should not be sprinkled throughout your code in an attempt to make it more palatable. The more threads you create the more overhead the operating systems require to keep track of them. A single-threaded process is much easier to code and debug. In an effort to keep your code from becoming too salty, Win32 provides APIs that can be used instead of creating another thread.

## OVERLAPPED I/O

Win32 has the concept of "overlapped" I/O. With overlapped I/O, it is not necessary to create a separate thread to perform I/O. Overlapping I/O requests

**148**

enable you to perform I/O to multiple devices simultaneously from a single thread. This asynchronous I/O can be performed on files, pipes, serial communications devices, or tape devices. When you request the I/O and pass in the address of an I/O completion routine, the I/O completion routine is called back when your I/O completes. The following code fragment is an example of "overlapped" I/O. The fifth parameter to ReadFileEx is the address of the callback, CompletionRoutine.

```
ReadFileEx(hFile, lpBuffer,
    nNumberOfBytesToRead,
    lpOverlapped,
    (LPOVERLAPPED_COMPLETION_ROUTINE) CompletionRoutine);
In CompletionRoutine, check dwErrorCode for success or failure.
VOID
CompletionRoutine(
    DWORD dwErrorCode,
    DWORD dwNumberOfBytesTransfered,
    LPOVERLAPPED lpOverlapped)
{
if (dwErrorCode)
    {
    // The I/O did not complete successfully
    // Call GetLastError() and perform Error routine.
    .
    .
    .
    }
else
    {
    // The I/O completed successfully.
    // Set a flag or a semaphore to
    // let waiting threads know I/O is complete.
    .
    .
    .
    }

}
```

Instead of wasting processor time polling for a significant event, Win32 provides APIs that can eliminate a separate, polling thread. The WaitForSingleObject and WaitForMultipleObject APIs are covered in the Synchronization section later in this chapter.

# STRUCTURES AND THE CREATEPROCESS API

Getting back to the CreateProcess API (we're now at the ninth parameter) is the STARTUPINFO structure. In Win32, you have the opportunity to describe the window characteristics for a new process. In Win16, you are limited to the nCmdShow parameter. In Win32, all "startup" properties can be manipulated via the STARTUPINFO structure.

## ENVIRONMENT VARIABLES

Environments in 32-bit Windows are not much different from environments in Windows, DOS or OS/2. At startup, each process receives a copy of the environment from its parent. For example, if the only environment variable you want CHILD.EXE to inherit is the path variable, it works like this:

```
LPTSTR pszEnviron = "PATH=C:\DOS";

fSuccess = CreateProcess(NULL, pszEnviron, NULL, NULL, TRUE, 0,
            NULL, // inherit parent's
                // environment
            NULL, &siStartInfo, &piProcInfo);
if (! fSuccess)
    ErrorExit("CreateProcess failed");
```

The GetEnvironmentStrings function returns a pointer to the environment block of the calling process. Treat this as a read-only block; do not modify it directly. Instead, use the SetEnvironmentVariable function to change an environment variable. The GetEnvironmentVariable function determines whether a specified variable is defined in the environment of the calling process, and, if so, the value of the variable.

**150**

## THE PROCESS_INFORMATION STRUCTURE

If CreateProcess succeeds, it returns a PROCESS_INFORMATION structure containing handles and identification numbers for the new process and its primary thread. The thread and process handles are created with full access rights, although you can restrict access if you specify a security descriptor.

## STOPPING THE GUI PROCESS

When you want to stop your GUI process, you still issue PostQuitmessage. This is the preferred method for ending your process. However, any thread in the process can call ExitProcess. If you are a console application and you want to quit, you can call ExitProcess or you can just return from main. If you return, the startup code calls ExitProcess for you. If you don't handle Ctrl-C or Ctrl-Break in your console program, the startup code also calls ExitProcess. As I said earlier, NT is unlike OS/2, because when a parent process terminates, the children are not affected. There is one exception to this rule: If neither parent nor child handles Ctrl-C or Ctrl-Break, and neither is a detached process, and the child has not created a new console application, then both applications will terminate when they receive the signal.

Consequently, if you cannot create a window in a GUI process or if you realize that this is the second copy of the process, you can explicitly return from a GUI process as well.

If the initial thread of the process calls ExitThread instead of returning or calling ExitProcess, the process will not cease until one of the other threads calls ExitProcess. This situation occurs when the logic of your code dictates that the initial thread exit while other threads are still processing. If this situation occurs, make sure one of your other threads calls ExitProcess or the resources for your process will be orphans. Notice that this is different from OS/2, which operates on the primary thread concept. (A process doesn't end in OS/2 until the primary thread ends.)

When your process ceases, any threads from other processes that are waiting on the process are allowed to run. All DLLs attached to the process are notified, unless TerminateProcess is called. This is the reason ExitProcess is preferred over TerminateProcess. Besides notifying DLLs, nothing else takes place after ExitProcess or TerminateProcess is called. All open handles to objects are closed and no further code is run in any thread.

Call GetExitCodeProcess if you want to find the termination status of a process. If the process is still active, you receive a STILL_ACTIVE return. If the process has terminated, the return is the exit code of ExitProcess or TerminateThread. If the process is terminated by a Crtl-C or a unhandled exception, the exit code is the exception code that caused the termination.

## SYNCHRONIZATION

Synchronization is the process of making sure that only one thread has control of a resource at a time. When I say resource, I am referring to objects such as global variables, public data members, or handles such as communication handles, console input handles, file handles, named pipe handles, and process and thread handles. This is not to be confused with resources that are linked in with your program, such as strings, icons, and dialog boxes. Since these resources are read-only, there is no need to perform synchronization on them.

## DIFFERENCES BETWEEN WIN16 AND WIN32

In most cases, Windows 3.x doesn't require explicit synchronization, because 3.x is not preemptive. Therefore, all Win16 threads are atomic (they run to completion), and all Win16 code can be considered to be in the critical section by default. The only time Win16 relinquishes the critical section is when you call a function such as PeekMessage or GetMessage. Since 32-bit Windows is preemptive, programming a multithreaded model brings up synchronization issues. If you do not synchronize your code, you may end up with what is known as a race condition. A race condition happens when two or more threads are reading from or writing to the same region of shared data. One thread should be blocking upon the completion of another thread, but isn't. The code works as long as the second thread finishes what it is doing—it "wins the race"—before the first thread accesses the resource. Unfortunately, Murphy's Law dictates that the second thread always wins the race during development and testing, but loses the race after it is in production. Race conditions are easy to visualize if you think about MP systems where both threads can be running simultaneously. Of course, races conditions can also occur on UP systems.

The remainder of the chapter discusses the APIs that Win32 provides to ensure that you have no race conditions in your code. But first, let's examine all the possible places where synchronization is needed.

- ▪▪ Between threads within a process
- ▪▪ Between threads in other processes
- ▪▪ Between multiple threads and GDI objects

Once you add the proper calls to ensure you have no race conditions, make sure you have no deadlocks. Deadlocks occur only when you have synchronization in your code. A typical deadlock occurs when thread A blocks waiting for thread B to terminate, but thread A is unaware that thread B is already blocked waiting for a resource thread A owns. The result is that neither thread can run and will block indefinitely.

When synchronizing threads, Win32 uses the following terms: signaled and not-signaled. The term signaled means an object is available, and not-signaled means it is unavailable. For example, if thread A is waiting for thread B to terminate, thread A will start executing again when thread B's process state becomes signaled (when Thread B terminates). Until that time, Thread B's object is Not-Signaled.

In Multithreaded MDI, we wait for the threads to become signaled, as the following code shows:

```
WaitForSingleObject(m_hThrd, INFINITE);
m_pMDIFrameWnd->SendMessage(WM_CHILDDESTROY, (UINT)m_hWnd, 0);
```

# SYNCHRONIZATION OBJECTS

The type of resource that you are synchronizing determines the type of synchronization object you use. Objects can be named or unnamed. The handle to an object is not system-wide. The handle is valid for all threads within a process, but threads in other processes cannot use the handle. Win32 provides a mechanism for sharing objects by naming them. If you use IPC (inter-process communication), naming an object makes it possible to share the object across processes. As with threads, you can decide whether children will inherit these objects.

Four types of synchronization objects are available:

■■ Critical-Section

■■ Event

■■ Mutex

■■ Semaphores

To synchronize execution, threads either block on one of these objects—that is, wait for it to become signaled—or call an API function to modify the state of the object.

While a thread is waiting on a object, it does not get any CPU time until the object becomes signaled. Hence the term "blocked." Some APIs offer a timeout value so you can abort the wait.

## CRITICAL SECTION OBJECTS

Use Critical Section objects when threads of a single process need to ensure that only one thread accesses a shared resource at any time. For example, if two threads need to perform file I/O, each thread has to request and receive the Critical Section before they can perform file I/O. The second and subsequent threads) that did not receive the Critical Section will block until the resource becomes available.

The basic steps are as follows:

1. InitializeCriticalSection. You must first declare a CS object
   CRITICAL_SECTION cs;
2. You then call the InitializeCriticalSection function once:
   InitializeCriticalSection(&cs);
3. This sets the object's state to NOT_SIGNALLED, allowing threads to use the resource.
4. EnterCriticalSection. At the point in the code that has resources you need to protect, you make a call to EnterCriticalSection. While you are

in the Critical Section, no other thread can execute this code. When they attempt to execute the code, they will be blocked.

5. LeaveCriticalSection. When you are finished, you must call LeaveCriticalSection so that other threads can access the code.

6. DeleteCriticalSection. When all threads are finished with the protected resources, call DeleteCriticalSection to free the CRITICAL_SECTION object.

If for some reason your thread terminates before it calls the LeaveCriticalSection, all other threads are precluded from running this code. Therefore, the proper procedure is to place this code within a try..finally block:

```
try{
EnterCriticalSection(&cs)
  .
  .
  .
}
finally
{
  .
  .
.LeaveCriticalSection(&cs);
}
```

Both try and finally are extensions to the C language to support Structured Exception Handling (SEH). Chapter 9, "Memory Management," contains a sidebar on SEH.

Think of Critical Section code as non-reentrant code. Non-reentrant means that two or more processes cannot execute the same function at the same time. In Win16 or DOS, the method for protecting a critical resource goes something like this:

```
If (gfCS)           //some global boolean
    return (FALSE);  // get out, not okay at this time
gfCS=TRUE;          // set to NOT_SIGNALLED to indicate we
                    // are in CS
```

**155**

```
        .                   //do critical processing
        .
    gfCS=FALSE;             //set back to SIGNALLED - we are getting
                            //out
```

However, this is rarely necessary in Win16. The only time you must protect your critical resources in a Win16 process is when you have some type of interrupt handler, such as the InterruptNotify from TOOLHELP.DLL.


## EVENT OBJECTS

Event objects notify a waiting thread that an event occurs. You can set or reset an event object. You can also pulse an event, which means to set momentarily and then reset the event object. Two types of resets are available: automatic reset and manual reset.

- If the event function is set to automatic reset the object releases the next available thread when it becomes signaled. Use automatic reset to set up a round-robin series of threads.

- A manual reset event object releases all available threads when it becomes signaled. An example of this is a communication program which uses one thread to read the raw incoming data and several worker threads are temporarily blocked waiting to read the cooked data. Perhaps one thread tests for the presence of an autostart file transfer, while another handles the protocol/formatting. When the communication thread fills the buffer, it manually resets the event, which allows the file transfer thread and communication protocol thread to do their work. When the communication thread needs to fill the buffer again it resets the event to not-signaled, which blocks the worker threads.

On the other hand, there may be a situation where you do not want all of the waiting threads to be freed. Perhaps you have a situation where you want just one of the waiting threads to be freed. Win32 provides an automatic reset for this situation. Automatic reset releases one of several waiting threads. In the communication program there may be a situation where you need to release only the protocol thread. In this case, you use automatic reset for the event.

## 156

Which of the waiting threads will be released? The thread with the highest priority is always released next, In the case of a tie, the next thread in the queue is released. Since Win16 has no event objects, the only alternative is to poll.

The function PulseEvent is available when you want to set a specified event to the signaled state and then immediately reset the event back to the not-signaled state.

■■ If your event is created as automatic reset, then only one waiting thread is released.

■■ If the event is created as manual reset, all waiting threads are released.

■■ If no threads are waiting to be released, the object state goes to not-signaled.

At first glance this doesn't seem very useful, but PulseEvent is very powerful. You can use PulseEvent to work around the problem of how to release waiting threads and then immediately block their next execution. When an event is pulsed, it remains set long enough to satisfy any thread that called WaitForSingleObject or WaitForMultipleObjects. If you try to accomplish this using two function calls (SetEvent and ResetEvent), you have a built-in race condition. You cannot guarantee that ResetEvent is called before the threads call one of the wait functions. Instead the following can happen:

| Your Process | Other Threads |
|---|---|
| SetEvent | Call WaitforSingleObject (now released, the thread performs its processing). Threads Call WaitforSingleObject again and perform more processing because the object is still SIGNALED. |
| ResetEvent | Application doesn't perform as expected due to race condition. |

## MUTEX OBJECTS

Mutexes are similar to Critical Section objects. The term mutex comes from the contraction of the words "mutual exclusion." The difference between Critical Section objects and mutexes is that mutexes can be used between processes, but Critical Section objects can be used only within the same process. You can use mutexes for threads within a single process. However, it's faster and more

**157**

efficient to use Critical Section objects. Instead of calling EnterCriticalSection, you call WaitForSingleObject or WaitForMultipleObjects. Both functions take a timeout parameter so you can avoid deadlocking, and avoid blocking forever. Consider this example:

1. Create Mutex.
2. Attempt to gain ownership.
3. Use critical resource.
4. Release Mutex. Be careful not to abandon your mutexes.

Like Critical Section objects, you should enclose your read/write operations with try..finally blocks. That way, if you encounter exceptions you can recover and release the mutex. You cause problems however, if you call TerminateThread in your try block. No code in the finally block is executed when the thread is terminated and your mutex will be abandoned. When you attempt to gain a mutex that has been abandoned by its owner, you get a return status of WAIT_ABANDONED. If you do get a WAIT_ABANDONED status, it's time to warn your user and terminate the program. In most cases, it is unwise to try to recover. Who knows why you original mutex died and left the wait object abandoned?

## SEMAPHORE OBJECTS

Semaphores are used when you need a counter to limit the number of threads that can use a resource. Semaphores in Win32 are more similar to semaphores in OS/2 than they are to semaphores in UNIX. A UNIX semaphore can signal on a particular value that is set by the developer. In Win32, a semaphore is signaled until its count becomes zero. Semaphores are the mechanism to use when you have multiple, identical resources to manage. You create a semaphore by calling the CreateSemaphore function:

```
HANDLE CreateSemaphore(lpsa, cSemInitial, cSemMax, lpszSemName)

LPSECURITY_ATTRIBUTES lpsa;      // optional security attributes
LONG cSemInitial;                // initial count
LONG cSemMax;                    // maximum count
LPTSTR lpszSemName;              // name of the semaphore
```

cSemInitial specifies an initial count and cSemMax specifies the maximum number of semaphores. If you want, you can use the lpszSemName parameter to name your semaphore. That allows other processes to share the semaphore.

Going back to the MDI sample program, suppose we wanted one window to display something different than "Hello Multithreaded World." To achieve this, you must create a semaphore that acts as a gate. As long as one thread is printing the alternative message, no other thread can print the message. Figure 4–4 shows the window displaying the new message. Listings 4–3 and 4–4 show the source. Naming the semaphore allows you to run multiple copies of the program, and having only one copy displays the alternative message. When the thread displaying the alternative message terminates, the resource gate becomes not-signaled and the next thread that attempts to get through will be able to display the message. As soon as you close the window displaying the alternative message, another window begins to display it.

**Figure 4–4** Multithreaded App with a semaphore

**Listing 4–3** Source to the multithreaded MDI frame window

```
// chap4.cpp : Defines the class behaviors for the application.
//

#include "stdafx.h"
#include "chap4.h"
```

```
#include "mainfrm.h"
#include "chap4doc.h"
#include "chap4vw.h"

#ifdef _DEBUG
#undef THIS_FILE
static char BASED_CODE THIS_FILE[] = __FILE__;
#endif

/////////////////////////////////////////////////////////////////////////
// CChap4App

BEGIN_MESSAGE_MAP(CChap4App, CWinApp)
    //{{AFX_MSG_MAP(CChap4App)
    ON_COMMAND(ID_APP_ABOUT, OnAppAbout)
            // NOTE - the ClassWizard will add and remove mapping macros here.
            //    DO NOT EDIT what you see in these blocks of generated code!
    //}}AFX_MSG_MAP
    // Standard file based document commands
    ON_COMMAND(ID_FILE_NEW, CWinApp::OnFileNew)
    ON_COMMAND(ID_FILE_OPEN, CWinApp::OnFileOpen)
    // Standard print setup command
    ON_COMMAND(ID_FILE_PRINT_SETUP, CWinApp::OnFilePrintSetup)
END_MESSAGE_MAP()

/////////////////////////////////////////////////////////////////////////
// CChap4App construction

CChap4App::CChap4App()
{
    // TODO: add construction code here,
    // Place all significant initialization in InitInstance
}

/////////////////////////////////////////////////////////////////////////
// The one and only CChap4App object

CChap4App theApp;

/////////////////////////////////////////////////////////////////////////
```

```
// CChap4App initialization

BOOL CChap4App::InitInstance()
{
    // Standard initialization
    // If you are not using these features and wish to reduce the size
    //  of your final executable, you should remove from the following
    //  the specific initialization routines you do not need.

    Enable3dControls();

    LoadStdProfileSettings(0);  // Load standard INI file options (including MRU)

    // Register the application's document templates.  Document templates
    //  serve as the connection between documents, frame windows and views.

    CMultiDocTemplate* pDocTemplate;
    pDocTemplate = new CMultiDocTemplate(
            IDR_CHAP4TYPE,
            RUNTIME_CLASS(CChap4Doc),
            RUNTIME_CLASS(CMDIChildWnd),            // standard MDI child frame
            RUNTIME_CLASS(CChap4View));
    AddDocTemplate(pDocTemplate);

    // create main MDI Frame window
    CMainFrame* pMainFrame = new CMainFrame;
    if (!pMainFrame->LoadFrame(IDR_MAINFRAME))
            return FALSE;
    m_pMainWnd = pMainFrame;

    // create a new (empty) document
    OnFileNew();

    if (m_lpCmdLine[0] != '\0')
    {
            // TODO: add command line processing here
    }

    // The main window has been initialized, so show and update it.
    pMainFrame->ShowWindow(m_nCmdShow);
```

```
        pMainFrame->UpdateWindow();

        return TRUE;
}


/////////////////////////////////////////////////////////////////////////////
// CAboutDlg dialog used for App About

class CAboutDlg : public CDialog
{
public:
        CAboutDlg();

// Dialog Data
        //{{AFX_DATA(CAboutDlg)
        enum { IDD = IDD_ABOUTBOX };
        //}}AFX_DATA

// Implementation
protected:
        virtual void DoDataExchange(CDataExchange* pDX);     // DDX/DDV support
        //{{AFX_MSG(CAboutDlg)
                // No message handlers
        //}}AFX_MSG
        DECLARE_MESSAGE_MAP()
};

CAboutDlg::CAboutDlg() : CDialog(CAboutDlg::IDD)
{
        //{{AFX_DATA_INIT(CAboutDlg)
        //}}AFX_DATA_INIT
}

void CAboutDlg::DoDataExchange(CDataExchange* pDX)
{
        CDialog::DoDataExchange(pDX);
        //{{AFX_DATA_MAP(CAboutDlg)
        //}}AFX_DATA_MAP
}
```

```
BEGIN_MESSAGE_MAP(CAboutDlg, CDialog)
    //{{AFX_MSG_MAP(CAboutDlg)
            // No message handlers
    //}}AFX_MSG_MAP
END_MESSAGE_MAP()

// App command to run the dialog
void CChap4App::OnAppAbout()
{
    CAboutDlg aboutDlg;
    aboutDlg.DoModal();
}


//
// The FormatMessage API and MB_SETFOREGROUND are discussed
// in the Console Chapter (Chapter 9).
//

void CChap4App::DisplayLastError(DWORD dwError)
{
  DWORD cMsgLen;
  CHAR *msgBuf; // buffer for message text from system
  CString strError;


  MessageBeep(MB_ICONEXCLAMATION);

  //
  // get the text description for dwError number from the system
  //
  cMsgLen = FormatMessage(FORMAT_MESSAGE_FROM_SYSTEM |
      FORMAT_MESSAGE_ALLOCATE_BUFFER | 40, NULL, dwError,
      MAKELANGID(0, SUBLANG_ENGLISH_US), (LPTSTR) &msgBuf, MAX_MSG_BUF_SIZE,
      NULL);
  if (!cMsgLen)
    AfxMessageBox(IDS_SETMESSAGE_ERROR, MB_ICONEXCLAMATION | MB_SETFOREGROUND);

  else
    {
```

```
    MessageBox(NULL, msgBuf, AfxGetAppName(), MB_ICONEXCLAMATION |
MB_SETFOREGROUND);
    //
    // free the message buffer returned to us by the system
    //
    LocalFree((HLOCAL) msgBuf);
    }
}


/////////////////////////////////////////////////////////////////////////
// CChap4App commands
```

**Listing 4—4** Source for thread class

```
// chap4vw.cpp : implementation of the CChap4View class
//

#include "stdafx.h"
#include "chap4.h"

#include "chap4doc.h"
#include "chap4vw.h"

#ifdef _DEBUG
#undef THIS_FILE
static char BASED_CODE THIS_FILE[] = __FILE__;
#endif


/////////////////////////////////////////////////////////////////////////
// CChap4View

IMPLEMENT_DYNCREATE(CChap4View, CView)

BEGIN_MESSAGE_MAP(CChap4View, CView)
    //{{AFX_MSG_MAP(CChap4View)
    ON_COMMAND(ID_THREADS_SUSPEND, OnThreadsSuspend)
    ON_COMMAND(ID_THREADS_RESUME, OnThreadsResume)
    //}}AFX_MSG_MAP
    // Standard printing commands
    ON_COMMAND(ID_FILE_PRINT, CView::OnFilePrint)
```

```
        ON_COMMAND(ID_FILE_PRINT_PREVIEW, CView::OnFilePrintPreview)
END_MESSAGE_MAP()

/////////////////////////////////////////////////////////////////////
// CChap4View construction/destruction

CChap4View::CChap4View()
{
m_bKillme = FALSE;
m_nColor = 0;
m_strTitle = "Hello, Multithreaded World!";
CChap4App * pApp = (CChap4App *)AfxGetApp();


#ifdef USE_AFX
m_pThreadWnd = AfxBeginThread(Threadfunc,this);

#else
        //
        // By creating the thread suspended and setting its priority
        // below normal we can keep the UI threads more responsive.
        //

        m_hThrd=CreateThread(NULL,

                                          0,
                                          this->Threadfunc,
                                          this,
                                          CREATE_SUSPENDED,
                                          &this->m_dwThreadID);
#endif


        if (!m_hThrd)
                pApp->DisplayLastError(GetLastError());

        SetThreadPriority(m_hThrd, THREAD_PRIORITY_BELOW_NORMAL);
        ResumeThread(m_hThrd);

}

CChap4View::~CChap4View()
```

```
{
}


////////////////////////////////////////////////////////////////////////
// CChap4View drawing

void CChap4View::OnDraw(CDC* pDC)
{
CChap4Doc* pDoc = GetDocument();
ASSERT_VALID(pDoc);

static int i=0;
CRect rect;

//
// Don't bother drawing if the MDI child window is minimized
//
if (!IsIconic())
     {
     pDC->SetTextColor(m_clrText);
     pDC->SetBkColor(::GetSysColor(COLOR_WINDOW));
     GetClientRect(rect);
     //
     // The following silliness just rotates around the screen where m_strTitle is
positioned
     //
     if (i==0)
            {
            i++;
            pDC->DrawText(m_strTitle, -1, rect, DT_SINGLELINE | DT_CENTER);
            }
     else
            {
            if (i==1)
                    {
                    i++;
                    pDC->DrawText(m_strTitle, -1, rect, DT_SINGLELINE |
DT_VCENTER);
                    }
            else
```

```
                    {
                    i=0;
                    pDC->DrawText(m_strTitle, -1, rect,DT_SINGLELINE | DT_RIGHT
| DT_VCENTER);

                    }

            }

        }



}

/////////////////////////////////////////////////////////////////////////
// CChap4View printing

BOOL CChap4View::OnPreparePrinting(CPrintInfo* pInfo)
{
        // default preparation
        return DoPreparePrinting(pInfo);
}

void CChap4View::OnBeginPrinting(CDC* /*pDC*/, CPrintInfo* /*pInfo*/)
{
        // TODO: add extra initialization before printing
}

void CChap4View::OnEndPrinting(CDC* /*pDC*/, CPrintInfo* /*pInfo*/)
{
        // TODO: add cleanup after printing
}

/////////////////////////////////////////////////////////////////////////
// CChap4View diagnostics

#ifdef _DEBUG
void CChap4View::AssertValid() const
{
        CView::AssertValid();
}
```

```
void CChap4View::Dump(CDumpContext& dc) const
{
      CView::Dump(dc);
}


CChap4Doc* CChap4View::GetDocument() // non-debug version is inline
{
      ASSERT(m_pDocument->IsKindOf(RUNTIME_CLASS(CChap4Doc)));
      return (CChap4Doc*)m_pDocument;
}
#endif //_DEBUG


/////////////////////////////////////////////////////////////////////////
// CChap4View thread function
//
// This function loops forever or until the boolean m_bKillme is set.
//


DWORD
CChap4View::Threadfunc(LPVOID)
{

static const COLORREF clrTextArray[] = { RGB (0, 0, 0), RGB (255, 0,   0),
                                  RGB (0, 255, 0), RGB (  0, 0, 255),
                                  RGB (255, 255, 255) };



BOOL fSem=FALSE;
while(1)
      {
      if (WaitForSingleObject ((((CChap4App *)AfxGetApp())->m_hSem, 0) == 0)  //find
out immediately
            {
            fSem = TRUE;
            m_strTitle = "Building Windows 95 Applications";
            MessageBox("Changing Message","SemaphoreTest");
            }
```

```
        if (m_bKillme)
                {
            if (fSem)
                    {
                m_strTitle = "Hello, Multithreaded World!";
                        if ((((CChap4App *)AfxGetApp())->m_hSem)
                            {
                ReleaseSemaphore((((CChap4App *)AfxGetApp())->m_hSem,1,NULL);
                ((CChap4App *)AfxGetApp())->m_hSem = NULL;
                            }
                    }
                //
                // Only one of the following lines is actually needed. Just
returning will
                // will be the equivalent of calling ExitThread. I have them both in
here
                // to show the options.
                //
                ExitThread(0);
                return 0;
                }

        if (m_nColor < IDM_WHITE)
                m_nColor++;
        else
                m_nColor=IDM_BLACK;

        m_clrText = clrTextArray[m_nColor - IDM_BLACK];
        Sleep(500);
        Invalidate();
        }

}


//
// Suspend the thread. Notice that since it is a different thread than the MDIChild
window
// you can still move, minimize, and maximize the window.
//
```

```
void CChap4View::OnThreadsSuspend()
{
      SetWindowText("Suspended");
      SuspendThread(m_hThrd);



}




void CChap4View::OnThreadsResume()
{
      ResumeThread(m_hThrd);
      SetWindowText("Thread Window");
}



//
// When the MDIChild goes away kill the thread associated with it.
//
BOOL CChap4View::DestroyWindow()
{
      m_bKillme=TRUE;
      WaitForSingleObject(m_hThrd, INFINITE);

      return CView::DestroyWindow();
}
```

# SYNCHRONIZATION AND GDI OBJECTS

GDI objects require special considerations. Be aware of the feature known as batching. To enhance performance, GDI32.DLL queues all GDI calls that return a BOOL. When your program reaches the batch limit, the GDI calls are turned over to the Win32 subsystem for processing. This means that the screen may not update immediately when you make a GDI call. For example, suppose your program drew a line, slept for 500 milliseconds, then drew a different color line. In theory, if you put this code in a loop you might expect to see a line blinking different colors. In practice you just see a line. This is not a bug in the Sleep API! Both the LineTo and MoveToEx functions are examples of GDI calls that are batched. What you see is the result of not reaching the batch limit. If this behavior is unacceptable, call GdiSetBatchLimit to control the caching of GDI calls. To turn batching off, call GdiSetBatchLimit with the batch limit set to one.

Another solution to the batching phenomenon is to call GDIFlush:

```
GDIFlush();
```

GDIFlush flushes all of the calls so they execute immediately, instead of waiting for the batch limit.

The other aspect of GDI programming in a multithreaded environment is the sharing of GDI objects (such as DCs). GDI objects are different from other objects in Win32. For performance, reasons you cannot name GDI objects, assign a security descriptor, or use the WaitforObjects APIs. Whether you are using MFC or not, you must take care to make sure that no two threads are accessing the same GDI object at the same time. A good rule of thumb is to treat GDI objects the same as other persistent objects. Now, it is fine to use GDI objects in different DCs in separate threads, just not the same DC. In the sample program, I avoided the issue altogether and kept all of the painting in the primary thread. Okay, we now have a process up and running, with multiple, preemptive, synchronized threads. The rest of the book shows you how to turn your processes into applications.

## CHAPTER 5

# MEMORY MANAGEMENT IN WIN32

In the past, understanding memory management schemes in Windows was a prerequisite for writing even the simplest program. Before Version 3.1, all Windows programmers had to be cognizant of the dreaded real mode. In Version 3.1, developer's have to constantly be aware of the cumbersome 64KB segment limits. Thankfully, Win32 memory management is light years ahead of its 16-bit cousin. In addition to continuing support for the Win16 APIs, the memory management facilities in Win32 provide several new ways to allocate and use memory. This chapter explains all of the APIs available to you and tells you the advantages and disadvantages of each. Later on, this chapter discusses cross-process memory management and shows you how to write an application to manage memory across processes in both Windows 95 and Windows NT.

## DIFFERENCES BETWEEN WINDOWS NT AND WINDOWS 95

Although Windows 95 supports most of the memory management functions that Windows NT supports, there are some differences. For starters, since Windows 95 doesn't concern itself with being a secure system, it doesn't have to take extra precautions to automatically zero-init memory and to guarantee that memory allocated by your process isn't available to other programs after your process terminates. Also, although the Win32 APIs make both operating systems appear to be the same code, they are not. Eschewing portability, most of the code that makes up the Windows 95 memory manager is assembly language.

## HOW WINDOWS 95 AND NT MANAGE VIRTUAL MEMORY

I'll get to the details after a quick overview of how Windows 95 and NT manage virtual memory. Although their implementations are slightly different, the concept of virtual memory is not new. Almost every operating system on the market today employs some type of virtual memory. However, just for clarity's sake, let me explain about a piece of the kernel called the physical memory manager. The physical memory manager's job is to make each process think that it has 4GB of physical memory. That's 2GB for your process with another 2GB reserved for the system (to load DLLs and such). Obviously, if you only have 32MB of physical memory not every process is going to get 4GB of physical memory. Yet, it is possible for every process to think it has 4GB. To accomplish this feat, the physical memory manager works in conjunction with the processor (or processors in an SMP machine) to provide a virtual address space to each process. Instead of pointing to physical memory, each virtual address is translated to a physical address by the physical memory manager. When requests for memory exhaust the amount of physical storage, the physical memory manager swaps inactive pages to a file on disk called the page file.

The physical memory manager keeps a list of virtual addresses in a structure known as the page map. A page is the smallest unit of memory you can allocate from the operating system. In Windows 95, pages are 4096 bytes (4KB). In NT, pages are 4KB for x86 systems and 8192 bytes (8KB) for MIPS, PowerPC and

ALPHA systems. The physical memory manager uses the page table to map virtual addresses to their corresponding physical addresses. This is where the term "separate address space" comes from. Address 0x0400000 in process A is just a virtual address and corresponds to a completely different physical address than address 0x400000 in process B. This is where some of the confusion lies. By implementing this scheme of virtual addresses, it is impossible for process B to "accidentally" write into process A's address space. To see what I mean by accidentally, let's take the example of a buggy program with a corrupted pointer. When the pointer is used, it reads (or writes ) to a virtual address. No matter what this virtual address is it will point to memory inside it's own address space. That's because pointers in Windows 95 and NT are 32-bits—which mean they have a range of 0 to 4GB. That coincidentally, is exactly the size of all Win32 processes. So no matter what value the pointer contains it will always be within the range of a Windows 95 or NT process space. (The chances are great that accessing this address will cause an access violation, so as a side benefit you are protected from yourself.)

By implementing virtual addresses, it is impossible for process B to accidentally write into process A's address space. I say "accidentally" because, as we shall see in a minute, Both Windows 95 and NT allow cross-process operations. If the processes cooperate they can deliberately read or write into each other's address space.

If processes use more virtual memory than there is corresponding physical memory, you have a memory overcommit situation. To remedy this, the physical memory manager copies pages of physical memory and writes them to a file called the page file. This phenomenon is known as swapping. Processes unknowingly have pages (4KB or 8KB portions) of their address space swapped to disk whenever an overcommit situation arises. When a process attempts to read a virtual address that corresponds to a page of memory that is in the page file, a page fault occurs. After each page fault, the processor and the physical memory manager work together to copy the page of memory from the page file back into physical memory. Each page in the page table, called a page table entry, has certain characteristics. For example, a page can have the following attributes:

- ▟ Fault on write: A page that has a page table entry of fault on write generates an exception whenever you attempt to write a virtual address that corresponds to physical memory within the range of the page.

- ■■ Fault on read: A page that has fault on read generates an exception whenever you attempt to read a virtual address within the range of the page.

- ■■ Fault on execution: Any attempt to execute code within the page will generate an exception. Only certain processors support this exception. (x86 processors do not).

To minimize swapping, each process always has a certain minimum number of pages in physical memory. The physical memory manager uses a least recently used algorithm and other optimization techniques to determine which pages to swap. This whole technique is transparent to processes. Processes worry only about their virtual address space.

In Windows 3.1 (which also supports virtual memory and swap files), memory is in one of two states: allocated or deallocated (free). Because it can either allocate or free memory, a Win16 process has some tradeoffs to make. Let's take the example of a Win16 application whose memory requirements fluctuate between 200KB and 400KB. Perhaps this application is a remote-mail program that uploads and downloads files. If the application just uploads mail, the memory required is 200KB. However, to download, it takes an additional 200KB. To avoid being a RAM hog, the program only allocates 200KB upon startup. Then, if the user has mail to download, the program "GlobalAllocs" another 200KB.

Unfortunately, between the time the user started the program and when the download started, the user also executed a spreadsheet program and started a huge recalculation—conveniently enough for our example, a recalc that used the rest of available memory. (If you are using a temporary swap file in Windows 3.1, this example would have to be a really big recalc because the temporary swap file can grow.) This causes the mail application to fail at a critical time. So, if a Win16 application wants to guarantee itself 400KB, it must allocate all 400KB when it first loads. Otherwise, another process may execute, allocating the remainder of free memory. Unfortunately, allocating memory when you really don't need it irritates your users because they run out of memory faster. If every application allocates all the memory it might possibly need, the chance for a memory overcommit situation increases dramatically. Overcommitting memory causes excessive swapping to disk (in other words, thrashing). However, failing at a crucial time, such as in the middle of a download, also annoys users. So what do you do?

The virtual memory management scheme of Win32 solves this problem by allocating memory in the page file before consuming RAM. Now your application allocates as much memory as necessary without sacrificing RAM, just disk space. By allocating the storage in the page file first, there will be no unnecessary thrashing. Now, when the time comes to use this memory (when the mail download begins), a lot of thrashing may occur, but at least you have guaranteed the application enough memory to continue.

Like Win16, Win32 memory is either free or allocated. However, when you allocate, you designate memory as reserved or committed. A page in memory marked reserved cannot be allocated by any other allocation operation (unless you free it). You cannot access a reserved page until you commit it. A committed page has corresponding physical storage (in memory or a page file) allocated to it. In addition, committed pages can be designated as read-only, read-write, or inaccessible.

## MEMORY APIs

There are four ways to allocate memory. Two methods you should recognize from other operating environments: C runtime APIs and the Global, or LocalAlloc, APIs. In addition, there are two new APIs: the Heap APIs and the Virtual APIs. I'll describe the Virtual API functions first, because the rest of the APIs are built on top of the Virtual APIs. Table 5–1 lists the Virtual APIs.

**Table 5–1** Virtual APIs

| | |
|---|---|
| VirtualAlloc | Allocates a range of virtual pages |
| VirtualFree | Frees a range of virtual pages |
| VirtualProtect(Ex) | Changes a process's virtual-memory protection |
| VirtualQuery(Ex) | Retrieves a process's virtual-memory information |
| VirtualLock | Locks a range of virtual pages |
| VirtualUnlock | Unlocks a range of virtual pages |

## VIRTUAL APIS

There are eight functions, as shown previously in Table 5–1, that allow a process to manipulate virtual memory. Unlike Win16, the Virtual functions are not handle-based. To allocate memory you call VirtualAlloc. VirtualAlloc returns a pointer. Depending upon which parameters you choose, you can immediately use the pointer. The function prototype looks like this:

```
LPVOID VirtualAlloc(LPVOID lpvAddress,
                    DWORD cbSize,
                    DWORD fdwAllocationType,
                    DWORD fdwProtect);
```

Here's what the parameters mean:

| Parameter | Use |
|---|---|
| lpvAddress | Specifies the starting address. If this parameter is NULL, the physical memory manager allocates the region for you. Otherwise, lpvAddress points to the desired starting address of the region. (That's right, desired. There could be something else in this location already. If so, the call will fail.) |
| cbSize | Determines how much memory to allocate. The most you can allocate is 2GB minus 1MB for the stack minus the size of the executable. |
| fdwAllocationType | Is a flag that determines the allocation method. Use MEM_COMMIT to gain access to physical storage. When you commit a page, the physical memory manager initially allocates space for it in the paging file. The physical memory manager loads a page into memory only after a process attempts to read or write to the page. Use MEM_RESERVE just to reserve the virtual address space. A virtual address marked "reserved" cannot be allocated by any other allocation operation (such as malloc or GlobalAlloc). A typical example of when you just reserve memory is when you reserve a range of virtual addresses for a dynamic array. This allows you to expand the array when needed, but doesn't force you to consume physical memory until necessary. This way, you only have to commit pages when the need arises (as the array expands). When you allocate memory as reserved, you must allocate on 64KB boundaries. If you do not, your request will be rounded to the nearest 64KB boundary. |

| | |
|---|---|
| | When committing memory, your request will be rounded down to the nearest page boundary. There is very little overhead in reserving the memory. When you reserve memory the physical memory manager creates a virtual memory descriptor. This descriptor is less than 50 bytes in length and resides in the system's 2GB. Reserving a virtual address space does nothing to guarantee that physical storage will be available when the time to commit the memory comes around. In our example of the e-mail package, just reserving the memory would not have solved the problem. |
| fdwProtect | Is a flag that allows you to control access to the pages you are allocating. The flags correspond to page table entries maintained by the processor. |
| PAGE_READONLY | Corresponds to the page table entry of fault on write. Any attempt to write to a page marked PAGE_READONLY causes an exception. |
| PAGE_READWRITE | Corresponds to a valid page table entry. A page marked PAGE_READWRITE has both read and write access. |
| PAGE_NOACCESS | Corresponds to a page table entry marked as fault on write, fault on read, and—if your processor supports it—fault on execution. Any attempt to read, write, or execute a page marked PAGE_NOACCESS causes an exception. If you are just reserving memory you must specify the PAGE_NOACCESS flag. |

Committing 64KB of read/write-able memory that is both committed and reserved using VirtualAlloc looks like this:

```
LPSTR pszVirtual = (LPSTR)VirtualAlloc(NULL,
                                       1024*64,
                                       MEM_COMMIT|MEM_RESERVE,
                                       PAGE_READWRITE);
```

Do not make assumptions about the size of a page. Remember, x86 machines have a 4KB page size, while RISC processors have at least an 8KB page size. Instead, call GetSystemInfo to retrieve the page size:

```
SYSTEM_INFO si
GetSystemInfo(&si);
wsprintf(lpsz,"Page size equals %",si.dwPageSize);
```

## VIRTUALFREE

Changing the status of a page from committed to reserved is known as a decommit and corresponds to the flag MEM_DECOMMIT. Changing the status of a page from reserved to free is known as a release and corresponds to MEM_RELEASE. Use the VirtualFree function if you want to decommit or release pages.

VirtualFree takes three parameters. The first parameter, lpvAddress, is the base address of the memory you want to decommit or release. If you call VirtualFree to release the memory, lpvAddress must point to the address returned from VirtualAlloc. If you decommit the memory, lpvAddress can point anywhere within the virtual address range. Just remember that VirtualFree frees on page boundaries.

Here's an example of decommitting, then releasing storage:

```
// This decommits the memory
If (VirtualFree(lpvAddress, PAGESIZE, MEM_DECOMMIT))
// this releases the entire buffer
    {
    bResult = VirtualFree(base, 0, MEM_RELEASE);
    }
```

If all of the pages in the block are committed, you can specify MEM_DECOMMIT | MEM_RELEASE to release them in one function call:

```
VirtualFree(base, 0, MEM_DECOMMIT | MEM_RELEASE);
```

For security reasons, performance, and overall good hygiene, if you do not call VirtualFree and your process terminates, the physical memory manager automatically releases all physical storage associated with committed pages.

## GUARD PAGES

The PAGE_GUARD flag allows to set up what is known as a guard page. A guard page is a page that protects the boundaries of a resource. Let's say you want to allocate memory for a 64KB array. To ensure that no thread in your process accidentally writes past the boundaries of the array, allocate two extra pages of memory. Place one page at the beginning of the array and the other at the end. Then make both guard pages. If you exceed the bounds of the array and attempt to read or write past the beginning or end of the array, you will trigger an exception. You can use guard pages to guard the bounds of arrays, stacks, heaps, and just about anything else you can think of. Any page in the virtual memory address can be a guard page.

To turn an already committed page into a guard page, use the VirtualProtect function. The VirtualProtect function changes the protection state of any committed page:

```
BOOL VirtualProtect(LPVOID lpvAddress,
                    DWORD cbSize,           // size of the region
                    DWORD fdwNewProtect,    // access
                    PDWORD pfdwOldProtect); // address of
                                            // variable to get
                                            // old protection
```

The cool thing about VirtualProtect is the fact that it works on any committed page, not just ones allocated by VirtualAlloc. However, VirtualProtect works on pages, so if you pass in a pointer that another function allocated, the entire page will change:

```
DWORD buflen;
char *base;
BOOL bResult;
DWORD dwOldProtect;
MEMORY_BASIC_INFORMATION MemInfo;

buflen = VirtualQuery(base, &MemInfo,
    sizeof(MEMORY_BASIC_INFORMATION));

if (MemInfo.State == MEM_COMMIT)
    bResult = VirtualProtect(base, MemInfo.RegionSize,
                    PAGE_READONLY, &dwOldProtect);
```

Listing 5–1 shows how to guard an array of characters.

**Listing 5–1** Guarding an array of characters

```
SYSTEM_INFO si;

GetSystemInfo(&si);
char achMsg[80];
DWORD dwOldProtect;
LPSTR pszVirtual = (LPSTR)VirtualAlloc(NULL,
                                (1024*64) +
                                (si.dwPageSize),
                                MEM_COMMIT|MEM_RESERVE,
                                PAGE_READWRITE);

  if (!VirtualProtect(pszVirtual + (1024*64),
                                si.dwPageSize,
                                PAGE_GUARD | PAGE_READWRITE,
                                &dwOldProtect))

      {

      wsprintf(achMsg,"Last Error =%d",GetLastError());
      MessageBox(NULL,achMsg,"VirtualProtect",MB_OK);
      }


__try {
      for (int i = 0; i < 0xFFFF; i++)
          pszVirtual[i] = 'A';
      pszVirtual[++i] = 0;
      }
__except (EXCEPTION_EXECUTE_HANDLER)
{
MessageBox(NULL, "Guard page worked","Memory Mgmt.", MB_OK);

  }
```

# THE SPARSE MEMORY SOLUTION

One of the hassles with most memory management APIs is what to do when you need more memory than you've have. The Virtual Memory APIs solve this problem by introducing the concept of sparse memory. Suppose you had an array of unknown length. Since its record size is 512 bytes, you might initially allocate space for one hundred records. During the course of execution you realize that you need more space. In other operating systems, the answer is to perform some type of reallocate (such as a GlobalRealloc in Windows 3.x). When you reallocate, the operating system may seek out a new spot in the memory map and allocate it. It then copies the data from the original to the new, deleting the original, and returning a pointer to the new back to the caller. This is a complicated process that requires action by the caller. Sparse memory makes it possible to kiss the GlobalReallocs of the world good-bye. To implement sparse memory, just reserve the maximum amount of space necessary, but don't commit it.

## VIRTUALQUERY

The VirtualQuery function is useful if you want to determine the characteristics of a page or region of pages in memory:

```
DWORD VirtualQuery(LPVOID lpvAddress, // address of region
                   PMEMORY_BASIC_INFORMATION pmbiBuffer,
                   DWORD cbLength);
```

The first parameter, lpvAddress, points to the virtual address that you want to query. VirtualQuery returns the information in the format of a structure called the MEMORY_BASIC_INFORMATION structure. Listing 5–2 shows this.

**183**

**Listing 5–2** Memory Basic Information Structure from WINBASE.H

```
typedef struct _MEMORY_BASIC_INFORMATION { // mbi
PVOID BaseAddress;              // base address of region
PVOID AllocationBase;          // allocation base address
DWORD AllocationProtect;       // initial access protection
DWORD RegionSize;              // size, in bytes, of region
DWORD State;                   // committed, reserved, free
DWORD Protect;                 // current access protection
DWORD Type;                    // type of pages
} MEMORY_BASIC_INFORMATION;
typedef MEMORY_BASIC_INFORMATION *PMEMORY_BASIC_INFORMATION;
```

Notice that you cannot specify a range of addresses to VirtualQuery. Instead, VirtualQuery returns details on a region of consecutive pages beginning at lpvAddress and continuing as long as the state of all pages is the same (MEM_COMMIT, MEM_RESERVE, or MEM_FREE flag), and the protection flag is the same (PAGE_READONLY, PAGE_READWRITE, or PAGE_NOACCESS):

```
DWORD buflen;
char *base;
BOOL bResult;
DWORD dwOldProtect;
MEMORY_BASIC_INFORMATION MemInfo;

buflen = VirtualQuery(base, &MemInfo,
                  sizeof(MEMORY_BASIC_INFORMATION));

if (MemInfo.State == MEM_COMMIT)
    bResult = VirtualProtect(base, MemInfo.RegionSize,
                        PAGE_READONLY, &dwOldProtect);
```

The VirtualProtectEx and VirtualQueryEx functions are just like their counterparts except they are for cross-process operations.

## VIRTUALLOCK

In the rare situation where your process must guarantee that its pages are always in RAM (perhaps a callback for an interrupt handler), you can call VirtualLock. VirtualLock locks the pages into memory, ensuring that they will not be swapped to the page file. The limit on VirtualLock is about thirty pages per process. If you need more than thirty pages, you will have to write a device driver.

As we go through the rest of the memory management APIs, you will find that the virtual memory APIs are the most flexible. As you'll see, the other memory APIs are built on top of the virtual memory APIs. The virtual memory APIs do have some disadvantages. Since the minimum allocation is the size of a page, the virtual APIs are not useful if you're allocating in small chunks of memory.

# GLOBAL AND LOCALALLOC IN WIN32

Win16 uses a handle-based memory allocation scheme. In versions prior to Windows 3.1, the operating system used handles instead of passing around physical address pointers to support real mode. The API carried forward to Windows 3.1, where you call GlobalAlloc to receive a handle, and then GlobalLock to retrieve a pointer to the memory. There is also a corresponding set of functions that begin with Local (LocalAlloc, LocalLock, etc.). In Win16, the Local functions work similarly to the Global functions, except the Local functions allocate memory from the process's data segment instead of the global heap. In Win16, there is a performance gain by using near pointers. Unfortunately, however, there is less than 64KB available to the Local functions.

Win32, supports both the Global and Local functions, and except for the function name, both are identical. Both sets of functions allow you to allocate a block of memory of any size—limited only by the available physical memory (RAM and page file). In Win32, the handle returned from Global or LocalAlloc is an index into a table of memory objects. An application still must call GlobalLock or LocalLock, passing in the handle to receive a pointer to the allocated memory. However, the change from a 16-bit segmented memory model to the 32-bit virtual memory model has made some of the functions and

**185**

their options unnecessary or meaningless. For instance, there are no longer NEAR or FAR pointers, since both local and global allocations return 32-bit virtual addresses. The memory returned by GlobalLock will not be aligned on a 64KB boundary as in Windows 3.1. Also, Win32 ignores the NOCOMPACT and NODISCARD flags.

You can grow memory dynamically the old fashioned way with the realloc function (GlobalRealloc or LocalRealloc). However, be aware that the pointer returned from the realloc function may be different from the pointer returned by the original allocation function. Windows 3.x moves data around in memory to accommodate a realloc ensuring that the pointer returned from the original allocation function stays valid. Windows 95 and NT just change the virtual addresses (it is as if they allocate memory equal to the new size and copy the contents of the old location to the new location). Therefore, be careful not to have aliases to the memory returned from the allocation function. An alias occurs when you have two or more variables that refer to the same location. If you do have aliases, your program will crash after you realloc. In the following example, the alias to the virtual address returned by GlobalAlloc doesn't get updated when GlobalRealloc gets called:

```
LPSTR psz, pGlobal;

pGlobal = (LPSTR)GlobalLock(hGlobal, GMEM_SHARE,1024);
psz = pGlobal;  //create alias
.
. //Depending upon what happens here
. // realloc may occur
.
pGlobal = (LPSTR)GlobaReAlloc(hGlobal, 2048, GMEM_MOVEABLE);
.
.
.
strcpy(psz,"some string");  // BUG waiting to happen
```

It is a good idea to get rid of aliases whether you are reallocing or not. Having aliases in your code precludes you from using full optimization when compiling. This occurs because optimizing compilers sometimes place pointers into registers to speed things up. If you have two pointers that point to the same location and the compiler doesn't know about it, the second pointer may not get updated when the original pointer does.

The Global and Local functions are great for compatibility with Win16, but you suffer disadvantages in Win32. Allocated memory stays committed until decommitted with GlobalFree or LocalFree. Allocated memory is always read-write. In Win16, when you allocate memory with the GMEM_SHARE or GMEM_DDESHARE flag, you can pass the pointer returned from GlobalLock to other processes. This still works in Win32, but there is an extra step involved, which I will explain in a moment.

## MANIPULATING MEMORY WITH THE STANDARD C LIBRARY

You can also manipulate memory by using the standard C library functions (malloc, free, etc.). With previous versions of Windows, these functions had potential dangers that do not exist with Win32. For example, malloc in Windows 3.0 allocates a fixed pointer that does not allow the memory to be moved. With virtual memory, this is no longer a problem. Similarly, the confusion around near and far pointers is no longer relevant. So, unless you want to allocate discardable memory, it is reasonable to use the standard C library functions. However, in a virtual memory management system, discardable memory is almost useless. Even though Win32 still supports discardable memory, you should avoid it. In many cases, discardable memory drains performance. Discardable means that the operating system should just overwrite a section of memory if it needs the space, and you, the programmer, will ask the operating system to reload the original file when you need it. Typically, resources like strings and bitmaps that tend to take up large amounts of space relative to their usage were candidates for discardable memory.

The idea was to keep as much memory available as possible, since memory was such a precious commodity under real-mode and Standard-mode Windows 3.0. Under Windows 95, Windows NT, and even enhanced mode Windows 3.1 this actually degrades performance. Consider the sequence a Windows 3.x application performs to load a discarded resource: The application attempts to GlobalLock the handle, and GlobalLock returns NULL. The application calls GlobalFlags, and finds out that the memory has been discarded by GMEM_DISCARD. The application then calls GlobalFree on the handle, and

GlobalAllocs another block for the resource. The process starts all over again when the application tries to GlobalLock the new handle. GlobalAlloc may cause pages to be swapped to disk to make enough room. The application then uses file I/O functions to read the data into memory. Keep in mind that all of this is taking place at the application level. The Win32 way is to store your data in a nondiscardable block. If another application needs memory, the physical memory manager pages your data to the page file. If the physical memory manager pages data when your application attempts to read from or write to the memory, it will be paged back in. The paging is in response to a "Not Present" fault from the processor.

For most real-world cases, all of this gobbledygook at the application level to support the "discardable" version is significantly greater than the code required for paging. When using the discardable memory flag in Global or LocalAlloc, you are responsible for locking down the memory before you use it, using Global or LocalLock. When using VirtualAlloc, the physical memory manager performs this action for you. If you try to use memory that's paged out, the physical memory manager loads it for you. The physical memory manager does this transparently to your application. So why do something manually that the operating system does automatically?

# NEW HEAP APIS IN WIN32

There are six new APIs in Win32 to create and manage a private heap. They are listed in Table 5–2.

**Table 5–2** New Heap APIs in Win32

| API | Use |
| --- | --- |
| HeapAlloc | Allocates memory from a heap |
| HeapCreate | Creates a heap |
| HeapDestroy | Destroys a heap |
| HeapFree | Frees memory allocated from a heap |
| HeapReAlloc | Reallocates memory from a heap |
| HeapSize | Returns the size of a heap object |

Like the Global and LocalAlloc functions, the Heap functions are handle-based. Like the Virtual APIs, you can commit and reserve memory. Use the Heap functions when you want to allocate memory on a per-thread basis or otherwise want to keep memory separated. Threads can create private heaps and then use the Heap APIs to manage the memory in those heaps.

The HeapCreate function creates the heap:

```
HANDLE
HeapCreate(DWORD flOptions,          // heap allocation flag
           DWORD dwInitialSize,      // initial heap size
           DWORD dwMaximumSize);     // maximum heap size
```

The dwInitialSize parameter sets the initial amount of committed memory and dwMaximumSize sets the amount of reserved memory. The memory is automatically set to read-write. If you like, you can use the VirtualProtect function to change the status of the pages. However, this is really not necessary, because if allocation requests exceed the initial size, additional pages are automatically committed from this reserved space (assuming that the physical storage is available). If you set the dwMaximumSize parameter in HeapCreate to zero, you get a heap that expands dynamically as needed (limited by available memory). To start using a portion of the committed memory you call HeapAlloc. Unlike a handle allocated by GlobalAlloc with the GMEM_SHARE attribute, you cannot share the handle returned from HeapCreate among processes. However, this makes it very convenient for a DLL to create a private heap for each process that links to it.

Use the HeapAlloc function to retrieve a pointer to a portion of the committed memory. The parameter dwBytes indicates how many bytes you wish to allocate. The dwFlags parameter is a flag that specifies two things.

The HEAP_GENERATE_EXCEPTIONS bit determines whether NT should generate an exception if HeapAlloc fails. With the introduction of Structured Exception Handling (see "Structured Exception Handling" in this chapter), an exception is an easy way to trap errors. Instead of constantly checking return codes for NULL and such, you can just set up an exception handler that will get control whenever an error occurs. If the HEAP_GENERATE_EXCEPTIONS bit is clear, then HeapAlloc returns a NULL upon failure.

The other bit in the dwFlags parameter is the HEAP_ZERO_MEMORY flag. If this bit is set the memory allocated by HeapAlloc is automatically filled with zeroes. The following call allocates 10KB of zero filled memory:

```
lpsz = (LPSTR) HeapAlloc(hHeap,
                         HEAP_ZERO_MEMORY,
                         10 * 1024);
```

You use this same pointer returned by HeapAlloc in subsequent calls to HeapFree (to free the memory) and to HeapSize (to determine the size of an allocated memory block). If HeapSize returns a number greater than requested, it is okay to use the memory. For example, if you request 4000 bytes and HeapSize returns 4096, it is okay to use all 4096 bytes.

## HEAPREALLOC FOR ALLOCATING MORE MEMORY

If it turns out that, during the call to HeapCreate, you specified a value for dwMaximumSize that was too small, you can call HeapReAlloc to reallocate a larger block of memory. When the HeapReAlloc returns, it may return a new address for the region of memory it reallocated. This happens if the system had to move the region to accommodate the HeapReAlloc. If this is unacceptable, you can specify the HEAP_REALLOC_IN_PLACE_ONLY flag. Both HeapReAlloc and HeapAlloc return a pointer to a specific virtual address in the process's address space, not a handle. Windows 95 and NT guarantee that the pointer returned by these functions never changes. By that, I mean that physical memory may move, but the virtual address never changes.

Since your code is dealing with pointers, the system cannot just blindly move other regions of memory during this call in an effort to reallocate, because the pointers to the other regions of memory would become invalid. Therefore, if there is not enough space to reallocate in place, HeapReAlloc with the HEAP_REALLOC_IN_PLACE will fail. As with HeapAlloc, you can specify that HeapReAlloc generate an exception when it fails. The following call attempts to reallocate in place, and if this is not possible, it generates an exception:

```
try{
```

```
lpsz = (LPSTR) HeapReAlloc(hHeap,
            HEAP_GENERATE_EXCEPTIONS |
            HEAP_REALLOC_IN_PLACE_ONLY,
            (LPSTR) lpMem,
            dwBytes);
}
except(EXCEPTION_EXECUTE_HANDLER)
{
MessageBox("Could not realloc in place");
}
```

One of the benefits of private heaps is that they grow automatically as memory is allocated. Heaps grow all the way up to the limits of available physical storage and the reserved address space.

## HEAPDESTROY FOR DESTROYING THE HEAP

One drawback to the heap APIs is that once you commit pages, they stay committed until you call HeapDestroy or the process terminates.

To destroy the heap, call HeapDestroy as follows:

```
BOOL HeapDestroy(HANDLE hHeap);
```

Of course, you could call VirtualProtect to decommit pages manually. But, once you start maintaining the heap yourself, you've lost the effectiveness of the heap and would be better off just using straight virtual memory API calls.

Another drawback is that HeapAlloc allocates memory that is not moveable within the heap. So if you are churning a lot of memory (allocating and deallocating), you will fragment your heap.

## MFC C++ NEW AND DELETE FUNCTIONS

Now that you know what Win32 offers in the way of memory management, you may wonder how MFC takes advantage of it. The C++ new operator maps to malloc, which maps to HeapAlloc. C++ delete maps to free, which maps to

HeapFree. MFC also takes care of the HeapCreate and HeapDestroy functions for you. It is perfectly acceptable to have a combination of new functions, delete functions, and other memory management APIs in your code. So, if you are creating your own classes and want to use either the Virtual, Heap, Global, Local, or C runtime APIs, you won't have conflicts with the new and delete functions.

I'll go over each of these operations and describe the situations which makes each one appropriate to use. I've also provided a sample application that demonstrates each of these techniques.

## MANAGING MEMORY ACROSS PROCESSES

Remember, NT is a discretionary access control system. If you do not want other user-mode processes to have access to the data in your process, there is no way they can get it. However, if you allow access to your process, another process can read and write into your process almost same as it does in Win16.

Let's examine a typical Win16 scenario in which two processes need to share memory:

1. Process A allocates some memory via the GlobalAlloc(GMEM_SHARE...) API call.

2. Process A then communicates the handle returned from GlobalAlloc to Process B (let's say via a registered message).

3. Process B GlobalLocks the handle and, using the pointer returned from GlobalLock, starts accessing the buffer.

This scenario takes place daily in the Windows 3.1 world. Process A also has the option of allocating memory, again via GlobalAlloc(GMEM_SHARE,...), then GlobalLocking the memory and passing the returned pointer to Process B.

However, this same situation fails in Windows 95 and NT and probably causes an access violation. This is because the pointer returned from GlobalLock is a pointer into Process A's memory. This pointer is relevant to Process A only and has no meaning in Process B. This is because the addresses used by a process are virtual addresses and do not represent the physical location of an object in memory. The kernel maintains a map for each process that translates virtual addresses into the corresponding physical addresses. This is how Windows 95 and NT maintain separate address spaces for each process. Don't worry! Both operating systems allow cross-process operations, including passing handles and pointers. This next section shows how.

To accomplish the equivalent Windows 3.1 transfer of data between processes you have several options:

- Use remote procedure calls.
- Use a memory mapped file.
- Share memory in a shared memory DLL.
- Send another process the WM_COPYDATA message.
- Using ReadProcessMemory and WriteProcessMemory, you can send a handle retrieved from GlobalAlloc(GMEM_SHARE,...), a pointer returned from GlobalLock, a static pointer, and a pointer returned from VirtualAlloc.

The first method, remote procedure calls (actually local remote procedure calls) is covered thoroughly in Chapter 7, "Remote Procedure Calls," so I'll skip the details here.

Cross-process operations with memory-mapped files.

One method you can use to share data between processes is to use memory-mapped files. The WIN32 calls associated with a physical file are dealt with in Chapter 9, "Console Programming." This section describes how to create a block of named shared memory using the memory-mapped API.

The following function calls are necessary to share memory between processes using mapped files:

CreateFileMapping
MapViewOfFile
MapViewOfFileEx
OpenFileMapping
UnMapViewofFile

Here's how to create a block of named shared memory using the memory-mapped API.

Have the first process create a named file mapping object. You must name the object when you create it in order to share the object among processes. To create a named mapped file object, call CreateFileMapping:

```
HANDLE CreateFileMapping(
        HANDLE hFile,                  // handle of file
        LPSECURITY_ATTRIBUTES lpsa,    // security
        DWORD fdwProtect,              // protection
        DWORD dwMaximumSizeHigh,       // high-order
                                       // 32 bits of
                                       // object size
        DWORD dwMaximumSizeLow,        // low-order
                                       // 32-bits of
                                       // object size
        LPCTSTR lpszMapName);          // name of object
```

The first parameter is the handle to the file-mapping object. Set this parameter to 0xFFFFFFFF. When the handle is 0xFFFFFFFF, the system uses the paging file instead of a real file for storage. This tells the system that you are creating an object to share among processes, The second parameter sets the security attributes for the object. The third parameter specifies the protection for the object.

Like virtual memory, the protection can be PAGE_READONLY or PAGE_READWRITE. If multiple processes have write access to the shared memory, they must provide their own synchronization. Otherwise the data can be corrupted if two processes attempt to write at the same time. Mapped files can also specify PAGE_WRITECOPY, which indicates that the receiving process will receive a copy of the mapped file upon altering its contents. By specifying PAGE_WRITECOPY, the creating process can guarantee that its original data remains pristine, while allowing other processes the freedom to manipulate a copy if they so desire.

The maximum size of a file mapping object is 2**64 and the fourth and fifth parameters specify the high and low 32 bits of the size of the object. The last parameter, lpszMapName, specifies the name of the object. Other processes must know lpszMapName to access the mapping object. The IpszMapName variable exists in its own address space, and does not collide with the names of other objects (events, semaphores, and so on). You can pass

**194**

a NULL into lpszMapName and still share the object, but it is a pain. To do this you would have to duplicate the handle and somehow communicate it to the other processes.

The following example shows how to create a 4096-byte named mapping object called SharedMem:

```
HANDLE hMapObj = CreateFileMapping((HANDLE) 0xFFFFFFFF,
                        NULL, // not inherited
                        PAGE_READWRITE,
                        0, // buffer size, hi order
                        0x1000, // buffer size, lo order
                        "SharedMem"); // object name
```

After you create the file mapping object, use the MapViewOfFile function call to map the data into your process's address space:

```
LPVOID MapViewOfFile(
            HANDLE hMapObject,    // handle returned from
                                  // OpenFileMapping or
                                  // CreateFileMapping
            DWORD fdwAccess,      // access mode
            DWORD dwOffsetHigh,   // high offset
            DWORD dwOffsetLow,    // low offset
            DWORD cbMap);         // count of bytes to map
```

The first parameter, hMapObject, is the handle returned from CreateFileMapping. The second parameter, fdwAccess, is a flag that specifies the access mode. There are three types of access, and they correlate to the access you specified when you called CreateFileMapping:

■ FILE_MAP_WRITE: Specifies read and write access. If you specified PAGE_READWRITE in CreateFileMapping, then you can use this parameter.

■ FILE_MAP_READ: Specifies read-only access. If you specified PAGE_READWRITE or PAGE_READ in CreateFileMapping, then you can use this parameter.

■ FILE_MAP_ALL_ACCESS: Same as FILE_MAP_WRITE.

**195**

◼◼ FILE_MAP_COPY: Specifies copy on write access. If you specified PAGE_WRITECOPY in CreateFileMapping, then you use this parameter.

The third and fourth parameters specify the 64-bit offset into the object. You must request offsets in multiples of 64KB. Actually, you must allocate according to the processor's allocation granularity. Currently, all processors that NT runs on have a 64KB allocation granularity. To be well behaved, you should call GetSystemInfo to find the correct allocation granularity:

```
SYSTEM_INFO si
GetSystemInfo(&si);
AfxMessageBox("Allocation granularity = %h bytes",
si.dwAllocationGranularity);
```

The last parameter specifies how many bytes to map. If you set this parameter to zero, the system maps the entire file. MapViewOfFile returns an LPVOID, which you can cast to suit your needs.

The following example shows how to map a view of a buffer:

```
//
// map view of shared buffer
//

LPSTR pszMapView = (LPSTR) MapViewOfFile(hMapObj,
                    FILE_MAP_READ | FILE_MAP_WRITE,
                    0,   // offset, high order
                    0,   // low order
                    0);  // 0 means entire file
```

Notice that the allocation granularity becomes an issue only when you want to map less than the entire file.

Okay, that takes care of the creating process. Now, let's see what other processes must do to access the shared data.

Have other processes call OpenFileMapping and MapViewOfFile. To access the shared object, other processes must know the name of the object and call the OpenFileMapping function:

```
HANDLE OpenFileMapping(
         DWORD dwDesiredAccess, // access mode
         BOOL bInheritHandle,   // inherit flag
         LPCTSTR lpName);       // address of name of
                                // file-mapping object
```

To make sure that other processes don't attempt to open the file mapping before the first process can create it, you must use some type of synchronization.

Here's how other processes would gain access to SharedMem:

```
//
// open named mapping object for read/write access
//
HANDLE hMapObj = OpenFileMapping(
                   FILE_MAP_WRITE,  // read/write
                                    // access
                   FALSE,           // no inheritance
                   "SharedMem");
```

Once other processes have the handle to the mapping object, they call MapViewOfFile to map a view of the object just as the creating process does.

MapViewOfFile returns different virtual addresses for each process. To specify the virtual address where the file will be mapped, use the MapViewOfFileEx function, rather than MapViewOfFile:

```
LPVOID MapViewOfFileEx(
          HANDLE hMapObject,
          DWORD fdwAccess,
          DWORD dwOffsetHigh,
          DWORD dwOffsetLow,
          DWORD cbMap,
          LPVOID lpvBase);
```

The last parameter specifies the virtual address you want the file to be mapped into.

When your process finishes using the shared memory, call UnmapViewOfFile to destroy the view in its address space:

```
BOOL
UnmapViewOfFile(LPVOID lpBaseAddress);
The only parameter, lpBaseAddress, must be identical to the pointer
returned from MapViewOfFile.
The following fragment uses UnmapViewOfFile to free the file view
within the process's address space.
if (!UnmapViewOfFile(pszMapView))
{
AfxMessageBox("Could not unmap view of file.");
}
```

The mapped file API sits directly on top of the physical memory manager. Underneath the covers, the mapped views of all processes are actually looking at the same pages of physical storage. These pages are marked as sharable, but just because the pages are sharable doesn't necessarily mean other processes (ones that didn't map a view) can access this data.

## SHARED-MEMORY DLLS

Another method of sharing data between cooperating processes utilizes a shared-memory DLL. A shared-memory DLL allows processes to access read-write data similar to the way Windows 3.1 DLLs share data. However, since data in a Win32 DLL is by default instance data, you must take extra steps to set it up as shared:

1.  Create a named data section. The easiest way to do this (if you are using Visual C++) is to use the data_seg pragma. One of the quirks of using the data_seg pragma is that the data must be initialized. But this is a good idea anyway for all variables, not just shared data. Besides preventing you from accidently using the data before it's initialized (which is a very hard bug to track down sometimes), The Microsoft compiler places all uninitialized data into separate section in your executable (the .BSS data section.) This means that programs with large amounts of unitialized data compile slower and due to some work that takes place in the start up code, may actually load slower. Therefore, make sure all of your shared data is initialized.

The data_seg pragma specifies the default segment that data resides in so that when you are finished specifying your shared data, use the data_seg pragma with no arguments to tell the compiler to reset the allocation back to the original default data section.

The following example shows how to place the character array, achShared, into the MYSEC data section:

```
#pragma data_seg("MYSEC")
char achShared[4096]={0};
#pragma data_seg()
```

2. Specify the sharing attributes for the named data section in your DEF file. The following DEF file entry shows how to make the MYSEC section a shared data section:

```
LIBRARY   TEST

DATA      READ WRITE

SECTIONS
        .MYSEC READ WRITE SHARED
```

Data sections are not shared by default, so any data that is not in the MYSEC section will be instance data. That is, each process that attaches to the DLL will receive its own copy of the data. When one process changes its instance of the data, it is not reflected in any other process's instance data.

3. Export the data appropriately in either the DEF file or your program (depending upon what your compler supports). The following DEF file entry shows how to export achShared as a constant data variable:

```
EXPORTS
    achShared   CONSTANT
```

4. Applications reference the shared data as external variables.

Once you have set up the shared memory DLL, any application that desires to reference shared data variables must reference the variables as external, as the following example shows:

```
extern __export "C" {char *achShared[];}
```

Also, notice the extra level of indirection involved. An application that wants to change the elements in the achShared array does so in the following manner:

```
**achShared='A';
```

or

```
m_pStatic = (CEdit *)GetDlgItem(IDC_SHARED);
m_pStatic->GetLine(0,*achShared,80);
```

The one drawback to using a shared memory DLL is that the data cannot be made to grow dynamically. In other words, this type of data is static only.

## WM_COPYDATA FOR TRANSFERRING READ-ONLY DATA

If it is read-only data that you want to transfer, use the Win32 WM_COPYDATA message. The primary purpose of WM_COPYDATA is to allow processes to pass private messages that contain read-only data. Windows 95 or NT provide no inherent synchronization during the transfer of data with the WM_COPYDATA message. To compensate for this, the SDK documentation recommends that you use SendMessage instead of PostMessage:

```
SendMessage(hwnd, WM_COPYDATA, wParam, lParam);
```

The idea is that the receiving application won't return until it has copied the data, making it impossible for the sending application to delete or modify the data before the receiving application has a chance to read it. However, this scenario only works if the sending application is single-threaded. If the sending application is multithreaded, you must synchronize to guarantee your data's integrity. If you don't, the receiving application receives garbage.

To implement the WM_COPYDATA message, set the wParam parameter of SendMessage to the window handle that contains the data. The lParam parameter points to a COPYDATASTRUCT structure:

```
typedef struct tagCOPYDATASTRUCT {
    DWORD dwData;
    DWORD cbData;
    PVOID lpData;
} COPYDATASTRUCT;
```

The COPYDATASTRUCT structure contains three fields. The first field is a DWORD for user-defined data. The third field, lpData, is a PVOID to the data, and the second field is a DWORD that specifies the size in bytes of the data pointed to by lpData.

## READPROCESSMEMORY AND WRITEPROCESSMEMORY

Another way to read and write data across processes is to use the ReadProcessMemory and WriteProcessMemory functions directly. This method is useful for applications that have been ported from 16-bit applications that shared memory using pointers and handles.

All that is required is an open handle to the process you want to interact with. This handle must be created with the PROCESS_VM_OPERATION, PROCESS_VM_READ, and PROCESS_VM_WRITE flags. To retrieve a handle to a process, use the OpenProcess function:

```
HANDLE
OpenProcess(DWORD fdwAccess,      // access rights
            BOOL fInherit,         // inheritable?
            DWORD ProcessID);      // process identifier
```

The first parameter determines the access rights. To be able to read and write into another process, call OpenProcess in the following manner:

```
HANDLE hTargetProcess = OpenProcess(
                          STANDARD_RIGHTS_REQUIRED|
                          PROCESS_VM_READ|
                          PROCESS_VM_WRITE|
                          PROCESS_VM_OPERATION,
                          FALSE,
                          dwProcessId);
```

The second parameter is a Boolean that specifies whether any new processes you create will inherit this handle or not. The third parameter is the process ID of the process you want to interact with.

In order for OpenProcess to succeed, the process you are interacting with must have been created with these flags.

Once you have a valid handle to a process, use ReadProcessMemory to read the process's memory:

```
BOOL ReadProcessMemory(
     HANDLE hProcess,             //open handle of the process
     LPVOID lpBaseAddress,        // virtual address to read
     LPVOID lpBuffer,             // address of buffer to place read data
     DWORD cbRead,                // number of bytes to read
     LPDWORD lpNumberOfBytesRead); // actual number of
                                  // bytes read
```

Use this same handle to write into the process's memory:

```
BOOL WriteProcessMemory(
     HANDLE hProcess,             // open handle of process
     LPVOID lpBaseAddress,        // virtual address to write
     LPVOID lpBuffer,             // address of buffer to
                                  // write
     DWORD cbWrite,               // number of bytes to write
     LPDWORD lpNumberOfBytesWritten); // actual number of
                                  // bytes written
```

The lpBaseAddress parameter is the location in the process's address space where ReadProcessMemory and WriteProcessMemory will begin reading or writing.

The cbRead (or cbWrite) parameter specifies how much memory to read or write. All of the memory in the range must be available. This means that, if you want to read 10KB, all 10KB must be marked as either PAGE_READONLY or PAGE_READWRITE—otherwise the function fails. Consequently, if you want write into another process's address space, the entire range must be marked as PAGE_READWRITE.

Using the ReadProcessMemory and WriteProcessMemory method, you can communicate between processes much the same way you do in Windows 3.1.

To illustrate how ReadProcessMemory , WriteProcessMemory work I've created two sample applications, Send and Receive.

SEND.EXE provides seven ways to transmit memory to RECV.EXE:

1.  From the pointer returned from GlobalLock

2.  Via a handle retrieved from GlobalAlloc(GMEM_SHARE,...)

3.  From a static pointer

4.  From a pointer returned from VirtualAlloc

5.  Via the WM_COPYDATA message

6.  By using a mapped file

7.  From a shared memory DLL

Send uses registered messages to communicate with Receive. Each different method of transmitting data corresponds to different registered message. Both Send and Receive are applications created with Visual C++ 2.0, and both use the Microsoft Foundation Class Libraries (MFC). Receive uses the MFC ON_REGISTERED_MESSAGE message map to handle the registered messages:

```
ON_REGISTERED_MESSAGE(theApp.m_nMsgVirtual,
                      OnRegMsgVirtual)
ON_REGISTERED_MESSAGE(theApp.m_nMsgGlobal,
                      OnRegMsgGlobal)
ON_REGISTERED_MESSAGE(theApp.m_nMsgGlobalPtr,
                      OnRegMsgHandle)
ON_REGISTERED_MESSAGE(theApp.m_nMsgStatic,
                      OnRegMsgStatic)
```

Send transmits the data the same way a Win16 application would—by posting a message:

```
//
// Post a registered msg to recv.exe
// and pass the Process ID and HANDLE to GlobalAlloc'd
// memory
//
::PostMessage(HWND_TOPMOST,
            theApp.m_nMsgGlobal,
            (UINT)GetCurrentProcessId(),
            (LONG)theApp.hGlobal);
```

However, Send also transmits one very important piece of data in wParam: the process's ID. By passing the process ID, Send enables Receive to GlobalLock the memory, invoke OpenProcess, and then call ReadProcessMemory:

```
LPSTR lpszApp = (LPSTR)GlobalLock((HANDLE)hGlobal);
HANDLE hTargetProcess=OpenProcess(STANDARD_RIGHTS_REQUIRED|
                        PROCESS_VM_READ |
                        PROCESS_VM_WRITE |
                        PROCESS_VM_OPERATION,
                        FALSE,
                        dwProcessId);

if (!ReadProcessMemory((HANDLE)hTargetProcess,
                    (LPSTR)lpszApp,
                    s.GetBuffer(80), 80, &cb))
    {
    wsprintf(achMsg,"Last error: %d",GetLastError());
    AfxMessageBox(achMsg,"Error in read process ");
    return TRUE;
    }
```

If ReadProcessMemory fails with an extended error of 998 (ERROR_NO_ACCESS), it is typically because the process handle does not have the proper access. Remember, NT is a discretionary access control system. If a user-mode process chooses to, it can modify its Access Control

List to prevent you from accessing it address space. That's why I stated that it takes cooperating processes to share memory. Notice that RECV.EXE calls ReadProcessMemory and WriteProcessMemory for virtual, static, and globally alloc'd pointers. This is to show all the methods that are available to read and write across processes. It is important to note that since the RECV physically change memory in SEND's virtual address space, it must synchronize access to the data. I have chosen to use SendMessage instead of PostMessage to transmit the registered message because SEND is a single-threaded application. This is a cheap way of achieving synchronization (there is no way SEND can alter data if it is waiting for RECV to return). However, if you use these techniques in your multithreaded application, you need to add a mutex object to fully synchronize your data.

The lpBaseAddress parameter is the location in the process's address space where ReadProcessMemory and WriteProcessMemory will begin reading or writing.

The cbRead (or cbWrite) parameter specifies how much memory to read or write. All of the memory in the range must be available. This means that, if you want to read 10KB, all 10KB must be marked as either PAGE_READONLY or PAGE_READWRITE -otherwise the function fails. Consequently, if you want write into another process's address space, the entire range must be marked as PAGE_READWRITE.

# SAMPLE APPLICATIONS: READING AND WRITING MEMORY

Using the ReadProcessMemory and WriteProcessMemory method, you can communicate between processes much the same way you do in Windows 3.1. This chapter's sample application is actually two executables, send and receive. Figure 5–1 shows the SEND.EXE main window.

SEND.EXE provides seven ways to transmit memory to RECV.EXE:

1. From the pointer returned from GlobalLock
2. Via a handle retrieved from GlobalAlloc(GMEM_SHARE,...)
3. From a static pointer
4. From a pointer returned from VirtualAlloc

**205**

5. Via the WM_COPYDATA message
6. By using a mapped file
7. From a shared memory DLL

**Figure 5–1** The SEND.EXE main Window

Send uses registered messages to communicate with Receive. Each different method of transmitting data corresponds to different registered message. Receive uses the MFC ON_REGISTERED_MESSAGE message map to handle the registered messages: ON_REGISTERED_MESSAGE(theApp.m_nMsgVirtual, OnRegMsgVirtual) ON_REGISTERED_MESSAGE(theApp.m_nMsgGlobal, OnRegMsgGlobal) ON_REGISTERED_MESSAGE(theApp.m_nMsgGlobalPtr, OnRegMsgHandle)

ON_REGISTERED_MESSAGE(theApp.m_nMsgStatic, OnRegMsgStatic)

Send transmits the data the same way a Win16 application would—by posting a message:

```
//
// Post a registered msg to recv.exe
// and pass the Process ID and HANDLE to GlobalAlloc'd
// memory
//
::PostMessage(HWND_TOPMOST,
```

```
theApp.m_nMsgGlobal,
(UINT)GetCurrentProcessId(),
(LONG)theApp.hGlobal);
```

However, Send also transmits one very important piece of data in wParam: the process's ID. By passing the process ID, Send enables Receive to GlobalLock the memory, invoke OpenProcess, and then call ReadProcessMemory:

```
LPSTR lpszApp = (LPSTR)GlobalLock((HANDLE)hGlobal);

HANDLE hTargetProcess=OpenProcess(STANDARD_RIGHTS_REQUIRED|
                        PROCESS_VM_READ |
                        PROCESS_VM_WRITE |
                        PROCESS_VM_OPERATION,
                        FALSE,
                        dwProcessId);

if (!ReadProcessMemory((HANDLE)hTargetProcess,
                    (LPSTR)lpszApp,
                    s.GetBuffer(80), 80, &cb))
    {
    wsprintf(achMsg,"Last error: %d",GetLastError());
    MessageBox(achMsg,"Error in read process ");
    return TRUE;
    }
```

If ReadProcessMemory fails with an extended error of 998 (ERROR_NO_ACCESS), it is typically because the process handle does not have the proper access.

Listing 5–3 contains the source for SEND.EXE, and Listing 5–4 contains the source for RECV.EXE. You'll notice that RECV.EXE calls ReadProcessMemory and WriteProcessMemory for virtual, static, and globally alloc'd pointers. This is to show that you can read and write across processes. It is important to note that since you are physically changing memory in SEND's virtual address space, you must synchronize access to the data. I have chosen to use SendMessage instead of PostMessage to transmit the registered message because SEND is a single-threaded application. This is a cheap way of achieving synchronization (there is no way SEND can alter data if it is waiting for RECV to return).

**207**

However, if you use these techniques in your multithreaded application, you need to add a mutex object to fully synchronize your data.

**Listing 5–3** Send.cpp

```
// send.cpp : Defines the class behaviors for the application.
//

#include "stdafx.h"
#include "send.h"
#include "senddlg.h"

#ifdef _DEBUG
#undef THIS_FILE
static char BASED_CODE THIS_FILE[] = __FILE__;
#endif

/////////////////////////////////////////////////////////////////////////////
// CSendApp

BEGIN_MESSAGE_MAP(CSendApp, CWinApp)
    //{{AFX_MSG_MAP(CSendApp)
            // NOTE - the ClassWizard will add and remove mapping macros here.
            //    DO NOT EDIT what you see in these blocks of generated code!
    //}}AFX_MSG
    ON_COMMAND(ID_HELP, CWinApp::OnHelp)
END_MESSAGE_MAP()

/////////////////////////////////////////////////////////////////////////////
// CSendApp construction

CSendApp::CSendApp()
{
    // TODO: add construction code here,
    // Place all significant initialization in InitInstance
}

/////////////////////////////////////////////////////////////////////////////
// The one and only CSendApp object

CSendApp theApp;
```

```
///////////////////////////////////////////////////////////////////////////
// CSendApp initialization

BOOL CSendApp::InitInstance()
{
    // Standard initialization
    // If you are not using these features and wish to reduce the size
    //  of your final executable, you should remove from the following
    //  the specific initialization routines you do not need.

    Enable3dControls();
    LoadStdProfileSettings();  // Load standard INI file options (including MRU)

    CSendDlg dlg;
    m_pMainWnd = &dlg;
    int nResponse = dlg.DoModal();
    if (nResponse == IDOK)
    {
            // TODO: Place code here to handle when the dialog is
            //  dismissed with OK
    }
    else if (nResponse == IDCANCEL)
    {
            // TODO: Place code here to handle when the dialog is
            //  dismissed with Cancel
    }

    // Since the dialog has been closed, return FALSE so that we exit the
    //  application, rather than start the application's message pump.
    return FALSE;
}
```

**Listing 5–4** SendDlg.cpp

```
// senddlg.cpp : implementation file
//

#include "stdafx.h"
#include "send.h"
#include "senddlg.h"
```

```
#ifdef _DEBUG
#undef THIS_FILE
static char BASED_CODE THIS_FILE[] = __FILE__;
#endif
extern "C" {char *achShared[];}
#define _MAX_FIELD 80
//////////////////////////////////////////////////////////////////////
// CAboutDlg dialog used for App About

class CAboutDlg : public CDialog
{
public:
    CAboutDlg();

// Dialog Data
    //{{AFX_DATA(CAboutDlg)
    enum { IDD = IDD_ABOUTBOX };
    //}}AFX_DATA

// Implementation
protected:
    virtual void DoDataExchange(CDataExchange* pDX);      // DDX/DDV support
    //{{AFX_MSG(CAboutDlg)
    virtual BOOL OnInitDialog();
    //}}AFX_MSG
    DECLARE_MESSAGE_MAP()
};

CAboutDlg::CAboutDlg() : CDialog(CAboutDlg::IDD)
{
    //{{AFX_DATA_INIT(CAboutDlg)
    //}}AFX_DATA_INIT
}

void CAboutDlg::DoDataExchange(CDataExchange* pDX)
{
    CDialog::DoDataExchange(pDX);
    //{{AFX_DATA_MAP(CAboutDlg)
    //}}AFX_DATA_MAP
}
```

```
BEGIN_MESSAGE_MAP(CAboutDlg, CDialog)
    //{{AFX_MSG_MAP(CAboutDlg)
            // No message handlers
    //}}AFX_MSG_MAP
END_MESSAGE_MAP()


/////////////////////////////////////////////////////////////////////////////
// CAboutDlg message handlers

BOOL CAboutDlg::OnInitDialog()
{
    CDialog::OnInitDialog();
    CenterWindow();

    // TODO: Add extra about dlg initialization here

    return TRUE;  // return TRUE  unless you set the focus to a control
}


/////////////////////////////////////////////////////////////////////////////
// CSendDlg dialog

CSendDlg::CSendDlg(CWnd* pParent /*=NULL*/)
    : CDialog(CSendDlg::IDD, pParent)
{
    //{{AFX_DATA_INIT(CSendDlg)
    m_strMapped = _T("");
    m_strHandle = _T("");
    m_strGlobal = _T("");
    m_strCopy = _T("");
    m_strShared = _T("");
    m_strStatic = _T("");
    m_strVirtual = _T("");
    //}}AFX_DATA_INIT
    // Note that LoadIcon does not require a subsequent DestroyIcon in Win32
    m_hIcon = AfxGetApp()->LoadIcon(IDR_MAINFRAME);
}

void CSendDlg::DoDataExchange(CDataExchange* pDX)
{
```

```
        CDialog::DoDataExchange(pDX);
        //{{AFX_DATA_MAP(CSendDlg)
        DDX_Control(pDX, IDC_MAPPED, m_CtlMapped);
        DDX_Text(pDX, IDC_MAPPED, m_strMapped);
        DDX_Text(pDX, IDC_HANDLE, m_strHandle);
        DDX_Text(pDX, IDC_GLOBALPTR, m_strGlobal);
        DDX_Text(pDX, IDC_COPY, m_strCopy);
        DDX_Text(pDX, IDC_SHARED, m_strShared);
        DDX_Text(pDX, IDC_STATICPTR, m_strStatic);
        DDX_Text(pDX, IDC_VIRTUAL, m_strVirtual);
        //}}AFX_DATA_MAP
}


BEGIN_MESSAGE_MAP(CSendDlg, CDialog)
        //{{AFX_MSG_MAP(CSendDlg)
        ON_WM_SYSCOMMAND()
        ON_WM_PAINT()
        ON_WM_QUERYDRAGICON()
        ON_BN_CLICKED(IDTRANSMIT, OnTransmit)
        //}}AFX_MSG_MAP
END_MESSAGE_MAP()


///////////////////////////////////////////////////////////////////////
// CSendDlg message handlers

BOOL CSendDlg::OnInitDialog()
{
        CDialog::OnInitDialog();
        CenterWindow();

        // Add "About..." menu item to system menu.

        // IDM_ABOUTBOX must be in the system command range.
        ASSERT((IDM_ABOUTBOX & 0xFFF0) == IDM_ABOUTBOX);
        ASSERT(IDM_ABOUTBOX < 0xF000);

        CMenu* pSysMenu = GetSystemMenu(FALSE);
        CString strAboutMenu;
        strAboutMenu.LoadString(IDS_ABOUTBOX);
        if (!strAboutMenu.IsEmpty())
        {
```

```
            pSysMenu->AppendMenu(MF_SEPARATOR);
            pSysMenu->AppendMenu(MF_STRING, IDM_ABOUTBOX, strAboutMenu);
    }
CSendApp * pApp = (CSendApp *)AfxGetApp();


m_nMsgVirtual = RegisterWindowMessage("Virtual");
m_nMsgGlobal = ::RegisterWindowMessage("Global");
m_nMsgHandle = ::RegisterWindowMessage("Handle");
m_nMsgStatic = ::RegisterWindowMessage("Static");
m_nMsgProcess = ::RegisterWindowMessage("Process");
m_nMsgMapped = ::RegisterWindowMessage("Mapped");
m_nMsgShared = ::RegisterWindowMessage("Shared");
pApp->m_hMapObj = CreateFileMapping((HANDLE) 0xFFFFFFFF,
                                    NULL, // not inherited
                                    PAGE_READWRITE,
                                    0, // buffer size, hi order
                                    0x1000, // buffer size, lo order
                                    "SharedMem"); // object name


 pApp->m_pszMapView = (LPSTR) MapViewOfFile(pApp->m_hMapObj,
                    FILE_MAP_READ | FILE_MAP_WRITE,
                    0,       // offset, high order
                    0,       // low order
                    0);      // 0 means entire file



ASSERT(pApp->m_pszMapView);

//
// Initialize the handle to Global memory
//

pApp->m_hGlobalHandle = GlobalAlloc(GMEM_SHARE,1024);
pApp->m_pszGlobalHandlePtr=(LPSTR)GlobalLock(pApp->m_hGlobalHandle);
lstrcpy (pApp->m_pszGlobalHandlePtr,"GlobalLocked memory");

//
// Initialize more Global memory
// Instead of the Handle we'll pass the pointer
// to this memory directly.
//
```

**213**

```
pApp->m_hGlobal = GlobalAlloc(GMEM_SHARE,1024);
pApp->m_pszGlobal=(LPSTR)GlobalLock(pApp->m_hGlobal);

lstrcpy (pApp->m_pszGlobal,"GlobalLocked memory");

//
// Allocate 4KB of virtual memory
//

pApp->m_pszVirtual = (LPSTR)VirtualAlloc(NULL,_BUFSIZE,
                                        MEM_COMMIT|MEM_RESERVE,
                                      PAGE_READWRITE);

//
// Initialize Static memory
//
static char achStatic[_BUFSIZE];
pApp->m_pszStatic = (LPSTR)achStatic;

//
// Initialize WM_COPYDATA memory
//
static char achCopy[_BUFSIZE];
pApp->m_pszCopy = (LPSTR)achCopy;


return TRUE;  // return TRUE  unless you set the focus to a control
}



void CSendDlg::OnSysCommand(UINT nID, LPARAM lParam)
{
     if ((nID & 0xFFF0) == IDM_ABOUTBOX)
     {        ShellAbout(m_hWnd, "Send",
         "From Name of Book goes here\r\nby Kevin Goodman",
            LoadIcon(AfxGetInstanceHandle(),
             MAKEINTRESOURCE(AFX_IDI_STD_FRAME)));

     }
```

```
        else
        {
                CDialog::OnSysCommand(nID, lParam);
        }
}


// If you add a minimize button to your dialog, you will need the code below
//   to draw the icon.  For MFC applications using the document/view model,
//   this is automatically done for you by the framework.

void CSendDlg::OnPaint()
{

        if (IsIconic())
        {
                CPaintDC dc(this); // device context for painting

                SendMessage(WM_ICONERASEBKGND, (WPARAM) dc.GetSafeHdc(), 0);

                // Center icon in client rectangle
                int cxIcon = GetSystemMetrics(SM_CXICON);
                int cyIcon = GetSystemMetrics(SM_CYICON);
                CRect rect;
                GetClientRect(&rect);
                int x = (rect.Width() - cxIcon + 1) / 2;
                int y = (rect.Height() - cyIcon + 1) / 2;

                // Draw the icon
                dc.DrawIcon(x, y, m_hIcon);
        }
        else
        {
                CDialog::OnPaint();
        }
}

// The system calls this to obtain the cursor to display while the user drags
//   the minimized window.
HCURSOR CSendDlg::OnQueryDragIcon()
{
        return (HCURSOR) m_hIcon;
```

```
}

void CSendDlg::OnTransmit()
{
if (!UpdateData())
     return;
CSendApp * pApp = (CSendApp *)AfxGetApp();
//
// Perform FindWindow to get hwnd of receive
//


  CWnd *pWndRecv =  FindWindow("#32770","Receive");
  if (!pWndRecv)
    {
    MessageBox("Please start receive.exe ");
    return;
    }




//
// Send a msg to let recv.exe know that it is okay to
// call OpenFileMapping
//
strcpy(pApp->m_pszMapView,m_strMapped);

if (pWndRecv->SendMessage(m_nMsgMapped, 0, 0))
     m_strMapped = pApp->m_pszMapView;




//
// Retrieve the text from the WM_COPYDATA field
//
if (!m_strCopy.IsEmpty())
     strcpy(pApp->m_pszCopy,m_strCopy);
```

```
//
// Create a COPYDATASTRUCT for WM_COPYDATA
//

static COPYDATASTRUCT cds;
cds.lpData=pApp->m_pszCopy;
cds.cbData=strlen(pApp->m_pszCopy);

pWndRecv->SendMessage(WM_COPYDATA, NULL, (LONG)&cds);



//
// Retrieve the text from Global Pointer field
//

strcpy(pApp->m_pszGlobalHandlePtr, m_strHandle);


if (pWndRecv->SendMessage(m_nMsgHandle,
                             (UINT)GetCurrentProcessId(),
                             (LONG)pApp->m_hGlobalHandle))
   {
     m_strHandle = pApp->m_pszGlobalHandlePtr;
   }



  strcpy(pApp->m_pszGlobal, m_strGlobal);


//
// Send a msg to pWndRecv
// and pass the Process ID and pointer returned
// from GlobalLocked memory
//

  if (pWndRecv->SendMessage(m_nMsgGlobal,
            (UINT)GetCurrentProcessId(),
```

```
                    (LONG)pApp->m_pszGlobal))
      {
       m_strGlobal = pApp->m_pszGlobal;
      }




//
// Retrieve the text from Virtual Pointer field
//
       strcpy(pApp->m_pszVirtual,m_strVirtual);



//
// Send a registered msg to recv.exe
// and pass the Process ID and pointer to VirtualAlloc'd
// memory
//

   if (pWndRecv->SendMessage(m_nMsgVirtual,
               (UINT)GetCurrentProcessId(),
               (LONG)pApp->m_pszVirtual))
      {
        m_strVirtual = pApp->m_pszVirtual;
      }




//
// Retrieve the text from the Static Pointer field
//

   strcpy(pApp->m_pszStatic, m_strStatic);

//
// Send a registered msg to recv.exe
// and pass the Process ID and pointer to static
// memory
//
```

```
    if (pWndRecv->SendMessage(m_nMsgStatic,
                (UINT)GetCurrentProcessId(),
                (LONG)pApp->m_pszStatic))
    {

        m_strStatic = pApp->m_pszStatic;
    }

//
// Retrieve the text from the Shared DLL field
//


    strcpy(*achShared,m_strShared);


//
// Send a msg to recv.exe
// recv.exe knows the data is in the variable achShared
//

    if (pWndRecv->SendMessage(m_nMsgShared,
                                        0,
                                        0))
    {
    m_strShared = *achShared;
    }


    UpdateData(FALSE);

}
```

### Listing 5–5 Recv.cpp

```
// recv.cpp : Defines the class behaviors for the application.
//

#include "stdafx.h"
```

```
#include "recv.h"
#include "recvdlg.h"

#ifdef _DEBUG
#undef THIS_FILE
static char BASED_CODE THIS_FILE[] = __FILE__;
#endif

/////////////////////////////////////////////////////////////////////////
// CRecvApp

BEGIN_MESSAGE_MAP(CRecvApp, CWinApp)
    //{{AFX_MSG_MAP(CRecvApp)
        // NOTE - the ClassWizard will add and remove mapping macros here.
        //    DO NOT EDIT what you see in these blocks of generated code!
    //}}AFX_MSG
    ON_COMMAND(ID_HELP, CWinApp::OnHelp)
END_MESSAGE_MAP()

/////////////////////////////////////////////////////////////////////////
// CRecvApp construction

CRecvApp::CRecvApp()
{
    // TODO: add construction code here,
    // Place all significant initialization in InitInstance
}

/////////////////////////////////////////////////////////////////////////
// The one and only CRecvApp object

CRecvApp theApp;

/////////////////////////////////////////////////////////////////////////
// CRecvApp initialization
    //
    UINT CRecvApp::m_nMsgVirtual = ::RegisterWindowMessage("Virtual");
    UINT CRecvApp::m_nMsgGlobal = ::RegisterWindowMessage("Global");
    UINT CRecvApp::m_nMsgHandle = ::RegisterWindowMessage("Handle");
    UINT CRecvApp::m_nMsgStatic = ::RegisterWindowMessage("Static");
    UINT CRecvApp::m_nMsgMapped = ::RegisterWindowMessage("Mapped");
```

```
      UINT CRecvApp::m_nMsgShared = ::RegisterWindowMessage("Shared");

BOOL CRecvApp::InitInstance()
{
      // Standard initialization
      // If you are not using these features and wish to reduce the size
      //  of your final executable, you should remove from the following
      //  the specific initialization routines you do not need.

      Enable3dControls();
      LoadStdProfileSettings();  // Load standard INI file options (including MRU)

      //
      // initialize registered messages.

      CRecvDlg dlg;
      m_pMainWnd = &dlg;
      int nResponse = dlg.DoModal();
      if (nResponse == IDOK)
      {
              // TODO: Place code here to handle when the dialog is
              //  dismissed with OK
      }
      else if (nResponse == IDCANCEL)
      {
              // TODO: Place code here to handle when the dialog is
              //  dismissed with Cancel
      }

      // Since the dialog has been closed, return FALSE so that we exit the
      //  application, rather than start the application's message pump.
      return FALSE;
}
```

**Listing 5–6** RecvDlg.cpp

```
// recvdlg.cpp : implementation file
//

#include "stdafx.h"
#include "recv.h"
```

```
#include "recvdlg.h"

#ifdef _DEBUG
#undef THIS_FILE
static char BASED_CODE THIS_FILE[] = __FILE__;
#endif

#define _MAX_FIELD 80
LPCSTR CRecvDlg::STARS = "**************************";


///////////////////////////////////////////////////////////////////////////
// CAboutDlg dialog used for App About

class CAboutDlg : public CDialog
{
public:
     CAboutDlg();

// Dialog Data
     //{{AFX_DATA(CAboutDlg)
     enum { IDD = IDD_ABOUTBOX };
     //}}AFX_DATA

// Implementation
protected:
     virtual void DoDataExchange(CDataExchange* pDX);      // DDX/DDV support
     //{{AFX_MSG(CAboutDlg)
     virtual BOOL OnInitDialog();
     //}}AFX_MSG
     DECLARE_MESSAGE_MAP()
};

CAboutDlg::CAboutDlg() : CDialog(CAboutDlg::IDD)
{
     //{{AFX_DATA_INIT(CAboutDlg)
     //}}AFX_DATA_INIT
}

void CAboutDlg::DoDataExchange(CDataExchange* pDX)
{
     CDialog::DoDataExchange(pDX);
```

```
    //{{AFX_DATA_MAP(CAboutDlg)
    //}}AFX_DATA_MAP
}


BEGIN_MESSAGE_MAP(CAboutDlg, CDialog)
    //{{AFX_MSG_MAP(CAboutDlg)
            // No message handlers
    //}}AFX_MSG_MAP
END_MESSAGE_MAP()


/////////////////////////////////////////////////////////////////////////
// CAboutDlg message handlers

BOOL CAboutDlg::OnInitDialog()
{
    CDialog::OnInitDialog();
    CenterWindow();

    // TODO: Add extra about dlg initialization here

    return TRUE;  // return TRUE  unless you set the focus to a control
}


/////////////////////////////////////////////////////////////////////////
// CRecvDlg dialog

CRecvDlg::CRecvDlg(CWnd* pParent /*=NULL*/)
    : CDialog(CRecvDlg::IDD, pParent)
{
    //{{AFX_DATA_INIT(CRecvDlg)
    m_strMapped = _T("");
    m_strCopy = _T("");
    m_strGlobal = _T("");
    m_strHandle = _T("");
    m_strShared = _T("");
    m_strStatic = _T("");
    m_strVirtual = _T("");
    //}}AFX_DATA_INIT
    // Note that LoadIcon does not require a subsequent DestroyIcon in Win32
    m_hIcon = AfxGetApp()->LoadIcon(IDR_MAINFRAME);
}
```

**223**

```
void CRecvDlg::DoDataExchange(CDataExchange* pDX)
{
    CDialog::DoDataExchange(pDX);
    //{{AFX_DATA_MAP(CRecvDlg)
    DDX_Text(pDX, IDC_MAPPED, m_strMapped);
    DDX_Text(pDX, IDC_COPY, m_strCopy);
    DDX_Text(pDX, IDC_GLOBALPTR, m_strGlobal);
    DDX_Text(pDX, IDC_HANDLE, m_strHandle);
    DDX_Text(pDX, IDC_SHARED, m_strShared);
    DDX_Text(pDX, IDC_STATICPTR, m_strStatic);
    DDX_Text(pDX, IDC_VIRTUAL, m_strVirtual);
    //}}AFX_DATA_MAP
}


BEGIN_MESSAGE_MAP(CRecvDlg, CDialog)
    //{{AFX_MSG_MAP(CRecvDlg)
    ON_WM_SYSCOMMAND()
    ON_WM_PAINT()
    ON_WM_QUERYDRAGICON()
    ON_MESSAGE( WM_COPYDATA, OnCopyData )
    //}}AFX_MSG_MAP
    ON_REGISTERED_MESSAGE(CRecvApp::m_nMsgVirtual, OnRegMsgVirtual)
    ON_REGISTERED_MESSAGE(CRecvApp::m_nMsgGlobal, OnRegMsgGlobal)
    ON_REGISTERED_MESSAGE(CRecvApp::m_nMsgHandle, OnRegMsgHandle)
    ON_REGISTERED_MESSAGE(CRecvApp::m_nMsgStatic, OnRegMsgStatic)
    ON_REGISTERED_MESSAGE(CRecvApp::m_nMsgMapped, OnRegMsgMapped)
    ON_REGISTERED_MESSAGE(CRecvApp::m_nMsgShared, OnRegMsgShared)

END_MESSAGE_MAP()


/////////////////////////////////////////////////////////////////////////
// CRecvDlg message handlers

BOOL CRecvDlg::OnInitDialog()
{
    CDialog::OnInitDialog();
    CenterWindow();

    // Add "About..." menu item to system menu.

    // IDM_ABOUTBOX must be in the system command range.
```

```
        ASSERT((IDM_ABOUTBOX & 0xFFF0) == IDM_ABOUTBOX);
        ASSERT(IDM_ABOUTBOX < 0xF000);

        CMenu* pSysMenu = GetSystemMenu(FALSE);
        CString strAboutMenu;
        strAboutMenu.LoadString(IDS_ABOUTBOX);
        if (!strAboutMenu.IsEmpty())
        {
                pSysMenu->AppendMenu(MF_SEPARATOR);
                pSysMenu->AppendMenu(MF_STRING, IDM_ABOUTBOX, strAboutMenu);
        }

        // TODO: Add extra initialization here

        return TRUE;  // return TRUE  unless you set the focus to a control
}

void CRecvDlg::OnSysCommand(UINT nID, LPARAM lParam)
{
        if ((nID & 0xFFF0) == IDM_ABOUTBOX)
        {
        if ((nID & 0xFFF0) == IDM_ABOUTBOX)
        {       ShellAbout(m_hWnd, "Receive",
            "From Name of Book goes here\r\nby Kevin Goodman",
                LoadIcon(AfxGetInstanceHandle(),
                    MAKEINTRESOURCE(AFX_IDI_STD_FRAME)));
        }
        else
        {
                CDialog::OnSysCommand(nID, lParam);
        }
}

// If you add a minimize button to your dialog, you will need the code below
//  to draw the icon.  For MFC applications using the document/view model,
//  this is automatically done for you by the framework.

void CRecvDlg::OnPaint()
{
        if (IsIconic())
        {
```

```
            CPaintDC dc(this); // device context for painting

            SendMessage(WM_ICONERASEBKGND, (WPARAM) dc.GetSafeHdc(), 0);

            // Center icon in client rectangle
            int cxIcon = GetSystemMetrics(SM_CXICON);
            int cyIcon = GetSystemMetrics(SM_CYICON);
            CRect rect;
            GetClientRect(&rect);
            int x = (rect.Width() - cxIcon + 1) / 2;
            int y = (rect.Height() - cyIcon + 1) / 2;

            // Draw the icon
            dc.DrawIcon(x, y, m_hIcon);
    }
    else
    {
            CDialog::OnPaint();
    }
}


// The system calls this to obtain the cursor to display while the user drags
//  the minimized window.
HCURSOR CRecvDlg::OnQueryDragIcon()
{
    return (HCURSOR) m_hIcon;
}


//
//
//
LONG
CRecvDlg::OnRegMsgMapped(UINT /*wParam*/, LONG /*lParam*/)
{
 CRecvApp *pApp = (CRecvApp *)AfxGetApp();
 m_hMapObj = OpenFileMapping(FILE_MAP_WRITE,

                                        NULL,          // not inherited
                                        "SharedMem"); // object name

//
// Map a view of the file
//
```

**226**

```
m_pszMapView = (LPSTR) MapViewOfFile(m_hMapObj,
                    FILE_MAP_READ | FILE_MAP_WRITE,
                    0,      // offset, high order
                    0,      // low order
                    0);     // 0 means entire file

ASSERT (m_pszMapView);
m_strMapped = m_pszMapView;
int nLen = strlen(m_pszMapView);
strncpy(m_pszMapView,STARS,nLen);
UpdateData(FALSE);
return TRUE;
}


LONG
CRecvDlg::OnRegMsgShared(UINT /*wParam*/, LONG /*lParam*/)
{

m_strShared = *achShared;
UpdateData(FALSE);

return TRUE;




}



LONG
CRecvDlg::OnRegMsgVirtual(UINT dwProcessId, LONG lpszApp)
{
static DWORD cb=0;

HANDLE hTargetProcess=OpenProcess(STANDARD_RIGHTS_REQUIRED|
                    PROCESS_VM_READ|
                    PROCESS_VM_WRITE| PROCESS_VM_OPERATION,
                                        FALSE,
                    dwProcessId);
if (!ReadProcessMemory((HANDLE)hTargetProcess,(LPSTR)lpszApp,
                    m_strVirtual.GetBuffer(_MAX_FIELD),_MAX_FIELD,&cb))
    {
```

```
        m_strVirtual.ReleaseBuffer();
    return FALSE;
        }

m_strVirtual.ReleaseBuffer();
UpdateData(FALSE);

if (!WriteProcessMemory(hTargetProcess,(LPSTR)lpszApp, (LPSTR)STARS,
                    m_strVirtual.GetLength(),&cb))
    return FALSE;

return TRUE;
}


//
//
//
LONG
CRecvDlg::OnRegMsgHandle(UINT dwProcessId, LONG hGlobal)
{
static DWORD cb=0;


HANDLE hTargetProcess=OpenProcess(STANDARD_RIGHTS_REQUIRED|
                    PROCESS_VM_READ|
                    PROCESS_VM_WRITE| PROCESS_VM_OPERATION,
                                        FALSE,
                    dwProcessId);
//
// Since hGlobal is a handle you must GlobalLock
// to get a pointer
//



LPSTR lpszApp = (LPSTR)GlobalLock((HANDLE)hGlobal);

//
// lpszApp points into hTargetProcess's address space
// Use ReadProcessMemory to dereference the pointer
//
```

```
if (!ReadProcessMemory((HANDLE)hTargetProcess,(LPSTR)lpszApp,
                    m_strHandle.GetBuffer(_MAX_FIELD),_MAX_FIELD,&cb))
    {
    m_strHandle.ReleaseBuffer();
    return FALSE;
    }
m_strHandle.ReleaseBuffer();
UpdateData(FALSE);

if (!WriteProcessMemory(hTargetProcess,(LPSTR)lpszApp,
                    (LPSTR)STARS,m_strHandle.GetLength(),&cb))
    return FALSE;

return TRUE;
}


/////////////////////////////////////////////////////////////////
//
// Upon receipt of the registered message call ReadProcessMemory
// Then, just to show that you can, overwrite the data with
// asterisks by calling WriteProcessMemory
//
/////////////////////////////////////////////////////////////////


LONG
CRecvDlg::OnRegMsgGlobal(UINT dwProcessId, LONG lpsz)
{
static DWORD cb=0;

HANDLE hTargetProcess=OpenProcess(STANDARD_RIGHTS_REQUIRED|
                    PROCESS_VM_READ|
                    PROCESS_VM_WRITE| PROCESS_VM_OPERATION,
                                        FALSE,
                    dwProcessId);

if (!ReadProcessMemory((HANDLE)hTargetProcess,

(LPSTR)lpsz,m_strGlobal.GetBuffer(_MAX_FIELD),_MAX_FIELD,&cb))
    {
    m_strGlobal.ReleaseBuffer();
```

```
        return FALSE;
        }
m_strGlobal.ReleaseBuffer();
UpdateData(FALSE);

if (!WriteProcessMemory(hTargetProcess, (LPSTR)lpsz, (LPSTR)STARS,
                        m_strGlobal.GetLength(), &cb))
    return FALSE;

return TRUE;
}



//
//
//
LONG
CRecvDlg::OnRegMsgStatic(UINT dwProcessId, LONG lpszApp)
{
static DWORD cb=0;

HANDLE hTargetProcess=OpenProcess(STANDARD_RIGHTS_REQUIRED|
                        PROCESS_VM_READ|
                        PROCESS_VM_WRITE| PROCESS_VM_OPERATION,
                                              FALSE,
                        dwProcessId);
if (!ReadProcessMemory((HANDLE)hTargetProcess,(LPCSTR)lpszApp,
                        m_strStatic.GetBuffer(_MAX_FIELD),_MAX_FIELD,&cb))
      {
      m_strStatic.ReleaseBuffer();
    return FALSE;
      }
m_strStatic.ReleaseBuffer();
UpdateData(FALSE);

if (!WriteProcessMemory(hTargetProcess,(LPSTR)lpszApp,
                        (LPSTR)STARS,m_strStatic.GetLength(),&cb))
    return FALSE;

return TRUE;
}
```

```
//
// WM_COPYDATA is read only so we won't attempt to alter the source
//

LONG
CRecvDlg::OnCopyData(UINT /*hWndfrom*/, LONG cds)
{
DWORD cb=0;
m_strCopy = (LPSTR)((COPYDATASTRUCT *)cds)->lpData;
UpdateData(FALSE);

return TRUE;
}
```

### Listing 5–7 Shared.c

```
#include <windows.h>
#pragma data_seg(".MYSEC")
char achShared[4096]={0};
#pragma data_seg()
BOOL WINAPI
DllInit(HANDLE hInst, DWORD fdwReason, LPVOID lpReserved)
{
return TRUE;
}
```

### Listing 5–8 Shared.def

```
LIBRARY    SHARED

DATA       READ WRITE

SECTIONS
    .MYSEC READ WRITE SHARED


EXPORTS
    achShared  CONSTANT
```

# APPLICABILITY TO WINDOWS 95

I wonder how many developers have shied away from NT because of the mistaken notion of how restrictive NT is. Perhaps this is why Microsoft has chosen the memory management scheme they have for Windows 95. In Windows 95, the system reserves 1GB of every process space specifically for sharing memory between processes. With the exception of global handles, each of the method presented here will work on Window 95.

# SUMMARY

According to Microsoft documents, the consensus method of IPC is either OLE2 or memory mapped files. However, they should not be considered the only alternatives. The advantage of one memory API over the other might be just your individual preference and situation. For example, do you like using handles, or pointers? How much flexibility do you need? How simple do you find the API of that memory group to use? Are you trying to maintain code between Win16 and Win32? Armed with this knowledge, you'll be able to correct someone when they mispeak about "separate protected address spaces."

Often, the advantage of one memory API over the other might be just preference. For example, do you like using handles, or pointers? How much flexibility do you need? How simple do you find the API of that memory group to use? If you are trying to maintain code between Win16 and Win32, the Global and Local functions make sense. If you are porting from DOS or UNIX, the C runtime functions make sense. But if you wish to take full advantage of the Win32 API, only the Heap or Virtual APIs will suffice.

As you can see from the SEND and RECV sample programs, there are several ways to share memory between processes. I can't count how many times I've cringed when I've read or heard about how restrictive NT is because of its "separate protected address spaces." It's true that no renegade program can accidentally write into your address space (or worse yet, your program cannot accidentally write into another program's address space). But if you have cooperating processes you can read and write memory almost at will. If you are thinking that this is a security violation, I remind you that C2-level security means discretionary access contol. Using the techniques provided in Chapter 12, "The Windows NT Security Architecture," you can apply an ACL to your process to prevent another process (perhaps a malicious one) from gaining access to your data.

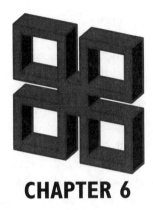

**CHAPTER 6**

# THE REGISTRY

Configuring and managing Windows NT or Windows 95 means working with and managing the Registration Database, known as the Registry. The Registry serves three purposes:

- To store information about the computer on which NT or Windows 95 is installed.
- To store information about the software that is installed on the computer.
- To store information about the users who are authorized to use the computer.

The Registry combines the functionality of the AUTOEXEC.BAT, CONFIG.SYS, WIN.INI, and SYSTEM.INI files, as well as the Windows 3.1 registration database and the BIOS equipment list interrupts. For compatibility reasons, these files still exist in Windows 95. For example, you can still load real-mode device drivers in Windows 95 via the "device=" list in CONFIG.SYS. In Windows NT these files are not longer used.

**233**

Several files, called hives, make up the Registry. In Windows 95, the two main hives are SYSTEM.DAT which stores system-specific information and USER.DAT which holds user-specific information. However, there is no need to access these files directly. Unlike Win16, which only has a few API calls to manipulate .INI file information (GetProfilexxx, GetPrivateProfilexxx and WriteProfilexxx WritePrivateProfilexxx), Win32 has a myriad of functions available to you. This chapter shows how to use the Win32 Registry APIs to store and access information about your and also explains why the Registry is necessary,). Your application also has the option of using the Registry to store private configuration information instead of private initialization (INI) files. This chapter shows when and where using the Registry is appropriate. It also explains how to take advantage of a feature of the Registry known as INI file mapping to write configuration code that is compatible with both Windows 3.1 and Windows NT.

In Windows NT only, the Registry also provides a way to access performance data and statistics. This chapter finishes up by showing how to use all of the functions necessary to store and retrieve configuration information as well as obtain performance statistics. At the end of the chapter is the listing for the Registrar, a sample application that demonstrates these techniques.

# WHY THE REGISTRY IS NECESSARY

Besides extending the capabilities of the Windows 3.1 registration database, the Registry provides features that are necessary for the following reasons:

■   Single-user INI files are obsolete. With the advent of multiple users and remote capabilities in Windows 95 and NT, the Windows 3.1 style INI files have become obsolete. Since many users can share the same application on one machine, it is necessary to provide every user with his or her own configuration data. Otherwise, personal settings and such would be lost each time a different user logged on. For example, suppose two people shared the same machine (perhaps one person used the computer during the day and another at night on the second shift.) In Windows 3.1, if the first shift employee changed the contents of their startup folder it would be reflected when the second shift user logged on. In Windows 95 and NT each employees could have their own configuration determined by their logon ID. So what ever the first shift employee did to their configuration settings, it wouldn't effect the second shift employee. However, keep in mind that this is only for configuration data. If the first shift employee deleted data off the local hard drive, it would be gone — for both users.

■■ Consistent location with a published API. The Registry defines specific locations for you to store configuration data (discussed shortly). By documenting these locations and documenting the Win32 functions necessary to access this information, Windows 95 and NT make it easy for users and technical support personnel to configure and manage their computers. The Win16 functions (RegCloseKey, RegCreateKey, RegDeleteKey, RegEnumKey, RegOpenKey, RegQueryValue, and RegSetValue) that you use on the Windows 3.1 registration database are compatible with the Registry. However, to take advantage of the new features of the Registry you will have to use the extended (Ex) version of some functions. The Win32 versions (see Table 6-1) of the functions that read and write profile strings are compatible with their Win16 counterparts.

**Table 6-1** Registry Functions Compatible with Win16

| Function | Use |
| --- | --- |
| GetPrivateProfileInt | Gets an integer from private file |
| GetPrivateProfileSection | Returns private key and value pairs |
| GetPrivateProfileString | Gets a string from a private file |
| GetProfileInt | Gets an integer from WIN.INI |
| GetProfileSection | Returns keys and values from WIN.INI |
| GetProfileString | Gets a string from WIN.INI |
| WritePrivateProfileSection | Writes a section to a private INI file |
| WritePrivateProfileString | Writes a string to a private INI file |
| WriteProfileSection | Writes a section to WIN.INI |
| WriteProfileString | Writes a string to WIN.INI |
| RegCloseKey | Closes a registration key |
| RegCreateKey | Creates or opens a key |
| RegDeleteKey | Deletes a key |
| RegEnumKey | Enumerates key values |
| RegOpenKey | Opens a key |
| RegQueryValue | Retrieves a name for a specified key |
| RegSetValue | Associates a text string with a specified key |

■ New Security procedures required. The fact that there is a consistent location in which end users and technical support personnel can expect to find configuration information doesn't preclude you from securing private data in Windows NT. Using the information in Chapter 12, "The Windows NT Security Architecture," and functions described later in this chapter, you can set descretionary access control lists (DACLs) on the data in the Registry that would normally be contained in your INI file. Unlike a physical INI file, this provides your configuration with information available to authorized users only.

■ Reliability measures must be taken. The CONFIG.SYS and AUTOEXEC.BAT files associated with MS-DOS and Windows 3.1 do not fit with Windows 95 or NT's emphasis on reliability. In MS-DOS it is easy for a naive or destructive user to alter the CONFIG.SYS or AUTOEXEC.BAT file and render the computer unbootable. Both Windows 95 and NT provide ways to ensure that your computer will never be rendered unbootable due to bad configuration data.

Edits to individual value entries are atomic, even across system crashes. Atomic means that any time a value entry is set, it is read the next time it is encountered (even after a crash), so it will have either the old value or the new value. Its type, name, and value go together. The system will not mix or corrupt data. A key's properties will always be consistent with the value entries actually present. For example, in Windows NT, the security descriptor on a key will always be either the new one or the old one, but never a mix of the two.

■ Accessing hardware information is now more complicated. Getting hardware information in MS-DOS, such as drive types, requires hardware-specific function calls that are unsuitable in an operating system ,such as NT, that supports a variety of processors. Windows 95's support for Plug-n-Play

■ Database size. The Registry can hold up to 32MB of information. This is a change from the early days of Windows when Windows would crash when WIN.INI grew larger than 64KB. The size of a key can vary, but it is more efficient than using the file system, where storing a lone byte of data costs between 512 and 8000 bytes. I have  not heard of any quotas imposed on the Registry currently, but you can bet if MondoWare's new application uses up 10 MB of the Registry, future releases will impose restrictions.

An individual value's entry data size is limited to 1MB, (In NT, a large part of this is for security.) I recommend that you store any individual objects larger than about 1KB as a separate file. Then create an entry in the Registry that contains the separate file's name. But, this is only a rule of thumb. The essential thing is that all configuration data be in the registry, and that nonconfiguration data be stored elsewhere.

# THE BASIC STRUCTURE OF THE REGISTRY

All of these factors contributed to the design of the Registry. The Registry is an object database consisting of keys and values. As shown in Figure 6–1, the basic structure of the Registry is a tree of nodes. Each node within the tree is called a key. Each key may have names and may contain other keys and values. A value is a name paired with a data object and a data type. All registry keys and value entries are case-insensitive, case-preserving, and stored in Unicode format.

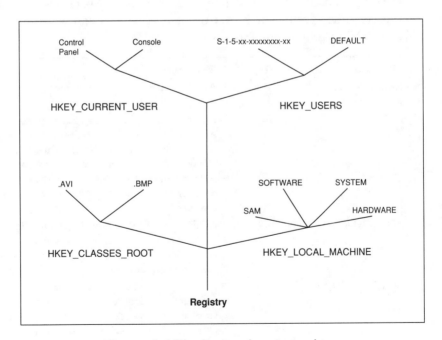

**Figure 6–1** The Registry's structural tree

**237**

## KEYS AND VALUE ENTRIES

Each key contains the following items:

- A name. A mandatory unique string used to gain access to the key.
- A class. An optional name for use in associating class method code with class instances stored in the registry.
- A time stamp. A value indicating the last time the key was modified.
- A security descriptor. Like other objects that take a security descriptor, this field is optional. All access control is on a key basis.
- A set of child keys. These go in the registry name space.
- A set of value entries. A private name space for each key.

Unlike in the Windows 3.1 registration database, where NULL is the only legal name, each value entry name may be up to 32,000 bytes (16,000 Unicode characters) long and may contain backslashes. The type is either system or a user-defined. The data can be stored or accessed in the following formats:

| | |
|---|---|
| REG_BINARY | Binary data. |
| REG_DWORD | Any 32-bit number. |
| REG_DWORD_LITTLE_ENDIAN | Any 32-bit number (same as REG_DWORD) that is stored with most significant byte of the word in the high-order word. Endian is normally determined by the hardware. Windows 95, which only runs on Intel class machines uses little endian format. The majority of hardware the NT runs on also uses this format. |
| REG_DWORD_BIG_ENDIAN | A REG_DWORD in big-endian format. Big-endian format is the opposite of little endian, in which the most significant byte of a word is the low-order word. |
| REG_EXPAND_SZ | A null-terminated string that contains unexpanded references to environment variables For example, my HKEY_CURRENT_USER\Environment\ include looks like this:"e:\msvc20\include; |

| | |
|---|---|
| | e:\msvc20\mfc\include; %include%". This string can be either ANSI or UNICODE string depending on whether you compile for UNICODE or not. |
| REG_LINK | Unicode symbolic link. |
| REG_MULTI_SZ | An array of null-terminated strings, terminated by two null characters. |
| REG_NONE | No defined value type. |
| REG_RESOURCE_LIST | A device-driver resource list. |
| REG_SZ | A NULL-terminated string. It is either ANSI or UNICODE string depending on whether you compile for UNICODE or not. |

The Registry treats data as either stable or volatile. The behavior for stable data is similar to a file system. Items exist until explicitly deleted. Volatile data, on the other hand, goes away upon rebooting. Notice that I wrote "rebooting." I did so because logging off is not sufficient to destroy the data. All children of a volatile key must also be volatile. Some parts of the registry (for example, HKEY_LOCAL_MACHINE\hardware in Windows NT) are forced to be entirely volatile.

## PREDEFINED HANDLES

The Registry uses predefined handles to point into its name space. Every Registry name reference is either directly or indirectly related to these handles. There are two major parts of the Registry's name space: per-user and per-machine data.

The predefined handle names that both Windows 95 and NT support are: HKEY_CLASSES_ROOT, HKEY_USERS, HKEY_CURRENT_USER and HKEY_LOCAL_MACHINE. Another handle, HKEY_PERFORMANCE_DATA, is a special handle that you use to gain access to performance data in Windows NT only. This handle will be discussed separately later in the chapter. Windows 95 defines an additional handle, HKEY_CURRENT_CONFIG, to store non user specific information that pertains to hardware. This next section discusses the predefined handles and a set of conventions you should follow to add registry support to your application..

## HKEY_USERS

Following with the tree analogy, the first predefined handle, HKEY_USERS, is the root list of users and contains keys for all per-user configuration information. This handle refers to a tree of information about the people who use this machine. The top level of the tree consists of a .DEFAULT key and one or more entries for specific people. The specific entries are created dynamically and are initially based on the content of the .DEFAULT key. The key names for the specific entries are SIDs that define the permissions given to the corresponding people.

## HKEY_CURRENT_USER

In Windows 3.1, the registration database is explicitly for system-wide OLE and Shell information only. However, just the opposite is true for the Windows NT Registry. HKEY_CURRENT_USER is for the express purpose of storing per-user information. HKEY_CURRENT_USER is the root of the current user's profile. After an application has been installed, almost all registry changes will involve HKEY_CURRENT_USER and will concern a specific user's preferences or history. The default items in HKEY_CURRENT_USER are Control Panel configuration information, Program Groups, Console settings, Environment variables, keyboard layout, and printers.

The information for HKEY_CURRENT_USER doesn't necessarily have to be stored on the local machine. In fact, it can be anywhere on the network. The information for HKEY_CURRENT_USER is stored under HKEY_USERS. HKEY_CURRENT_USER is the profile root for the current user. It contains program groups, control panel settings, and per-user application preferences.

## HKEY_CLASSES_ROOT

Object Linking and Embedding (OLE) and shell applications such as the Program Manager or File Manager in NT store information in HKEY_CLASSES_ROOT. It defines the associations between file extensions and document types as well as the command strings for shell and Dynamic Data Exchange (DDE) or OLE actions.

HKEY_CLASSES_ROOT is identical in format to the Windows 3.1 registration database. The format is shown in Table 6–2.

**240**

**Table 6–2** Format of HKEY_CLASSES_ROOT

| Class Name | | | Class Description |
|---|---|---|---|
| protocol | | | |
| | StdFileEditing | | |
| | | server | Command line for opening application |
| | | handler | Path and file name for handler DLL |
| | | verb | Play or edit |
| shell | | | |
| | **open** | | |
| | | command | Command line for opening application |
| | | ddeexec | DDE command used when opening document |
| | | application | DDE app name for starting conversation |
| | | topic | Topic of the DDE conversation |
| | | ifexec | DDE command if initiate fails |
| | **print** | | |
| | | command | Command line for opening application |
| | | ddeexec | DDE command used when printing document |
| | | application | DDE app name for starting conversation |
| | | topic | Topic of the DDE conversation |
| | | ifexec | DDE command if initiate fails |

In Windows 95 and NT, the information in HKEY_CLASSES_ROOT is stored under HKEY_LOCAL_MACHINE\SOFTWARE\Classes. In other words, HKEY_CLASSES_ROOT is just an alias to HKEY_LOCAL_MACHINE \SOFTWARE\Classes. You can use the Registry Editor, an application that ships with both Windows 95 NT, to verify this fact. Figure 6–2 shows a screen shot of the Registry Editor with both HKEY_LOCAL_MACHINE \SOFTWARE\Classes and HKEY_CLASSES_ROOT displayed.

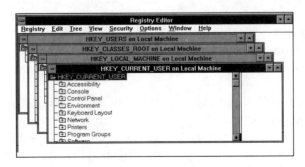

**Figure 6–2** Regedt32

241

## HKEY_LOCAL_MACHINE

HKEY_LOCAL_MACHINE is the root of where per-machine data is kept. The data stored here is always pertains to the local machine (hence the name). But, this does not mean that the configuration data is physically stored on the local machine. Both Windows 95 and Windows NT support the concept of the "Roving User". The roving user concept allows you to logon any machine on the network and see your same configuration on your home machine. This HKEY_LOCAL_MACHINE handle refers to a tree of keys and values that characterize the state of the local machine. It contains state information global to everyone who uses the machine.

There are five subkeys in HKEY_LOCAL_MACHINE:

1.  System.

    HKEY_LOCAL_MACHINE\system controls booting, driver loading, and run-time operating system behavior.

2.  Software.

    HKEY_LOCAL_MACHINE\software contains per-machine software data.

3.  Hardware.

    HKEY_LOCAL_MACHINE\hardware is strictly volatile and controls data about hardware and driver hardware use.

4.  Security.

    HKEY_LOCAL_MACHINE\SECURITY controls the security database (NT only).

5.  Security Account Manager (SAM). (NT Only)

    Remember that being the owner of an object does not automatically give you read-write access to the object. What you always have as the owner of an object is the right to change the security on the object. By always having this right, you can grant yourself access (Security Permissions menu) to the object and then access it.

System security, hardware, and software are all what is known as hives. A hive is a discrete body of keys, subkeys, and values that is rooted at the top of the registry hierarchy. For example, HKEY_LOCAL_MACHINE\Hardware is a volatile hive.) A hive is backed by a single file and log file. All hives appear at the same level in the registry name space. Only the information in the Software and System hives are read-write. The other keys are read-only. NOTE: You cannot add keys at this level.

The information in HKEY_CURRENT_USER overrides any information in HKEY_LOCAL_MACHINE. Therefore, whenever you have similar data in both HKEY_CURRENT_USER and HKEY_LOCAL_MACHINE, the data in HKEY_CURRENT_USER is the data you should use.

In addition to not supporting the Security and SAM branches, Windows 95 does not put any information into the hardware brance. Instead information about the current hardware is provided by the Chicago Plug and Play functions.

## CONTROL SETS TO MAKE SURE WINDOWS NT CAN BOOT

Earlier I stated that HKEY_LOCAL_MACHINE\System controls booting. The procedure is more complicated than it looks. The Registry uses a concept known as control sets to ensure that Windows NT is always capable of booting. A control set is stored as a subkey to HKEY_LOCAL_MACHINE\SYSTEM. There can be more than one control set and each contains all the pertinent information necessary to make Windows NT boot (like device drivers and such). The only subkey that is important to you is the CurrentControlSet subkey. When modifying system settings in the Registry, use the CurrentControlSet subkey. The CurrentControlSet subkey maps to one of the other control set subkeys, normally called ControlSet001, ControlSet002, or something like that.

To give you an idea how Windows NT ensures reliability when booting, I'll walk you through a typical installation problem. Let's take the example of the naive end-user who happens to notice some display drivers for NT up on an electronic BBS. To make our example seem more real, let's pretend that this user is a product manager for a software development company (no typical end-user would be this dumb). Mr. Product Manager decides to download the drivers and install them onto his system. Never mind that his display doesn't support the resolution of the drivers he's installing—he plunges ahead. After installing, he reboots and guess what happens? Windows NT boots anyway using the display drivers that were previously installed. Why? Because if there are any problems at boot time Windows NT reverts back to the last control set that booted NT successfully. The key HKEY_LOCAL_MACHINE\SYSTEM\Select\LastKnownGood value contains the last control set to successfully boot NT. If it contains 0x01, then the last known good control set is ControlSet001. If it contains 0x02, then the last known good control set is ControlSet002, and so on. This is helpful to know if you are developing software that is necessary to boot NT (like a device driver).

# INI FILE MAPPING

The recommended install location for Windows NT (if a user has installed Windows 3.1) is in the same directory as Windows 3.1. This fact presents a challenge to you if you want to maintain a common code base between your Win16 and Win32 code and take advantage of the Registry when running under Windows NT. A "common code base" means using functions such as ReadProfileString or WritePrivateProfileString, and these functions are ignorant of the Registry. To remedy this situation, NT supports the concept of IniFileMapping. The IniFileMapping information is stored in the Registry at:

```
HKEY_LOCAL_MACHINE\
    SOFTWARE\
    Microsoft\
    WindowsNT\
    Current Version\
    IniFileMapping.
```

To give you an idea of how this works, let's take the File Manager in NT as an example. In Windows 3.1, the File Manager stores configuration information in WINFILE.INI. The WINFILE.INI I have on my disk currently looks like this:

```
[Settings]
Window=0,0,648,488, , ,2
dir1=0,0,648,349,-1,-1,1,30,201,1814,357,C:\*.*
```

The INI file mapping for the File Manager is located at

```
HKEY_LOCAL_MACHINE\
Software\
```

```
Microsoft\
WindowsNT\
Current Version\
IniFileMapping\
winfile.ini.
```

The entries for my machine are the following:

```
Settings: REG_SZ: #USR:Software\Microsoft\File
                  Manager\Settings
AddOns: REG_SZ: SYS:Microsoft\Windows NT\CurrentVersion\File
                  Manager\AddOns
```

The entries break down like this:

```
Section:
Value type:
Key:
Subkey
```

In the case of the first entry, Settings corresponds to the section and REG_SZ indicates that the following is a string value. The string value #USR:Software\Microsoft\File Manager\Settings indicates that the actual values that a call to ReadPrivateProfileString returns are stored in HKEY_CURRENT_USER\Software\Microsoft\File Manager\Settings. The USR part of the string is shorthand for HKEY_CURRENT_USER. The pound sign prepended to USR means that the Registry set the values to be equal to what is in the Windows 3.1 INI file for each new user that uses the application for the first time.

Table 6–3 lists all of the shorthand variables available for IniFileMapping. The first time a user executes the Win32 File Manager, its default settings will automatically equal the Win16 File Manager's settings. This means that the actual WINFILE.INI file is used by the Windows 3.1 version of the File Manager only. The Win32 version uses the Registry. Through the magic of IniFileMapping, any calls made by the Win32 version of File Manager will be intercepted and routed to the Registry. This is convenient because you need not use the Registry APIs to add the AddOns entry.

**Table 6–3** INI File-Mapping Characters

| Character | Action |
| --- | --- |
| USR: | Shorthand for HKEY_CURRENT_USER |
| | For example, USR:Software\Microsoft\File Manager expands to HKEY_CURRENT_USER\Software\ Microsoft\File Manager. |
| SYS: | Shorthand for HKEY_LOCAL_MACHINE\Software. For example SYS:Microsoft\Windows NT\CurrentVersion\File Manager\AddOns expands to HKEY_LOCAL_MACHINE\Software\ Microsoft\WindowsNT\CurrentVersion\ File Manager\AddOns. |
| # | Use this character to force the Registry value to be set to the value in the Windows 3.1 INI file for each new user that uses the application for the first time. |
| ! | Prepending this character to either USR: or SYS: forces all profile writes to go both to the Registry and to the .INI file on disk. |
| @ | If the requested data is not found in the Registry, this character instructs profile reads to return failure (instead of reading the corresponding INI file). Use this when you have a configuration option that is only available in one operating system, but not the other. |

Thanks to IniFileMapping, any Profile API calls directed to WINFILE.INI automatically get mapped to the Registry. Thus the code

```
WritePrivateProfileString("AddOns","File Manager Extension",
                    "my_fmext.dll","winfile.ini");
```

will end up in Microsoft\Windows NT\CurrentVersion\File Manager\AddOns instead of the WINFILE.INI file.

To use IniFileMapping under NT, create a subkey of HKEY_LOCAL_MACHINE\

```
SOFTWARE\
Microsoft\
Windows NT\
CurrentVersion\
IniFileMapping
```

with the name of your INI file. Each time you write to your INI file with APIs like WritePrivateProfileString under NT, the writes go to the Registry instead. If your application runs under Windows 3.1, your WritePrivateProfileString calls do the usual thing and write to the actual INI file—all transparent to your application. The only thing you need to do different is to determine if you are running under Windows 3.1 or NT, and if you are running under NT, add the correct subkey to IniFileMapping. The rest of your code doesn't need to change.

Under NT, the files WIN.INI, SYSTEM.INI, CONTROL.INI, and WINFILE.INI are all mapped to the Registry. There is one case where IniFileMapping doesn't work the way you would expect it to. That is the case where you are using GetPrivateProfileString to determine what program is the shell (In NT, the default is the Program Manager):

```
GetPrivateProfileString("boot", "shell", "", szBuffer,
                        sizeof(szBuffer),"system.ini");
```

All reads and writes to the boot section of SYSTEM.INI are INI file-mapped to :

```
HKEY_LOCAL_MACHINE\
    SOFTWARE\
    MICROSOFT\
    Windows NT\
    Current Version\
    WOW\
    Boot\
    Shell
```

This means that you cannot change the shell using WritePrivateProfileString. You must use the Registry APIs. "Typical Things to Extract from the Registry" at the end of this chapter discusses the shell in more detail.

Windows 95 does not support INI File Mapping. Most likely Windows 3.1 users will be upgrading to Windows 95 not running along side it.

# SETTING YOUR ENVIRONMENT VARIABLES

One of the biggest pains in getting a Windows 3.1 application properly installed and configured is making sure you have your environment variables properly set. To make matters worse, in Windows 3.1 the PATH environment variable can only be 128 bytes long. This restriction is removed in both Windows 95 and NT, but it is still a pain to set environment variables. The Win32 SDK setup program does things a little differently depending on whether or not you are an administrator when you install. Both Windows 95 and NT have the concept of user-specific environment variables and system-wide environment variables.

User environment variables are stored in the following Registry key:

```
HKEY_CURRENT_USER\
Environment
```

System environment variables are stored in the following Registry key:

```
HKEY_LOCAL_MACHINE\
SYSTEM\
CurrentControlSet\
Control\
Session Manager\
Environment
```

The reason I say it's a pain is because you must force the user to log off and then back on again for the changes to take effect. Win32 has a function called RegNotifyChangeKeyValue that will do this, but according to \sdk\docs\win32api.csv, Windows 95 will not implement this API. You can broadcast a WM_WININICHANGE to shell applications (or any windows that process this message) to make them aware of the change, but any already-running process that doesn't process this message will be ignorant of the new environment variables.

Here's how to send a WM_WININICHANGE message to all top-level windows:

```
SendMessage( HWND_BROADCAST, WM_WININICHANGE,
             OL, (LPARAM) "Environment" );
```

# HOW TO STRUCTURE YOUR APPLICATION'S DATA

Applications manipulate key trees. At installation time an application should adjust HKEY_CLASSES_ROOT to define the documents that it handles together with their file extensions and its shell and DDE or OLE command strings. At the same time it needs to add information global to all users to the HKEY_USERS\DEFAULT key.

Subsequently, you store per-user information in the HKEY_CURRENT_USER subtree. That information will include preferences as well as historical information such as lists of recently opened files. Store the following in the Registry:

▪▪  Per user and per-machine data, each in its own place.

▪▪  Small data. Store this directly in the Registry. Refer to large data with file names and the like in the Registry.

▪▪  Any and all data which is fundamentally configuration data that you want to keep from session to session, such as user preferences.

Text should be Unicode. Use binary data where appropriate.

Do not store the following in the Registry:

▪▪  Things that belong in files. Use the file system to store the object and have the registry point to it.

▪▪  Executable images. A user's profile could end up on many machines, of varying CPU types.

▪▪  Duplicates of medium-sized objects over and over. Store them once and refer to them instead.

▪▪  Data that is not configuration data in the Registry. Use the Registry to point to it instead.

Use a key anywhere you need unique access rights. Consider grouping related quantities into small structures that are assigned to value entries. Do this to control the number of value entries. The Type field is arbitrary. Values below 0xf7777777 are intended for System use.

You are encouraged to use and conform to standard types, but the system does not interpret this field, so you may use arbitrary values. (Exception: RegQueryValue performs an ExpandSz on REG_EXPAND_SZ fields, so use RegQueryValueEx to avoid this.) Some tools will use the Type field. Be sure to use and conform to standard types if you depend on such tools.

Divide data into per-machine and per-user. Per-machine data goes in:

```
HKEY_LOCAL_MACHINE\
Software\Description\
company\
product\
version\
```

where company is the name of your company, product is the name of your product, and version is a name or number.

For example, Microsoft normally uses one of two conventions:

```
HKEY_LOCAL_MACHINE\Software\Microsoft\(product)\CurrentVersion
```

or just

```
HKEY_LOCAL_MACHINE\Software\Microsoft\(product)\
```

Either way, this information should be written at setup-install time.

The format of per-user data is similar except it goes in

```
HKEY_CURRENT_USER\
Software\
Description\
company\
product\
version\
```

Per-user data must be written at run time because it may not be the right profile at the setup install time .

# PROGRAMMING THE REGISTRY

Okay, now that you know where everything goes, this next section shows you how to read and write data programmatically via the new Win32 API functions.

Before you can access any information in the Registry you must obtain a handle to a key, which will be either a subkey of one of the four predefined handles (HKEY_CLASSES_ROOT, HKEY_CURRENT_USER, HKEY_USERS, and HKEY_LOCAL_MACHINE) or a subkey from a previously opened handle. To obtain a handle call RegOpenKeyEx:

```
LONG
RegOpenKeyEx(HKEY hkey,          // handle of open key
          LPCTSTR lpszSubKey,    //subkey to open
          DWORD dwReserved,      // reserved
          REGSAM samDesired,     // access mask
          PHKEY phkResult);      //handle for open key
```

For example, to retrieve a handle to HKEY_LOCAL_MACHINE\ SOFTWARE\Microsoft, call RegOpenKeyEx this way:

```
HANDLE hKeyMicrosoft;
RegOpenKeyEx(HKEY_LOCAL_MACHINE,
          SOFTWARE\\Microsoft,
          0,
          KEY_ALL_ACCESS,
          &hKeyMicrosoft);
```

The first parameter is for the open handle. The second parameter is for the subkey to open. The fourth parameter, samDesired, is for the security access mask. It can be any combinations of the constants in Table 6–4.

**Table 6–4** REGSAM Constants

| Constant | Purpose |
| --- | --- |
| KEY_ALL_ACCESS | Combination of KEY_QUERY_VALUE, KEY_ENUMERATE_SUB_KEYS, KEY_NOTIFY, KEY_CREATE_SUB_KEY, EY_CREATE_LINK, and KEY_SET_VALUE access. |
| KEY_CREATE_LINK | Permission to create a symbolic link. |

**Table 6–4** (continued)

| Constant | Purpose |
| --- | --- |
| KEY_CREATE_SUB_KEY | Permission to create subkeys. |
| KEY_ENUMERATE_SUB_KEYS | Permission to enumerate subkeys. |
| KEY_EXECUTE | Permission for read access. |
| KEY_NOTIFY | Permission for change notification. |
| KEY_QUERY_VALUE | Permission to query subkey data. |
| KEY_READ | Combination of KEY_QUERY_VALUE, KEY_ENUMERATE_SUB_KEYS, and KEY_NOTIFY access. |
| KEY_SET_VALUE | Permission to set subkey data. |
| KEY_WRITE | Combination of KEY_SET_VALUE and KEY_CREATE_SUB_KEY access. |

Another method to use to open a key is to call RegCreateKeyEx:

```
LONG
RegCreateKeyEx(HKEY hkey,                // open key
          LPCTSTR lpszSubKey,            // address of subkey name
          DWORD dwReserved,              // reserved
          LPTSTR lpszClass,              // class string
          DWORD fdwOptions,              // special options flag
          REGSAM samDesired,             //security access
          LPSECURITY_ATTRIBUTES lpSecurityAttributes,
          PHKEY phkResult,               // buffer for handle
          LPDWORD lpdwDisposition);      // disposition
                                         // value buffer
```

If the key specified in parameter two, lpszSubKey, doesn't exist, then RegCreateKeyEx will create it. The last parameter, dwDisp, returns the disposition of the key. The disposition is one of two values:

■■ REG_CREATED_NEW_KEY

　　The key was created successfully.

■■ REG_OPENED_EXISTING_KEY

　　The handle returned is to a key that already existed.

The following is an example of calling RegCreateKeyEx and checking the disposition:

```
if (RegCreateKeyEx(HKEY_LOCAL_MACHINE,
                   szBuf,
                   0,
                   NULL,
                   REG_OPTION_NON_VOLATILE,
                   KEY_QUERY_VALUE | KEY_SET_VALUE,
                   NULL,
                   &hk,
                   &dwDisp))
{
    return TRUE;
}

if (dwDisp == REG_OPENED_EXISTING_KEY)
{
    RegCloseKey(hk);
    return FALSE;
}
```

The fifth parameter, fdwOptions, indicates whether the key is volatile or not. The parameter can be one of the following values:

▪▪ REG_OPTION_VOLATILE

Use this option when the information to store does not need to be saved when the system is shut down or rebooted.

▪▪ REG_OPTION_NON_VOLATILE

Use this option when the information to store must be preserved between reboots.

No matter how you get an open handle, use RegCloseKey to close the key:

```
LONG RegCloseKey(HKEY hkey);      // handle of key to close
```

RegCloseKey does not perform a flush, so if you want your key explicitly committed to disk, call RegFlushKey:

```
LONG RegFlushKey(HKEY hkey);      // handle of key to flush
```

## QUERYING THE REGISTRY

Once you have the proper handle, you read information from the Registry by calling one of the query functions. Which function you call next depends upon whether you know the exact key and value you want to obtain or not. If you do know, call RegQueryValueEx:

```
LONG
RegQueryValueEx(HKEY hkey,           // handle of key to query
            LPTSTR lpszValueName,    // name to query
            LPDWORD lpdwReserved,    // reserved
            LPDWORD lpdwType,        // buffer for value type
            LPBYTE lpbData,          // data buffer
            LPDWORD lpcbData);       // data buffer size
```

RegQueryValueEx supersedes RegQueryValue and is the function you use to retrieve your data from the Registry.

The following example retrieves the boolean value, fSaveOnExit, from the Registry location:

```
HKEY_CURRENT_USER\
    SOFTWARE\
    "Digital DataWhack"\
    BugWhacker\
    CurrentVersion
lResult= RegOpenKeyEx(HKEY_CURRENT_USER, szPathBuffer, 0,
                KEY_READ,&hkGlobal);

if (lResult == ERROR_SUCCESS)
{
    cbData= sizeof(fSaveOnExit);
    RegQueryValueEx(hkGlobal, "SaveFlag", 0,
                &dwType, (LPBYTE) &fSaveOnExit,
                &cbData);
}
```

However, the real power of RegQueryValueEx is in its ability to query the size and type of the data. In the previous example, fSaveOnExit is a boolean value and you know its size is going to be sizeof(fSaveOnExit). However, for the case of REG_SZ or REG_MULTI_SZ, what you can do is call RegQueryValueEx twice—once to get the size of the value, then once to obtain it's value. This next example shows what I mean:

```
cbData= 0;

lResult= RegQueryValueEx(hkPerUser, LAST_FILE_SET, NULL,
                    &dwType, NULL, &cbData);

if (lResult != ERROR_SUCCESS || dwType  != REG_MULTI_SZ)
return FALSE;

pszFileList= (PSZ) _alloca(cbData);

if (!pszFileList) return FALSE;

lResult = RegQueryValueEx(hkPerUser, LAST_FILE_SET, NULL,
                    &dwType,(LPBYTE) pszFileList,
                    &cbData);

if (lResult != ERROR_SUCCESS)
    return FALSE;
```

The last parameter RegQueryValueEx, cbData, specifies the size in bytes of the information pointed to by the lpbData parameter. If the data is of type REG_SZ, REG_EXPAND_SZ, or REG_MULTI_SZ, cbData must include the size of the terminating NULL character.

To get detailed information on a specific subkey, call RegQueryInfoKey:

```
// Get Class name, Value count.
RegQueryInfoKey (hKey,          // Key handle.
                ClassName,      // Buffer for class name.
                &dwcClassLen,   // Length of class string.
```

```
            NULL,              // Reserved.
            &dwcSubKeys,       // Number of subkeys.
            &dwcMaxSubKey,     // Longest subkey size.
            &dwcMaxClass,      // Longest class string.
            &dwcValues,        // Number of values for key.
            &dwcMaxValueName,    // Longest Value name.
            &dwcMaxValueData,    // Longest Value data.
            &dwcSecDesc,         // Security descriptor.
            &ftLastWriteTime);   // Last write time
```

RegQueryInfoKey retrieves data that will help you in setting up buffer sizes and such. Besides returning the longest buffer size for subkey, class, value name, and data, it also retrieves the security descriptor and the time stamp for the key.

## ENUMERATING KEYS AND VALUES

If you are looking in no particular order or you are writing an application that displays all the available subkeys and values, use the RegEnumKeyEx and RegEnumValue functions to iterate through all the keys and value names. An example of this is REGEDT32.EXE, which ships with the SDK.

To enumerate subkeys, call RegEnumKeyEx. This function enumerates all of the subkeys of the first parameter, hkey, and returns the class of the subkey in the lpszClass parameter:

```
LONG
RegEnumKeyEx(HKEY hkey,          // handle of key to enumerate
           DWORD iSubkey,        // index of subkey to enumerate
           LPTSTR lpszName,      // buffer for subkey name
           LPDWORD lpcchName,    // size of subkey buffer
           LPDWORD lpdwReserved, // reserved
           LPTSTR lpszClass,     // buffer for class string
           LPDWORD lpcchClass,   // size of class buffer
           PFILETIME lpftLastWrite);   // time stamp
```

Once you have a particular subkey, call RegEnumValue to retrieve all the values for that subkey:

```
LONG
RegEnumValue(HKEY hkey,
        DWORD iValue,          // index of value to query
        LPTSTR lpszValue,      // buffer for value string
        LPDWORD lpcchValue,    // size of value buffer
        LPDWORD lpdwReserved,   // reserved
        LPDWORD lpdwType,      // buffer for type code
        LPBYTE lpbData,        // buffer for value data
        LPDWORD lpcbData);     // size of data buffer
```

## WRITING TO THE REGISTRY

Use RegSetValueEx to store data in an open Registry key:

```
LONG
RegSetValueEx(HKEY hkey,          // key to set value for
        LPCTSTR lpszValueName,    // value to set
        DWORD dwReserved,         // reserved- NULL
        DWORD fdwType,            // value type
        CONST BYTE * lpbData,     // value data
        DWORD cbData);            // size of value data
```

## SECURING REGISTRY ENTRIES

There are two ways to secure Registry entries in Windows NT (remember, Windows 95 doesn't support security). You can create the key with a security descriptor or you can add ACEs to an existing DACL. To retrieve a key's security descriptor, an application can use the RegGetKeySecurity function.

The RegSetKeySecurity function sets the security of an open registry key:

```
LONG
RegSetKeySecurity(HKEY hkey,                  // open handle of key to set
            SECURITY_INFORMATION si,    // descriptor contents
            PSECURITY_DESCRIPTOR psd);  // address of descriptor
    to for key
```

## SAVING AND RESTORING THE REGISTRY FROM A DISK FILE

At times you need to take your configuration with you. Perhaps you are upgrading to a new machine, or you are putting your development environment onto a second machine. In Windows 3.1, this requires cutting out pieces of WIN.INI, SYSTEM.INI, CONFIG.SYS, and AUTOEXEC.BAT, and then pasting them into the files in the new system. In NT only, you can use the RegSaveKey function to save a given key, its subkeys, and their values into a file:

```
LONG
RegSaveKey(HKEY hkey,          // handle of key to save
           LPCTSTR lpszFile,            // filename
           LPSECURITY_ATTRIBUTES lpsa);   // security
```

The first parameter, hkey, is any currently open key. The filename is the name on disk where the Registry information will be stored:

```
//
// Save HKEY_CURRENT_USER Key
//
lTest = RegSaveKey(HKEY_CURRENT_USER, "User.reg", NULL);
if (lTest != ERROR_SUCCESS)
    return lTest;
```

To restore a key from a file, call RegRestoreKey.

The RegRestoreKey function reads the registry information in a specified file and copies it over the specified key. This registry information may be in the form of a key and multiple levels of subkeys:

```
LONG
RegRestoreKey(HKEY hkey,       // handle of key to restore
           LPCTSTR lpszFile,   // filename of saved tree
           DWORD fdw);         // volatile flag
```

RegRestoreKey writes the key and its subkeys to the Registry, overwriting the previous information stored at that key.

If the key that you want to restore already exists and you do not want to permanently overwrite that information, you can call RegLoadKey instead:

```
LONG
RegLoadKey(HKEY hkey,
          LPCTSTR lpszSubKey,  // name of subkey
          LPCTSTR lpszFile);   // filename
```

RegLoadKey writes a key and its subkeys to the Registry from a file, but it also saves the existing information in the same file that you specified in parameter three, lpszFile.

When finished, you call RegUnLoadKey to restore the registry to its previous state:

```
LONG
RegUnLoadKey(HKEY hkey,
             LPCTSTR lpszSubKey);   // subkey to unload
```

## CONNECTING TO A REMOTE MACHINE

There is one instance in which you must open a handle to one of the predefined handles:

```
LONG
RegConnectRegistry(LPTSTR lpszComputerName,   // remote
                                              // computer
                   HKEY hkey,
                   PHKEY phkResult);   // buffer for remote
                                       // registry handle
```

RegConnectRegistry is a Windows NT only function call. It enables you to connect to a remote computer and query or set information with the HKEY_LOCAL_MACHINE or HKEY_USERS handles. When you are finished with the handle, you must call RegCloseKey to close the handle.

## UNINSTALLING THE SDK

A lot has been written in various publications about how to install your software, but I rarely see advice or recommendations to developers to include a uninstall program—that is a program to remove the contents of your software from a user's machine. It's a pain to try to uninstall software by hand. Deleting the directory the software is in is no problem (especially with the del /s command), but deleting DLLs out of the system directory and removing items from the Registry is usually beyond the abilities of the everyday user.

There are three steps that I can think of to uninstall the SDK: delete the program groups and del /s mstools, and remove the subdirectories from the environment variables using regedt32 under

```
HKEY_LOCAL_MACHINE\
SYSTEM\
CurrentControlSet\
Control\
Session Manager\
Environment
```

To delete a value from a key, use the RegDeleteValue:

```
LONG
RegDeleteValue(HKEY hkey,          // handle of key
               LPTSTR lpszValue);  // value name to delete
```

To delete a key, use the RegDeleteKey function:

```
LONG
RegDeleteKey(HKEY hkey,             // handle of key
             LPCTSTR lpszSubKey);   // subkey to delete
```

Deleted keys do not go away until the last handle is closed. You cannot delete again or create child keys under a value entry under or delete or use a value entry under a deleted key.

You have to know something about how the application was installed in order to be able to delete it. You have to know what changes were made to the registry, what registry keys were added, what directories were created, what DLLs were installed in the \winnt\system32 or \windows\system directories, and what program groups were created. This data will vary from application to application.

Now that you know the Registry exists, you may be tempted to explore the Registry to try and get a feel for where things are kept. This is a good idea. "Typical Things to Extract from the Registry" at the end of this chapter lists several of the more common items. However, don't be any more clever than you have to be. If there is a defined API for extracting information, use it. For example, if you want to know the directory where NT is installed, call GetWindowsDirectory or GetSystemDirectory, which act identical to their Win16 counterparts. You will drive yourself crazy trying to determine which key in the Registry holds the values you want. Besides, it makes maintaining code that is compatible with Windows 3.1 or Win32s difficult.

Another example is the mouse double-click speed. Sure, you could call RegQueryValueEx on

```
HKEY_CURRENT_USER\
Control Panel\
Mouse\
DoubleClickSpeed
```

but instead use

```
GetProfileString("windows","DoubleClickSpeed","500",
                 szBuffer, &cb);
```

Under Windows 3.1, you get what is in WIN.INI, but under Windows NT, via the magic of IniFileMapping, you will get what is stored in the Registry.

## PERFORMANCE DATA

Combined with your knowledge about your code, raw performance data can give you valuable information about the efficiency of your application. This information can help you with bottleneck detection and with capacity planning. For example, what type of resources is your application consuming? How long does it take to perform a particular operation? In Windows NT, you use the Registry to obtain this type of information. This is a departure from Windows 3.1 which doesn't really have an effective method of performance monitoring.

**261**

Windows 3.1 supports profiling with a set of eight Win16 functions that are now obsolete. These functions are:

ProfClear

ProfFlush

ProfInsChk

ProfSampRate

ProfSetup

ProfFinish

ProfStart

ProfStop

Windows NT also supports profiling, but the performance-monitoring method doesn't require you to make changes to your source in order for it to work.

Even if you don't specifically care about improving the performance of your application, accessing the performance data through the Registry is the only way to obtain basic system-related information. I'm referring to items such as the list of processes currently executing in the system and a list of threads that each process owns. This next section presents you with an overview of how to retrieve performance data, as well as sample code to determine a list of currently executing processes.

Performance data isn't physically stored in the Registry—the Registry is just a common collecting point. At runtime, the Registry queries several system objects to make performance data available to you. Because many different types of systems (installed for various languages) query for performance data, the data must be presented in a system- and language-independent fashion. To see how this works, let's examine how the data is returned from the Registry.

The first thing you do is call RegQueryValueEx with the predefined handle HKEY_PERFORMANCE_DATA and the subkey "Global". Since there is no way to know ahead of time how big the buffer is, you must be sure to check for an error code returning from RegQueryValueEx. If the error is ERROR_MORE_DATA, you'll have to reallocate your buffer and make the call again. Here is an example:

```
{

DWORD dwBuf
```

```
SYSTEM_INFO si
DWORD dwPerfDataLen;
GetSystemInfo(&si);
dwPerfDataLen = si.dwPageSize;

PPERF_DATA_BLOCK pPerfData = (PPERF_DATA_BLOCK) malloc (dwPerfDataLen);
if (pPerfData == NULL)
     return FALSE;

while (RegQueryValueEx (HKEY_PERFORMANCE_DATA, (LPTSTR) "Global", NULL,
              NULL, (LPBYTE) pPerfData, &dwBuf) == ERROR_MORE_DATA)
    {

        free (pPerfData);

        dwPerfDataLen += si.dwPageSize;

        pPerfData = (PPERF_DATA_BLOCK) malloc (dwPerfDataLen);
        if (!pPerfData)
            return FALSE;
        else
          {
          if (pPerfData->Signature[0] == (WCHAR)'P') &&
              (pPerfData->Signature[1] == (WCHAR)'E') &&
              (pPerfData->Signature[2] == (WCHAR)'R') &&
              (pPerfData->Signature[3] == (WCHAR)'F')))
              return TRUE;
          else
              return FALSE;
          }
      }
  }
```

There is no need to RegOpenKey the reserved handle
HKEY_PERFORMANCE_DATA, but you should RegCloseKey the handle
when you are finished in case network transports and drivers need to be
removed or installed. (This cannot happen while they are open for
monitoring.) The data that RegQueryValueEx returns is in the form of several

structures that show the counters that are available. The data is broken down into three basic categories: performance objects, performance instances, and performance counters.

- ■■ Performance Objects: Performance data objects are measurable items such as processes, threads and synchronization objects.

- ■■ Performance Instances: Instances refer to an individual object type in a class, such as a specific process or thread.

- ■■ Performance Counters: Represent a method of incrementing. All instances of a given type have identical performance counters.

This next section describes each of them. The returned data begins with a PERF_DATA_BLOCK structure (see Listing 6–1). Immediately following the PERF_DATA_BLOCK structure is NumObjectTypes of data sections, one for each type of object measured. Each object type section begins with a PERF_OBJECT_TYPE structure (see Listing 6–2). Figure 6–3 displays the logic behind the buffer returned by RegQueryValueEx.

```
1) PERF_DATA_BLOCK
    2) PERF_OBJECT_TYPE (NumObjectTypes many)
    {
        3) PERF_COUNTER_DEF (One or more times)
        {
            if only one instance
            {
                    PERF_COUNTER_BLOCK
                    counter data
            }
            else
            {
                    PERF_INSTANCE_DEF
                    PERF_COUNTER_BLOCK
                    counter data
            }
        } // end of 3
    } // end of 2
```

**Figure 6–3** The definition of the RegQueryValueEx buffer

**Listing 6–1** PERF_DATA_BLOCK structure

```
typedef struct _PERF_DATA_BLOCK {
    WCHAR       Signature[4];      // Signature: Unicode "PERF"
    DWORD       LittleEndian;      // 0 = Big Endian, 1 = Little Endian
    DWORD       Version;           // Version of these data structures
                                   // starting at 1
    DWORD       Revision;          // Revision of these data structures
                                   // starting at 0 for each Version
    DWORD       TotalByteLength;   // Total length of data block
    DWORD       HeaderLength;      // Length of this structure
    DWORD       NumObjectTypes;    // Number of types of objects
                                   // being reported
    LONG        DefaultObject;     // Object Title Index of default
                                   // object to display when data from
                                   // this system is retrieved (-1 =
                                   // none, but this is not expected to
                                   // be used)
    SYSTEMTIME      SystemTime;    // Time at the system under
                                   // measurement
    LARGE_INTEGER PerfTime;        // Performance counter value
                                   // at the system under measurement
    LARGE_INTEGER PerfFreq;        // Performance counter frequency
                                   // at the system under measurement
    LARGE_INTEGER PerfTime100nSec;  // Performance counter time in 100
nsec
                                   // units at the system under
measurement
    DWORD       SystemNameLength;  // Length of the system name
    DWORD       SystemNameOffset;  // Offset, from beginning of this
                                   // structure, to name of system
                                   // being measured
} PERF_DATA_BLOCK, *PPERF_DATA_BLOCK;
```

**Listing 6–2** PERF_OBJECT_TYPE structure from WINPERF.H

```
typedef struct _PERF_OBJECT_TYPE {
    DWORD       TotalByteLength;   // Length of this object definition
                                   // including this structure, the
                                   // counter definitions, and the
```

```
                            // instance definitions and the
                            // counter blocks for each instance:
                            // This is the offset from this
                            // structure to the next object, if
                            // any
  DWORD      DefinitionLength;   // Length of object definition,
                            // which includes this structure
                            // and the counter definition
                            // structures for this object: this
                            // is the offset of the first
                            // instance or of the counters
                            // for this object if there is
                            // no instance
  DWORD      HeaderLength;       // Length of this structure: this
                            // is the offset to the first
                            // counter definition for this
                            // object
  DWORD      ObjectNameTitleIndex;
                            // Index to name in Title Database
  LPWSTR     ObjectNameTitle;    // Initially NULL, for use by
                            // analysis program to point to
                            // retrieved title string
  DWORD      ObjectHelpTitleIndex;
                            // Index to Help in Title Database
  LPWSTR     ObjectHelpTitle;    // Initially NULL, for use by
                            // analysis program to point to
                            // retrieved title string
  DWORD      DetailLevel;        // Object level of detail (for
                            // controlling display complexity);
                            // will be min of detail levels
                            // for all this object's counters
  DWORD      NumCounters;        // Number of counters in each
                            // counter block (one counter
                            // block per instance)
  LONG       DefaultCounter;     // Default counter to display when
                            // this object is selected, index
                            // starting at 0 (-1 = none, but
                            // this is not expected to be used)
```

```
    LONG       NumInstances;        // Number of object instances
                                    // for which counters are being
                                    // returned from the system under
                                    // measurement. If the object defined
                                    // will never have any instance data
                                    // structures
(PERF_INSTANCE_DEFINITION)

                                    // then this value should be -1, if the
                                    // object can have 0 or more instances,
                                    // but has none present, then this
                                    // should be 0, otherwise this field
                                    // contains the number of instances of
                                    // this counter.
    DWORD      CodePage;            // 0 if instance strings are in
                                    // UNICODE, else the Code Page of
                                    // the instance names
    LARGE_INTEGER  PerfTime;        // Sample Time in "Object" units
                                    //
    LARGE_INTEGER  PerfFreq;        // Frequency of "Object" units in
                                    // counts per second.
} PERF_OBJECT_TYPE, *PPERF_OBJECT_TYPE;
```

The data sections are made up of an PERF_OBJECT_TYPE, followed by one or more PERF_COUNTER_DEFINITIONs, followed by the data for the counters. After the definitions for the counters for the object types are the instances for that object type. For example, there are normally multiple instances of the object type process. However, it is possible for a counter to have no instance definitions if that counter has only one occurrence.

However, if the counters have more than one instance, then after each instance definition is the counter data for that instance. Here is where the actual data for each counter defined for the object type of which the instance is a member is stored. PERF_OBJECT_TYPE. NumCounters is equal to the number of counter for each instance.

The size of the various instance definitions is not constant, since each instance-definition structure is followed by the null-terminated name of the instance (zero-padded to a DWORD boundary). Therefore, the instance definition contains an offset to its first counter data item, and also to its name.

### GETTING COUNTER DATA

To understand how to get the counter data, you will need four pointers:

- ■■ A pointer to a PPERF_INSTANCE_DEFINITION
- ■■ A pointer to a PPERF_COUNTER_DEFINITION
- ■■ A pointer to a PPERF_OBJECT_TYPE
- ■■ A pointer to a PPERF_COUNTER_BLOCK

The counter data is offset PPERF_COUNTER_DEFINITION.CounterOffset bytes from the CounterBlock. To get a pointer to the counter block use the following algorithm: If the PPERF_INSTANCE_DEFINITION is not NULL, then the CounterBlock is offset PPERF_INSTANCE_DEFINITION.ByteLength bytes from the PPERF_INSTANCE_DEFINITION block. Otherwise, if the PPERF_INSTANCE_DEFINTION is NULL, then the CounterBlock is offset PPERF_OBJECT_TYPE. DefinitionLength bytes from the PPERF_OBJECT_TYPE block.

Once your retrieve the CounterBlock, here's how to retrieve the counter data:

```
PVOID GetCounterData ()
{
PPERF_COUNTER_BLOCK pCounterBlock = (PPERF_COUNTER_BLOCK)
                                            GetCounterBlock();

return (PVOID)((PCHAR)pCounterBlock + m_pCounter->CounterOffset);
}
```

# SAMPLE PROGRAM: THE REGISTRAR

If all of these structures have you wishing you had saved some of those brain cells you burned off by partying too much in college, don't worry. To show you how this all works, I've put together a sample program called the Registrar that displays the name and process ID of the currently executing processes. See Listing 6–3 which contains registry.cpp and registry.h. The Registrar has an added treat: it encapsulates all of the performance data in a CPerf class, which is derived from CRegistry, which encapsulates many of the Registry functions.

**Listing 6–3** Source for the CPerf and CRegistry classes

```
///////////////////////////////////////////////////////////////////////////
//
//
// Registry.h : Defines the class behaviors
// KJG
//
//
///////////////////////////////////////////////////////////////////////////
#ifndef __REGISTRY_H__
#define __REGISTRY_H__

#include <winperf.h>



#define  PROCESS 230
#define  PROCESSID 784



class CRegistry
{
public:

HKEY m_hKey;


CRegistry(HKEY hKey);


long RegSet(LPSTR sSubKey, BOOL fValue, DWORD cbValue);

long RegSet(LPSTR sSubKey, DWORD dwValue, DWORD cbdata);

long RegSet(LPSTR sSubKey, LPSTR sValue,  DWORD cbValue, DWORD fdwType);
```

```
long RegQuery( LPSTR sSubKey, BOOL *fValue, BOOL fAdd);

long RegQuery(LPSTR sSubKey, DWORD *dwValue);

long RegQuery(LPSTR sSubKey, char *szValue, DWORD *cbdata);
};


class CPerfRegistry :  public CRegistry
  {

    PPERF_DATA_BLOCK m_pPerfData;
    PPERF_OBJECT_TYPE m_pObject;
    PPERF_COUNTER_DEFINITION m_pCounter;
    PPERF_INSTANCE_DEFINITION m_pInstance;
    public:

      CPerfRegistry();
      ~CPerfRegistry();

      void FirstObject(){m_pObject = (PPERF_OBJECT_TYPE)((PCHAR)m_pPerfData +
                                    m_pPerfData->HeaderLength);}
      void NextObject(){m_pObject =  (PPERF_OBJECT_TYPE)((PBYTE) m_pObject +
                                    m_pObject->TotalByteLength);}


      void FirstCounter()
                    {m_pCounter =
                    (PPERF_COUNTER_DEFINITION)((PCHAR) m_pObject +
                    m_pObject->HeaderLength);}
      void NextCounter()
                    {m_pCounter =
                    (PPERF_COUNTER_DEFINITION)((PCHAR) m_pCounter +
                    m_pCounter->ByteLength);}

      void FirstInstance()
                    {m_pInstance =
                    (PPERF_INSTANCE_DEFINITION)((PCHAR) m_pObject +
                    m_pObject->DefinitionLength);}
```

```
        PCHAR GetCounterBlock()
                {return ((PCHAR) m_pInstance + m_pInstance->ByteLength);}

        void NextInstance()
                {
                PPERF_COUNTER_BLOCK pCounterBlock =
                (PPERF_COUNTER_BLOCK)((PCHAR) m_pInstance +
                m_pInstance->ByteLength);
        m_pInstance = (PPERF_INSTANCE_DEFINITION)((PCHAR) pCounterBlock +
                        pCounterBlock->ByteLength);
        }




LPWSTR InstanceName(LPWSTR lpwInstanceName)
{
        return (lpwInstanceName = (LPWSTR)((PCHAR)m_pInstance +
                                        m_pInstance->NameOffset));
}




LPSTR InstanceName(LPSTR lpInstanceName)
{
        WCHAR *lpwInstanceName = InstanceName(lpwInstanceName);

         //
        // Name is in Unicode. Convert to Ascii
        //


        wcstombs(lpInstanceName, (const WCHAR *) lpwInstanceName,
            m_pInstance->NameLength / sizeof(WCHAR));

        return lpInstanceName;

}



DWORD NumObjectTypes(){return m_pPerfData->NumObjectTypes;}
DWORD NumInstances(){return m_pObject->NumInstances;}
```

**271**

```
BOOL FindObject (DWORD TitleIndex)
{

DWORD i = 0;

    if (!m_pObject)
            FirstObject();

    while (i < m_pPerfData->NumObjectTypes)
        {
        if (m_pObject->ObjectNameTitleIndex == TitleIndex)
            return TRUE;

        NextObject();
        i++;
        }

    return FALSE;
}




//
//
//
//  FindCounter
//
//      Find a counter specified by dwTitleIndex.
//
//

BOOL
FindCounter (DWORD dwTitleIndex)
{
DWORD i = 0;

    FirstCounter();
    while (i < m_pObject->NumCounters)
        {
```

```
            if (m_pCounter->CounterNameTitleIndex == dwTitleIndex)
                return TRUE;

            NextCounter();
            i++;
            }

        return FALSE;

    }

    PVOID GetCounterData ()
    {
    PPERF_COUNTER_BLOCK pCounterBlock = (PPERF_COUNTER_BLOCK) GetCounterBlock();
        return (PVOID)((PCHAR)pCounterBlock + m_pCounter->CounterOffset);

    }

    };
    #endif
```

## SUMMARY

The Registry provides consistent storage and a defined API for storing and retrieving a variety of configuration information. The APIs allow you to programmatically view, update, or modify configuration data.

However, not every piece of data is within easy reach of the Registry. I wish Microsoft had included an easier way to get a list of the user groups on the current machine and a way to determine which users are in those groups. This information is essential when you want to build a list of all the groups to which a user belongs. Unfortunately, to perform this task you will have to resort to the LAN Manager APIs which are documented only in the LANMAN32.HLP file.

# TYPICAL THINGS TO EXTRACT FROM THE REGISTRY

Following are some tips and some code for extracting normal everyday items from the Registry.

To find out if your program is running on an NT Advanced Server, use a registry API to query the

```
HKEY_LOCAL_MACHINE\
    SYSTEM\
    CurrentControlSet\
    Control\
    ProductOptions
```

The value will be LANMANNT if the NT Advanced Server is running; otherwise it will be WINNT.

Under Windows 3.1, you can retrieve the registered user and company as resources 513 and 514 in USER.EXE. The equivalent information in NT is stored in the Registry in

```
HKEY_LOCAL_MACHINE\
    SOFTWARE\
    Microsoft\
    Windows NT\
    CurrentVersion\
    RegisteredOrganization
```

and

```
HKEY_LOCAL_MACHINE\
    SOFTWARE\
    Microsoft\
    Windows NT\
    CurrentVersion\
    RegisteredOwner
```

In order to change which program is the startup shell, you have to change the value stored at :

```
HKEY_LOCAL_MACHINE\
     SOFTWARE\
     MICROSOFT\
     Windows NT\
     Current Version\
     Winlogon\
     Shell
```

Here is the listing

```
long
GetOwnerInfo(LPTSTR szRegOrg.LPDWORD cbOrg, LPTSTR szRegOwner,
LPDWORD cbOwner)
{
HEKY hkey;
TCHAR achOrg{1024};
DWORD dwOrg = sixzeof(archOrg);
TCHAR achUser[1024];
DWORD dwUser = sizeof(dwUser);
LONG lerr

lerr = RegOpenKeyEx( HEKY_LOCAL_MACHINE,
                "SOFTWARE\\Microsoft\\Windows NT\\CurrentVersion",
             0,
                  KEY_READ,
                  &hkey);
if (leff != ERROR_SUCCESS)
  return lerr;

lerr = RegQueryValueEx(hkey,
                  "RgisteredOrganization",
                  NULL
                  NULL, szRegOrg, cbOrg);
if (lerr !=ERROR_SUCCESS)
  return lerr;
```

```
lerr = RegQueryValueEx( key, "RegisteredOwner", NULL, NULL,
szRegOwner, cbOwner);
if (leff != ERROR_SUCCESS)
  return lerr;
}
.
```

As I stated earlier, you must use the Registry APIs to make the change because WritePrivateProfileString acts upon

```
HKEY_LOCAL_MACHINE\
     SOFTWARE\
     MICROSOFT\
     Windows NT\
     Current Version\
     WOW\
     Boot\
     Shell
```

Even though this has no effect on which shell Windows NT executes, you should change this value (with either WritePrivateProfileString or the RegSetValueEx) to maintain compatibility with applications that are still calling GetPrivateProfileString .

A post-mortem debugger is a tool that gains control whenever an unhandled exception occurs in an application. This tools then attaches itself to the process that caused the exception and produces output that helps in determining the cause of the bug. To change which program the system calls when an unhandled exception occurs, use:

```
HKEY_LOCAL_MACHINE\
     SOFTWARE\
     Microsoft\
     Windows NT\
     CurrentVersion\
     AeDebug.
```

For example, to make the 32-bit version of Dr. Watson the post-mortem debugger, change the value to this:

```
drwtsn32 -p %ld -e %ld -g
```

To make WinDebug the post-mortem debugger, enter this string:

```
windbg -p %ld -e %ld
```

The change won't take place until you reboot.

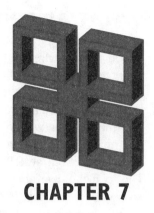

**CHAPTER 7**

# REMOTE PROCEDURE CALLS

I once worked for a company whose mission was to make life easier for users of Windows 3.x on a network. That company and others like it will have to find a new mission if they want to succeed in the Windows 95 and NT markets because Microsoft has taken great pains to make these two operating systems easier for network users. This chapter will concentrate on one specific feature that Microsoft has added to accomplish that task, *remote procedure calls* (RPCs).

I won't spend too much time going over the basics of RPCs. Instead, this chapter will concentrate on the interface definition language, binding, the runtime APIs, using pointers, and differences between OSF/DCE and Win32 RPCs APIs. The sample program finishes up by showing a typical RPC implementation. In this case, a remote make program so you can do your builds on available server machines.

# WHAT ARE RPCS?

If you are not already familiar with RPCs, a quick overview is in order. A remote procedure call is a form of *interprocess communication* (IPC) that takes place on networks. The intelligence built into the RPC mechanism enables you to abstract out the network interface and call a function located on the network as if the function were on your own machine. To your application, an PC looks like any other function or procedure. However, instead of executing like a normal function, an RPC is actually just a placeholder for the real function. This placeholder function, called a *stub*, calls RPC runtime library routines (also called *RPC runtime DLLs* because of where they are located) to resolve the location on the network and executes the call in the remote address space. Meanwhile, your client application thinks it is calling its own function. You can even make remote procedure calls within a single machine. These types of RPCs are called local procedure calls, or *LPCs*. However, it is important to note that, unlike function calls made to regular DLLs, a remote procedure call is not mapped into the calling (client) process's address space. It actually executes in the address space of the remote (server) process.

Here's how it all works:

1   The client stub transfers any data and the function to the client PC runtime DLL. The client RPC runtime DLL finds a server that can satisfy the RPC command.

2   If an appropriate server can be found, the client RPC runtime DLL sends the function and its data to the server.

3.   A corresponding RPC runtime DLL on the server receives the function and its data and proceeds to call the server's placeholder function (the server stub).

4.   The server stub retrieves the data, converts it to an appropriate format if necessary, and calls the actual function.

5.   When the function is completed, the RPC server runtime DLL retrieves the return value and any data (from the stub, which got it from the destination function) and delivers it to the client RPC runtime DLL.

6.   The client RPC runtime DLL returns to the client application, updating the return code and any data (via the client stub).

Since all of the transport and protocol commands are taken care of by the RPC runtime DLLs, developing client-server applications is made much simpler and you can take advantage of all of the available processing power on the network. Although you will still have to have someone in your organization who is network-savvy, you can eliminate the need for separate-network-specific releases of your software. The Win32 SDK ships with RPC utilities for developing for 32-bit RPC servers, 32-bit RPC clients, and 16-bit RPC clients. The 32-bit tools install automatically as part of the Win32 SDK install. The 16-bit development tools install under Windows 3.1.

The RPC model offers a number of advantages over programming, say, NetBIOS directly, including better handling of network failures and an easier calling convention. The RPC programming model is designed to be similar to the C calling convention.

## WIN32 RPCS VS. OSF/DCE

RPCs are part of the Open System Foundation's *Distributed Computing Environment* (DCE). RPC clients developed on Windows 95, NT, DOS, or Windows 3.x can communicate with any other DCE server, including DECs, HPs, Suns, Crays, and so on.

Although Chapter 85 of the *Windows NT Programmer's Reference* (Volume 2) states that "the RPC provided by the Win32 API is compliant with the Open Software Foundation (OSF) Distributed Computing Environment (DCE)," that is not quite true. Compliance implies that Microsoft built its version of RPCs with the OSF source code. In fact, Microsoft developed its RPC facility from the ground up. One of the effects of this is the fact that clients developed with SDK cannot connect directly to DCE servers using the name service (discussed in more detail shortly). The OSF DCE environment uses the DCE Cell Directory Service (CDS) for its RPC name service. To allow interoperation between DCE computers and RPC client applications that call RPC name service API functions, you must use a gateway to the DCE CDS.

Microsoft RPCs also do not support the OSF DCE Core Services such as Directory Service, the Time Service, or the OSF DCE Extended Services, including the Distributed File Services. The Microsoft RPCs currently support the connection-oriented services. Consequently, clients developed on any of these boxes can communicate with Windows 95 or NT servers. One important note, however. Windows 95 does not support the server side using named pipes.

Older implementations of RPCs, such as the non-DCE-compliant version provided by Digital Equipment Corporation, which is based on and is compatible with the RPC component of Apollo's Network Computing System (NCS) Version 1.5, are not supported.

Another difference is that DCE RPC defines two RPC protocols, one for running over connection-oriented transport protocols such as TCP/IP, and one for running over connectionless transports such as UDP/IP. Unfortunately, NCS only supports the connectionless transport and Microsoft RPCs only support the TCP/IP protocol. The protocol that is common between DCE and NCS has a number of virtues, and perhaps Microsoft will consider supporting it at some point. However, given what I assume to be the relatively small number of deployed NCS applications, the motivation for doing so would presumably have to be those virtues, and not compatibility with NCS.

## RPCS AND DATA CONVERSION

The good news is that RPCs automatically support data conversion to account for different hardware architectures and for byte-ordering between dissimilar environments. RPCs solve the data-translation problems that you would expect to find in any medium to large size network. The automatic conversion of data and the fact the remote procedures run in the process space of the server means it is quite common to see a client call a remote procedure that executes on a server of a machine that has a completely different architecture (How would you like to get that Cray down the hall to do ray-tracing algorithms for you?)

# DEVELOPING RPC APPLICATIONS

Since all applications that use RPCs consist of the interface, the client and the server, let's tackle them in that order.

## DEFINING AN INTERFACE WITH THE MICROSOFT INTERFACE DEFINITION LANGUAGE

The Interface Definition Language (IDL) is the solution to the problem of how to transfer data in a network with dissimilar environments. The IDL is a platform-independent language that provides machine-independent data types. The IDL file contains type definitions and function prototypes that describe how data is transmitted on the network. By using the interface definition language, you avoid problems such as an integer being 32-bits on Windows 95 or , but only 16-bits on Windows 3.x.

Microsoft has its own implementation of IDL called the *Microsoft Interface Definition Language* (MIDL). Once you create an interface, you compile it with the MIDL compiler. The MIDL compiler generates header and stub files for both the client and the server.

Figure 7–1 shows the structure of an IDL file. First is the interface header, which contains interface header attributes and the interface name. Interface header attributes specify RPC features that uniquely apply to the interface. Inside the interface header attributes is the *universal unique identifier* (UUID). For each new interface you write, you must generate an UUID. To generate a UUID, run the *uuidgen* program.

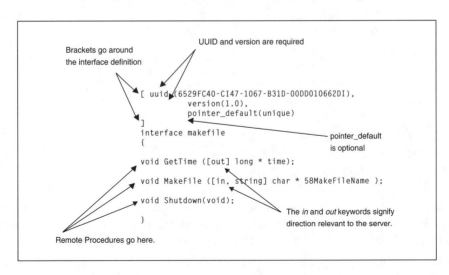

**Figure 7–1** The structure of an IDL file

**283**

Examine the following command line:

```
uuidgen -omyidl.idl
```

It produces output similar to the following:

```
[ uuid(2F5F6520-CA46-1067-B319-00DD010662DA),
  version(1.0),
]
interface INTERFACE
{
}
```

One of the reasons that the older DECrpc is not compatible with Microsoft RPCs is because a UUID in DECrpc is defined as a 16-byte quantity.

## THE GUID STRUCTURE

The Microsoft implementation of the UUID is the GUID structure:

```
typedef struct _GUID{
    unsigned long Data1;
    unsigned short Data2;
    unsigned short Data3;
    unsigned char Data4[8];
} GUID;typedef GUID UUID;
```

GUID stands for *Globally Unique Identifier* and it is type-defined to UUID. You should consider the GUID structure as opaque and not manipulate the data in the structure directly.

The GUID is a required attribute of the interface definition. After the GUID comes the optional attribute, *version* number. If you do not specify a version number, the MIDL compiler defaults to 1.0. Like other version numbers, the version attribute identifies a particular version when multiple versions of an interface exist.

Following the version number is the attribute *pointer_default*. This attribute is used so that pointers can be transmitted correctly. The *pointer_default* attribute determines the default pointer attribute for all pointers except if there are functions with pointers in the parameter list. So *pointer_default* is significant for pointers that appear inside of structures, unions, or arrays when you have a pointer to a pointer (such as char **argv*) as a parameter to a function or when a function returns a pointer type and does not have a pointer attribute as a function attribute.

After the interface header is the body. The body of an interface definition consists of import statements, constant definitions, data type definitions, and procedure declarations.

The interface body starts with the keyword *interface* and is followed by a required name. For the sample application, the interface name is "MAKEFILE":

```
interface MAKEFILE
```

After the interface name come the procedure declarations. Procedure declarations are like prototypes for the remote procedure calls that the server exports with some added information. For example, since it is more efficient to transmit data only if it is going to be accessed, procedure declarations use the parameter attributes *in* an *out* to signify whether data is transmitted to the server [*in*], or to the client [*out*], or to both [*in, out*]. Here are some examples:

```
//
// Procedure declaration with one parameter.
//
void Shutdown([in] DATA_HANDLE_TYPE hBinding);


//
// Procedure declaration with one string parameter
//

void TestProc([in, string] unsigned char *pszString);


//
//Procedure declaration with three parameters.
//
void InOutProc([in]        short     s1,
               [in, out]   short     *ps2,
               [out]       float     *pf3);
```

Unlike C or C++, in which a base type can vary from platform to platform, RPC base types are platform independent. Table 7–1 lists the available base types. You create aliases for other types by using data-type definitions, just as you do in C and C++. The data-type definitions and constant definitions also go in the interface body. All data transmitted on the network during a remote procedure call must resolve to a base type. following are examples of various data-type definitions.

A typical structure for a linked list:

```
typedef struct _DOUBLE_LINK_LIST {
    short sNumber;
    struct _DOUBLE_LINK_LIST * pNext;
    struct _DOUBLE_LINK_LIST * pPrevious;
} DOUBLE_LINK_LIST;
```

A structure for a linked list in which one member (*asNumber* in the following example) is an array:

```
typedef struct _DOUBLE_XMIT_TYPE {
    short sSize;
    [size_is(sSize)] short asNumber[];
} DOUBLE_XMIT_TYPE;
```

A structure for a linked list that will be transmitted as an array:

```
//
// transmit a double-linked list as an array
//
typedef [transmit_as(DOUBLE_XMIT_TYPE)] DOUBLE_LINK_LIST
DOUBLE_LINK_TYPE;
```

A typedef for a handle used in procedure declarations:

```
const short BUFSIZE = 1024;

typedef [context_handle] void *PCONTEXT_HANDLE_TYPE;

short RemoteOpen( [out] PCONTEXT_HANDLE_TYPE *pphContext,
```

```
                    [in, string] unsigned char *pszFile
               );

short RemoteRead( [in]  PCONTEXT_HANDLE_TYPE phContext,
                  [out] unsigned char achBuf[BUFSIZE],
                  [out] short *pcbBuf
               );
```

**Table 7–1**  RPC Base Types

| Base type | Default sign | Description |
|-----------|--------------|-------------|
| byte | n/a | 8-bit data item |
| char | unsigned | 8-bit unsigned data item |
| double | n/a | 64-bit floating-point number |
| float | n/a | 32-bit floating-point number |
| handle_t | n/a | primitive handle type |
| long | signed | 32-bit signed integer |
| short | signed | 16-bit signed integer |
| small | signed | 8-bit signed integer |
| void * | n/a | 32-bit context handle pointer type |
| wchar_t | unsigned | 16-bit unsigned data item |

## ASSOCIATING TYPE ATTRIBUTES TO DEFINED TYPES

The extensions to typedef declarations allow you to associate type attributes to defined types. They include the usage attributes and data-type attributes:

▪▪   Usage attributes

There are two usage attributes: string and ignore. The string attribute indicates that the parameter is a pointer that points to a string. The ignore attribute indicates that the parameter will not be used by the receiving end and therefore should not be transmitted.

▪▪   Data-type attributes

**287**

The data-type attributes that Microsoft supports are handle, context_handle, and transmit_as. The handle attribute specifies the name of a binding-handle type that you define. Use this type of handle when you want control over binding information. The following is an example of using the handle attribute:

```
typedef struct _DATA_TYPE {
    unsigned char * pszUuid;
    unsigned char * pszProtocolSequence;
    unsigned char * pszNetworkAddress;
    unsigned char * pszEndpoint;
    unsigned char * pszOptions;
} DATA_TYPE;

typedef [handle] DATA_TYPE *DATA_HANDLE_TYPE;

void MyHandleProc([in] DATA_HANDLE_TYPE hBinding,
                  [in, string] unsigned char *pszString);
```

You must provide your own binding and unbinding routines to use the *handle attribute*. This is how the stub routines convert between primitive and user-defined handle types. In the example above, I created a user-defined handle and named it *DATA_TYPE*. The binding and unbinding routines are named *DATA_TYPE_bind* and *DATA_TYPE_unbind*. When the remote procedure has a user-defined handle as a parameter or as an implicit handle, the client stubs call the binding routine before calling the remote procedure. The client stubs call the unbinding routine after the remote call.

*Context handles* are different from regular binding handles in that in, addition to providing binding information, they also are used by a server application refer to a specific state of a client. You specify a context handle with the *context_handle* attribute.

The *transmit_as* attribute notifies the stub routines that you want to convert the data before transmitting it. This is useful when you have a data type in which you want to have the client or server rebuild the pointers after transmitting. For example, in applications that require linked lists you use the [*transmit_as*] attribute to gain control before and after the linked list is transmitted. This method enables you to transmit the data yourself as a sized

array. This way, the pointers will be rebuilt on the server side. The
[*transmit_as*] attribute requires four functions (which you must write) to
perform the translation. The names must start with the name of the new type. If
your attribute is *transmit_as*(NEW_TYPE) then the names of the four functions
are as follows

```
void
NEW_TYPE_to_xmit((__RPC_API NEW_TYPE*),(__RPC_API NEW_TYPE**));
```

If the name of your presented type is NEW_TYPE, then *NEW_TYPE_to_xmit*
is the name of the function that converts from the presented type to the
transmitted type.

```
void
NEW_TYPE_from_xmit((__RPC_API NEW_TYPE*),(__RPC_API NEW_TYPE*));
```

The *NEW_TYPE_from_xmit* converts from the transmitted type back to the
presented type.

```
void
NEW_TYPE_free_inst((__RPC_API NEW_TYPE*));
```

NEW_TYPE_free_inst frees any storage used by the callee for the presented type.

```
void
NEW_TYPE_free_xmit((__RPC_API NEW_TYPE*));
```

*NEW_TYPE_free_xmit* frees the storage used by the caller for the transmitted type.

In the client, when the stub calls your *NEW_TYPE_to_xmit* function, copy
your data objects from your new type into a type that can be transmitted across
the network.

On the server side, the stub allocates space for you and then calls your
*NEW_TYPE_from_xmit* function so you can translate the transmitted data back
to *NEW_TYPE*.

The server stub calls your *NEW_TYPE_free_inst* function to free the storage
of *NEW_TYPE* on the server side.

The client stub calls your *NEW_TYPE_free_xmit* to free the *NEW_TYPE* storage on the client side.

The [*transmit as*] allows you great flexibility in the way you store and manipulate data in your clients by allowing you to translate the data to a base type that can be communicated over the network. However, you cannot use [*transmit_as*] with context handles, and the only array type supported is a fixed array.

Once you develop your interface definition you are ready to tackle the client or the server pieces. Let's take the client next.

## THE RPC CLIENT

In order for the client to execute a remote procedure, it must be able to find the server on the network. Clients choose a server to connect to using a process known as *binding*. After a client binds to a server, it receives a handle called the *binding handle*.

There are several different ways in which a client can bind to the server. The following describes each method and tells you when it is appropriate to use each.

### Auto Handles

When your application doesn't require a specific server, use auto handles. Auto handles are analogous to using the yellow pages to get a phone number. When you are looking for somewhere to eat, looking under "Restaurants" in the yellow pages is a good way to do it. When you want to execute a particular function and you don't care which server the function exists on, then use auto handles to bind.

When you use an auto handle, the stub file takes care of binding and binding handles for you. In your client code, just call the function as if it were a local function. Then specify auto handle in the attribute configuration file (ACF). The client stub will define the handle and manage the binding.

For example, our remote make program can be implemented using an auto handle. The client application does not care which server provides the make facilities. It merely wants to get the processing power from any available server.

You specify the use of auto handles by including the *auto_handle* attribute in the ACF file. The remote make example uses the following ACF file:

```
/* ACF file */
[auto_handle]
interface auto
{
}
```

If you don't specify a handle attribute in the ACF (or if you don't have an ACF file), then auto handle is the default. Also, once you specify auto handle, don't use the auto handle as an argument to any remote procedure call.

```
/* IDL file */
[ uuid (6B29FC40-CA47-1067-B31D-00DD010662DA),
  version(1.0),
  pointer_default(unique)
]
interface auto
{
void Makefile([in] char *makefile_name);
}
```

The great thing about auto handles is that you don't have to manage them. But, that means they provide you with the least flexibility.

```
/* auto handle client application (fragment) */

#include <stdio.h>
#include <time.h>
#include "auto.h"     // header file generated by the MIDL compiler


void main(int argc, char **argv)
{
    time_t t1;
    time_t t2;
    char * pszTime;
    ...

    RpcTryExcept {
          Makefile("test.mak");
```

```
        Shutdown();     // Shutdown is a remote procedure
    }
    RPCExcept(1)    {
    ...
    }
    RPCEndExcept

    exit(0);
}
```

In order to use auto handles, you must have a location service running on a server that your client can get connected to. The Microsoft implementation of the name service, the Microsoft Locator, manages auto handles.

## Name service

When you are looking for the phone number of just any place to eat, the yellow pages will do. But when you want to phone a specific restaurant such as Clay's Sports Cafe on Roswell Road in Sandy Springs, Georgia, it's easier to get the phone number from the white pages than it is from the yellow pages. The same is true of using the name service to find a particular server. When using the name service to bind, you must know the name of the server you want to bind with.

The name-service functions allow a server to register its interface in a database. When a server registers its interface, a client can query the database, supplying a logical name and an optional object UUID, to obtain a binding handle to the server instance.

The RPC name service makes distributed applications easy to administer. When the server side of the distributed application is moved to another computer, clients do not have to be reconfigured. As long as the database entry name and object UUIDs remain the same, client applications can access the server application as they did before.

## Attribute configuration files (ACF)

Normally, both clients and servers share MIDL output. But there at times you will want to customize a particular client, a server, or both. For example, if you have binding information that is relevant to just one client, then you don't want to put this information into the IDL. Instead, place the binding information in an attribute configuration file (ACF). Use an ACF file when you want to configure your application for a particular operating environment without affecting its network characteristics. By keeping the ACF information separate from the IDL, you can separate the interface specification from environment-specific settings. This method ensures that the IDL file will always be portable between computers. It's in the ACF file where you specify which binding you are going to use. When you don't have an ACF file or if you do and it does not specify an auto or implicit handle attribute, the MIDL defaults to auto handle.

## CLIENT API FUNCTIONS FOR BINDING

Once you have chosen a binding method, if all goes well the client runtime library will find a server to connect to. By "going well," I mean that UUIDs, version numbers, protocols, and so on all match. The following sections details the calls a client makes when it is using the name service to bind. Remember, the name service database is like the white pages in that you must "look up" binding information. Win32 provides several functions to assist you in this process:

▟   RpcNsBindingImportBegin

```
RPC_STATUS RPC_ENTRY
RpcNsBindingImportBegin(unsign long EntryNameSyntax,
                        unsigned char *  EntryName,
                        RPC_IF_HANDLE  IfSpec,
                        UUID *  ObjUuid,
                        RPC_NS_HANDLE *  ImportContext);
```

Since the same interface can be supported on more than one system, you must select the particular server that you want (remember we want Clay's in Sandy Springs—not the Clay's in Kennesaw). *RpcNsBindingImportBegin* starts the search and creates an import context. You use the *import context* in subsequent routines to select the binding information.

**293**

### ▪▪ RpcNsBindingImportNext

```
RPC_STATUS RPC_ENTRY
RpcNsBindingImportNext(
    RPC_NS_HANDLE   ImportContext,
    RPC_BINDING_HANDLE *  Binding);
```

Using the import context, the *RpcNsBindingImportNext* function accesses the locator database (there is still no communication with the server yet) and returns a binding handle of a compatible server if one is available. To determine if the returned handle is the one you want, you have a couple of options. One way is to just use the new handle and "see" if it works. The downside to this method is that, if the binding handle is not compatible (perhaps this particular binding handle uses a different protocol sequence than you are expecting), it will generate an exception. To avoid such unpleasantness you must surround your call within the RPC version of structured exception handling, the *RpcTryExcept* call. Here's the syntax for the *RpcTryExcept* call:

```
RpcTryExcept
        {
        guarded statements
        }
RpcExcept(expression)
        {
        exception statements
        }
RpcEndExcept;
```

If it looks similar to a regular *try* statement, it should. The *RpcTryExcept* is just a macro for *try,* defined in RPC.H:

```
#define RpcTryExcept \
    try \
        {
```

By using structured exception handling, you can ignore the error returns and the fact that the function may bomb and call it anyway. If it does bomb (that is, cause an exception), then you can recover in the *RpcExcept* part of the macro.

The following code example shows how to use this technique:

```
RPC_STATUS status;
RPC_NS_HANDLE hnsRemote;
RPC_BINDING_HANDLE hRemote;
short fContinue = TRUE;

RpcNsBindingImportBegin(RPC_C_NS_SYNTAX_DEFAULT,
                        "/.:/make_sample",
                        nRemote_ClientIfHandle,
                        NULL,
                        &hnsRemote);

    for (;;)  // loop until we are out of bindings or
              // we find one
    {
    status = RpcNsBindingImportNext(hnsRemote, &hRemote);
    if (status == RPC_S_NO_MORE_BINDINGS)
        return(status);

    if (status == RPC_S_OK) // found a binding
    {
        RpcTryExcept
    {
            MakeFile(hRemote, "Generic.mak");
        }
        RpcExcept(EXCEPTION_EXECUTE_HANDLER)
        {
            // You gain control here if an exception occurs
            // free the binding now that you know that you
            // don't want to use it.
        RpcBindingFree(&hRemote);
```

```
        }
        RpcEndExcept
    }


    }
```

The other method of determining if the returned handle is the one you want is to decode the binding handle yourself. This is useful in cases where you want to bind using a particular protocol sequence. The function *RpcBindingToStringBinding* converts a binding handle to a string:

```
RPC_STATUS RPC_ENTRY
RpcBindingToStringBinding(
    RPC_BINDING_HANDLE  Binding,
    unsigned char * *   StringBinding);
```

Once you have a string representation of the binding handle, pass it as a parameter to *RpcStringBindingParse*:

```
RPC_STATUS RPC_ENTRY
RpcStringBindingParse(
    unsigned char *   StringBinding,
    unsigned char * * ObjectUuid ,
    unsigned char * * ProtSeq ,
    unsigned char * * NetworkAddr ,
    unsigned char * * EndPoint ,
    unsigned char * * NetworkOptions);
```

The following code example shows how to use this technique:

```
    RPC_STATUS status;
    RPC_NS_HANDLE hnsRemote;
    RPC_BINDING_HANDLE hRemote;
    short fContinue = TRUE;

RpcNsBindingImportBegin(RPC_C_NS_SYNTAX_DEFAULT,
                    "/.:/make_sample",
                    nRemote_ClientIfHandle,
```

```
                        NULL,
                        &hnsRemote);

   for (;;)  // loop until we are out of bindings or
                   // we find one
   {
        status = RpcNsBindingImportNext(hnsRemote, &hRemote);
        if (status == RPC_S_NO_MORE_BINDINGS)
            return(status);


        if (status == RPC_S_OK) // found a binding
        {
//
//pchStringBinding and pchProtSeq are unsigned char *
//
            RpcBindingToStringBinding(hRemote, &pchStringBinding);
            RpcStringBindingParse(pchStringBinding,
                            NULL,
                            &pchProtSeq ,
                            NULL,
                            NULL,
                            NULL);
            if (memcmp(pchProtSeq,"ncacn_ip_tcp")==0)
                break;
            else
            {
                status = RpcBindingFree(&hRemote);
            }

    }

   return (MakeFile(hRemote, "Generic.mak"));
```

One additional function that you must use is *RpcBindingFree,* which frees the
memory that is associated with each *RpcNsBindingImportBegin:*

```
RPC_STATUS RPC_ENTRY
RpcBindingFree(RPC_BINDING_HANDLE *  Binding);
```

**297**

A call to *RpcBindingFree* must accompany calls to any of the following functions:

■■ RpcBindingCopy

■■ RpcBindingFromStringBinding

■■ RpcServerInqBindings

■■ RpcNsBindingImportNext

■■ RpcNsBindingSelect

■■ RpcNsBindingImportDone

When you are finished looping through all of the bindings, call *RpcNsBindingImportDone* to delete the import context:

```
RPC_STATUS RPC_ENTRY
RpcNsBindingImportDone(
    RPC_NS_HANDLE *  ImportContext);
```

## THE RPC SERVER

The mission of an RPC Server is simple. It contains the implementations for the remote procedures that the clients use. But before a client can make a remote procedure call, the server has some initialization to perform.

You must first register your server's interface with the RPC runtime library. The *RpcRegisterIf* function is provided for this purpose:

```
RPC_STATUS RPC_ENTRY
RpcServerRegisterIf(
    RPC_IF_HANDLE  IfSpec,
    UUID *  MgrTypeUuid,
    RPC_MGR_EPV *  MgrEpv);
```

Once you establish your server interface, you must choose a protocol sequence to create the binding information. Table 7–2 lists the protocols that an RPC server supports. One of the first initialization tasks an RPC server must perform is to select a protocol sequence. To receive RPC calls from a client, your server must register at least one protocol sequence with the RPC runtime library. The easiest way is to call *RpcServerUseAllProtseqs* that tells the RPC runtime library to use every protocol that is supported:

```
RPC_STATUS RPC_ENTRY
RpcServerUseAllProtseqs(
    unsigned int  MaxCalls,
    void *  SecurityDescriptor);
```

The first parameter, *MaxCalls,* indicates how many concurrent remote procedure call requests you want the server to accept. You specify the default with the constant *RPC_C_PROTSEQ_MAX_REQS_DEFAULT,* which is defined as 10 in RPCDCE.H.

**Table 7–2** Protocol Names

| NCA Name | Protocol |
|----------|----------|
| ncacn_ip_tcp | TCP/IP |
| ncacn_nb_tcp | TCP over NetBIOS |
| ncacn_np | named pipes |
| ncalrpc | local RPC |
| ncacn_dnet_nsp | DECnet* |
| ncacn_spx | SPX** |

To register only one specific protocol, call the *RpcServerUseProtseq* function:

```
RPC_STATUS RPC_ENTRY
RpcServerUseProtseq(
    unsigned char *  ProtSeq,
    unsigned int  MaxCalls,
    void *  SecurityDescriptor);
```

After registering protocol sequences, call *RpcServerInqBindings* to obtain a vector containing all of the server's binding handles:

```
RPC_STATUS RPC_ENTRY
RpcServerInqBindings(
    RPC_BINDING_VECTOR * *  BindingVector);
```

It is not enough for the client to be able to find your physical machine on the network. Clients must also know how to choose a particular process that is running on the machine. Therefore, your RPC server must also identify itself (to differentiate it from other RPC-server processes that may be running on the same physical server). An *endpoint* is the term used to define a particular server process running on a physical server:

```
RPC_STATUS RPC_ENTRY
RpcServerUseProtseqEp(
     unsigned char *  Protseq,
     unsigned int  MaxCalls,
     unsigned char *  Endpoint,
     void *  SecurityDescriptor);
```

The *RpcServerUseProtseqEp* tells the RPC server runtime DLL to specify a protocol sequence and a specified endpoint in the same function.

If you are using all protocol sequences, you can call the *RpcEpRegister* function to add the endpoint information:

```
#include <rpc.h>
RPC_STATUS RPC_ENTRY
RpcEpRegister(
     RPC_IF_HANDLE  IfSpec,
     RPC_BINDING_VECTOR *  BindingVector,
     UUID_VECTOR *  UuidVector,
     unsigned char *  Annotation);
```

Next, use *RpcNsBindingExport* to place the binding handles in the name-service database for access by any client in order to establish the name-service database entry:

```
RPC_STATUS RPC_ENTRY
RpcNsBindingExport(
     unsigned long  EntryNameSyntax,
     unsigned char *  EntryName,
     RPC_IF_HANDLE  IfSpec,
     RPC_BINDING_VECTOR *  BindingVec,
     UUID_VECTOR *  ObjectUuidVec);
```

Finally, call RpcServerListen so that your RPC server knows that clients will know you are ready to accept calls:

```
RPC_STATUS RPC_ENTRY
RpcServerListen(
     unsigned int  MinimumCallThreads,
     unsigned int  MaxCalls,
     unsigned int  DontWait);
```

Suppose you have an RPC server that gets bound to a client, and then another client comes along looking to bind to the same server. You may wonder how you can make the server detect this and spawn a copy of itself to handle the second client. Well, the RPC runtime does this for you automatically when you call *RpcServerListen*. The *MinimumCallThreads* parameter specifies the number of threads the server will spawn to handle clients' requests.

## Local Remote Procedure Calls (LRPCs)

RPCs are not limited to inter-network calls. Since RPCs are really just a method to call routines in a different process, there is no reason why the different process can't be on the same machine. This type of RPC is call the *Local Procedure Call*, or LRPC (I've sometimes seen is abbreviated to LPC).

If all your processes are going to be on the same machine (clients and servers), there are also other means for them to communicate, such as in the form of mapped files and named pipes. Although Chapter 9 delves interprocess communication methods for tightly coupled interfaces, LRPCs are an additional method to place in your bag of tricks. Using LPC has the benefit of speed when the clients and servers are on the same machine, but if you do have to split clients to run on machines other than the servers, you can simply add more protocol sequences for your RPC application to run over. For example, you can start off with the LRPC *ncalrpc,* protocol sequence and add named pipes or TCP/IP protocol sequences later.

There are two other additional benefits of LPRCs:

▪▪    They are valuable when you don't have a network card.

By installing the Remote Access Server (RAS) software that comes built-in with Windows NT, you can have a fully functioning network

**301**

running on the machine, even though there is no network card in your machine. This method works even when no RAS connection has been made to a remote RAS server. In addition to making LRPCs possible, this sort of approach is really convenient for developing network applications on a laptop or home machine. During the network installation of NT, refuse network card autodetect. Lie and say a network card is there (just pick a card out of the list). When you get to the Networks Dialog box later in setup, be sure to do choose "add software" and install RAS. Then, after returning to the Networks dialog box, remove the network adapter that you fibbed about before. Once you reboot you will be able to take advantage of LRPCs.

▪▪ LRPCs keep prying eyes off your function names.

With any other DLL that is in the PE file format, you can disassemble the DLL and learn what functions it imports and exports. However, this is not true about LRPC functions. For example, if you look at any of the protected subsystem executables, such as csrss.exe (Win32 subsystem), you'll find that they don't export anything.

# SAMPLE PROGRAM: DISTRIBUTED MAKE

Whenever a new generation of personal computers is announced, I always chuckle. Great, I think, here's another machine of whose capabilities I will use less than 1 percent. There are some real workhorse machines out there in corporate America that sit idle for at least eight hours a day (most developers I know only work an average of 16 hours). Of course, the real power-house machines—that is, those in Product Management—usually sit idle over twenty hours a day. What a waste. Back in the old days of mainframes, companies such as banks and insurance companies would frequently sell off their idle time. Well, RPCs are the '90s equivalent to time-sharing. Instead of letting all that horsepower remain idle, offer up that extra computing power to whoever needs it.

Here's how something like this works: Install an RPC server on each machine that has a tendency to sit idle. Then, from your machine, install the RPC client that makes calls into the server to take advantage of the extra computing power. The sample application, RMAKE (see Listing 7–1), uses the extra computing power to do builds. However, there are unlimited possibilities for this type of application. Any application that is compute-intensive qualifies. Here's another possibility: Each night after the developers go home (or in the case of some developers that I know, each *morning* after they go home), have them run an RPC test-server application. The client can then distribute Microsoft Test-type procedures to run on the available servers. If your fellow developers balk at having their machines used as guinea pigs, tell them that if they have so little confidence in their own code they won't have it running on their machines, perhaps they shouldn't check their source in.

One way to make things somewhat transparent to the user might be to install the compute-server applications as NT services on the servers. This way a user wouldn't have to intervene much after the install process. The server could just call *RpcServerListen* and block until someone over the net wakes it up.

**Listing 7–1** Remote Make fragment

```
//
// Remote Make
// KJG
//

#include <stdlib.h>
#include <stdio.h>
#include "wrmake.h"    // header file generated by MIDL compiler

void RMakeProc(unsigned char * pszString, unsigned int * rtn)
{

SECURITY_ATTRIBUTES lsa;
char s[80];
STARTUPINFO si;
PROCESS_INFORMATION pi;
LPSTARTUPINFO lpsi = &si;
LPPROCESS_INFORMATION lppi = &pi;

    lsa.nLength=sizeof(SECURITY_ATTRIBUTES);
    lsa.lpSecurityDescriptor=NULL;
    lsa.bInheritHandle=FALSE;
```

```
            if (!CreateProcess(NULL, pszString,
                                   NULL,
                                   NULL,
                               FALSE,
                                   CREATE_NEW_CONSOLE,
                                   NULL,
                                   NULL,
                                   lpsi,
                                   lppi))
          {
          *rtn = GetLastError();
          }
    else
        {
      WaitForSingleObject(pi.hProcess,INFINITE);
      GetExitCodeProcess(pi.hProcess,&rtn);
        }

CloseHandle(pi.hThread);
CloseHandle(pi.hProcess);

}

void Shutdown(void)
{
    RPC_STATUS status;

    status = RpcMgmtStopServerListening(NULL);
    if (status) {
        exit(status);
    }

    status = RpcServerUnregisterIf(NULL, NULL, FALSE);
    if (status) {
        exit(status);
    }
}
```

## SUMMARY

RPC provides interprocess communications with a function interface and support for automatic data conversion and for communications with other operating systems. Using RPC, you can create high-performance, tightly coupled distributed applications.

## NAMING CONVENTIONS

All of the DCE runtime functions use the old K&R-style naming convention— that is, all lowercase with underbars to separate words in the function. Microsoft has chosen to name its functions more consistently with the rest of the Win32 API. All RPC function names have basically the same name as the DEC RPC function, but instead of underbars, the character after the underbar is capitalized. For example, DCE API function names are derived by converting the first character of the DCE RPC function name and every character that follows an underscore character to uppercase and then removing underscore characters. For example, the DCE API function

```
rpc_server_listen
```

becomes

```
RpcServerListen
```

To help you port an OSF/DCE-compliant RPC application to Win32, use the DCEPORT.H header file. This file (which doesn't ship with the SDK—you have to download it from CompuServe) contains macros to convert the DCE style functions into the Win32 style. Here's what *rpc_server_listen* looks like:

```
#define rpc_server_listen(max_calls,status) \
            *status =
RpcServerListen(rpc_c_listen_min_threads_default,\
            max_calls,0)
```

RPC data-structure names are also different from the DCE names. The Win32 names are derived from the DCE names by converting all characters to uppercase and removing the trailing suffix _t. To show you what I mean, here is a snippet from DCEPORT.H :

```
/*
** Define various DCE RPC types
*/
#define rpc_if_handle_t                 RPC_IF_HANDLE
#define rpc_ns_handle_t                 RPC_NS_HANDLE
#define rpc_authz_handle_t              RPC_AUTHZ_HANDLE
#define rpc_auth_identity_handle_t      RPC_AUTH_IDENTITY_HANDLE
#define rpc_mgr_epv_t                   RPC_MGR_EPV __RPC_FAR *
#define rpc_object_inq_fn_t             RPC_OBJECT_INQ_FN
#define rpc_auth_key_retrieval_fn_t     RPC_AUTH_KEY_RETRIEVAL_FN
```

**CHAPTER 8**

# EXCEPTIONS IN WINDOWS 95 AND WIN32

Bruce Eckel, the C++ pioneer, once said that structured exception handling was invented because "..functions with return values that can be used to carry error information are rare, and programmers who check those values are even rarer."[1] By using structured exception handling you can ignore error returns and the fact that functions may bomb and call them anyway. If they do bomb (that is, cause an exception) you can recover. Structured exception handling enables you to write code that concentrates on the normal case, while allowing you to ignore the abnormal cases until they happen.

Before we get into the how's and why's, let me define some terms. There are two types of exceptions: hardware and software. A hardware exception is an abnormal event that forces the processor to stop executing your process temporarily. Usually just long enough to make a decision whether to circumvent the abnormal event and continue running your process or to terminate your process. Structured exception handling allows *you* to make that decision—not the operating system. Most hardware exceptions are dependent upon the processor you are running on, but they are usually the result of an error in an instruction sequence, such as an invalid opcode or an attempt to access an invalid memory address. Software exceptions are exceptions that are explicitly generated by software, instead of the processor. When you use a software exception, your process "creates" the abnormal event.

Hardware and software exceptions are not a new thing. Many operating systems like Windows 3.1 and languages such as C++ have the concept of exceptions. But, before Win32, it used to be important to know the difference between hardware and software exceptions. That's because operating systems like 16-bit Windows require you to have separate logic to deal with hardware and software exceptions (the TOOLHELP.DLL mechanism for hardware exceptions and Try/Catch SDK function calls for software exceptions).

As for C++ exceptions, almost all of the good compilers have them, but they should not be confused with structured exception handling. So far, no compiler vendor has implemented Windows NT structured exceptions within C++ exceptions. MFC currently implements a CException class that only understands software exceptions generated by MFC member functions. However, there is nothing stopping you from using both structured exception handling and MFC CExceptions within your C++ code.

If you are wondering why all the fuss about structured exception handling especially when there are other methods available, take a look at the following example. This sample is designed to handle all possible error conditions during a string copy operation.

```
LPTSTR HappyFunStrCpy(LPTSTR lpszString1, LPTSTR lpszString2)
{
//
// Make sure you can read from lpszString2
//
if (lpszString2 != NULL && !IsBadReadPtr(lpszString2,
                         lstrlen(lpszString2)));
//
// Make sure you can write to lpszString1. Make sure that
// the buffer that lpszString1 points to is large enough
// for strlen(lpszString2) bytes
// of lpszString2
//
```

```
        if (lpszString1 != NULL &&
                !IsBadWritePtr((LPVOID)lp,lstrlen(lpszString2));
                return strcpy(lpszString1, lpszString2);
        else
                return NULL;
    else
        return NULL;
    }
```

Now take a look at the same code using structured exception handling in Win32.

LPTSTR HappyFunStrCpy(LPTSTR lpszString1, LPTSTR lpszString2)

```
{
  try
    {
    return strcpy(lpszString1, lpszString2);
    }
  except (EXCEPTION_EXECUTE_HANDLER)
    {
    return NULL;
    }
}
```

Much simpler, isn't it? I'll get into the syntax in a moment, but basically this function states "I'm going to execute strcpy and return back to the calling function. If anything goes wrong (that is if an exception happens) during the execution of strcpy report back to me and I will return NULL." One advantage you should see immediately is that the path for the normal case is much shorter. If all goes well during the execution of strcpy, then you have incurred almost no overhead. The abnormal case, that is the case where an exception happens, incurs some overhead. But hey, if your are passing around bad data, zippy code is the least of your problems.

Besides clearer, more maintainable code, another reason to use structured exception handling is the preemptive multitasking nature of 32-bit Windows. It makes functions such as IsBadReadPtr unstable.

Thread AThread BIsBadReadPtr(lpszShared,MAX_PATH_SIZE)(returns FALSE)Thread A's time slice expires.free(lpszShared)strcpy (lpszName,lpszShared);(ACCESS VIOLATION).IsBadReadPtr, when used without structured exception handling, can fail in a multithreaded environment.This makes all of the IsBadXxx functions (IsBadCodePtr, IsBadStringPtr, and IsBadWritePtr), suspect in Win32, but for compatibility they're still supported. SEHSafeStrCpy also solves this problem. As a matter of fact, any exception to the rule you can come up with will be taken care of by the SEHSafeStrCpy function—without making changes to the code.

Are you starting to imagine all the places you can use structured exception handling in your code? Besides parameter validation, here are a few ideas I've come up with for uses for structured exception handling.

**Protecting critical resources.** If an exception happens without structured exception handling, your program will terminate without closing files handles, releasing synchronization objects or freeing memory. With structured exception handling you can guarantee that your cleanup functions will be called.

**Protecting precious data.** A good way to get your database corrupt is to have an exception right in the middle of an update. Using structured exception handling, you can trap the exception, make some determinations, then either flush the database or not. You decide depending upon the situation.

**During development.** A great use for structured exception handling is during development. You can create a debug version of your code that, when an exception happens, displays a dialog with detailed debug information. You can even prompt your testers for information about what they were doing to cause the exception. Sort of like your own private Dr. Watson. The Beta version of Visual C++ used structured exception handling to delete temporary files should the compiler cause an exception during compilation.

**As a catch-all.** One way to implement structured exception handling is to wrap your entire application with it. In other words,

```
WINAPI WinMain(...)
{
```

```
try
    {
    // your entire application
    }
except (EXCEPTION_EXECUTE_HANDLER)
    {
    MessageBox(NULL, "XYZ app: Internal error",
                "XYZ app", MB_OK);
    return 0;
    }
}
```

A note of caution, however. Exception handlers are thread-specific. Structured exception handling works only within the thread that generated the exception. But there is nothing stopping you from employing structured exception handling in every thread you create.

You can even make an operating system more robust using structured exception handling. That's what Microsoft did. Much of both Windows 95 and Windows NT kernel and subsystems employs structured exception handling.

One point I need to mention is that the implementation of structured exception handling is partly the compiler's responsibility. Later, I'll show you how you can take advantage of structured exception handling in your code. And, although I'd love to show you how to build a compiler that supports structured exception handling, I'm just going to show you what goes on beneath the covers to give you a feel for how the compiler and the operating system cooperate to implement structured exception handling.

# EXCEPTIONS IN 32-BIT WINDOWS

Believe it or not, another reason Microsoft implemented structured exception handling is to make your code more robust. Mere error returns can be ignored, but an exception gains your immediate attention. Bugs in your 16-bit Windows code that used to slip through testing and into production will jump right out and stare you in the face in Win32.

To show you what I mean, let me describe what actually takes place when an exception happens. If your Win32 code causes an exception, the processor immediately suspends execution of your thread. The processor then exits user-mode, enters kernel-mode and begins executing an exception handler known as the exception dispatcher. If you are not handling exceptions, (that is not using structured exception handling) you have what is known as an unhandled user mode exception. For all unhandled user mode exceptions the exception dispatcher executes the system exception handler. The system exception handle displays a dialog box similar to the one in Figure 8–1 and then terminates your program.

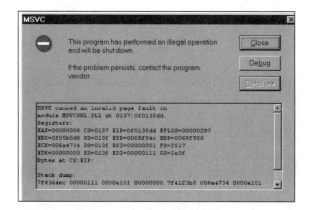

**Figure 8–1** No! Don't contemplate a new career. It's just an unhandled exception.

## UNHANDLED EXCEPTIONS IN THE KERNEL

An unhandled kernel mode exception in either Windows 95 or NT is considered a fatal bug and the following will happen: The operating system will terminate itself, switch to an all blue character mode screen (containing a dump of registers and other debug info), then attempt to connect with the kernel debugger. The blue screen is affectionately called the "blue screen of death."

## EXCEPTION HANDLERS AND FILTERS

Okay, since I've impressed upon you the need to have structured exception handling in your code, let me show you how to do it.

To implement structured exception handling in Visual C++, Microsoft defined extensions to the C/C++ language. The first extension, the try-except clause, enables you to replace the system exception handler with one of your own. It introduces two new keywords, __try and __except:

```
__try        {
     .
     .              // guarded section
     .
     }
__except(filter) {
     .
     .              // exception handler
     .
     }
```

The HappyFunStrCpy function is an example using structured exception handling to handle a typical hardware exception. Here's another:

```
__try {
     char *p = &data;
     *p = 'A';
     .
     }
__except(EXCEPTION_EXECUTE_HANDLER)
     {
     MessageBox(NULL, "p is an invalid pointer",
               "XYZ app", MB_OK);
     return 0;
```

In this example, if the variable p points to an invalid virtual address, an exception will occur. When it does, the MessageBox in the exception handler will execute. Now, the difference between this exception handler and the system exception handler (the one that executes when you have and unhandled exception) is that our process can continue executing. Which means it will not be terminated like a process with an unhandled exception.

By the way, Table 1 lists all the possible hardware exceptions that can be generated under 32-bit Windows. I should point out that some exceptions such as page faults are not in the list. Page faults (a fault is a type of exception), are part of the normal occurrence of a virtual memory management system and are never seen by a user mode program. In other words, page faults are handled only in kernel mode.

Just because the previous example only called MessageBox in the exception handler, don't think that all you can do. On the contrary, you can do just about anything you want. The exception dispatcher even provides you with specific information about the exception. Because when an exception occurs, the exception dispatcher gets control and saves some facts about the exception and the current hardware state into two structures. Table 8–2, at the end of this chapter, describes all of the variables in both structures. The first structure, is the EXCEPTION_RECORD structure, which specifies why the exception occured, the address the exception occurred at, and a few other details. Both hardware and software exceptions use this structure. The CONTEXT structure describes the hardware state (registers and so on) at the time the exception occurred. This structure is different depending upon which machine your code is executing on. The kernel then passes you a pointer to both of these structures in the EXCEPTION_ POINTERS structure. (also described in Table 2). EXCEPTION_RECORD and the three flavors of CONTEXT (Intel for Windows 95, Intel MIPS and Alpha for NT) are all defined in winnt.h. Using the information provided in EXCEPTION_RECORD you can decide if you want to handle the exception or not.

Up until now, my examples of exception handlers all pass EXCEPTION_EXECUTE_HANDLER to the filter meaning they want it to handle the exception, but you actually have a choice. If an exception occurs within a try block, the exception filter gets evaluated. The exception filter is just an expression that must evaluate to one of three options:

1.  Your filter can "accept" the exception by evaluating to a 1 (EXCEPTION_EXECUTE_HANDLER). This instructs the dispatcher call your exception handler. There are other ways to evaluate to a 1 besides passing in EXCEPTION_EXECUTE_HANDLER. For example, the GetExceptionCode function retrieves the exception that caused the execution of the except block. In this next example, if an access violation occurs in the try block, the exception handler will execute.

```
__try
{
// some code that may cause an exception
}
__except(GetExceptionCode() == ACCESS_VIOLATION)
{
// if the exception is an access violation, this
// code will execute
}
```

GetExceptionCode is an intrinsic function that is only available to you in the filter part of a try-except statement. All it does is retrieve the variable ExceptionCode from the EXCEPTION_RECORD structure. Another intrinsic function is GetExceptionInformation. GetExceptionInformation returns a pointer to the entire EXCEPTION_POINTERS structure.

2.  Dismiss the exception. If your filter evaluates to -1 (EXCEPTION_CONTINUE_EXECUTION), it means you have taken care of the reason for the exception. In this case, the exception dispatcher restores the machine state from the context record and starts executing code from the point that caused the exception.

3.  A value of zero (EXCEPTION_CONTINUE_SEARCH) means that you do not want to handle the exception. In this case, the exception dispatcher searches for another handler to handle the exception. That's right, you can have more than one exception handler. If you do not handle the exception, then the exception dispatcher looks for another exception handler by working backwards through the call stack. If the exception dispatcher doesn't find a handler willing to evaluate to EXCEPTION_EXECUTE_HANDLER, then it is considered an unhandled exception.

## UNWINDING

One question that you should be asking, is how does the stack get cleaned up? Depending on where your code is when an exception happens and which exception filter decides to execute its handler, the stack could be in who-knows-what-state.

Take a look at this example:

```
void First(int a, int b, int c, int d)
{
Second(int a, int b, int c, int d);
}

void Second(int a, int b, int c, int d)
{
// some code that causes an access violation
}

__try
{
//
Second(1,2,3,4);
}
__except(GetExceptionCode() == ACCESS_VIOLATION)
{
// if the exception is an access violation, this
// code will execute
return NULL;
}
```

In the try block, First is called passing four parameters. First in turn calls Second also passing four parameters. Second causes an access violation. It is now necessary for the exception dispatcher to somehow get First's and Second's parameters off the stack so the exception handler can return NULL and not have it go off into la-la land. This is all taken care of by a feature of structured exception handling called unwinding. There are actually two types of unwinds: global and local. A global unwind takes place when there are nested functions and an exception takes place. A local unwind takes place when there are multiple handlers within one function. I'll get to examples of a local unwind in a moment. In either case, just remember that the stack is going to be clean by the time your handler's code gets executed.

It's the compiler's job to help the exception dispatcher perform the unwinds. This means that although the object code must follow certain rules, compilers are are free to implement the syntax of structured exception handling anyway they like. The syntax of Visual C++ compiler is just one possible method. As we shall see in a moment, structured exception handling is not limited to C or C++. Although I'm not going explain how to build structured exception handling support into a compiler, it is important to see the role that a compiler plays.

Let's go back to the HappyFunStrCpy function, The output of HappyFunStrCpy compiled with the /Fa parameter on a x86 machine. (And you thought you wouldn't need assembly knowledge anymore) To make the output more readable, I added some comments and constants and deleted the extraneous stuff. The first thing you'll notice looking at SEH.ASM is the extra variables, structures, and functions the compiler adds to your code.

The first item of interest is called the registration node. The registration node is broken into two pieces: a system-defined piece and a language-specific piece. Among the variables in the registration node are a pointer to the next registration node and a pointer to the language handler function.

```
struct registration_node{
    .
    .
    .
struct registration_node *next.
    .
    .
void (*language_handler)();
    .
    .
    .
}
```

Their locations within the registration node are unimportant and, until officially documented, subject to change. Visual C++ sets the language handler to the run-time function _except_handler2.

The next item of interest is the exception stack which stores registration nodes. In SEH.ASM this variable is called __except_list.

The next interesting variable is the _HappyFunStrCpy structure. The _except_handler2 function uses the variable try_count in this structure to determine if there are nested trys. Then _except_handler2 uses the next variable in the _HappyFunStrCpy structure to determine if this is a exception handler or a termination handler (I'll explain termination handlers in a moment). If it's an exception handler this variable points to the address of the filter, otherwise it is NULL. The third variable is a pointer to either the except handler or the termination handler.

When the dispatcher searches for handlers, it simply walks the exception stack calling the language handler in each node. This is why I stated that structure exception handling wasn't limited to C or C++. As you can see, since the dispatcher is just calling a callback function in the registration node, any number of implementations could be provided. The _except_handler2 function uses the information in _HappyFunStrCpy to perform the actual work of calling termination handlers, exception handlers, and unwinding.

The last point of interest is the following line:

```
cmp  DWORD PTR $T12873[ebp], EXCEPTION_ACCESS_VIOLATION
```

This is the assembly language output of this C statement:

```
GetExceptionCode() == EXCEPTION_ACCESS_VIOLATION
```

GetExceptionCode turns out to be a variable instead of a function to retrieve the exception. That's GetExceptionCode why is only allowed within the constructs of a termination handler.

```
        .model FLAT
        PUBLIC      _HappyFunStrCpy
        EXTRN       __except_handler2:NEAR
        EXTRN       __except_list:DWORD
        EXTRN       _strcpy:NEAR
        .data
;;;;;;;;;;;;;;;;;;;;;;;;;;;;;;;;;;;;;;;;;;;;
; Scope Table Structure
;;;;;;;;;;;;;;;;;;;;;;;;;;;;;;;;;;;;;;;;;;;;
_HappyFunStrCpy
try_count    DD      0ffffffffH
FilterPtr    DD      FLAT:$filter
Excpt_or_fnly        DD      FLAT:$handler
;;;;;;;;;;;;;;;;;;;;;;;;;;;;;;;;;;;;;;;;;;;;
```

```
.code
$T12871 = -4
$T12872 = -28
$T12873 = -32
_lpszString1$ = 8
_lpszString2$ = 12
_HappyFunStrCpy PROC NEAR
; Line 26
    push    ebp
    mov     ebp, esp
    sub     esp, 20H
    push    ebx
    push    esi
    push    edi
;;;;;;;;;;;;;;;;;;;;;;;;;;;;;;;;;;;;;;;;;;
; Registration Node initialization
;;;;;;;;;;;;;;;;;;;;;;;;;;;;;;;;;;;;;;;;;;
    mov     DWORD PTR $T12871[ebp], esp
    mov     DWORD PTR $T12872[ebp+16], ebp
    mov     DWORD PTR $T12872[ebp+12], -1
    mov     DWORD PTR $T12872[ebp+8], OFFSET FLAT:_HappyFunStrCpy
    mov     DWORD PTR $T12872[ebp+4], OFFSET FLAT:__except_handler2
;;;;;;;;;;;;;;;;;;;;;;;;;;;;;;;;;;;;;;;;;;
; "push" Registration Node onto except stack
;;;;;;;;;;;;;;;;;;;;;;;;;;;;;;;;;;;;;;;;;;
    mov     eax, DWORD PTR fs:__except_list
    mov     DWORD PTR $T12872[ebp], eax
    lea     eax, DWORD PTR $T12872[ebp]
    mov     DWORD PTR fs:__except_list, eax
;;;;;;;;;;;;;;;;;;;;;;;;;;;;;;;;;;;;;;;;;;;;
; Line 28 Beginning of try
;;;;;;;;;;;;;;;;;;;;;;;;;;;;;;;;;;;;;;;;;;;;
    mov     DWORD PTR $T12872[ebp+12], 0
    push    DWORD PTR _lpszString2$[ebp]
    push    DWORD PTR _lpszString1$[ebp]
    call    _strcpy
    add     esp, 8
    jmp     $L12863
```

```
; Line 29
$L12864:
    mov     DWORD PTR $T12872[ebp+12], -1
    jmp     $L12869
$filter:
    mov     eax, DWORD PTR $T12872[ebp+20]
    mov     eax, DWORD PTR [eax]
    mov     eax, DWORD PTR [eax]
    mov     DWORD PTR $T12873[ebp], eax
; Line 32
    cmp     DWORD PTR $T12873[ebp], EXCEPTION_ACCESS_VIOLATION
    mov     eax, 0
    sete    al
    ret     0
    jmp     $L12866
$handler:
    mov     esp, DWORD PTR $T12871[ebp]
; Line 33
    sub     eax, eax
    jmp     $L12863
; Line 34
    mov     DWORD PTR $T12872[ebp+12], -1
$L12869:
; Line 35
$L12863:
$L12866:


;;;;;;;;;;;;;;;;;;;;;;;;;;;;;;;;;;;;;;;;;
; "pop" Registration Node off except stack
;;;;;;;;;;;;;;;;;;;;;;;;;;;;;;;;;;;;;;;;;
    mov     ecx, DWORD PTR $T12872[ebp]
    mov     DWORD PTR fs:__except_list, ecx
    pop     edi
    pop     esi
    pop     ebx
    leave
    ret     0
_HappyFunStrCpy ENDP
```

```
_TEXT         ENDS
END
```

## DON'T SWALLOW EXCEPTIONS.

Now that you have seen how easy it is to implement structured exception handling you may be tempted to guard every function call. One word of advice. Don't accidently handle an exception that some other handler is depending on. This means that you shouldn't blindly call EXCEPTION_EXECUTE_HANDLER in your filter functions. In practice it is important that you either handle the exception or pass it on. For example, the following code "swallows" the exception.

```
__try
  {
  .
  .
  .
  return TRUE;
  }
__except (EXCEPTION_EXECUTE_HANDLER)
  {
  return FALSE;
  }
```

If functions that call you are depending upon structured exception handling then your handler just ate their exception. If you want to handle a specific exception, make sure you take advantage of the filter function. This next example, only handles access violations, passing on all others.

```
__try
  {
  .
  .
  .
  return TRUE;
  }
__except (GetExceptionCode() == EXCEPTION_ACCESS_VIOLATION ?
```

**321**

```
                              EXCEPTION_EXECUTE_HANDLER :
                              EXCEPTION_CONTINUE_SEARCH )
   {

   .

   .

   return FALSE;
   }
```

# SOFTWARE GENERATED EXCEPTIONS

Until now, I have been discussing hardware generated exceptions, but software generated exceptions are another reason not to swallow exceptions. Software generated exceptions are an easy way to have application-defined exceptions. Both kernel-mode and user-mode threads can generate software exceptions. For example, HeapCreate (one of the Win32 Heap allocation routines) has a flag called HEAP_GENERATE_EXCEPTIONS that determines what to do when one of the other Heap functions fail. If the HEAP_GENERATE_EXCEPTIONS flag is clear, functions, such as HeapAlloc, return NULL upon failure. But, if HEAP_GENERATE_EXCEPTIONS is set, then the Win32 virtual memory manager will raise an exception to indicate a function failure, such as an out-of-memory condition, instead of returning NULL. This way, you can set up an exception handler that will get control whenever an error occurs, instead of constantly checking the returns of all of your functions for NULL.

You can also use the RaiseException function to generate your own software-based exceptions.

```
VOID RaiseException(DWORD dwExceptionCode,
                    DWORD dwExceptionFlags,
                    DWORD cArguments,
                    DWORD lpArguments);
```

The first parameter, dwExceptionCode, sets the user-defined exception code. The second parameter can be either EXCEPTION_NONCONTINUABLE, which indicates that you cannot recover from this exception, or zero which indicates that you can. The final two parameters allow you to pass application-defined data as arguments. These parameters enable a process to use structured exception handling to handle private, software-generated, application-defined exceptions. If you decide to generate your own application-defined exceptions, follow the standard set in WINERROR.H for the exception codes you choose:

```
//
// Values are 32 bit values layed out as follows:
//
//   3 3 2 2 2 2 2 2 2 2 2 2 1 1 1 1 1 1 1 1 1 1
//   1 0 9 8 7 6 5 4 3 2 1 0 9 8 7 6 5 4 3 2 1 0 9 8 7 6 5 4 3 2 1 0
//  +---+-+-+-----------------------+-------------------------------+
//  |Sev|C|R|     Facility          |           Code                |
//  +---+-+-+-----------------------+-------------------------------+
//
// where
//
//      Sev - is the severity code
//
//          00 - Success
//          01 - Informational
//          10 - Warning
//          11 - Error
//
//      C - is the Customer code flag - set to 1
//
//      R - is a reserved bit - set to 0
//
//      Facility - is the facility code
//
//      Code - is the facility's status code
//
```

If you haven't defined any application specific exceptions, you can use RaiseException to emulate one of the hardware-based exceptions.

Here's how simulate a hardware-based exception, such as an access violation:

```
RaiseException(EXCEPTION_ACCESS_VIOLATION,
                    0,    //continuable exception
                    0, NULL); //no arguments
```

## TERMINATION HANDLERS

Using RaiseException give you the power to decide when to generate an exception. Evaluating the filter within an excepton handler enables you to decide whether to execute your exception handler or not. However, you only get to decide if there is an exception. This means that your exception handler is not guaranteed to be called. Take a look at this next example:

```
try
    {
            EnterCriticalSection(&CriticalSection);
        .
        .
        .
    }
except(EXCEPTION_ACCESS_VIOLATION ?
    EXCEPTION_EXECUTE_HANDLER :
    EXCEPTION_CONTINUE_SEARCH)
    {
            LeaveCriticalSection(&CriticalSection);

    }
```

In this example, the try block calls EnterCriticalSection to request access to some protected data. If there is an exception, then LeaveCriticalSection will be called in the exception handler. But if all goes well, LeaveCriticalSection will not get called leaving the CriticalSection object locked.

To combat this problem use a termination handler. A termination handler is always called. It doesn't matter whether your function executes cleanly or causes an exception (or anybody else's function causes an exception for that matter) the termination handler will execute.

To implement termination handling, Microsoft defined another extension to the C/C++ language called the finally block. Here's the syntax:

```
__try {
.
.                    // guarded section
.
}
__finally {
.
.                    // termination handler
.
}
```

A termination handler is the place to guard precious resources such as memory and synchronization objects.

```
CString *ps;
__try
{
    .
    .
    pS = new CString;        WaitForSingleObject(m_hSem,INFINITE)
    .
    .
}
__finally
{
    delete pS;
    ReleaseSemaphore(m_hSem,1,NULL);
}
```

When your program enters the try block—called the guarded section—of a try-finally construct it can leave it normally or abnormally.

If there are no exceptions, the code executes to the closing brace and it terminates normally. The second situation is an abnormal termination, which occurs when the code leaves the try body by any other means. The following are all examples of abnormal terminations: return, goto, longjmp or an exception. Your termination handler is still guaranteed to be called, but there is a performance penalty. Since your termination handler is called every time you enter the function, you want to avoid the performance penalty whenever possible. Earlier I stated that a local unwind takes place when there are multiple exception handlers within a function and an exception takes place. Well, a local unwind also takes place when you abnormally terminate a termination handler. It's the local unwind that causes the performance hit.

Note that you cannot create objects on the stack or the unwind will get messed up. If you do try, Visual C++ will generate an error C2712—try in functions that require unwinding. If you must prematurely exit the try block, use the new __leave keyword. The __leave keyword causes execution to immediately exit the try block and enter the finally block without performing a local unwind. In the following example, if you cannot get a semaphore then the SomeOtherFunction won't execute. Instead, the finally block will immediately execute.

```
__try
{
hSem = CreateSemaphore(NULL,1,1, SEM_NAME);
if (hSem == NULL )
        __leave;
    SomeOtherFunction()

.

}
__finally
{
if (AbnormalTermination())
   MessageBox(NULL,
     "leave is not considered an abnormal termination",
     MB_OK); //MessageBox will not be called
if (!hSem)
   ReleaseSemaphore(hSem, 1, NULL);


}
```

The AbnormalTermination function is an intrinsic that determines whether the try block terminated normally or abnormally

```
__try
{
```

```
        if (!foo())
            return;
        SomeOtherFunction()

            .

            .

    }
    __finally
    {
        if (AbnormalTermination())
            MessageBox(NULL,
                "return is considered an abnormal termination",
                MB_OK); //MessageBox will be called
    }
```

NOTE: There is one case in which your termination handler will not be called. It's when you call ExitThread or ExitProcess (or if some other thread calls TerminateThread or TerminateProcess during execution of the try block). Use this method only as a last resort. If your termination handler doesn't execute, memory may be left floating or other resources left dangling.

## EXCEPTION PRECEDENCE

Now that I've gone over exception handling and termination handling the only thing left is the order which handlers are called. Just like exception handlers you can have any number of nested termination handlers. You can even mix and match the two. But when an exception occurs who gets called when? It goes like this: If an exception occurs and the exception dispatcher finds a handler to accept the exception, it executes all termination handlers between the point of the exception and the point of the accepting handler. Since this can be confusing, I'll show what I mean in examples. The first example is where you have nested termination handlers.

```
    __try
    {
        __try
        {
            //
```

```
        }
        __finally
        {
                // #1 The termination handler is executed.
        }
    }
    __finally
    {
        //#2 The second termination handler is executed

    }
```

This is a pretty straight-forward case. Termination handlers are executed as you leave each try block. The next case might not be so straight forward. It's where you have both termination handlers and exception handlers and an exception occurs.

```
    puts("Beginning of the function");
    __try
    {
        __try
        {
        RaiseException(EXCEPTION_ACCESS_VIOLATION, 0, NULL) //#1
        }
        __finally
        {
        puts("In finally");   //#3
        }
    }
    __except(puts("In the exception filter"), 1) //#2
            {
                puts("in the except handler"); //#4
            }
```

The output is:

Beginning of the function
In first try

In second try

In the exception filter

In finally

In the exception handler

First, when the exception is raised (#1), it is trapped and evaluated by the filter function. Next, when the filter evaluates to EXCEPTION_EXECUTE_HANDLER (#2), all termination handlers are executed (#3). The exception handler is executed after the last termination handler (#4).

# DEBUGGING WITH EXCEPTIONS

Here are a couple of tips if you are going to debug code that contains structured exception handlers. If your code generates an exception and you are debugging with either Windbg (the debugger that ships with the Win32 SDK) or the debugger in Visual C++, the debugger is notified of the exception first. The dispatch goes like this: debugger, your exception handler, second chance debugger, system exception handler. Therefore, if you are debugging a try block and an exception occurs, the debugger will gain control. If you want your handler to gain control, then you must inform the debugger not to handle the exception. If you are using the Windbg, you can turn off individual exceptions in the Options-exceptions dialog. Or from the command window you can enter gn for go - not handled. This enables you to debug your exception handler. If you are using the Visual C++ debugger, go to the Debug-Exceptions dialog to turn off individual exceptions (see figure 8–2).

If while you're browsing through the available exceptions in the Debug-Exceptions dialog box you notice an entry for Ctrl-C don't be alarmed. In a normal console process, Ctrl-C does not cause an exception. But if your process is being debugged it does. What happens is when the console server detects a Ctrl-C or break, it calls CreateRemoteThread to create a new thread in the your application to handle the event. This new thread then raises an exception if the process is being debugged. This makes it convenient for the debugger to catch Ctrl-Cs. This doesn't mean your application should use structured exception handling to catch Ctrl-C. Instead, use the documented SetConsoleCtrlHandler.

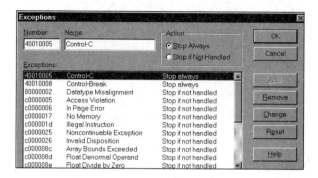

**Figure 8–2** VC++2.0 exception options dialog.

# STRUCTURED EXCEPTION HANDLING AND WIN32S.

Up until now I have been just talking about the structured exception handling capabilities under Windows 95 and NT. But, structured exception handling also works in Win32s. You have everything available to you in Win32s that you do in Win32 with one exception. Since structured exception handling relies upon the compiler for support you cannot use it within any 16-bit universal thunks sections that you have.

If your Win32s application has ever caused an unhandled exception, you'll notice that it is impossible to get a Windows 3.1 GPF (or a DRWATSON.LOG) from a Win32s application. Windows 3.1 treats unhandled exceptions within 32-bit sections of code as fatal errors and terminates Windows. (If you have ever written your own 32-bit code, perhaps in a VxD, for Windows 3.1 that caused an exception you now know why you were mysteriously deposited at the MS-DOS prompt.) For this reason Win32s places a try-except block around your entire Win32s-based program to trap any of your unhandled exceptions.

# CONCLUSION

The concept is good and 32-bit Windows provides an excellent implementation, but structured exception handling is not a cure-all. Sprinkling try-excepts and try-finallys thoughout your code like salt will not preempt the need for sound design and testing. However, when combined with proper design and testing, structured exception handling has the potential to make your code more stable and easily more maintainable.

**TABLE 8–1** Win32 Hardware Exceptions

**The following constants are from winbase.h**

### EXCEPTION_ACCESS_VIOLATION

This exception occurs if a thread attempts to load or store data to or from an address that is not accessible to the current process. This is the most common exception: reading or writing through a bad or NULL pointer will cause it. With a 4GB address space you may be wondering what address could considered bad? Well, only 2GB is available to a process and that some virtual addresses within that 2GB can be marked as PAGE_READONLY or PAGE_NOACCESS.

### EXCEPTION_DATATYPE_MISALIGNMENT

The MIPS or Alpha AXP architectures generate this exception when an instruction attempts to read or write data to or from an address that is not naturally aligned. Actually you won't see this exception in a user-mode program, but I am describing it here to make you aware of it. You won't see it because the developers of the Win32 subsystem code use structured exception handling to handle this exception and automatically pad the data. Unfortunately, this process if very slow. It takes over 1,000 instructions to do this!

### EXCEPTION_BREAKPOINT

A breakpoint exception occurs when a breakpoint instruction executes or a hardware-defined breakpoint is encountered (for example, an address stored in a breakpoint register is reached). This is for debuggers. On x86 processors, the breakpoint instruction is the ubiquitous int 3H assembly-language instruction. Calling the DebugBreak function causes this exception.

### FLOATING POINT EXCEPTIONS

By default, Windows NT turns off floating-point exceptions. To enable the floating-point processor to generate exceptions you must call the controlfp function to initialize the floating point trap. This function is the portable equivalent to control87() used in MS-DOS and 16-bit Windows. (Remember, there is no x87 on RISC machines!)

Here's how to initialize the floating-point trap to capture all exceptions except EM_DENORMAL and EM_INEXACT (defined in float.h) that is, in all cases where there is a true error.

```
controlfp(EM_INEXACT | EM_DENORMAL, MCM_EM);
```

## EXCEPTION_INT_DIVIDE_BY_ZERO

This exception is generated when a thread attempts to divide an integer by zero.

## EXCEPTION_PRIV_INSTRUCTION

A privileged instruction is an instruction that is only allowed in a kernel mode. Any attempt by a user mode thread to execute kernel mode code (such as an attempt to read or write to a port) will generate this exception. I got this exception alot when porting a 16-bit application to Windows NT. The following line of code was the culprit:

```
_asm
{
.
.
.
out dx,al
}
```

This harmless instruction in 16-bit Windows is now considered a security violation in Windows NT and is forbidden in user mode. If you want to access ports in Windows NT, you have to write a device driver.

## EXCEPTION_ILLEGAL_INSTRUCTION

Illegal instructions are instructions that have no meaning to the processor your running on. For example, on an x86, the instruction 0xCC equates to the mnemonic int 3. However, the instruction 0xFFFF has no meaning on an x86. Many times this exception occurs due to a serious bug in you program. For example if you program somehow messes up the stack, a function could return right into the middle of your data section. If your program does (but you didn't intend it to), sooner or later it will generate this exception. If this exception results from executing data--it's time to get out of dodge. There is no way to recover from this exception. Just free your memory and unlock your objects and maybe display a MessageBox to try to help you track down what's causing this problem. Hopefully, you will discover any occurrence of this exception before your application goes to production.

**TABLE 8–2** CONTEXT RECORD AND EXCEPTION RECORD defined in WINNT.H

```
typedef struct _EXCEPTION_POINTERS { /* exp */
    PEXCEPTION_RECORD ExceptionRecord;
    PCONTEXT ContextRecord;
```

```
} EXCEPTION_POINTERS;

typedef struct _EXCEPTION_RECORD {
    DWORD    ExceptionCode;
    DWORD ExceptionFlags;
    struct _EXCEPTION_RECORD *ExceptionRecord;
    PVOID ExceptionAddress;
    DWORD NumberParameters;
    DWORD ExceptionInformation[EXCEPTION_MAXIMUM_PARAMETERS];
} EXCEPTION_RECORD;

typedef EXCEPTION_RECORD *PEXCEPTION_RECORD;
typedef struct _CONTEXT {

    //
    // The flags values within this flag control the contents of
    // a CONTEXT record.
    //
    // If the context record is used as an input parameter, then
    // for each portion of the context record controlled by a flag
    // whose value is set, it is assumed that that portion of the
    // context record contains valid context. If the context record
    // is being used to modify a threads context, then only that
    // portion of the threads context will be modified.
    //
    // If the context record is used as an IN OUT parameter to capture
    // the context of a thread, then only those portions of the thread's
    // context corresponding to set flags will be returned.
    //
    // The context record is never used as an OUT only parameter.
    //


    DWORD ContextFlags;

    //
    // This section is specified/returned if CONTEXT_DEBUG_REGISTERS is
    // set in ContextFlags.  Note that CONTEXT_DEBUG_REGISTERS is NOT
    // included in CONTEXT_FULL.
```

```
    //

    DWORD    Dr0;
    DWORD    Dr1;
    DWORD    Dr2;
    DWORD    Dr3;
    DWORD    Dr6;
    DWORD    Dr7;

    //
    // This section is specified/returned if the
    // ContextFlags word contians the flag CONTEXT_FLOATING_POINT.
    //

    FLOATING_SAVE_AREA FloatSave;

    //
    // This section is specified/returned if the
    // ContextFlags word contians the flag CONTEXT_SEGMENTS.
    //

    DWORD    SegGs;
    DWORD    SegFs;
    DWORD    SegEs;
    DWORD    SegDs;

    //
    // This section is specified/returned if the
    // ContextFlags word contians the flag CONTEXT_INTEGER.
    //

    DWORD    Edi;
    DWORD    Esi;
    DWORD    Ebx;
    DWORD    Edx;
    DWORD    Ecx;
    DWORD    Eax;
```

```
//
// This section is specified/returned if the
// ContextFlags word contians the flag CONTEXT_CONTROL.
//

DWORD   Ebp;
DWORD   Eip;
DWORD   SegCs
DWORD   EFlags;
DWORD   Esp;
DWORD   SegSs;

} CONTEXT;
typedef CONTEXT *PCONTEXT;
```

1 Bruce Eckel, "C++ Into The Future," UNIX Review, May 1992, pp. 27-34.

**CHAPTER 9**

# PROGRAMMING CONSOLE APPLICATIONS

In 32-bit Windows, a *Console* process is a process that does not have a graphical user interface. Many companies are porting their MS-DOS applications or their UNIX applications. To help developers of these applications port more easily, Win32 supports a character mode API called the *console* API. This chapter gives you all the details you will need to know to decide whether to make a console application that has a character-based interface. This chapter teaches you how to take advantage of the console standard input, standard output, and error input-output operations. It shows how to redirect the standard input-output handles through pipes and files. It also shows how to integrate your console application with *MessageBoxes*, common dialogs, string resources, and printing. It finishes up by showing how to get your graphical application to send output to a console window.

If you are a developer of graphical applications, you may be wondering why, in this day and age, Win32 supports a character mode API, yet alone *another* character mode API? Well, for starters, any application that doesn't have a user interface is a candidate for a console program. So are command-line-only

**337**

applications. (Hey, I know how to type, so why should I wade through the file manager just to copy some files to my C drive?) But the main impetus for the console API is to allow the easy porting of character-mode applications from other environments.

Another question you might be asking is, "What is Microsoft's commitment to the console API?" After all, it is not in Win32s. But, since both Windows NT and Windows 95 support the console APIs you should be satisfied that the console API is not a dead-end API. (Windows 95 supports all of the APIs with the exception of the console CodePage APIs: *GetConsoleCP, GetConsoleOutputCP, and SetConsoleCP.*)

One feature that the console API provides is a method to implement character-oriented windows. Character-oriented Windows applications are applications that use a mouse to manipulate the user interface in character mode. Buttons and menus are drawn using characters that form lines and rectangles. If you are looking in this chapter for instructions on how to implement your own character-oriented Windows application, forget it. Those types of applications may sell in a character-based-only operating system like MS-DOS (without Windows 3.1) or in certain flavors of UNIX, but they have no chance of competing on the same desktop with graphical applications. Table 10–1 contains all of the Console API functions. In my opinion, if you are designing an application from scratch and its user interface is more complicated than a few command line parameters, design it as a graphical application.

**Table 9–1** Console APIs

| Function | Description |
| --- | --- |
| AllocConsole | Creates a console for the current process |
| CreateConsoleScreenBuffer | Returns a handle to a new screen buffer |
| FillConsoleOutputAttribute | Writes attributes to the screen buffer |
| FillConsoleOutputCharacter | Writes characters to the screen buffer |
| FlushConsoleInputBuffer | Clears the console input buffer |
| FreeConsole | Frees the current console |
| GenerateConsoleCtrlEvent | Sends a signal to a console process group |
| GetConsoleCP | Gets code page for console input |
| GetConsoleCursorInfo | Returns cursor size and visibility |
| GetConsoleMode | Returns console input or output mode |
| GetConsoleOutputCP | Gets code page for console output |

| | |
|---|---|
| *GetConsoleScreenBufferInfo* | Returns screen-buffer information |
| *GetConsoleTitle* | Returns console-window title |
| *GetLargestConsoleWindowSize* | Returns largest possible window size |
| *GetNumberOfConsoleInputEvents* | Retrieves number of console-queue events |
| *GetNumberOfConsoleMouseButtons* | Retrieves number of mouse buttons |
| *GetStdHandle* | Returns standard I/O handles |
| *PeekConsoleInput* | Previews console input data |
| *ReadConsole* | Reads console input data |
| *ReadConsoleInput* | Reads console input data |
| *ReadConsoleOutput* | Reads screen-buffer data |
| *ReadConsoleOutputAttribute* | Reads a console attribute string |
| *ReadConsoleOutputCharacter* | Reads a screen-buffer string |
| *ScrollConsoleScreenBuffer* | Scrolls data in the screen buffer |
| *SetConsoleActiveScreenBuffer* | Changes displayed screen buffer |
| *SetConsoleCP* | Sets code page for console input |
| *SetConsoleCtrlHandler* | Sets signal handler for console process |
| *SetConsoleCursorInfo* | Sets console cursor size and visibility |
| *SetConsoleCursorPosition* | Sets console cursor position |
| *SetConsoleMode* | Sets console input or output mode |
| *SetConsoleOutputCP* | Sets code page for console output |
| *SetConsoleScreenBufferSize* | Changes screen-buffer size |
| *SetConsoleTextAttribute* | Sets attributes for screen text |
| *SetConsoleTitle* | Sets console-window title string |
| *SetConsoleWindowInfo* | Sets console window size |
| *SetStdHandle* | Sets the standard device handles |
| *WriteConsole* | Writes to console screen buffer |
| *WriteConsoleInput* | Writes to console input buffer |
| *WriteConsoleOutput* | Writes directly to screen buffer |
| *WriteConsoleOutputAttribute* | Writes an attribute string to console |
| *WriteConsoleOutputCharacter* | Writes a character string to console |

However, let me quote you something about opinions from the guy who designed the user interface for DCA's Windows-based 3270 terminal emulator: "There are more opinions about user interfaces than there are elbows in the world. Considering that only human beings have opinions and even insects have elbows, that's a lot of opinions." But, there's more to a console program than just its user interface. This next sections details several other limitations of console applications.

# FEATURES NOT SUPPORTED IN A CONSOLE APPLICATION

This chapter gives you all the details you will need to know to decide whether to make a console application with a full user interface. But before you make your decision, you should know that console applications have limitations that graphical applications don't have. Console applications are Win32 applications, and many Win32 API calls work seamlessly. Still, you can't do simple things with a console window that you can with a graphical window. The major stumbling block is the fact that the user interface for console applications runs in the server side of the Win32 subsystem. This means that when a new console application is started, the console window is mapped into the 2GB of address space reserved for the kernel.

# HOOKS IN CONSOLE APPLICATIONS

If you call *SetWindowsHookEx* for a console application you will see results that are different from what you see when you set a hook in a graphical application. That means if application A sets a system-wide input hook (*WH_KEYBOARD*), and text is typed in a console window, application A's input hook won't get called. Here's a list of other hooks that are not supported.

■■ Message hooks (*WH_MSGFILTER*). Any hook that relies upon a message queue is not supported. For instance, when you ask for mouse messages, the system calls your MouseHookProc callback whenever an application calls the *GetMessage* or *PeekMessage* function and there is a mouse message to be processed. However, console applications do not call *GetMessage* or *PeekMessage*. Instead console applications normally use a *ReadConsoleInput* loop which waits for event messages. Thus, a mouse hook is not compatible with the console application's message handle scheme.

■■ Computer-based training hooks (*WH_CBT*). Computer-based training hooks are used to capture events before activating, creating, destroying, minimizing, maximizing, moving, or sizing a window. If you set a *WH_CBT* hook and specify all windows, messages from every window except console windows will respond. Thus computer-based training hooks are also not compatible with console windows.

Journal hooks, however, do work. They tap into the system message queue that all applications (both graphical and console) use. Currently Windows NT supports journaling by forcing the console input thread to communicate with the application that set the hook. In the case of a console application, the call to the hook functions are run in the context of the application that installed the hook. This forces Windows NT to synchronously talk to this process in order for it to work; if this process is busy or blocked (like sitting at a breakpoint), the console thread is hung. Similarly, if Windows NT allowed other hooks to freely hook any process, this same hung state could occur for these processes as well. The reason journaling is allowed to hook consoles is that journaling already requires synchronization between all processes in the system and a mechanism to disengage the journaling process (via the **Ctrl+Esc**, **Alt+Esc** and **Ctrl+Alt+Del** keystrokes) is provided to prevent a hung-system message queue.

## TIMERS AND CONSOLE APPLICATIONS

You also shouldn't use timers in a console application. Timers require a message loop to dispatch the timer message to the timer procedure (which console applications normally don't have). However, later in this chapter I will show you how to emulate timer functions by using *Sleep* or the multimedia timer.

## CONSOLE INTERACTION WITH OTHER WINDOWS

There is no way to get notification that your console window is being maximized, minimized, dragged around, or resized. Console applications also don't take notice of things like window position or focus. A window hierarchy does not exist between console windows and graphical windows. Later on I'll show you how to take special precaution when spawning graphical applications from a console because the new application could end up behind the console application.

## SUBCLASSING AND CONSOLE APPLICATIONS

You cannot subclass the window in which your console application resides. Console windows are of the type *ConsoleWindowClass*. If you call *GetClassInfo* or *GetWindowLong* with the window handle of the "ConsoleWindowClass," you receive an *ERROR_ACCESS_DENIED* return code. This is because the window procedure for ConsoleWindowClass runs in the Win32 server, which means that—although the window procedure is technically in you same process space—it is outside of the 2GB your process can access (it's in the system's 2GB).

Now that all of the caveats are out of the way, let's look at what you can do.

# FEATURES OF CONSOLE APPLICATIONS

You can develop a console application using the C runtime API. But at this point you may be asking yourself why to even bother with a console application, especially when Windows NT supports MS-DOS, POSIX, and OS/2 subsystems? Well, there are several things you can do with a native console application that you cannot accomplish when running an application compiled for these other subsystems. Consider the following examples:

■■ Multithreaded applications. Unlike an MS-DOS application, you can create a multithreaded application with the console API. Threads created in a console application are like any other thread in the system. You can suspend, resume, or change the priorities of the thread.

■■ Unicode applications. Like their graphical counterparts, console applications support Unicode. MS-DOS, OS/2, and POSIX are limited to single-byte characters. (Windows NT only)

■■ Secure applications. Native console applications can take advantage of the Windows NT security APIs. Although it is for Windows NT only, this means that native console applications can have access control lists (ACLs) on their objects and can have privileges. In a secure environment it is impossible for any MS-DOS, POSIX, or OS/2 application to even change the system clock.

■■ 32-bit applications. Console applications are Win32 applications, which means they are full 32-bit applications (remember, the OS/2 subsystem only supports the 16-bit, 1.x version). This means that console applications can take full advantage of their 2GB process space and don't have to fool with segments or selectors.

▐▌ Use of Resources. Although not required, console applications can use resources just like any graphical application. By resources I mean string tables, icons, dialogs, and so on. Even if you don't plan to use any other resources, you should at least include an icon so you can properly display your console application in 3.1 or the shell in windows'95.

In essence, the decision to port your character-based application to the Win32 console API is similar to the decision you must make concerning porting your Win16 applications. You shouldn't consider the console API to be interchangeable with the graphical API. The Win32 subsystem does not prevent the mingling of these APIs sets, but the characteristics of each are in many cases unique to themselves and are at times at odds with each other. However, once you learn the rules, there are some things you can do with a console that may not be obvious.

## CONSOLE HANDLES

To manipulate console input and output buffers, you must first obtain a handle to the buffer. There are three different functions to use to open a console handle: *GetStdHandle, CreateFile,* and *CreateConsoleScreenBuffer.* This next section goes through each of the functions and tells when it is appropriate to use each.

### GetStdHandle

Use the *GetStdHandle* function to access the *STD_INPUT_HANDLE, STD_OUTPUT_HANDLE,* or the *STD_ERROR_HANDLE* handles:

```
MyStdOut = GetStdHandle(STD_OUTPUT_HANDLE);
```

The C runtime refers to these handles as standard input (stdin), standard output (stdout), and standard error (stderr), respectively. If the handles haven't been redirected, *GetStdHandle(STD_INPUT_HANDLE)* returns a handle to the console input buffer, and *GetStdHandle(STD_OUTPUT_HANDLE)* and

*GetStdHandle(STD_ERROR_HANDLE)* refer to the console's output buffer, which is the screen. However, any of the three handles can be redirected with *SetStdHandle* function:

```
HANDLE NewStdIn;
HANDLE NewStdOut;
HANDLE NewStdErr;

SetStdHandle(STD_INPUT_HANDLE,NewStdIn);
SetStdHandle(STD_OUTPUT_HANDLE,NewStdOut);
SetStdHandle(STD_ERROR_HANDLE,NewStdErr);
```

If a handle has been redirected, *GetStdHandle* returns the redirected handle. To guarantee that you are actually getting a handle to the console input buffer or the console screen buffer, use the constants *CONIN$* and *CONOUT$*, as in the following example:

```
Handle hConsoleIn = GetStdHandle(CONIN$);
Handle hConsoleOut = GetStdHandle(CONOUT$);
```

The handles returned by *GetStdHandle* have GENERIC_READ | GENERIC_WRITE access unless *SetStdHandle* has been used to set the handle to have lesser access. Using *SetStdHandle* allows a process to spawn a child and redirect the child's handles to something other than stdin or stdout. In a minute, I'll show you how to spawn a console application from a graphical process and redirect stdin and stdout back to the graphical process.

### CreateFile

In addition to creating disk-based files, the *CreateFile* function enables you to retrieve handles to a console's input buffer and output buffers. Like *GetStdHandle*, you can use *CONIN$* and *CONOUT$* to get handles to the console input and output buffers even if stdin and stdout have been redirected:

```
HANDLE hFile = CreateFile(CONIN$,
                    GENERIC_READ | GENERIC_WRITE,
                    FILE_SHARE_READ | FILE_SHARE_WRITE,
                    NULL,
```

```
                    OPEN_EXISTING,
                    fdwAttrsAndFlags,
                    hTemplateFile);
```

For compatibility reasons, you can also call *CreateFile* with "CON" as the file name. When the second parameter is set to *GENERIC_WRITE*, this opens a console output handle. When the second parameter is *GENERIC_READ*, it opens a console input handle. Don't accidentally specify both *GENERIC_READ* and *GENERIC_WRITE* when the first parameter is "CON" or you'll get an error:

```
    if ((hConsoleInput = CreateFile("CON",
                        GENERIC_READ,
                        FILE_SHARE_READ | FILE_SHARE_WRITE,
                        0L, OPEN_EXISTING,
                        FILE_ATTRIBUTE_NORMAL, 0L))
        == (HANDLE) -1 )
        {
        printf("\nUnable to open console output handle.\n");
        return(FALSE);
        }
```

If you want to guarantee that you can get to the screen buffer (perhaps you must print an error message), then your process cannot continue if *CreateFile* fails:

```
    // This function opens up a handle to CONOUT$ so that we can
    // be guaranteed to get error messages to the console even
    // if the standard handles are redirected.

    void myError(HANDLE h, char *api, int line)
    {
    char buf[512];
    BOOL fSuccess;
    DWORD cBytesWritten;
    HANDLE hConout;

    sprintf(buf, "%s: Error %d from %s on line %d\n", __FILE__,
            GetLastError(),api, line);
```

```
fSuccess = WriteFile(h, buf, strlen(buf), &cBytesWritten,
                     NULL);
if (!fSuccess)
    {
    hConout = CreateFile("CONOUT$", GENERIC_READ |
                         GENERIC_WRITE,
                         FILE_SHARE_READ | FILE_SHARE_WRITE,
                         NULL, OPEN_EXISTING,
                         FILE_ATTRIBUTE_NORMAL, NULL);
    sprintf(buf, "%s: Error %d from %s on line %d\n",
            __FILE__,GetLastError(), api, line);
    WriteFile(hConout, buf, strlen(buf), &cBytesWritten,
            NULL);
    CloseHandle(hConout);
    }
return;
}
```

## CreateConsoleScreenBuffer

The third way to retrieve a console handle is to use the *CreateConsoleScreenBuffer* function:

```
HANDLE
CreateConsoleScreenBuffer(DWORD fdwAccess,
                          DWORD fdwShareMode,
                    LPSECURITY_ATTRIBUTES lpsa,
                    DWORD fdwType,
                    PVOID pvReserved);
```

You can have any number of screen buffers created by *CreateConsoleScreenBuffer*, but only one screen buffer can be the active buffer (the buffer that you see on the screen) at a time. To display a screen buffer, call *SetConsoleActiveScreenBuffer:*

```
BOOL
SetConsoleActiveScreenBuffer(hConsoleOutput);
```

Changing which buffer is displaying does not change which handle is considered standard out.:

```
int main()
{
DWORD cBytesWritten;
HANDLE hStdErr, hStdOut, hConout;
BOOL fSuccess;
char *stdErrMsg = "Hello from child to standard error!\n";
char *stdOutMsg = "Hello from child to standard output!\n";

hConout = CreateFile("CONOUT$", GENERIC_READ |
                     GENERIC_WRITE, FILE_SHARE_READ |
                     FILE_SHARE_WRITE, NULL, OPEN_EXISTING,
                     FILE_ATTRIBUTE_NORMAL, NULL);
//
// no reliable way of reporting errors to the console
// if we can't open a console handle
//
if ((int) hConout == -1)
    Beep(5000,500);
hStdErr = GetStdHandle(STD_ERROR_HANDLE);
if (hStdErr == INVALID_HANDLE_VALUE)
    myError(hConout, "GetStdHandle", __LINE__);
hStdOut = GetStdHandle(STD_OUTPUT_HANDLE);
if (hStdOut == INVALID_HANDLE_VALUE)
    myError(hConout, "GetStdHandle", __LINE__);
fSuccess = WriteFile(hStdErr, stdErrMsg, strlen(stdErrMsg),
                     &cBytesWritten, NULL);
if (!fSuccess)
    myError(hConout, "WriteFile", __LINE__);
fSuccess = WriteFile(hStdOut, stdOutMsg, strlen(stdOutMsg),
                     &cBytesWritten, NULL);
if (!fSuccess)
    myError(hConout, "WriteFile", __LINE__);
CloseHandle(hConout);
return(0);
}
```

No matter which of the three previous methods you choose to open the handle, use the *CloseHandle* function to close the handle, as in this example:

```
CloseHandle(hFile);
```

# C RUNTIME LIBRARY SUPPORT FOR CONSOLE INPUT AND OUTPUT

In addition to the handles provided by *CreateFile*, *GetStdHandle*, and *CreateConsoleScreen*Buffer, you can also manipulate console input and output via C runtime file handles. You obtain a C runtime file handle through the C runtime calls *_open* or *_sopen*. C runtime handles should only be used in C runtime calls. There are times when you want to convert between a C runtime handle and an operating system handle. An example of this is the situation where you want to use *fgets* to read input one line at a time, but also want to usc *CreateFile* to open the file. You must use *CreateFile* if you want to open a secure file—that is attach a security descriptor. For example:

```
HANDLE hConout = CreateFile("CONOUT$", GENERIC_READ |
                      GENERIC_WRITE,
                      FILE_SHARE_READ | FILE_SHARE_WRITE,
                      lpsa, // Use a security descriptor
                      OPEN_EXISTING,
                      FILE_ATTRIBUTE_NORMAL, NULL);
```

That's right, you can open a file with the Win32 API and manipulate it with C runtime functions. However to do so, you must convert the handle returned by CreateFile into a handle that C runtime functions understand. To convert between an operating system file handle and a C runtime handle, use the following C runtime call:

```
CRTstdout _open_osfhandle(hConout);
FILE *f = fdopen(CRTstdout, "a");
fgets(s.GetBuffer(0),s.GetLength(),f);
```

The C runtime routine *_open_osfhandle* takes an operating system file handle (like the one returned from *CreateFile*) and returns a C runtime file handle. Then you can use *_fdopen* to get a FILE for use in *fgets* and other stream-type C runtime functions.

**348**

When you are finished with the handle created by *CreateFile*, use *CloseHandle*. If the stream you are associated with is stdin, stdout, or stderr, you do not have to use the *flcose* function to close the C runtime handle.

**Note:** This same scheme can be used with disk-based files. If it is, you must explicitly close the C runtime handle with a call to *fclose*.

The following shows an example of opening a file with *CreateFile* and using *open_osfhandle* as a parameter to *fstat* to get file information:

```
LoadMyFile(PSTR pszFullFileName)
{
HFILE hf;
OFSTRUCT OfStruct;
struct stat FileStatus;
DWORD dwFileSize;

if ((hf = (HFILE)OpenFile(pszFullFileName,
                          (LPOFSTRUCT)&OfStruct,
                          OF_READ) == (HFILE)-1)
    {
    // Error Message Can't open
    return FALSE;
    }

fstat((INT)_open_osfhandle((long)(hf), (int)(O_RDONLY)),
    &FileStatus);
dwFileSize = (DWORD)FileStatus.st_size;

MyStdinCrtHandle = _open_osfhandle((long)StdinPipe, 0);
assert(MyStdinCrtHandle != -1);
MyStdoutCrtHandle = _open_osfhandle((long)StdoutPipe, 0);
assert(MyStdoutCrtHandle != -1);
```

You can also convert a C runtime handle (one created via *_open*) into an operating system handle via *get_osfhandle*:

```
int CRTConOut = _open(STDOUT,_O_RDWR);
HANDLE hConout = _get_osfhandle(CRTConOut);
```

# GETLASTERROR VS. ERRNO

The C runtime library routines use the global value errno to store error returns. The Win32 API enables you to retrieve extended error information via the *GetLastError* call. When mixing C runtime calls with Win32 API calls, do not get the mechanisms to test for error values confused. The return value from *GetLastError* is undefined if you call it after a call to a C runtime library call. The reason is that some C runtime calls map directly to Win32 calls, but others do not. That means that a C runtime call could be calling a Win32 call behind your back. Other times the C runtime could just return an error without calling the Win32. Unlike *GetLastError*, not every C runtime function sets the errno variable. (The C/C++ language help file is real good about stating which function sets errno.) If a function succeeds, the value of *errno* and the return from *GetLastError* are undefined.

The constants for the errno variables are declared in the Errno.h. Each errno value is associated with a text message. You can use C runtime function *strerror* to retrieve a text message associated with each errno. Unfortunately, the return from *strerror* is not language independent. To remedy this, use the function *CRTError*, whose use is demonstrated in Listing 10–1. It converts errno to a constant that can be used as a parameter to the Win32 *FormatMessage* function. Normally, you use *FormatMessage* in the following manner:

```
hFile = CreateFile(...);
if (hFile == INVALID_HANDLE_VALUE )
    {
    PVOID lpBuffer;
    FormatMessage( FORMAT_MESSAGE_FROM_SYSTEM
            | FORMAT_MESSAGE_ALLOCATE_BUFFER,
            NULL, GetLastError(),
            MAKELANGID(LANG_NEUTRAL, SUBLANG_NEUTRAL),
            (LPSTR)&lpBuffer, 0, NULL );
    printf("Error CreateFile: %s", (LPSTR)lpBuffer );
    VirtualFree((LPSTR)lpBuffer, 0, MEM_RELEASE );
    }
```

However, when formatting a C runtime error, use *CRTError* instead:

```
hFile = CreateFile(...);
if (hFile == INVALID_HANDLE_VALUE )
```

```
{
FormatMessage( FORMAT_MESSAGE_FROM_SYSTEM
        FORMAT_MESSAGE_ALLOCATE_BUFFER,
        NULL, CRTError(errno),
        MAKELANGID(LANG_NEUTRAL, SUBLANG_NEUTRAL ),
        (LPSTR)&lpBuffer, 0, NULL );
printf("Error CreateFile: %s\n", lpBuffer );
VirtualFree( lpBuffer, 0, MEM_RELEASE );
}
```

**Listing 9–1** *CRTError*

```
#include <windows.h>
#include <errno.h>

DWORD CrtError(DWORD errno)
{

switch (errno)
    {
    case EACCES:
    return ERROR_ACCESS_DENIED;

    case EDEADLOCK:
    return ERROR_POSSIBLE_DEADLOCK;

    case EEXIST:
    return ERROR_FILE_EXISTS;


    case EMFILE:
    return ERROR_TOO_MANY_OPEN_FILES;

    case ENOENT:
    return ERROR_FILE_NOT_FOUND;

    case ENOEXEC:
    return ERROR_BAD_FORMAT;
```

**351**

```
        case ENOMEM:
        return ERROR_NOT_ENOUGH_MEMORY;

        case ENOSPC:
        return ERROR_HANDLE_DISK_FULL;

        case ENOTEMPTY:
        return ERROR_DIR_NOT_EMPTY;

        case ERANGE:
        return ERROR_INSUFFICIENT_BUFFER;


        case E2BIG:
        case EBADF:
        case EDOM:
        case EINVAL:
        default:
        return ERROR_INVALID_PARAMETER;
        };


    }
```

Table 9–2 lists the *errno* values that the C runtime library returns under Windows NT. If you look in STDLIB.H you will notice many more constants, but these extra constants are just present for the sake of compatibility (with XENIX and MS-DOS).

## CreateThread vs. _beginthread

Although it is perfectly acceptable to use *CreateThread* in a console application, if your program uses C runtime library routines it is preferable to use the *_beginthread* function:

```
unsigned long
_beginthread( void( *start_address )( void * ),
        unsigned stack_size, void *arglist );
```

Like *CreateThread*, *_beginthread* takes a pointer to a function as the starting address of the new thread. You can also pass in the size of the stack that you want allocated and a pointer to an argument list. However, *_beginthread* does not allow you to assign a security descriptor. You also cannot create the new thread suspended as *CreateThread* can. The reason *_beginthread* is necessary is because it performs some internal library initialization that helps other C runtime routines deal with threads. When you link with the multithreaded C runtime libraries, *_beginthread* initializes the global *errno* value, the runtime signal function, and any floating-point variables that must be unique for each thread. Unlike a single-threaded application, *errno* is actually a pointer to a function in a multithreaded application that uses the C runtime. You must compile your application with the *_MT* switch to take advantage of the multithreaded C runtime libraries. Listing 9–2 is an excerpt from STDLIB.H, which shows what happens when you compile with the *_MT* switch.

**Listing 9–2** errno is different in a multithreaded environment.

```
/* declare reference to errno */

#ifdef   _MT
extern int * _CRTAPI1 _errno(void);
#define errno(*_errno())
#else
extern int errno;
#endif
```

Call the *_endthread* function so the system can garbage collect these variables when your thread is finished with them.

```
void _endthread( void );
```

# USING GUI FEATURES IN A CONSOLE APPLICATION

As I said before, it will be difficult for a console application to compete against a similar graphical application on the either Windows 95 or the NT desktop.

However, a console application is better than no application at all. If you are porting a character-based application from another operating system to Windows 95 or NT, making it a console application may be the quickest way to get to market. One simple way to differentiate yourself is employ some basic graphical features in your console application. The first thing you must do is find the window handle for the console that your application resides in. The easiest way to do this is with *GetConsoleTitle* and *FindWindow*. *GetConsoleTitle* gets the caption for the console window that your application resides in:

```
char s[80];
GetConsoleTitle(s,sizeof(s));
hConWnd = FindWindow("ConsoleWindowClass",s);
if (!hConWnd)
   {
   printf("FindWindow failed");
   }
```

Once you have the handle to the console's window, you can manipulate any of the *WM_SYSCOMMAND* functions using *PostMessage*. For example, the following minimizes the console window:

```
PostMessage(hConWnd, WM_SYSCOMMAND, SC_MINIMIZE, 0l);
```

You can also call *MoveWindow* to move the console window around the screen. If the coordinates that you specify are smaller than the size of the console window, the console will automatically put up scroll bars. If you make the window larger than the size of the default console window, your application will not be able to take advantage of the extra client space until you call *SetConsoleWindowInfo* to increase the buffer size:

```
SMALL_RECT srctWindowRect;
HWND hConWnd=NULL;
srctWindowRect.Left = 0;
srctWindowRect.Top = 0;
srctWindowRect.Bottom = 125;
srctWindowRect.Right = 80;
SetConsoleWindowInfo(hConout, TRUE, &srctWindowRect);
```

The three other places that can be implemented quite easily are help windows, simple messages, and dialogs, each of which is described below.

Windows users have grown accustomed to having help available. You spawn help in a console application the same way you do in a graphical application, with *WinHelp*. While you are busy porting the application, your documentation department can be creating the help file. Following is an example:

```
WinHelp (GetFocus(), "Con32.HLP", HELP_KEY,
         (DWORD)(LPSTR)szHelpTopic);
```

You can call *MessageBox* from anywhere in your console application. To ensure that the message box appears on top of your console application, use the new *MB_SETFOREGROUND* as one of the styles for the message box:

```
MessageBox(NULL,"Hello", "From the Console",
         MB_OK | MB_SETFOREGROUND);
```

The most important place to use *MessageBox* in a console application is when it first loads to make sure you are not running under Win32s:

```
int main(void)
{
//
// If running Win32s — ABORT
//
if (GetVersion() & 0x80000000)
   {
   MessageBox(NULL,"XYZ Application requires 32-bit Windows",
             "You need to upgrade.",
             MB_OK | MB_FOREGROUND);

   return 0;
   }
//
// rest of application
//
```

```
    .
    .
    .
}
```

Win32s does not provide support for the console API, but it does allow console applications to load and run. If your console application does not check for Win32s, erratic things can happen. The user will be confused because no output can be displayed. Also, since Windows 3.1 is nonpreemptive, if your console application goes into a loop (perhaps checking for keyboard input) you will hang Windows 3.1.

One character-based application that I use quite frequently is Brief from Borland International. Before Visual C++ shipped, I used Brief extensively in Windows NT. One thing I don't like about Brief is that when I am editing one file and I press the Alt-E key sequence to edit another file, Brief wants me to type in the full path name of the new file to edit. A great feature to add to applications that run as console applications (like Brief) would be the common open file dialog. That way you could take advantage of the "Browse" option of the common dialog without forcing your entire application to be graphical.

Both the Open and Save As dialogs and the Print and Print Setup Dialogs provide usefulness to a console application. However, the other common dialogs (Color, Font, and Find and Replace) don't match up as nicely.

The Color dialog returns a *COLORREF* which doesn't correspond to a console applications color scheme. Console applications use the *SetConsoleTextAttribute* to change the color attributes in the console:

```
BOOL
SetConsoleTextAttribute(HANDLE hConsoleOutput,
                WORD wAttr); // text and backgrnd colors
```

The font dialog paradigm doesn't fit because console applications are not "what you see is what you get" (WYSIWYG) applications. Console applications change their fonts via the System menu.

In addition to the common dialogs, your console application can have any number of dialogs that you create.

# CONSOLE WINDOWS IN CONJUNCTION WITH GRAPHICAL APPLICATIONS

Even if your application is already graphical, there are many places where you may want to create a separate console window that works in conjunction with your other windows. If all you want to accomplish is the output of some text into a window, allocating a console and using the console API to output the text is a viable solution. Windows NT differs from Windows 3.1 in that no display drivers ship with NT that support monochrome monitors. Also, the Windows NT debug model is such that the *OutDebugString* doesn't work unless you are running under a debugger. So, writing to a separate console is a simple alternative to *OutputDebugString* that works whether you are debugging or not.

Before you begin writing to the new console you must first allocate it. You do that with the *AllocConsole* function:

```
BOOL AllocConsole(void);
```

When you finish with the console window, destroy it via *FreeConsole:*

```
BOOL FreeConsole(void);
```

You are only allowed to allocate one console per process. After the first successful call to *AllocConsole*, each subsequent call will fail and any output you create will go to the first console window. If your process terminates before calling *FreeConsole*, the system performs an implicit *FreeConsole* for you.

## DIRECTING OUTPUT TO A CONSOLE WINDOW

Once you have a console, you send output to it with the *WriteConsole* function. *WriteConsole* writes a character string to a console screen buffer beginning at the current cursor location:

```
BOOL WriteConsole(HANDLE hConsoleOutput,
                CONST VOID *lpvBuffer,  // source address
                DWORD cchToWrite,      // number of chars
                LPDWORD lpcchWritten,  // chars written
                LPVOID lpvReserved);   // reserved
```

When you put the two together, you have a very convenient method to send text output to a window:

```
BOOL MyOutputDebugString(char *s)
{
DWORD StdHandle;
DWORD cChars;
if (AllocConsole())
    {
    StdHandle = GetStdHandle(STD_OUTPUT_HANDLE);
    WriteConsole( StdHandle, s,strlen(s), &cChars, NULL);
    }
else
    return FALSE;
```

*WriteConsole* is a simple function to use. However, it would be even more convenient to use the C runtime APIs in the console window. To do so successfully, you must understand how console windows are initialized. As we learned in Chapter 4, "Processes," you use the *CreateProcess* function to create new processes. One of the parameters to *CreateProcess* is the *STARTUPINFO* structure:

```
typedef struct _STARTUPINFO { /* si */
    DWORD   cb;
    LPTSTR  lpReserved;
    LPTSTR  lpDesktop;
    LPTSTR  lpTitle;
    DWORD   dwX;
    DWORD   dwY;
    DWORD   dwXSize;
    DWORD   dwYSize;
    DWORD   dwXCountChars;
```

```
    DWORD   dwYCountChars;
    DWORD   dwFillAttribute;
    DWORD   dwFlags;
    WORD    wShowWindow;
    WORD    cbReserved2;
    LPBYTE  lpReserved2;
    HANDLE  hStdInput;
    HANDLE  hStdOutput;
    HANDLE  hStdError;
} STARTUPINFO, *LPSTARTUPINFO;
```

Your console window will behave differently—that is, what shows up in the console window will be different—depending on how you launch your graphical application. When you run your application from the command line of a console (what Windows 95 and NT refer to as the MS-DOS window), CMD.EXE is the process that calls *CreateProcess*. When CMD.EXE calls *CreateProcess*, it sets the standard input-output handles in *STARTUPINFO* such that the handles will interact with a console window if one exists. This means that the *iob[]* array of *FILE* structs (what the stdout and stdin macros access) are properly initialized. On the other hand, if you launch your application using START, the program manager, file manager in NT or the Explorer in Windows 95, these handles are not initialized. Any attempt to use them sends the standard input-output into the bit-bucket. This problem is easily solved if you control the application that spawns your process. Simply use the *STARTF_USESTDHANDLES* flag in the *dwFlags* field to ensure the standard input-output handles are properly initialized. For this to work, the *fInheritHandles* flag in *CreateProcess* must be set to TRUE. Unfortunately, you have no control over the program manager, file manager, or users who use the START command. To get around this you must physically set the standard input-output handles yourself:

```
int hcrt;
FILE *hf;

AllocConsole();
hcrt = _open_osfhandle((long) GetStdHandle(STD_OUTPUT_HANDLE),
_O_TEXT);
hf = _fdopen(hcrt, "w");
*stdout = *hf;
```

What this does is open up a new low-level C runtime handle to the correct console output handle. Next it associates a new stream with that low-level handle. Then you replace the stdout handle with the new stream handle. This fixes any problems with C runtime calls that use stdout such as *printf, puts,* and so on. This technique will *not* fix problems with standard low-level C runtime handles 0, 1, and 2. It turns out that it is not possible to change handles 0, 1, and 2 to point to the correct console handles. So, do not use the low-level C runtime calls such as *_write* to perform standard input-output. Instead, stick with the stream calls such as *fopen, printf,* and so on.

Once you have taken care of the C runtime handles, you can use C runtime APIs to write text in the console window:

```
puts("\n This will also go to the console\n");
```

However, if you run out and write an application to do this, you will be surprised to learn that your output doesn't show up in the console window. That is because the stream calls such as *fopen, puts,* and *printf* automatically buffer their output. There are two techniques for overcoming this, *fflush* and *setvbuf.*

First, you can use the *fflush* function to flush the output stream. This will force all of the output in the stream to automatically be displayed:

```
fflush();
```

Or you can turn buffering off by calling *setvbuf:* The *_IONBF* flag indicates no buffering:

```
setvbuf(stdout, NULL, _IONBF, 0);
```

The default buffer is 512 bytes. If you are sending a significant amount of data to the console, you will easily fill the buffer and may not need either call.


## RECEIVING CONSOLE INPUT

One thing you can do with a console window that you cannot do when you write output to the monochrome monitor in 16-bit Windows is get keyboard input. To get keyboard input from a console window you have a few options. But first you should be aware of the caveats:

▪▪   No normal window hierarchy exists between the console window and its graphical parent window. The first time your process calls *AllocConsole*, the console window will be created on top of any windows your process might have. If you physically change the z-order (for example, by clicking on your main window), the next time you ask for keyboard input in your console window, it won't automatically come to the front or get the focus.

▪▪   The keyboard input procedure should be in a separate thread. Otherwise your main window will be stalled waiting for the console window. This means that input to the main graphical window will be queued until you return from the keyboard-input procedure. For example, if you click on the main window the mouse messages and *WM_COMMAND* messages will stack up until the request for keyboard input is satisfied. This also means that your main window will not be able to repaint. That's why you want to place all of the calls that receive console keyboard input into a separate thread.

▪▪   If you close the process, you automatically close the console window and vice-versa. Normally, destroying a child window has no effect on the parent window. But if the console window is in your processes only thread, then your process will exit. However, there is one instance in which a console window won't close if the process closes. That's the case where you spawn a child process that inherits the handles to the console from the parent process. In this case the console will not close until the child closes:

```
HANDLE hSTDIN = GetStdHandle(STD_INPUT_HANDLE);

INPUT_RECORD lr;
DWORD Bytes;
BOOL ret;
while (TRUE)
{
    FlushConsoleInputBuffer( hSTDIN );
    if (PeekConsoleInput( hSTDIN, &lr, 1, &Bytes ))
        if (lr.EventType == KEY_EVENT)
            break;
}
```

# REDIRECTING STANDARD INPUT-OUTPUT

One other method to integrate console applications and graphical applications concerns redirecting standard input-output. That's what the 32-bit edition of Visual C++ does when it spawns the console applications necessary to build an application (the make utility, compiler, linker, and so on). By redirecting the output handle of these console applications, Visual C++ captures their output and places it in the Output Window instead of having a separate console window for the output.

This makes console applications very versatile. For users who prefer the command line, they can type in the name of the program (or programs) at the command line and the console applications work as expected. But for users who prefer the integrated environment, they simply press a button to start the console application. The beauty of this is the fact that the console application requires no changes.

If you want to integrate your graphical applications with your console applications, here are a few rules you should follow:

- ▚ In your *CreateProcess* call, specify *CREATE_NEW_CONSOLE*, or you should create a console by calling *AllocConsole* before starting the child. If you choose to do this, you can simply specify *STARTF_USESTDHANDLES* in the *STARTUPINFO*. You can then set *hStdInput, hStdOutput*, and *hStdError* as appropriate. This is easier than redirecting the standard handles in the parent. The child process will cause an exception if it writes to an invalid stdout handle.

- ▚ Duplicate the write handle without inheritance, and close the original inheritable write handle before starting the child. This allows the child to see *EOF* when you later close the parent's write handle.

Listing 9–3 is an example of a graphical application that spawns a console application and redirects its output back into the graphical window.

### Listing 9–3 Redirect

```
// run.cpp : Defines the class behaviors for the application.
// This application shows how to redirect console output to a window
//

#include <afxwin.h>
```

```
#include "resource.h"

#include "run.h"


//////////////////////////////////////////////////////////////////////
////////
//
// theApp:
// Just creating this application object runs the whole application.
//

CTheApp theApp;

//////////////////////////////////////////////////////////////////////
////////


//
// CMainWindow constructor:
// Create the window with the appropriate style, size, menu, etc.
//

CMainWindow::CMainWindow()
{
   LoadAccelTable( "MainAccelTable" );
   Create( NULL, "Redirect Console Application",
     WS_OVERLAPPEDWINDOW, rectDefault, NULL, "MainMenu" );
}


//
//  OnPaint:
//  CPaintDC's constructor needs the window (this).
//
void CMainWindow::OnPaint()
{
        CPaintDC dc( this );

}
```

**363**

```
// OnRun:
// This member function is called when a WM_COMMAND message with an
// IDM_RUN code is received by the CMainWindow class object.  The
// message map below is responsible for this routing.
//

void CMainWindow::OnRun()
{
    SECURITY_ATTRIBUTES lsa;
    STARTUPINFO         si;
    PROCESS_INFORMATION pi;
    LPPROCESS_INFORMATION lppi=&pi;


HANDLE hWritePipe, hWritePipe2;


    lsa.nLength=sizeof(SECURITY_ATTRIBUTES);
    lsa.lpSecurityDescriptor=NULL;
    lsa.bInheritHandle=TRUE;

    m_edit.SetWindowText((LPSTR)"Initializing...\r\n\r\n");

    //
    // Create an anonymous pipe
    //

    if (!CreatePipe(&m_hReadPipe,&hWritePipe,&lsa,0))
      {
       m_edit.SetWindowText("Couldn't create Pipe\r\n");
      return;
      }

   DuplicateHandle(GetCurrentProcess(),    // source process
       m_hReadPipe,                        // handle to duplicate
       GetCurrentProcess(),                // destination process
       NULL,
       0,
```

```
       FALSE,                           // not inheritable
       DUPLICATE_SAME_ACCESS);

   DuplicateHandle(GetCurrentProcess(),
       hWritePipe,                      // handle to duplicate
       GetCurrentProcess(),             // destination process
       &hWritePipe2,                    // used by child as stderr
       0,
       TRUE,                            // it's inheritable
       DUPLICATE_SAME_ACCESS);


       //
       // set STARTF_USESTDHANDLES and STARTF_USESHOWWINDOW to be able
       // to redirect AND not have the console window display.
       //


       si.cb=sizeof(STARTUPINFO);
       si.lpReserved=NULL;
       si.lpTitle=NULL;
       si.lpDesktop=NULL;
       si.dwX=si.dwY=si.dwYSize=si.dwXSize=0;
       si.dwFlags=STARTF_USESTDHANDLES|STARTF_USESHOWWINDOW;
       si.wShowWindow = SW_HIDE;
       si.hStdInput =NULL;
       si.hStdOutput=hWritePipe;
       si.hStdError =hWritePipe2;
       si.lpReserved2=NULL;
       si.cbReserved2=0;

       //
       // Create Process: for demonstrations purposes spawn nmake.
       //

       if (!CreateProcess(NULL,
                     "CMD /c nmake.exe",
                 NULL,
```

```
                    NULL,
                    TRUE,
                    0,
                    NULL,
                    NULL,
                    &si,
                    &pi))
      {
        m_edit.SetWindowText("Couldn't Create Process");
      return;
      }
      this->m_hThrd=CreateThread(NULL,
                                  0,
                                  this->Threadfunc,
                                  this,
                                  0, //CREATE_SUSPENDED,
                                  &this->threadid);

  //
  // Close unneccesary Handles
  //

    CloseHandle(pi.hThread);
    CloseHandle(pi.hProcess);
    CloseHandle(hWritePipe);
    CloseHandle(hWritePipe2);
//////////////////////////


}


// Threadfunc:
//
DWORD
CMainWindow::Threadfunc(void *)
{
    DWORD cchReadBuffer;  // number of bytes read or to be written
```

```
//
// Read until ERROR_BROKEN_PIPE
//

  HGLOBAL hh = m_edit.GetHandle();
  HGLOBAL hhh = (LPSTR)LocalReAlloc(hh,8192,GHND);
  LPSTR ph = (LPSTR)LocalLock(hhh);
  strcpy(ph,INIT);
  ph = ph+strlen(INIT);

  for (;;)
      {
       if (!ReadFile(m_hReadPipe,
                ph,
                4096,
                &cchReadBuffer,  // number of bytes actually read
                NULL))
            if (GetLastError() == ERROR_BROKEN_PIPE)
               break;
      ph=ph+cchReadBuffer;
      }
  LocalUnlock(hh);
  m_edit.SetHandle(hh);

  CloseHandle(m_hReadPipe);
   return 0;
}



//
// If the main window changes size, update the edit Window.
//

void CMainWindow::OnSize(UINT nFlags, int cx, int cy)
{
   CRect rc;

   GetClientRect(&rc);
```

```
   rc.InflateRect(GetSystemMetrics(SM_CXBORDER),
GetSystemMetrics(SM_CYBORDER));
   m_edit.MoveWindow(rc);
    CFrameWnd::OnSize(nFlags, cx, cy);

}
 void CMainWindow::OnSetFocus(CWnd* pWndOldFocus)
{
   m_edit.SetFocus();
   CWnd::OnSetFocus(pWndOldFocus);
}


//
// OnCreate:
//

int CMainWindow::OnCreate(LPCREATESTRUCT lpCreateStruct)
{
   LOGFONT    lfEditFont;
    HFONT     hFont;
   CRect rect(0, 0, 0, 0);

   m_edit.Create(WS_BORDER | WS_VISIBLE | WS_HSCROLL | WS_VSCROLL |
      ES_AUTOHSCROLL | ES_AUTOVSCROLL | ES_MULTILINE | ES_NOHIDESEL |
      WS_MAXIMIZE, rect, this, 0xCAC);

   m_edit.SetFocus();
//
// create fixed pitch font as default font
//
        lfEditFont.lfHeight = 16;
        lfEditFont.lfWidth = 0;
        lfEditFont.lfEscapement = 0;
        lfEditFont.lfOrientation = 0;
        lfEditFont.lfWeight = 400;
        lfEditFont.lfItalic = FALSE;
        lfEditFont.lfUnderline = FALSE;
```

```
        lfEditFont.lfStrikeOut = FALSE;
        lfEditFont.lfCharSet = ANSI_CHARSET;
        lfEditFont.lfOutPrecision = OUT_DEFAULT_PRECIS;
        lfEditFont.lfClipPrecision = CLIP_DEFAULT_PRECIS;
        lfEditFont.lfQuality = DEFAULT_QUALITY;
        lfEditFont.lfPitchAndFamily = FIXED_PITCH | FF_MODERN;
        *lfEditFont.lfFaceName = 0;

//
// create the logical font
//
        if (hFont = CreateFontIndirect (&lfEditFont))
            m_edit.SendMessage (WM_SETFONT, (UINT)hFont, 0);

    return CWnd::OnCreate(lpCreateStruct);
}


// CMainWindow message map:
// Associate messages with member functions.
//
// It is implied that the ON_WM_PAINT macro expects a member function
// "void OnPaint()".
//
// It is implied that members connected with the ON_COMMAND macro
// receive no arguments and are void of return type, e.g., "void
// OnAbout()".
//
BEGIN_MESSAGE_MAP( CMainWindow, CFrameWnd )
   ON_WM_CREATE()
   ON_WM_PAINT()
   ON_WM_SIZE()
   ON_WM_SETFOCUS()
   ON_COMMAND( IDM_RUN, OnRun )
END_MESSAGE_MAP()


/////////////////////////////////////////////////////////////////////
///
// CTheApp
```

```
// InitInstance:
// When any CTheApp object is created, this member function is
automatically
// called.  Any data may be set up at this point.
//
// Also, the main window of the application should be created and
shown here.
// Return TRUE if the initialization is successful.
//
BOOL CTheApp::InitInstance()
{

    m_pMainWnd = new CMainWindow();
    m_pMainWnd->ShowWindow( m_nCmdShow );
    m_pMainWnd->UpdateWindow();

    return TRUE;
}
```

# DETECTING EVENTS

Earlier I stated that console events were not notified when the console window is dragged around, minimized, or maximized. But console applications are not totally ignorant of their surroundings. By setting a console control handler, you can instruct the system to call a callback when the following events occur. You set a console control handler in a manner similar to the C runtime *signal* function. To install a console control handler, call the *SetConsoleCtrlHandler* function:

```
BOOL
SetConsoleCtrlHandler(PHANDLER_ROUTINE pHandlerRoutine,
                 BOOL fAdd);    //add or remove handler
```

*SetConsoleCtrlHandler* takes two parameters. The first is a pointer to a callback routine. When an event takes place, it will call this function. The callback function has the following prototype:

```
BOOL HandlerRoutine(DWORD dwCtrlType);
```

When an event occurs, the parameter, *dwCtrlType* will equal one of the following:

▪▪ CTRL_BREAK_EVENT

This event can be generated two ways. If the user presses Ctrl-Break or if you call the function *GenerateConsoleCtrlEvent* (which is discussed in a moment).

▪▪ CTRL_C_EVENT

The system generates this event if the user presses Ctrl-C or if you call the function *GenerateConsoleCtrlEvent*. That is assuming that the current console mode is set for *ENABLE_PROCESS_INPUT*. If the console mode is set for *ENABLE_PROCESS_INPUT,* the system processes Ctrl-C and does not place the keystrokes into the console's input buffer. You can set the console mode by calling *SetConsoleMode*. This next example shows how to call *GetConsoleMode* to get the current mode and *SetConsoleMode* to enable processed input:

```
DWORD dwOutputMode;

GetConsoleMode(hConsole, &dwOutputMode);

bSuccess = SetConsoleMode(hConsole, dwOutputMode |
                          ENABLE_PROCESSED_OUTPUT)
```

You can programmatically generate a Ctrl-C or a Ctrl-Break event by calling the *GenerateConsoleCtrlEvent* function:

```
BOOL
GenerateConsoleCtrlEvent(DWORD fdwEvent, //
                         DWORD IDProcessGroup);
```

The first parameter is either *CTRL_C_EVENT* or *CTRL_BREAK_EVENT*. The second parameter is the process ID of the process you want to send the control event to. The second parameter is called the *IDProcessGroup* because it sends the event to a process and all of its descendants. You can set a process group with the *CREATE_PROCESS_GROUP* flag in the call to *CreateProcess*.

■■ CTRL_CLOSE_EVENT

The system generates this event in one of three ways: When the user double-clicks on the system menu of the console, chooses Close from the system menu of the console, or if another process calls *TerminateProcess* passing in the handle to the console's process.

■■ CTRL_LOGOFF_EVENT

The system generates this event when a user is logging off.

■■ CTRL_SHUTDOWN_EVENT

The system generates this event when the system is shutting down.

If you handle the event, return TRUE. Otherwise return FALSE so the next handler in the chain (if any) can be called. By handling *CTRL_LOGOFF_EVENT* and *CTRL_SHUTDOWN_EVENT* and closing your application programmatically, you can avoid the "This application cannot respond to the End Task request" dialog. If you want this dialog to appear, return TRUE from your control handler.

You can also use the *GetProcessShutdownParameters* and *SetProcessShutdownParameters* functions to prevent the dialog from displaying. If you specify the *SHUTDOWN_NORETRY* flag and you returned TRUE from your control handler, your application will terminate. The following shows how you can use *GetProcessShutdownParameters* to retrieve the current settings and then use *SetProcessShutdownParameters* to change them:

```
DWORD dwLevel;
DWORD dwFlags;

if (GetProcessShutdownParameters(&dwLevel, &dwFlags))
   SetProcessShutdownParameters(dwLevel,dwFlags |
            SHUTDOWN_NORETRY);
else
   .
```

## CONSOLE EVENTS VS. SIGNALS

Although the SDK documentation and help files treat Win32 console events and the C runtime signals as synonymous, there are a few differences. Instead of *SetConsoleCtrlHandler* the C runtime provides signal. The major difference is the fact that the C runtime signal function traps Ctrl-C, but not Ctrl-Break. Like SetConsoleCtrlHandler, the signal function takes as a parameter a pointer to a callback function:

```
void (__cdecl *signal(int sig, void( __cdecl *func )
                    (int sig [, int subcode ])))(int sig);
```

If you are porting your application from UNIX or MS-DOS, you already have signals in your code. Since the *signal* function is so similar to *SetConsoleCtrlHandler* you might be wondering if you can have both *signal* and *SetConsoleCtrlHandler* point to the same callback. That way you can keep your C runtime code intact and use the console events to detect Ctrl-Break and such. Unfortunately, this isn't possible because the manifest constants for console events and signals overlap. For example, *SIGINT*, which means Ctrl-C in the C runtime is defined as

```
#define SIGINT      2    /* interrupt */
```

in Signal.h and *CTRL_CLOSE_EVENT* is also defined as 2 in Wincon.h.

## USING TIMERS

You also shouldn't use regular timers in a console application. *SetTimer* can work within a console application, but it requires a thread in the almighty *GetMessage* loop:

```
while (GetMessage (&msg, NULL, 0, 0))
{
    TranslateMessage (&msg) ;
    DispatchMessage (&msg) ;
}
```

Because this requires a thread looping, there is no real advantage to adding a timer to a console application over using these other options:

▪▪    Waiting on an event.

**373**

Timers require a message loop to dispatch the timer message to the timer procedure. In a console application, this behavior can be easily emulated with a thread that is set to wait on an event. Waiting for events is covered thoroughly in Chapter 1, "The Life of a Process," so I won't go over them again here.

■■ Sleep.

If you want an event to occur regularly and do not require exact timing, use the *Sleep* function:

```
VOID
Sleep(DWORD dwMilliseconds);   // sleep time in milliseconds
```

However, the system only guarantees that the amount you specify in *dwMilliseconds* is the minimum amount of time your thread will be dormant. Depending upon what your threads priority is and where it is in relation to the scheduler, it may be longer before your thread "wakes" up. If you need more precision, use a multimedia timer.

■■ Multimedia timers.

Multimedia timers do not require a message loop and have higher resolution. However, multimedia timers may be overkill, especially in a console application. Normally, multimedia timers are used when playing back video or .WAV files.

If you find you have a need for such precision, use the *timeSetEvent* function to set the timer:

```
UINT
timeSetEvent(UINT wDelay,        // specifies event period
             UINT wResolution,   //delay accuracy
             LPTIMECALLBACK lptc, // callback function
             DWORD dwUser,       // user-defined data
             UINT fCallbackType); // callback type flags
```

The *fCallbackType* is either *TIME_ONESHOT* or *TIME_PERIODIC* to indicate whether to call the lptc callback function once or once per *wDelay*. You can also set the *wResolution* parameter to indication the accuracy of the delay.

# DETACHED PROCESSES

Detached processes run in the background. Applications that need no interaction with the user should be launched as detached processes. A detached process doesn't have access to any console, which means its standard input-output handles all point to NULL.

To create a detached process you call *CreateProcess* with the *fdwCreate* parameter set to *DETACHED_PROCESS:*

```
//
// Creating a detached process
//
BOOL
CreateProcess(lpszImageName,
        lpszCommandLine,
        NULL,
        NULL,
        FALSE,
        DETACHED_PROCESS,
        lpvEnvironment,
        lpszCurDir,
        lpsiStartInfo,
        lppiProcInfo);
```

If a detached process finds it must communicate with the user, it can call *MessageBox* to display a message. Or it can call *AllocConsole* to create a new console to print a message to the screen or get input from the user.

One of the challenges with detached processes is determining how to kill the detached process from a foreground application. The simple solution is to call *TerminateProcess* with a handle to the background process. However, if the detached process must clean up before it terminates, you can't just destroy it with *TerminateProcess*. One of the easiest approaches would be to create an event object for each background process. You could use the name of the process or something similar for the event name. The background process that calls *CreateEvent* would place the event object in a nonsignalled state. It then spins off a thread that calls *WaitForSingleObject(hObject, INFINITE)*. The application that is going to terminate the background process uses *OpenEvent* to obtain the handle to the event object. It then places the event object in a

**375**

signaled state. When the thread in the background process wakes because its object being was signaled, the thread can perform an orderly shutdown of the background process.

# PRINTING FROM A CONSOLE APPLICATION

Whether you are creating from scratch or you are porting your character-based code from another operating system, most likely you will have a need to print. Printing from a console application can be done two ways: You can retrieve a handle to a printer port via *CreateFile* and *WriteFile*, or you can use the same method that graphical applications use:

```
fh = CreateFile ( "lpt1", GENERIC_WRITE, 0, NULL,
                OPEN_EXISTING, FILE_ATTRIBUTE_NORMAL, NULL );
if (!WriteFile(fh, text, strlen(text), &dwWritten, NULL))
{
    wsprintf(text, "WriteFile failed %ld\n",
            GetLastError());
    printf(text);
    CloseHandle(fh);
    return(0);
}
```

But if you choose this method, you will bypass the 32-bit Windows printer driver. Output will still be spooled, thereby eliminating the chance of mixing pages of your process's output with some other process's output. But there will be no conversion of your output. This means that you will have to embed you own escape sequences into your printer output to get it to look right on the printer. In essence, you will have to write a printer driver for each and every printer you choose to support. This is clearly not acceptable. Therefore, the correct method is to use the *StartDoc-EndDoc* combination normally reserved for Windows applications. To do this you will need to create a device context that corresponds to the printer, as in this example:

```
if (!(ghdc = CreateDC (szDriverName, szDeviceName,
                szPort, NULL)
    {
        MessageBox (ghwndMain, "CreateDC() failed",
                    ERR_MOD_NAME, MB_OK);
        return;
    }
    break;
```

The easiest way to get the *szDriverName, szDeviceName,* and *szPort* name are by calling the common print dialog. Once you have a valid DC you can use the *StartDoc* and *EndDoc.* However, when using *StartDoc* and *EndDoc* you must use functions that send output to device contexts. This set of functions does not include the C runtime library.

Listing 9–4 is a complete listing for a console application that prints its output to a printer that the user chooses via the print dialog.

**Listing 9–4** Printing via the common dialog

```
//
//
//

#include <windows.h>
#include <stdio.h>
#include <conio.h>
#include <string.h>
#include <winspool.h>
#include <commdlg.h>


BOOL HandlerRoutine(DWORD dwCtrlType);

BOOL    CALLBACK AbortProc    (HDC, int);

#define BUFSIZE        256
const char *szTitle = "Console Printing at its finest!";
```

```
HDC     hdc;                          // device context to print on
BOOL    bAbort;                       // AbortProc return code



char    szDeviceName[BUFSIZE];        // current device name
char    szPort     [BUFSIZE];         // current port
char    szDriverName[BUFSIZE];        // current driver name


void main (int argc, char **argv[])
{
  DOCINFO di;
  RECT    rect;
  HPEN    hpen;
  HBRUSH  hbr;
  PRINTDLG  pd;

   //
   // Initialize everything and call common printer dialog
   //

   memset ((void *) &pd, 0, sizeof(PRINTDLG));
   pd.lStructSize = sizeof(PRINTDLG);
   pd.hwndOwner   = NULL;
   pd.Flags       = PD_RETURNDC;
   pd.hInstance   = NULL;

   if (PrintDlg(&pd) ==TRUE)
      {
        if (pd.hDevMode)
         GlobalFree (pd.hDevMode);

      if (!pd.hDC)
         {
           MessageBox (NULL, "PrintDlg (PD_RETURNDC) failed",
                   "ERR", MB_OK);
           return;
```

```
            }
        else
            hdc = pd.hDC;


//
// put up Abort & install the abort procedure
//
 SetConsoleCtrlHandler((PHANDLER_ROUTINE)HandlerRoutine,TRUE);

  puts("Printing... Press Crtl-C to abort...");

   bAbort = FALSE;

   SetAbortProc (hdc, AbortProc);

//
// create & select pen/brush
//

hpen = CreatePen (PS_SOLID, 10, RGB(255,255,255));
SelectObject (hdc, hpen);
hbr  = CreateHatchBrush (HS_SOLID, RGB(255,255,255));
SelectObject (hdc, hbr);

SetTextColor (hdc, RGB(0,0,0));

SetMapMode (hdc, MM_TEXT);

rect.top        = 0;
rect.left       = 0;
rect.right      = GetDeviceCaps (hdc, HORZRES);
rect.bottom     = GetDeviceCaps (hdc, VERTRES);
di.cbSize       = sizeof(DOCINFO);
di.lpszDocName  = szTitle;
di.lpszOutput   = NULL;

StartDoc  (hdc, &di);
```

**379**

```
   StartPage (hdc);

     TextOut (hdc, 150, 150, szTitle, sizeof(szTitle));

   EndPage   (hdc);
   EndDoc    (hdc);
   DeleteDC  (hdc);

   _getch();
   }
else
   puts("Printing Cancelled\n");


}


BOOL HandlerRoutine(DWORD dwCtrlType)
{
switch (dwCtrlType)
   {
   case CTRL_C_EVENT:
   case CTRL_BREAK_EVENT:
       bAbort = TRUE;
       puts("\nAborting!");
       return TRUE;
       break;
   default:
      break;
   }
   return FALSE;
}

/////////////////////////////////////////////////////////////////
///////////
//
//  Your basic AbortProc  modified slightly since we don't have an
//  abort dialog
//
```

```
//
///////////////////////////////////////////////////////////////////
///////////

BOOL CALLBACK AbortProc (HDC hdc, int error)
{
  MSG msg;

  while (!bAbort && PeekMessage (&msg, NULL, 0, 0, PM_REMOVE))

    {
      TranslateMessage (&msg);
      DispatchMessage (&msg);
    }

  return !bAbort;
}
```

## DETERMINING A CONSOLE PROGRAM AT RUNTIME

Normally, it shouldn't matter at runtime whether a program is console or graphical. But there is one instance in which it is important to know if an application is a console application. That's the case where you want to provide a DLL that services both console applications and graphical applications and you need to determine whether to utilize the C Runtime library or not.

The way to do this is to determine what type of application is attaching to your DLL during *DLL_PROCESS_ATTACH*. The *GetModuleFileName* function retrieves the name of the executable attaching to your DLL:

```
DWORD
GetModuleFileName(HMODULE hinstModule,
                  LPTSTR lpszPath,
                  DWORD cchPath);
```

Passing a NULL in the first parameter, *hinstModule* indicates that you want the name of the executable used to create the calling process. Use this name as input into *CreateFile:*

```
HANDLE
CreateFile(LPCTSTR lpszName,
          DWORD fdwAccess,              // access mode
          DWORD fdwShareMode;           // share mode
          LPSECURITY_ATTRIBUTES lpsa,
          DWORD fdwCreate;              // creation flags
          DWORD fdwAttrsAndFlags;       // file attributes
          HANDLE hTemplateFile);        //template file
```

Here's the entire *DllInit* function:

```
DllInit(HANDLE hInst, DWORD fdwReason, LPVOID lpReserved)
{
  if (fdwReason == DLL_PROCESS_ATTACH)
    {
    char szProgName[MAX_PATH];
    GetModuleFileName(NULL,szProgName,sizeof(szProgName));
    //
    hFile = CreateFile(lpszProgName, &ofFile, OF_READ );
    ASSERT (hFile != NULL);
//

    _llseek(hFile, 0L, 0);
    _llseek(hFile, (LONG) IMAGE_SECOND_HEADER_OFFSET,
            SEEK_SET);
    _lread(hFile,  &NTSignature, 4);
    _llseek(hFile, 0L, 0);
    _llseek(hFile, (LONG) NTSignature, SEEK_SET);
    _lread(hFile,  &NTSignature, 4);

    if (NTSignature == IMAGE_NT_SIGNATURE)
      {
      _llseek(hFile, 0x58, 1); //seek to subsystem
      _lread(hFile, &Subsystem, 2);
      if (Subsystem == IMAGE_SUBSYSTEM_WINDOWS_CUI)
        {
        .
        .// Console application
```

```
      .
    }
if (Subsystem == IMAGE_SUBSYSTEM_WINDOWS_GUI)
    {
      .
      .// GUI application
      .
    }


}
```

Another way to accomplish this is to take advantage of memory-mapped files. Chapter 5, "Win32 Memory Management," introduced memory-mapped files backed by the page-file. This next section will show you how to use memory-mapping for disk-based files.

Mapping disk-based files into memory enables to you eliminate the slow _lseek_ and *SetFilePointer* type calls and replace them with a pointer to directly access memory. Once you have the pointer, all other operations (such as a seek) take place by manipulating the pointer:

```
if (!(hMap = CreateFileMapping((HANDLE) hFile,
                NULL,
                PAGE_READONLY,
                0,
                0,
                NULL)))

{
MessageBox(NULL, "Can't create file mapping object!",
            TITLE, MB_ICONSTOP | MB_OK);
return 01;
}

if (!(pMap = (LPSTR) MapViewOfFile(hMap, FILE_MAP_READ,
            0, 0, 0)))

    {
    MessageBox(NULL, "Can't map view of file!",
```

**383**

```
                        TITLE, MB_ICONSTOP | MB_OK);
        return 01;
        }


PIMAGE_DOS_HEADER pDosHeader;
PIMAGE_FILE_HEADER pFileHeader;
PIMAGE_NT_HEADERS pNTHeader;



//
// calculate address of DOS real mode (MZ) file header
//
    pDosHeader = (PIMAGE_DOS_HEADER) pMap;


//
// calculate address of PE file header
//
    pNTHeader = (PIMAGE_NT_HEADERS)pDosHeader +
                    pDosHeader->e_lfanew;

    if((pDosHeader->e_magic != IMAGE_DOS_SIGNATURE) ||
        (pNTHeader->Signature != IMAGE_NT_SIGNATURE))
    {
    MessageBox(NULL, "Not a 32-bit Windows program or DLL!",
                    TITLE, MB_ICONSTOP | MB_OK);
    return 01;
    }
```

# SUMMARY

Character-based applications are still alive in 32-bit Windows. By supporting the C runtime API, Microsoft has made it easier to port a UNIX or MS-DOS based application to 32-bit Windows than it would be to port that same application to the graphical Win32 APIs. However, Microsoft could have made it easier to integrate a console application into the desktop. The restrictions placed on console applications (not being able to access the window procedure of the console window) seem unnecessary or could have been avoided. However, if you are using a detached process or a command-line process, the console APIs (being a subset of the Win32 APIs) provide you with a quick way to become a Win32 application.

**CHAPTER 10**

# AND THE BEAT GOES ON

No operating system is developed in a vacuum. In order to understand why Windows 95 is what it is, one should look back at the recent history of Microsoft operating systems. The operating system prior to Windows 95 that Microsoft released is Windows NT. NT may stand for new technology, but it has a lot of history behind it. It is the operating system that I had hoped would be released in 1987, instead of OS/2. The reasons for wanting a new operating system were obvious. And I wasn't the only one who knew this. Microsoft also knew that DOS, the operating system installed on millions of computers, was reaching its peak of usefulness. The limitations of DOS were well known. Designed for the 8088 chip, DOS was (and, as of this writing, still is) limited to real mode, and is single threaded. Any number of things can happen to an application or to DOS itself that can cause a lockup. Based on a decision made years before to place screen memory starting at segment A000h, DOS is limited to 640KB for application address space (the infamous 640KB limit). Microsoft made several attempts to extend DOS' life prior to 1987 with limited success. Finally, in 1987, Microsoft & IBM jointly announced OS/2. At the same time, IBM announced the PS/2. The PS/2 was IBM's next generation of personal

**387**

computers. PS/2s have a proprietary bus making them incompatible with cards that fit in the older, AT style PCs. Coincidentally, OS/2 has a similar design flaw. Just as the PS/2 required users to abandon their current hardware, OS/2 version 1.0, required users to abandon their existing software. Sure, OS/2 1.0 had a DOS compatibility box, but since the operating system was designed around Intel's 80286 chip, you could run OS/2 or DOS applications but not both at the same time.

OS/2 1.0 also introduced the Presentation Manager (PM) application programming interface (API), which was incompatible with the Windows 1.x API. To make matters worse, Windows 2.0 was released and contained the same API as Windows 1.x. Due to real world constraints Microsoft decided not to adopt the PM API for Windows. They couldn't pull the rug out from under the feet of independent software vendors (ISVs) who had just converted their applications from the Macintosh to Windows. No company could completely rewrite their program twice for the same operating system. So Windows 2.0 remained as an extension to the Windows 1.x API set. Super. This meant you couldn't run your favorite DOS applications under OS/2, since the character mode API is incompatible with the DOS API. And the graphical user interface (GUI) API is incompatible with the Windows API. To compound matters, the companies confused some developers and end-users by placing a '/2' at the end of both product names. Many thought that only PS/2 computers could run OS/2. This of course, isn't true. All OS/2 1.x requires is an 80286 (or higher) computer, not an **IBM** 80286 computer.

How could a company such as Microsoft have missed the boat so badly? Well, for starters, the PM API is better than the Windows API. It is hard to look at a Windows API function and tell what type of call it is. Windows 3.1 is composed of three main dynamic-link libraries: KERNEL.EXE, GDI.EXE and USER.EXE. Each exports is own set of functions. There is no apparent correlation between a function name of a Windows API call and module to which it belongs to. Since the function names are not grouped together, it is difficult to find the function in the manual. It is also difficult to get support on a particular function. Most Microsoft developer support avenues require you to know ahead of time which category the function is in.

My favorite example of this derives from a conversation I had with a UNIX programmer trying to learn Windows 3.1:

Former UNIX Developer now neophyte Windows programmer: "My sprintf functions seem to be bombing."

ME: "<explaining segment models> Are you medium model? You'll need to use wsprintf."

Former UNIX Developer...: "<groan> Okay, I've got that, but now wstrlen is giving me an unresolved external."

ME:"Oh, if you want to use the medium model version of strlen you need to use lstrlen"

Former UNIX Developer...: "<sounding agitated> Okay, so which do I use for strstr? --lstrstr or wstrstr?

ME "Neither. Use _fstrstr."

Former neophyte Windows Developer now UNIX programmer once again: "And you actually make money doing this?"

However, aside from the API naming anomalies, the designers of Windows 1.0 should be given credit. The designers of the 1.0 API were working under incredible constraints. Simulating protected mode and swapping segments in and out while in real mode is a formidable task. Windows 1.0 performance considerations necessitated separate dialogprocs, windowprocs and buttons, read-only code segments, etc. If you were working on the PM API and no longer under the constraint of real mode you would want to correct that—wouldn't you?

Well, the PM API designers decided they would. One of the things they did was group function names logically. All base API calls in PM start with the prefix 'DOS' (for example, DosOpen, DosClose, etc.) All window management calls begin with a 'WIN' prefix (for example, WinGetMsg, WinCreate, etc.) One of the things they did was clean up keyboard handling, buttons, dialogs, and so on. Everything in OS/2 is a window. Dialogs are windows, buttons are windows. The designers of OS/2 decided that you would love the new API so much you wouldn't mind porting all of your DOS/Windows code to OS/2. And, heck, in the cases where porting wasn't feasible you would just *rewrite*. It was a big assumption and only a handful of applications were ported. OS/2 did not sell the next "thousand great applications" as Bill Gates predicted. That distinction went to Windows 3.0. Windows 3.0 is so successful because it is one of the first successful graphical environments to run concurrently with MS-DOS programs. By taking advantage of the enhanced mode of the Intel 80386 processor, DOS programs can run in a window upon the Windows desktop. By the virtue of installing directly over DOS, Windows removed some of the fears users had over choosing between OS/2 or DOS. In addition, the Windows 3.0

**389**

API is a superset of the Windows 2.x API, and 2.x applications will run under 3.0. Windows 3.0 became extremely successful in the marketplace. As great as it is, however, Windows 3.0 brought with it the infamous Unrecoverable Application Error (UAE). The design of Windows 3.0 allowed a UAE, which is usually a protection violation, to corrupt other applications and sometimes Windows itself. However, Windows is better than anything else out there, and developers flocked to it in droves.

Then came the split between IBM and Microsoft. Unless you were behind the Iron Curtain or had your head stuck in a UNIX box, you know that the two companies had some disagreements and, for the most part, dissolved their joint development agreement. Instead of co-developing the next version of OS/2, IBM decided to develop the operating system (OS) alone. Microsoft continued to develop Windows and also gained control of a future version of OS/2 referred to as either "Portable OS/2" or "NTOS/2".

IBM's OS/2, version 2.0, was the next entry into the PC operating system arena. OS/2 2.0 is a 32-bit operating system, and it requires an Intel 386 or 486 based computer. PM 1.x applications port relatively easily to the new version. While Windows 3.0 applications run under OS/2 2.0, no considerations is made for Windows 3.0 programs at the API level. By the time IBM released OS/2 2.0, the next *five* thousand great applications had been written to Windows 3.0. Even developers who wanted to port applications to the PM API found limitations in OS/2 2.0. While the underlying OS is preemptive, PM is still non-preemptive. Multithreaded PM applications must have restrictions on them to make sure they don't freeze. For example, non-message queue threads cannot send messages to window procedures in message queue threads. This forces developers to be constantly aware of input state. Designed to run only on 386 and 486 platforms, OS/2 2.0 is marketed as a 32-bit OS. However, in order to accelerate time to market, the device drivers and graphics system in OS/2 2.0 are still 16-bit drivers.

Many developers and potential developers started to ask questions:

■■ If a high-end 486 PC wasn't fast enough for their application, could they move to a PC with multiple 486s?

■■ Or, could they move to another type of chip altogether?

**Note:** OS/2 2.0 is over a million lines of assembly language, which ties it to the x86 platform.

Unfortunately, without a rewrite, the answer is probably not. OS/2 2.0 is written in assembly language, which ties it to the x86 platform. Multi-processor support is something that must be designed into the OS. It cannot be easily tacked on later1. However, multi-processor support is a lot easier than moving to a new platform and OS/2 will probably support multiple 486s before it can run on another type of processor.

While these questions were nagging at potential OS/2 2.0 developers, Microsoft released Windows 3.1. Some new APIs, including support for multimedia and pen computing, were added to the new version of Windows. Parameter validation was added, which makes it more difficult, but not impossible, for applications to crash Windows. Microsoft added parameter validation to Windows 3.1 in an effort to reduce the number of exceptions within the Kernel, GDI, and User .DLLs. Parameter validation ensured that no bogus handle or bad pointer could corrupt Windows itself. Unfortunately, rejecting a bad parameter is difficult with the API setup the way it is. When a GP fault occurs, Windows 3.1 no longer displays the UAE box. Instead, Windows issues a popup giving the code segment and the offset of the offending instruction. Comforting, isn't it? Have you noticed how I haven't been calling Windows an operating system? Even though Microsoft keeps insisting Windows is a DOS-extender, it is not an operating system. DOS-extenders start from the DOS command line (in real mode) and switch themselves into protected mode. Windows just happens to be the best DOS-extender I have ever seen, but it is not an operating system. As developers became more familiar with 3.1 they found out it really is just a pretty face on top of DOS. And DOS is the very operating system we are trying to get away from in the first place! There are other design flaws as well. In addition to the ones that plague DOS, Windows has some of the same flaws that plague OS/2 2.0, such as single threaded input model, non-preemption, and tied to one x86 processor at a time.

The following code, known as the Terminator, shows just how easy it is to accidently freeze Windows 3.1. If you are a Windows developer, you probably have your own code that has already wreaked havoc on Windows. I include this just to show how human frailties, like forgetting to set capture off and forgetting to yield, can bring Windows to its knees. You don't necessarily have to be brave enough to run this under Windows 3.1. If you do execute the Terminator, you must press CRTL-ALT-DEL to terminate the Terminator. Until you do, Windows will be in what appears to be a frozen state. CTRL-ESC won't work and neither will ALT-TAB, or ALT-ESC

**Listing 10–1** The Terminator.

```
//


#include <afxwin.h>
#include "resource.h"

#include "term.h"
     CString s = "You are Terminated!";


/////////////////////////////////////////////////////////////////////////

// theApp:
// Just creating this application object runs the whole application.
//
CTheApp theApp;


/////////////////////////////////////////////////////////////////////////

// CMainWindow constructor:
// Create the window with the appropriate style, size, menu, etc.
//
CMainWindow::CMainWindow()
{
     LoadAccelTable( "MainAccelTable" );
     Create( NULL, "The Terminator",
             WS_OVERLAPPEDWINDOW, rectDefault, NULL, "MainMenu" );
}


// OnPaint:
// This routine draws the string "You are terminated!" in the center of the
// client area. It is called when Windows sends a WM_PAINT message.
// Note that creating a CPaintDC automatically does a BeginPaint and
// an EndPaint call is done when it is destroyed at the end of this
// function. CPaintDC's constructor needs the window (this pointer).
//
void CMainWindow::OnPaint()
{
```

```
        CPaintDC dc( this );
        CRect rect;

        GetClientRect( rect );
        dc.SetTextAlign( TA_BASELINE | TA_CENTER );
        dc.SetTextColor( ::GetSysColor( COLOR_WINDOWTEXT ) );
        dc.SetBkMode(TRANSPARENT);
        dc.TextOut( ( rect.right / 2 ), ( rect.bottom / 2 ),
                                s, s.GetLength() );


}

// OnAbout:
// This member function is called when a WM_COMMAND message with an
// IDM_ABOUT code is received by the CMainWindow class object.  The
// message map below is responsible for this routing.
//
// We create a CModalDialog object using the "AboutBox" resource (see
// term.rc), and invoke it.
//
void CMainWindow::OnAbout()
{
    CModalDialog about("AboutBox", this );
    about.DoModal();
}

// CMainWindow message map:
// Associate messages with member functions.
//
// It is implied that the ON_WM_PAINT macro expects a member function
// "void OnPaint()".
//
//
BEGIN_MESSAGE_MAP( CMainWindow, CFrameWnd )
    ON_WM_PAINT()
    ON_COMMAND( IDM_ABOUT, OnAbout )

END_MESSAGE_MAP()
```

**393**

```
////////////////////////////////////////////////////////////////////////
// CTheApp

// InitInstance:
// When any CTheApp object is created, this member function is automatically
// called. Any data may be set up at this point.
//
// Also, the main window of the application should be created and shown here.
// Return TRUE if the initialization is successful.
//
BOOL CTheApp::InitInstance()
{
    TRACE( "Terminator\n" );

    m_pMainWnd = new CMainWindow();
    m_pMainWnd->ShowWindow( m_nCmdShow );
    m_pMainWnd->UpdateWindow();
    m_pMainWnd->Invalidate(TRUE);
    m_pMainWnd->UpdateWindow();

    m_pMainWnd->SetCapture();
    for (;;);    // The user intended to have a loop that did some lengthy
                 // processing so he turned the capture on to get stray
                 // keystrokes.
                 // Unfortunately a stray semicolon will cause this to loop
                 // forever.
    .
    .        //Some long processing goes here.
    .
    return TRUE;
}


// term.h : Declares the class interfaces for the application.
//          Term is a simple program which consists of a main window
//          and an "About" dialog which can be invoked by a menu choice.
//          Due to a bug in program logic Term accidently goes into a loop
//          after setting the capture on.
```

```
#ifndef __TERM_H__
#define __TERM_H__


/////////////////////////////////////////////////////////////////////


// CMainWindow:
// See term.cpp for the code to the member functions and the message map.
//
class CMainWindow : public CFrameWnd
{
public:
    CMainWindow();

    afx_msg void OnPaint();
    afx_msg void OnAbout();

    DECLARE_MESSAGE_MAP()
};


/////////////////////////////////////////////////////////////////////


// CTheApp:
// See term.cpp for the code to the InitInstance member function.
//
class CTheApp : public CWinApp
{
public:
    BOOL InitInstance();
};


/////////////////////////////////////////////////////////////////////


#endif // __TERM_H__
```

Basically, I started with the GENERIC sample and added a few function calls to freeze Windows. Now I doubt anyone would sell a lot of copies if this is all their application did, but it certainly is possible to have this happen by accident. Remember this application because we will come back to it after explaining NT.

# DON'T MAKE THE SAME MISTAKE TWICE.

This brings us to the first release of Windows NT. Windows NT is actually the portable OS/2 that I spoke of earlier. Which API do you think NT is based on: the OS/2 API or an API of the product that sells a million copies a month? When Microsoft and IBM split, Microsoft switched the development emphasis of Windows NT away from an OS/2 oriented API (as well as the name) to a new API. This new operating system and new API allows Microsoft to build on the success of Windows and, to some extent, atone for the sins of the past. Microsoft was not going to make the same mistake twice and abandon a legion of loyal developers and users. Now you will understand, when, later in the book, I present a new API call whose name doesn't seem to make sense. You'll understand when you see examples with separate dialog procs and window procs. You'll know all this was done for the sake of compatibility.

# COMPATIBILITY WITH WIN16

Compatibility is an easy word to say and a hard task to achieve. For example, NT looks just like Windows 3.1. That's why when NT was first released its official name was "Windows NT 3.1". Microsoft made a sincere effort to protect the customer's investment. So many corporations have standardized on Windows, it would be foolish to think they would willingly move to another User Interface (UI).

Okay, looking like Window is only half the battle. An operating system must also run Windows applications. It also runs DOS, LANMAN, character-based POSIX and character-based 16 bit OS/2 programs as well. Users are not forced to choose between NT and another OS. Anyway, that's what Microsoft marketing hype will tell you. OS/2 is only supported on Intel platforms, and even though NT supports DOS, LANMAN, and POSIX on all platforms, Microsoft does not want you to continue to develop new applications for these operating systems. On the contrary, support for DOS, OS/2 and POSIX is so you can use your favorite tools and editor while you build new NT applications. However, it is very nice to know that if you do have a DOS or OS/2 utility you are in love with you will be able to bridge the gap until a NT version ships.

# BASED ON 32-BITS

Corporations aren't the only ones who have invested in Windows. The designers also wanted to protect the investment of independent software vendors (ISVs), because so many of them have standardized on Windows APIs. To do so, they created a new API, called Win32, that enables ISVs to easily move their applications to NT. Win32 is basically a 32-bit version of the Windows 3.x API. Now that Win32 has arrived, Microsoft is referring to the Windows 3.x APIs as Win16. The primary goal of Win32 is to be upwardly compatible with Win16. Although it takes more than just recompiling your code, it is easier to port applications from Win16 to Win32 than it is to port from Win16 to PM. There are relatively few changes in the syntax between Win32 and Win16. The largest is the widening of many parameters from 16 to 32 bits. Another difference is that all of the APIs in Win32 return an error status. Extended support is also available using the GetLastError() call. This forced some APIs to change from Win16, but it means that if your code checks the return status it is impossible to use an invalid handle. For example, the function, MoveTo has been dropped because its prototype didn't allow for a return value. Chapter 3, "Porting Applications to Win32," explains the other issues involved in porting applications from Win16 to Win32.

Compatibility is important, but if an operating system doesn't offer new features, no one will buy it. Win32 introduces new features and functionality beyond the scope of the features in Win16. Win32 is designed to be a shield between applications and the underlying operating system. This shield allows NT to be radically different from either DOS or OS/2. As I mentioned earlier, NT is based on 32-bits. For programmers who are used to the 16-bit segmentation of Intel based systems, this widening can give you agoraphobia. First of all, the segmentation issues disappear completely. Offsets are 32 bits; and segments, while still 16 bit, lose their importance to the developer. As far as the developer is concerned, the segment registers no longer have any meaning. In other words, since you no longer care what the values of the CS, DS, and SS segment registers are, you no longer have to code with them in mind. Back in my DOS programming days, we called this Tiny Model. In Tiny Model, the code, data, and stack segments combine to form one 64KB block. In NT, Tiny Model is now 4 gigabytes wide, which means you can allocate memory greater than 64KB if you want. The operating system does not have to jump through hoops to accommodate you. You can allocate 20MB of memory using malloc() from your C runtime library if you wanted—something not possible in Windows 3.x. Chapter 2, "32-Bit Programming Rules," covers 32-bit programming in detail.

# MULTITHREADED PROCESS STUCTURE

Another major improvement over Windows 3.x is NT's multi-threaded process structure. In Windows 3.x, each executable accounts for one thread of execution. Since an executable (process) can have only one thread, the terms thread and process are treated synonymously and are often used interchangeably. To have more threads you must have more processes. This means that one Windows 3.x application sometimes spawns several processes with each running as a separate executable. Since Windows 3.x has only one address space, the processes get each others handles and share memory. In Windows NT, each process can have multiple threads, and each thread is preemptively scheduled by NT's scheduler. OS/2 also has the concept of multiple threads per process and is similiar to NT, except that processes in NT run in separate address spaces, while the processes in OS/2 run in the same address space. Processes, threads and synchronization are covered in great detail in Chapter 4, "The Life Of a Process."

# SEPARATE ADDRESS SPACE

Don't let all this talk of separate, protected address spaces scare you. NT does allow cross-process operations. The only difference in NT is you must have security clearance to do so. In chapter 12, "The NT Security Architecture," I show you how to get the security clearance. Your thread, with the correct privilege level, can read and write into another process. Subsystems can also control their client's virtual machine, and can read from and write into the client address space. For example, the POSIX subsystem suspends processes, finds the stack for the processes and changes it. This is how the POSIX subsystem implements signals.

Since NT no longer relies upon MS-DOS for base functionality, such as creating a file, APIs now replace all of the old INT 21H functions that exist in

**398**

DOS and Windows 3.x. I will be using several examples of these API calls throughout the book.

## STABILITY

But what about the UAEs and system hangs? All the features and 32-bit APIs in the world mean little if an operating system allows misbehaved applications to crash the system. To solve this problem, NT uses a client-server model to ensure that no process can accidently or deliberately corrupt the operating system. Win32 is a subsystem, and all subsystems operate in User mode. User mode is, more or less, a client to the kernel's server (called Kernel mode). Win32 is one of several subsystems to be offered by NT in its first release. The others are POSIX and OS/2. DOS and Windows 3.x applications run in Windows on Windows (WOW). WOW is not a true subsystem, but a User-mode program. NT also uses an asynchronous input model, which means that an application that has the focus and "forgets" to yield (doesn't call *PeekMessage* or *GetMessage*) to other applications will, at worst, succeed only in hanging itself. Other applications will continue to run oblivious to the plight of the misbehaving application. This means that any application that generates a general protection (GP) violation disappears, but the system keeps running. If you return to the Terminator program and run it under NT, you will see different results. With full preemption taking place, all applications get their time slice no matter what a single application does. Nothing notifies you that the Terminator is stuck until you attempt to run a second 16-bit program. When you run a second application you receive the dialog box shown in figure 10–1 stating that the Win16 subsytem is not responding.

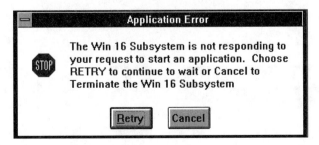

**Figure 10–1** NT cannot not be brought down by a failing subsystem

This occurs because all Win16 applications run in the same address space. Many 16-bit Windows programs break if they aren't allowed to share memory. Just as in Windows 3.x, where one application can corrupt Windows, a bad application in the Win16 subsystem can disable the entire Win16 system. In NT, the difference is that the Win16 subsystem is the only piece affected. The rest of NT and the other subsystems remain unaffected. Also NT, is aware that the Terminator is in trouble. If you double-click on the system menu, NT displays the dialog box in shown in figure 10–2.

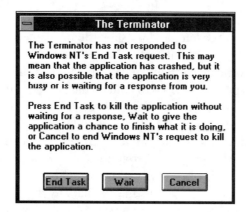

**Figure 10–2** NT is aware that the Terminator is in trouble

Since some good applications take longer than NT expects to respond to the WM_CLOSE message (for example, you will get this message if you attempt to terminate an application via the task manager and the application has a MessageBox displayed), NT lets you choose whether to terminate the program or not. If you choose "End Task," the program terminates no matter what condition it is in. When the program is no longer in the picture, the Win16 subsystem begins working correctly again.

# SUPPORT FOR DIFFERENT ARCHITECTURES

Another unique feature among PC-based operating systems is NT's ability to isolate the hardware from the software developer. A piece of the operating system, called the hardware abstraction layer (HAL), allows NT to operate on

**400**

multiple platforms. The HAL also frees hardware vendors from the bonds of supporting old software with each new chip design. This allows vendors to be innovative. The HAL isolates DMA, timers, caches and second-level interrupt dispatching. Unless you are developing device driver applications, you may never encounter the HAL. I bring it up to make a point. Different HALs mean different computer architectures. If you follow some basic rules (which I point out in Chapter 1, "32-bit Programming Rules"), your application will run on every type of platform that NT supports. All of the samples in this book have been tested on the x86, DEC AXP and MIPS R4x00 platforms. Because the samples are written to Win32, you can run them on any machine.

## SILICON GRAPHIC CORPORATION MIPS R4X00

Support for the MIPS R4x000 chip ships on both WorkStation and NT Server as well as the Win32 Software Development Kit (SDK). The MIPS chips use a RISC architecture and it's virtual address range is up to 64-bits. However, NT uses the MIPS chips in 32-bit mode.

## DIGITIAL EQUIPMENT CORPORATION ALPHA AXP

The Alpha AXP is a new microprocessor from Digital Equipment Corporation. The Alpha AXP also uses a RISC architecture and its virtual address range is also up to 64-bits, and NT also uses the Alpha AXP in 32-bit mode.

The nice feature of both the MIPS and DEC machines is their strong PC compatibility. When the Alpha migration folks gave me a peek at the innards of Alpha AXP, it looked like an ordinary PC. Aside from the processor itself, everything else can be purchased off the shelf.

## SYMMETRIC MULTI-PROCESSING

Now that NT runs on RISC-based systems, does that mean that the future of CISC-based x86 machines is limited? Not necessarily. NT is also a symmetric multi-processing (SMP) system. NT supports multiple processors of like type (for example, four 486 processors with the same clock frequency). Performance "scales" with each additional processor. On an SMP machine with four processors, a process has the potential to run four times as fast as the same process on a uni-processor (UP) system. I say potential because if there are kernel-intensive operations taking place, performance may be slighted degraded. Therefore, if your process causes a 15 percent degradation, it runs 3.40 times faster than the same process on a UP system (.85 * 4). No matter which processor you are using, your application has the same view of physical memory. A thread can be dispatched without worrying that if it runs on this processor, it won't see the memory it just allocated on another processor. The kernel can execute on any CPU, which means that because multiple system calls can take place simultaneously there are no bottlenecks.

# SECURITY

Many government agencies and organizations with mission critical information have avoided Windows 3.x due to its lack of security features. This is why NT is designed to be a secure system. The following chart defines the possible levels of security as defined by the Department of Defense.

**Table 10–1** Security Levels

| Security Levels |
| --- |
| **Division D Minimal Protection.** |
| For any system that fails to meet the requirements of a higher class. |
| **Division C Discretionary Protection** |
| Class C1 |
| Logon control |
| Discretionary access control |
| Class C2 |
| All of C1 plus |
| Users own objects |
| Users control access to objects they own. |
| Individual identification (logons) |
| Users are accountable for access-related actions - auditing |
| Memory initialized before use. (Memory is zeroed out, unless you are loading from disk.) |
| Auditing capabilities by system administrator. |

### Division B Mandatory Protection

Class B1

Labeled Security Protection.

Class B2

Structured Protection.

Although the NT design allows for B1 security, the security is not implemented in the first release. Depending upon what the Department of Defense decides, it's possible that no current Window 3.x program can run in a system that is B1-secure. Initially, NT will be the equivalent of C2-secure. This level of security provides for discretionary access control on all potentially shared resources or objects. A consequence of C2 security is that you must log on when you want to use NT. To ensure that applications cannot display fake logon dialog box to trick you out of your password, the familiar CTRL-ALT-DELETE keystroke combination now has a new meaning. Instead of rebooting, CTRL-ALT-DELETE now calls the logon manager, which displays the dialog in figure 10.3.

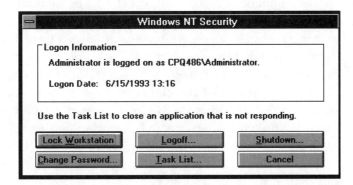

**Figure 10–3** Dialog displayed when you press CTRL-ALT-DELETE

In addition, the dialog in figure 10.4 is displayed each time you boot NT:

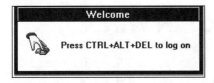

**Figure 10–4** Get used to this dialog box. It precedes every logon

**403**

The evaluation process for C2 security is lengthy and NT has not yet been certified. However, to you, the developer, it means that your NT application is also open to these new C2-secure markets. To support this new security system, NT includes a new file system called the NT File System (NTFS). NT also supports FAT and HPFS, however, NTFS is the only file system that will be approved in C2-secure installations. Therefore, if your users are in an installation that wants to be certified C2-secure, all of their sensitive data must be placed on the NTFS volume. In addition to security, NTFS includes several other new features. NTFS has 64-bit file sizes, which breaks the existing 4GB limit imposed on HPFS and FAT file systems. The capacity of an NTFS disk is 16 quadrillion bytes!

NTFS has a file recovery scheme that is superior to the HPFS recovery system. Since it is a transaction-based file system, the NTFS crash recovery takes only seconds. If you have ever had a power failure or some other abnormal shutdown on HPFS, you know that verifying that the disk is clean takes a minimum of twenty minutes for a minimum-size server disk (600MB SCSI). NTFS also supports symbolic links that will be familiar to POSIX programmers. All file names are now Unicode to support multi-byte characters. Unicode is the name chosen by a consortium of companies (of which Microsoft is a member) for its double-byte character set. Each Unicode character is 16 bits wide, meaning that the Unicode character set has space for 65,535 characters. This represents all of the characters in use today. Win32 also supports applications that use Unicode. NTFS supports long file names like HPFS; however, if you have programs that use the familiar 8.3 FAT file convention, they are also supported. The difference is that NTFS can support both file types simultaneously. NTFS is similiar to HPFS, in that, if you need to dual-boot, your entire disk cannot be NTFS.

As a side note, don't throw away that old 16-bit 80286 machine because it won't run NT. Sell it as a D-level secure, UP system.

# WHAT IS NOT IN WIN32

Another way to understand what Win32 includes is to learn what it doesn't include. Most of the functions that did not port to Win32 contained logic tied to the x86 platform. Since NT now supports multiple platforms, any call that assumes an x86 architecture no longer makes sense. The following are examples of deleted functions:

- x86 Specific functions.

  Any function that references a selector is obsolete.

- Int 21H function calls.

  The assembly language interface of MS-DOS is dead.

- Read-Only Code Segments.

  Read-only code segments are a vestige of real mode. One way to save memory in a real mode program is to discard code segments when memory is low. The fastest way to ensure the code segments can be discarded is to make them read-only. Functions that turn read-only code segments into read/write segments are no longer needed.

- MakeProcInstance.

  Another remnant of x86 processors MakeProcInstance is obsolete, but for portability reasons does not cause an error in NT.

- Functions present in Windows 3.1 only for compatibility reasons. Functions, such as, GetAtomHandle are in Windows 3.1 for compatibility with Windows 2.x only.

- Functions superseded by EX-type functions. Many functions changed to accommodate a new return value. This includes functions like MoveTo (MoveToEx). If your favorite function doesn't work in Win32, see if it has an "Ex" added to it.

- WEP

  The Wep call became obsolete when NT changed the way it handles DLLs. In Windows 3.x there is a lot of confusion about what the Wep does. Known as the Windows Exit Procedure Windows calls the Wep when a process is detaching from the DLL, only if the process loads the DLL using LoadLibrary(). If the process implib'ed the DLL, the Wep isn't called. Got that? Thankfully, the NT method for attaching to and detaching from DLLs is much cleaner. In NT, the function in your DLL, which declare at link time to be the DllEntryPoint, is called when a process or thread is attaching or detaching. When a process attaches to a DLL, the code and data from the DLL is mapped into the address space of the process.

**405**

# WIN32 vs WINDOWS NT vs WINDOWS 95

It is important to note that there is a difference between a product and an API. A product is something that is shrink-wrapped and you pay money for. For example, NT and Windows 95 are products. An API is something you code to. Win32 is an API. Win32 was first available in the product Windows NT 3.1. The reason I bring this up is that Win32 is available on platforms other than NT. In Chapter 14, "Win32s," I discuss Win32s, which is a subset of the Win32 API that can run under Windows 3.1. (The *s* in Win32s stands for *subset* not the plural of Win32.) In the remainder of this book, when I want to refer to the 16-bit Windows 3.1, I will call it Win16. When I explain something about a window on the screen I will call it a window.

NT has all the features in it that you would expect from a *real* operating system. Now I said real, not perfect. NT, like all operating systems, has its flaws.

- ■■ NT is perceived as taking up too much memory. It doesn't matter how great your operating system is, if the majority of machines do not have enough RAM to run it.

- ■■ In duplicating the look and feel of Windows 3.1, NT has taken on the look of an operating system badly in need of a facelift.

So where does this lead us? To Chicago, of course. Chicago, as most everyone knows, is the code name for Windows 95. Windows 95 both picks up where NT left off and fills the gap between Windows 3.1 and NT.

Microsoft is betting that new user interface of Windows 95 will make PCs much easier to use. But the operating system is just half the story. The other half is your application. In order for PCs to be easier to use, your application needs to be easier to use.

**Table 10–2** Win32 Feature set on Windows 95, NT and Win32s

| Feature | Windows 95 | Windows NT | Win32s | Comments |
|---|---|---|---|---|
| OLE 2.0 32-bit functionality | Yes | Yes* | Yes* | *32-Bit OLE 2.01 will ship with Windows NT "Daytona" and Win32s 1.2 in Q2 1994 |
| Visual Editing | Yes | Yes | Yes | Easy, consistent way to |

| | | | | |
|---|---|---|---|---|
| | | | | create compound documents |
| OLE Drag/Drop | Yes | Yes | Yes | Streamlines existing clipboard operation, enables drag & drop with "Windows '95" Shell |
| Automation | Yes | Yes | Yes | Enables cross-application programmability |
| Populate OLE Compound Files | Yes | Yes | Yes | Populate the summary stream in compound files |
| Associate documents with app | Yes | Yes | Yes | Use OLEclass ID to associate documents with applications |
| Register icons | Yes | Yes | Yes | Register small and large icons for "Windows '95" integration |
| Register verbs | Yes | Yes | Yes | Register for drag/drop open or others verbs for context sensitive menus |
| Support Print-to | Yes | Yes | Yes | Print-to in registry for drag/drop printing |
| Windows Sockets/NetBIOS | Yes | Yes | Yes | Defines network programming interface |
| Memory mapped files | Yes | Yes | Yes | Copy a file's contents into virtual memory. Good for sharing data. |
| Common Dialogs | Yes | Yes | Yes | Common Dialogs have 3-D look on "Windows '95" |
| Find | Yes | Yes | Yes | |
| Replace | Yes | Yes | Yes | |
| Print | Yes | Yes | Yes | |
| Print setup | Yes | Yes | Yes | |
| Color | Yes | Yes | Yes | |
| Structured exception handling | Yes | Yes | Yes | See Chapter 8 |
| Configuration/Setup | Yes | Yes | Yes | Support express install; minimal install; uninstall; use registry not WIN.INI |
| National Language Support (NLS) | Yes | Yes | Yes | |
| *32-bit Flat Memory model* | *Yes* | *Yes* | *Yes* | |
| *Separate address space* | *Yes* | *Yes* | *No* | |
| *Asynchronous input model* | *Yes* | *Yes* | *No* | |

**407**

**Table 10–2** (Continued)

| Feature | Windows 95 | Windows NT | Win32s | Comments |
|---|---|---|---|---|
| Preemptive multitasking | Yes | Yes | No | Win32s runs on Windows 3.1 and is non-preemptive multitasking |
| User & GDI System Resources | Expanded | Unlimited | Win3.1 limits | "Windows '95" has 32-bit heaps for User and GDI, expanded listbox limits |
| 3d look | Yes | 2D | 2D | Applications running on Windows NT and Win32s can code own 3D look |
| Property sheets exposed by shell | Yes | Won't appear | Won't appear | "Windows '95" shell will display property sheets for objects |
| Context menu on button 2 | Yes | Yes | Yes | User interface guideline |
| Long Filenames (LFN) | Yes | Yes | Won't appear | Win32 API handles this, make sure buffers are large enough |
| Unified Naming Convention (UNC) | Yes | Yes | Yes* | For example, \\server\share. *Win32s supports this on WindowsÔ for Workgroups |
| Focus on documents | Yes | Yes | Yes | User interface guidline; write document centric applications |
| Simple MAPI/CMC | Yes | Yes | Universal Thunk | Can code own Simple MAPI/CMC support on Win32s with the Universal Thunk |
| Network API | Yes | Yes | Universal Thunk | Can code own WNet API support on Win32s using the Universal Thunk. |
| Named Pipes | Yes (client) | Yes | No* (Stubs) | "Windows '95" will support client side named pipes, Windows NT has both server and client side support. * Can code own client side named pipes using Win32s Universal Thunk |
| Remote Procedure Calls (RPC) | Yes | Yes | No* | Client and server OSF DCE |

| | | | | |
|---|---|---|---|---|
| | | | | compliant RPC. * Can code own client side RPC using Win32s Universal Thunk. |
| Threads | Yes | Yes | No (Stubs) | Chapter 4 discusses Threads. |
| Paths/Beziers | Yes | Yes | No (Stubs) | In "Windows '95", only MoveTo, LineTo, PolyBezier/to are recorded in a path see Chap13. GDI |
| Win32 COMM API | Yes | Yes | No (Stubs) | Win32 interface to communications functions |
| Console support | Yes* | Yes | No (Stubs) | Win32 interface that provides consoles that manage I/O for char-mode apps. * "Windows '95" supports all console API except the code page APIs. See Chapter 9 |
| Print APIs | Yes (No forms) | Yes | No (Stubs) | Win32 API available for print spooler |
| Multimedia API | Yes | Yes | Windows 3.1 level | Win32s supports most Windows 3.1 multimedia API |
| Remote Access Services | Yes | Yes | No | |
| Enhanced metafiles | Yes | Yes | No | Device independent resolution and pictures |
| Common Controls | Yes | Yes | Yes | Available for Win32s and Windows NT via redistributable DLLs when "Windows '95" ships |
| Tabs | Yes | Yes | Yes | Used for Property sheets see Chapter 11 |
| Drag list boxes | Yes | Yes | Yes | Allows you to drag listbox items around with in the listbox |
| Toolbar | Yes | Yes | Yes | |
| Status bar | Yes | Yes | Yes | |
| Column heading | Yes | Yes | Yes | Sizable, sortable button headers for columns |
| Spin buttons | Yes | Yes | Yes | Up/down arrow buttons for increasing/decreasing contents |

**409**

**Table 10–2** (Continued)

| Feature | Windows 95 | Windows NT | Win32s | Comments |
|---|---|---|---|---|
| Slider | Yes | Yes | Yes | Moveable slider control |
| Scrolling button indicator | Yes | Yes | Yes | For scrolling toolbar buttons |
| Rich Text Object | Yes | Yes | Yes | Rich text control, expands limits, allows different font sizes and types |
| Progress indicator | Yes | Yes | Yes | Gas gauge |
| Tree View | Yes | Yes | Yes | Used by explorer mode (+/-) to expand/contract directories |
| List View | Yes | Yes | Yes | Small and large icon views, used in "Windows '95" shell |
| New Common Dialogs | Yes | Yes | Yes | Available for Win32s and Windows NT via redistributable DLLs when "Windows '95" ships |
| Open | Yes | Yes | Yes | New common dialogs support tree and details views. Also supports long filenames and UNC names (as Windows NT dialogs do today) |
| Save as | Yes | Yes | Yes | |
| Plug and Play event aware | Yes | Won't get events | Won't get events | Monitor events to accommodate resources coming and going |
| Viewers | Yes | Not used | Not used | Provide viewers for your data types |
| "Windows '95" style help | Yes | Won't appear | Won't appear | New help features |
| Context menu help | Yes | Won't appear | Won't appear | |
| New authorable buttons | Yes | Write own code | Write own code | |
| MAPI 1.0 | Yes | Yes | No | MAPI 1.0 will be available for Windows NT at "Windows '95" ship |
| More Multimedia (ACM/VCR/VfW1.1) | Yes | Yes | No | Multimedia, Compression, Video for Windows. |
| Telephony API 1.0/ Unimodem API | Yes | No* | No | Voice data and port contention. *Will be available for Windows NT |

| | | | | |
|---|---|---|---|---|
| | | | | withing 6 months of "Windows '95" ship. |
| File merge/Reconciliation | Yes | No (Cairo) | No | Add file merge to your applications to enhance mobile computing |
| Image Color Matching API | Yes | No (Cairo) | No | Use for consistent color across devices such as displays, printers, scanners, etc. |
| Pen | Yes | No (Cairo) | No | The "Windows '95" shell , but who cares. |
| "Windows '95" help  Cue Cards | Yes | No (Cairo) | No | Pop up context help for objects on screen |
| Container namespace in explorer | Yes | No (Cairo) | No | Container in directory hierarchy that contains specific non-ordered objects,  (i.e. mail, control panel, printers) |
| Unicode Win32 API | No (Stubs) | Yes | No (Stubs) | Global character encoding |
| Event logging | No (Stubs) | Yes | No (Stubs) | Centralized way for applications to record important events, and to view logs of those events |
| Service control manager API | No (Stubs) | Yes | No (Stubs) | Manage installed services, logon and security information. etc. |
| World transforms | Scaling  Only | Yes | No (Stubs) | "Windows '95" provides scaling, but not shearing or rotation |
| Async file I/O | No* | Yes | No (Stubs) | * "Windows '95" will map these to standard file i/o APIs |
| Security API | No (Stubs) | Yes | No (Stubs) | *See security Chapter* |
| *32-bit Coordinate System* | *No* | *Yes* | *No* | *See Chapter 13, GDI* |
| *Security (C2 certifiable)* | *No* | *Yes* | *No* | *See security Chapter.* |
| *Portable to non-Intel platforms* | *No* | *Yes* | *No* | *MIPS, Alpha, and eventually PowerPC* |
| *Scalable to symmetric multiprocessors* | *No* | *Yes* | *No* | |

Note Cairo (Microsoft's best guessed secret) is the code name for a future version of NT.

## CHAPTER 11

# THE WINDOWS 95 SHELL

## THE SHELL GAME

Many users of Windows 3.1 do not realize that programs such as the Program Manager and File Manager are not part of the operating system. Program Manager is what is known as a *shell* program. In Windows 3.1, Program Manager is just another windows program (PROGMAN.EXE). It just happens to be the first program you see in Windows 3.1 because of the "Shell=" statement in SYSTEM.INI. As millions of Norton Desktop for Windows (NDW) users can attest to, the shell is easily replaceble. NDW became popular, in part, because it has several ease-of-use features that Program Manager doesn't have. Microsoft's policy was that if Program Manager didn't do what you wanted it to do, replace it with your own shell. In Windows 95, Microsoft has taken a different approach. Although you can still replace the shell, the Explorer, it also can be extended to enhance its functionality. Throughout this chapter, when I refer to the shell, I am referring to the Explorer. Any shell application that replaces the Explorer would have to provide the same functionality--much the same way that any Windows 3.1 or Windows NT shell application that replaces Program Manager must provide all of Program Managers functionality.

You may be thinking so why are we talking about shells here? What's that got to do with Win32? Well, besides the new user interface (see the sidebar, "The Explorer"), the Win32 API sports calls that are specific to shell programs, called shell extensions (see Listing 11–1). The shell extensions described in this chapter allow applications to solve the problem of providing a consistent look to the user for all of the files that make up your application, whether the files are local or on the network. Extending the shell enables you to personalize how Explorer users view all the files that make up your application.

**Listing 11–1** Win32 APIs to support Shell Extensions

```
IContextMenu::AddRef
IContextMenu::InvokeCommand
IContextMenu::QueryContextMenu
IContextMenu::QueryInterface
IContextMenu::Release
IExtractIcon::AddRef
IExtractIcon::ExtractIcon
IExtractIcon::GetIconLocation
IExtractIcon::QueryInterface
IExtractIcon::Release
IShellExtInit::AddRef
IShellExtInit::Initialize
IShellExtInit::QueryInterface
IShellExtInit::Release
IShellFolder::AddRef
IShellFolder::BindToObject
IShellFolder::BindToStorage
IShellFolder::CompareIDs
IShellFolder::CreateViewObject
IShellFolder::EnumObjects
IShellFolder::GetAttributesOf
IShellFolder::GetUIObjectOf
IShellFolder::GetDisplayNameOf
IShellFolder::ParseDisplayName
```

```
IShellFolder::QueryInterface
IShellFolder::Release
IShellFolder::SetNameOf
IShellPropSheetExt::AddPages
IShellPropSheetExt::AddRef
IShellPropSheetExt::QueryInterface
IShellPropSheetExt::Release
IShellView::AddPropertySheetPages
```

Why do you need to personalize? Take a look at the following issues solved by Shell extensions:

▪▪ Adding menu items to the context menu

The context menu is the menu that pops up when a Explorer user right-clicks the mouse over one of your applications files (see Figure 11–1). By providing what is known as a *context-menu handler* your application can add menu items to the context menu. Another form of the context-menu handler is the *drag-drop* handler. Drag-drop handlers allow you to customize the standard drag-drop menu that pops up when a user drags and drops one of your file objects.

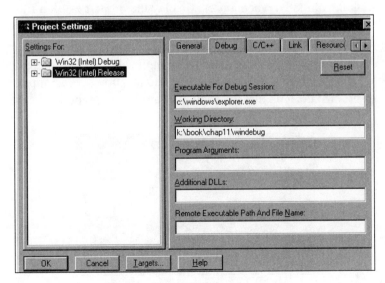

**Figure 11–1** A Context menu

■■ Ensuring that all pertinent files go with a particular folder when it is copied.

Ever take home what you thought was all the source files you needed to build your project only to discover once you got home you forgot REALIMPORTANT.CPP?

Ever hear about the user who deleted critical files for your application because they had really old time stamps? Wouldn't you like to be notified *before* something your application requires gets deleted, copied or renamed? Wouldn't it be great if a user required your approval before moving, or renaming one of your files. Well, by providing a copy-hook handler you can get that notification. Once an application has a *copy-hook handler* installed, the shell will call the handler before the shell moves, copies, deletes or renames a folder object. If you don't want the operation to take place you can tell the shell to refuse the operation.

■■ Additional feedback in identifying your applications files.

Even with the addition of long filenames, it may become difficult for users to determine exactly what purpose one of your file objects serve. This is the impetus for the context-menu available to Shell users. One of the menu items displayed in the context menu is the Properties dialog. Normally, when a users display the properties for a file they see a dialog similar to Figure 11–2. By implementing a *property-sheet handler* you can add new pages to the property sheet

Another way you can increase the recognizability of your application is with an *Icon-handler.* An Icon-handlers allows your application to customize the icon that the shell displays for your applications files.

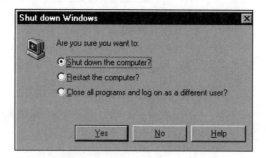

**Figure 11–2** A Property dialog

## HOW SHELL EXTENSIONS WORK

Shell extensions work by exploiting the power of object linking and embedding (OLE) version 2.x in the form of component objects. Shell extensions must be implemented as in-process object servers, that is, they must be DLL servers because the Explorer looks for only this type only. If you want to use an EXE-type server in order to use your extension objects as part of a stand-alone application, there's no reason your application can't call *CoCreateInstance* to instantiate and use them. But to work with the shell, the extensions need to be in DLLs. Like all OLE interfaces, each of the interfaces that you employ must include the QueryInterface, AddRef, and Release member functions. When coding a shell extension in C++ the standard practice is to use multiple inheritance to derive all the necessary interfaces.

```
class CMyShellExtension : public IExtractIcon,
                          IContextMenu,
                          IShellExtInit,
                          IPersistFile,
                          IShellPropSheetExt,
                          ICopyHook
```

Because of this you must call IsEquallIID to determine which interface the shell is querying.

```
STDMETHODIMP
CMyShellExtension::QueryInterface(REFIID riid, LPVOID FAR *ppv)
{
    *ppv = NULL;

    if (IsEqualIID(riid, IID_IShellExtInit) ||
                IsEqualIID(riid, IID_IUnknown))
    {
        OutputDebugString("QueryInterface()->IID_IShellExtInit\r\n");

        *ppv = (LPSHELLEXTINIT)this;
    }
    else if (IsEqualIID(riid, IID_IContextMenu))
    {
        TRACE0("QueryInterface()->IID_IContextMenu\r\n");
```

**417**

```
        *ppv = (LPCONTEXTMENU)this;
    }
    else if (IsEqualIID(riid, IID_IExtractIcon))
    {
        TRACE0("QueryInterface()->IID_IExtractIcon\r\n");

        *ppv = (LPEXTRACTICON)this;
    }
    else if (IsEqualIID(riid, IID_IPersistFile))
    {
        TRACE0("QueryInterface()->IPersistFile\r\n");

        *ppv = (LPPERSISTFILE)this;
    }
    else if (IsEqualIID(riid, IID_IShellPropSheetExt))
    {
        TRACE0("QueryInterface()->IShellPropSheetExt\r\n");

        *ppv = (LPSHELLPROPSHEETEXT)this;
    }
    else if (IsEqualIID(riid, IID_IShellCopyHook))
    {
        TRACE0("QueryInterface()->ICopyHook\r\n");

        *ppv = (LPCOPYHOOK)this;
    }

    if (*ppv)
    {
            AddRef();

            return NOERROR;
    }

    TRACE0("QueryInterface()->Unknown Interface!\r\n");

    return E_NOINTERFACE;
}
```

The AddRef and Release functions are pretty staightforward. AddRef increments the reference counter of the object and Release decrements the counter. When the counter reaches zero, the object is deleted.

```
STDMETHODIMP_(ULONG) CMyShellExtension::AddRef()
{
    TRACE0("CMyShellExtension::AddRef()\r\n");

    return ++m_cRef;
}

STDMETHODIMP_(ULONG) CMyShellExtension::Release()
{
TRACE0("CMyShellExtension::Release()\r\n");
m_cRef--;
if (m_cRef > 0)
    return m_cRef;

delete this;

return 0L;
}

STDMETHODIMP_(ULONG) CMyShellExtensionClassFactory::AddRef()
{
    return ++m_cRef;
}

STDMETHODIMP_(ULONG) CMyShellExtensionClassFactory::Release()
{
    if (--m_cRef)
        return m_cRef;

    delete this;

    return 0L;
}
```

Once you have set up the OLE housekeeping, there are two more things you must do to implement a shell extension. First, write code the for each interface that you wish to expose; second, register your shell extension in the Registry. This next section details how build a shell extension DLL using MFC and explains how to code the necessary interfaces.

After explaining how to code the interfaces I'll cover how to register the extensions in the Registry.

# CREATING A SHELL EXTENSION DLL USING MFC

You must implement the following steps to create your shell extension DLL using MFC:

- Create a new project in Visual C++ 2.0 to create a _USRDLL.
- Explicitly export the functions DllCanUnloadNow and DllGetClassObject
- Initialize the shell extension
- Implement the following shell extension interfaces:
  IExtractIcon
  IShellPropSheetExt
  IContextMenu
  Drag-Drop Handler (IContextMenu)
  ICopyhook
  IShellExtInit
- Keep track off the Dll's instance count.

## USE APPWIZARD TO CREATE A _USRDLL

In Visual C++ 2.0, there are two types of DLLs that can use MFC. The first type is called _AFXDLL, and is referred to by Visual C++ as an extension DLL. Do not use this type. _AFXDLLs are useful when the executable that loads the DLL wants to derive from the MFC classes stored in the DLL. Since that is not our case we will use _USRDLL. _USRDLLs are useful to provide a "C" wrapper around your functions, while using C++ internally. This type of DLL is perfect for a shell extension.

Export two functions: *DllCanUnloadNow* and *DllGetClassObject*

Each shell extension must implement *DllCanUnloadNow,* and *DllGetClassObject.*

```
#include "chap11.h"

#define new DEBUG_NEW

///////////////////////////////////////////////////////////////////
///
// Public C interface
///////////////////////////////////////////////////////////////////
///

//-----------------------------------------------------------------
---
// DllCanUnloadNow
//-----------------------------------------------------------------
---

STDAPI DllCanUnloadNow(void)
{
    TRACE0("In DLLCanUnloadNow\r\n");

    return (CShellExtensionDLL::m_cRefThisDll == 0 ? S_OK : S_FALSE);
}
```

The shell periodically calls your DllCanUnloadNow function when it needs memory. By maintaining a reference count you can determine if it is okay to unload your extension from memory. By returning S_OK from DLLCanUnloadNow you are giving the shell permission to call FreeLibrary on your DLL.

DllGetClassObject is where you expose your class factory to the shell.

```
STDAPI DllGetClassObject(REFCLSID rclsid, REFIID riid, LPVOID *ppvOut)
{
```

```
            TRACE0("In DllGetClassObject\r\n");

        *ppvOut = NULL;

        if (IsEqualIID(rclsid, CLSID_ShellExtension))
        {
        CMyShellExtensionClassFactory *pacf =
                                    new CMyShellExtensionClassFactory;
        if  (pacf)
            return pacf->QueryInterface(riid, ppvOut);
        else
                return CLASS_E_OUTOFMEMORY;
        }
#ifdef _DEBUG
        else
                AfxMessageBox(IDS_CLASS_NOTAVAIL);
#endif


        return CLASS_E_CLASSNOTAVAILABLE;
    }
```

## INITIALIZE THE SHELL EXTENSION.

Each of the shell extension interfaces must be initialized. The shell initializes the copy-hook handler interface directly so you don't have to code anything explicitly. But for each of the other extensions you must write an initialization method. To initialize a property sheet extension, context menu extension, or drag-drop handler use the IShellExtInit::Initialize method.

```
HRESULT STDMETHODCALLTYPE
IShellExtInit::Initialize(LPCITEMIDLIST pidlFolder,
                            LPDATAOBJECT lpdobj,
                                HKEY hkeyProgID);
```

The parameter, pIDFolder, specifies the parent folder, pDataObj is the set of items selected in that folder and hRegKey specifies the type of the focused item in the selection.

The shell calls Initialize after it creates an instance of a property sheet extension, context menu extension, or drag-drop handler. The meanings of the parameters vary depending upon what shell extension is initializing. For example, when initializing a property sheet or context menu pidlFolder specifies the folder that contains the selected file objects. The lpdobj parameter is the selected file objects and hkeyProgID is the file class of the file object that has the focus. When initializing drag-drop handlers, pidlFolder is the drop target. The lpdobj parameter is for the dropped items and hkeyProgID specifies the file class of the destination folder.

To initialize an icon handler use the IPersistFile interface. This interface is identical to the IPersistFile interface in OLE 2.x . Our shell returns uses only the Load method returning E_FAIL or S_FALSE for GetClassID, IsDirty, Save, SaveCompleted and GetCurFile. That's because our shell does not alter the icons in anyway (they are treated as read only).

Okay, now that we have everything initialized let's look at the implementations.

## ICON HANDLERS

Most executable programs have icons associated with them. In Windows 3.1 or Windows NT, the Program Manager groups consist of icons that were extracted from the executables (that is, Program Manager literally reads the executable file and makes a copy of the icon). Windows 3.1 and Windows NT also have the concept of default icons. Default icons are the icons supplied to Program Manager based on associationse. An example of an association is a .DOC file and Microsoft Word. Whenever a .DOC file appears in a Program Manager group it appears with the icon for Microsoft Word. There are flaws with this scheme, however. Since Program Manager keeps a copy of every icon for its own purposes there is a chance that the icon will become out of sync with the executable. This happened to me when I upgraded Word for version 2.0 to 6.0 on my Windows NT machine. All of my .DOC files stored in a

Program Manager group didn't automatically get the new version 6.0 icon. Actually the problem arose because I installed Word in Windows 3.1, then switched over to NT.

In Windows 95, the Explorer also allows an application to customize the icon that the shell displays for the application's file types. But instead of making copies of the icons for all file associations, the explorer uses an icon interface to allow applications to decide which icons they want to display. For backward compatiblity, you can still specify a default icon. But you can also use a shell extension DLL. To add a default icon, add a DefaultIcon key to the HKEY_CLASSES_ROOT\program\ key. This specifies the executable (or DLL) that contains your icon, and the index of the icon with the file. For example:

```
HKEY_CLASSES_ROOT\
Chap11\
DefaultIcon\
 = c:\chap11\chap11.dll,1
```

When you set up an icon this way the shell handles displaying the icons. This is the same as in Windows 3.1 or Windows NT.

By using the *IExtractIcon* interface you have the ability to display icons on a per-instance basis. That is you can have different icons for file objects of the same class. To do this you supply an icon handler. When you implement the IExtractIcon interface, the shell will call your icon handler when it is about to display an icon for file type. When the shell is about display an icon for a file finds the ProgID and ClassID of the file object. Then if the file has a ClassID, it gets the icon location string from the "DefaultIcon" registry key. In addition to the per-class method employed by Windows 3.1 and Windows NT: filename, index (Progman,1), Windows 95 introduces a per-instance icon: %1,index (%1,1). If a per-instance icon is specified, the shell then creates an icon extraction handler object for it, and extracts the icon from it. To extract the icon the shell calls IExtractIcon::GetIconLocation first, then calls IExtractIcon::ExtractIcon.

Therefore, your IExtractIcon interface must supply two functions: GetIconLocation and ExtractIcon.

```
STDMETHODIMP GetIconLocation(UINT   uFlags,
                             LPSTR  szIconFile,
```

```
UINT    cchMax,
int     *piIndex,
UINT    *pwFlags)
```

The shell calls GetIconLocation to locate the icon that you want displayed. The third parameter, szIconFile, refers to the file where the icon resides, and the fourth parameter, piIndex, is a pointer to the index of icons. In Listing 11–3, GetIconLocation returns an index to the first icon in the shell extension DLL.

**Listing 11–3** IExtractIcon::GetIconLocation

```
STDMETHODIMP CMyShellExtension::GetIconLocation(UINT    uFlags,
                                                LPSTR   szIconFile,
                                                UINT    cchMax,
                                                int     *piIndex,
                                                UINT    *pwFlags)
{

    TRACE0("CMyShellExtension::GetIconLocation()\r\n");

    GetModuleFileName(AfxGetInstanceHandle(), szIconFile, cchMax);
     *piIndex = 0;

    return S_OK;
}
```

The shell calls *ExtractIcon* when the icon is not contained in an executable or DLL. A typical example of this is when you have .ICOs on disk. You can use this method to extract both 16x16 and 32x32 icons. If you support per-instance icons store the icon location in a DLL or executable rather than have an icon image in each file object you need to implement only the GetIconLocation member and return S_FALSE for ExtractIcon. You need to implement ExtractIcon member only if you decide to store the icon images within files objects.

```
STDMETHODIMP CMyShellExtension::ExtractIcon(LPCSTR pszFile,
                                            UINT   nIconIndex,
                                            HICON  *phiconLarge,
```

```
                              HICON  *phiconSmall,
                              UINT   nIconSize)
```

In our case we just return S_FALSE to indicate that we don't extract icons. (Remember, we passed the index to our DLL in GetIconLocation. The shell knows how to extract icons from executables and DLLs)

```
STDMETHODIMP CShellExt::ExtractIcon(LPCSTR pszFile,
                              UINT   nIconIndex,
                              HICON  *phiconLarge,
                              HICON  *phiconSmall,
                              UINT   nIconSize)
{
    TRACE0("CShellExt::Extract()\r\n");

    return S_FALSE;
}
```

## ■■ IShellPropSheetExt interface.

The next interface to implement is the IShellPropSheetExt interface. This interface allows you to add pages to the property sheet (see figure 11–2) When a user selects properties for one of your files the shell calls your property-sheet handler. This allows you to add additional pages (up to 24) to the property sheet. Use the AddPage method to add sheets to the property page.

AddPages(LPFNADDPROPSHEETPAGE lpfnAddPage, LPARAM lParam)

The shell calls the AddPages when it is about to display a property sheet.

```
STDMETHODIMP
CShellExtensionDLL::AddPages(LPFNADDPROPSHEETPAGE lpfnAddPage,
                              LPARAM lParam)
{
    PROPSHEETPAGE psp;
    HPROPSHEETPAGE hpage;

    psp.dwSize      = sizeof(psp);    // no extra data.
```

```
psp.dwFlags      = PSP_USEREFPARENT | PSP_USERELEASEFUNC;
psp.hInstance    = (HINSTANCE)g_hmodThisDll;
psp.pszTemplate  = MAKEINTRESOURCE(DLG_FSPAGE);
psp.pfnDlgProc   = FSPage_DlgProc;
psp.pcRefParent  = &g_cRefThisDll;
psp.pfnRelease   = FSPage_ReleasePage;
psp.lParam       = (LPARAM)hdrop;

hpage = CreatePropertySheetPage(&psp);
if (hpage) {
  if (!lpfnAddPage(hpage, lParam))
     DestroyPropertySheetPage(hpage);
}

return NOERROR;
}
```

# CONTEXT-MENU HANDLERS

Implement the context-menu handler interface, IContextMenu, to add menu items to the drop-down menu. The shell displays this menu when a user right-clicks on your file object. (Clicks with the right mouse button). Any menu items that you add can be either class-specific (that is, applicable to all files of a particular type) or instance-specific (that is, applicable to an individual file).

The shell passes your context-menu handler a handle to a menu and you add items with the *AddItem* call. However, although your handler could change or remove existing items—don't. You never know if other handlers will be adding items. The shell may even add items.

There are three member functions that implement a context-menu handler:

▪ QueryContextMenu

▪ InvokeCommand

▪ GetCommandString

**427**

## *QUERYCONTEXTMENU*

The shell calls QueryContextMenu right before it displays a context menu for a file object.

The first parameter to QueryContextMenu is the handle to the context menu. This makes it easy to instantiate a CMenu object to create a new menu:

```
CMenu* pMenu = CMenu::FromHandle(hMenu);
```

Once you have a pointer to the menu insert menu items by position (MF_POSITION) directly into the drop-down menu by calling InsertMenu.

```
pMenu-
>InsertMenu(indexMenu++,MF_SEPARATOR|MF_BYPOSITION);
                                pMenu->InsertMenu(indexMenu++,
                                MF_STRING|MF_BYPOSITION, idCmd++,
                                     (LPSTR)(LPCSTR)strMenu);
```

Menu items must be string items (MF_STRING). As a result, the fuFlags parameter to InsertMenu must be MF_POSITION | MF_STRING for each menu item the context-menu handler inserts. Here's the entire function.

```
STDMETHODIMP CMyShellExtension::QueryContextMenu(HMENU hMenu,
                                UINT indexMenu,
                                UINT idCmdFirst,
                                UINT idCmdLast,
                                UINT uFlags)
{
    TRACE0("CMyShellExtension::QueryContextMenu()\r\n");

    UINT idCmd = idCmdFirst;
     CString strMenu;
    BOOL bAdded=FALSE;

     if (uFlags & CMF_VERBSONLY || uFlags & CMF_DEFAULTONLY)
            return NOERROR;
```

```
//
// CMF_ constants are all less < 16 so & off the unimportant bits
//
uFlags = uFlags & 0x0F;
TRACE1("QueryContextMenu: uFlags = %x\r\n",uFlags);
switch (uFlags)
{
case CMF_NORMAL:
    {

        TRACE1("CMF_NORMAL...uFlags=%d\r\n",uFlags);
        strMenu.LoadString(IDS_NORMAL);
        bAdded = TRUE;
        break;
}
case CMF_VERBSONLY:
    {
        //
        // The Docs say to ignore this variable. It indicates that
        // the user has clicked on a shortcut. We should never get
        // here due to the following code.
        //
        // if (uFlags & CMF_VERBSONLY || uFlags & CMF_DEFAULTONLY))
        //   return NOERROR;
        //
        // However, I included following for demonstration purposes

        TRACE1("CMF_VERBSONLY...uFlags=%d\r\n",uFlags);
            strMenu.LoadString(IDS_SHORTCUT);
            bAdded =TRUE;
            break;
    }
case CMF_EXPLORE:
    {
        TRACE1("CMF_EXPLORE...uFlags=%d\r\n",uFlags);
```

```
                        strMenu.LoadString(IDS_EXPLORER);
                        bAdded =TRUE;
                        break;
            }
    default:
    case    CMF_DEFAULTONLY:
            //
            // Means that a user has double-clicked.
            // We should never get here due to the code above.
            //
            // if (uFlags & CMF_VERBSONLY || uFlags & CMF_DEFAULTONLY))
            //  return NOERROR;
            //
            // However, I included the following for debug purposes
            //
            //
            TRACE1("CMF_DEFAULTONLY...uFlags=%d\r\n",uFlags);
                    break;
    };


    //
    // Use the hMenu passed to us to either insert or
    // append a menu item.
    //

    if (bAdded)
    {

            CMenu* pMenu = CMenu::FromHandle(hMenu);
            pMenu->InsertMenu(indexMenu++,MF_SEPARATOR|MF_BYPOSITION);
                            pMenu->InsertMenu(indexMenu++,
                            MF_STRING|MF_BYPOSITION, idCmd++,
                                    (LPSTR)(LPCSTR)strMenu);



            //
            // You could alternatively append the menu items...
            //
```

```
        /*
pMenu->AppendMenu(MF_SEPARATOR);

pMenu->AppendMenu(MF_STRING,indexMenu++,(LPSTR)(LPCSTR)strMenu);
        */

        //
        // Just remember to return the of menu items that you added.
        //
    return ResultFromScode(MAKE_SCODE(SEVERITY_SUCCESS, 0,
                                    (USHORT)(idCmd-idCmdFirst)));



        }

    return NOERROR;
}
```

## INVOKECOMMAND

When the user selects one of your new menu items, the shell calls the *IContextMenu::InvokeCommand* member to let it process the command. If you register multiple context-menu handlers for a file type, the value of the ContextMenuHandlers key will determine the order of the commands.

```
InvokeCommand(HWND    hwndParent,
    LPCSTR pszWorkingDir,
    LPCSTR pszCmd,
    LPCSTR pszParam,
    int    iShowCmd);
```

Here's an example of what I mean:

```
STDMETHODIMP
```

CMyShellExtension::InvokeCommand(LPCMINVOKECOMMANDINFO lpcmi)

```
    {
        TRACE0("CMyShellExtension::InvokeCommand()\r\n");

        HRESULT hr = E_INVALIDARG;

        // If HIWORD(lpcmi->lpVerb) then we have been called
        // programmatically and lpVerb is a command that should be
        // invoked.  Otherwise, the shell has called us, and
        // LOWORD(lpcmi->lpVerb) is the menu ID the user has
        // selected.  Actually, it's (menu ID - idCmdFirst) from
        // QueryContextMenu().

        if (!HIWORD(lpcmi->lpVerb))
        {
            UINT idCmd = LOWORD(lpcmi->lpVerb);
                TRACE1("InvokeCommand %x",idCmd);

            switch (idCmd)
                {
                case 0:
                    hr = DoMenu(lpcmi->hwnd,
                                    lpcmi->lpDirectory,
                                    lpcmi->lpVerb,
                                    lpcmi->lpParameters,
                                    lpcmi->nShow);
                    break;
                        /*
                        Addition menu item handlers would go here.
                        case n:

                            hr = DoMenun(lpcmi->hwnd,
                                    lpcmi->lpDirectory,
                                    lpcmi->lpVerb,
                                    lpcmi->lpParameters,
                                    lpcmi->nShow);

                        */
            }
```

```
    }
    return hr;
}



//
//  FUNCTION: The shell calls GetCommandString to display command
//            strings
//

STDMETHODIMP CMyShellExtension::GetCommandString(UINT idCmd,
                                        UINT uFlags,
                                        UINT FAR *reserved,
                                        LPSTR pszName,
                                        UINT cchMax)
{
    TRACE1("GetCommandString() uFlags = %x\r\n",uFlags);

    switch (uFlags)
    {
    case GCS_HELPTEXT:

    switch (idCmd)
            {
            case 0:
                        LoadString(AfxGetInstanceHandle(),
                                IDS_MENUSTRING,
                                pszName,
                                cchMax);
                        break;

            //
            // UnComment out the following if you have more menu items.
            //
            /*
            case 1:
                LoadString(AfxGetInstanceHandle(),
                                IDS_MENUSTRING2, pszName, cchMax);
                        break;
```

```
                case n:
                    LoadString(AfxGetInstanceHandle(),
                                    IDS_MENUSTRINGn, pszName, cchMax);
                        break;


            */
            };
    };
    return NOERROR;
}
STDMETHODIMP CMyShellExtension::DoMenu(HWND hParent,
                                LPCSTR pszWorkingDir,
                                LPCSTR pszCmd,
                                LPCSTR pszParam,
                                int iShowCmd)
{
    TRACE0("CMyShellExtension::DoMenu()\r\n");

    MessageBox(hParent, "Our Menu selected!", AfxGetAppName(), MB_OK);

    return NOERROR;
}
```

It's possible to add items to the context menu for a document based both on the document type *and* the folder in which it is contained  For example, suppose you would like to add a "Permissions..." item to the context menu for all items living on a Netware server and a property page that would allow you to modify the Netware permissions for the selected document. The LPDATAOBJECT that gets passed to IShellExtInit::Initialize allows you to get the fully qualified path to the file(s) clicked on.  From there, you can determine if the file is on a network drive, and add menu items as appropriate.


## ICONTEXTMENU (DRAG-DROP HANDLERS)

A Drag-drop handler is another type of IContextMenu interface. When a user drags and drops a file object with the right mouse button,  a drag-drop menu appears. Drag-drop handlers work in the same way as context-menu handlers.

## ICOPYHOOK INTERFACE

By registering a copy-hook handler you can get notification before the shell moves, copies, deletes, or renames one of your folder objects. What makes copy-hook handlers great is the fact that you don't actually have to do the moving, copying or deleting. You just get to provide the permission before the shell copies, moves or deletes. If you return IDNO or IDCANCEL from your handler the shell the file operation won't complete.

As I said before, the shell initializes the copy-hook handler interface directly. To implement a copy-hook handler use the *CopyCallBack,* function.

```
CopyCallback(HWND hwnd,
             WORD wFunc,
             WORD wFlags,
             LPCSTR pszSrcFile,
             DWORD dwSrcAttribs,
             LPCSTR pszDestFile,
             DWORD dwDestAttribs);
```

You can return one of three constants

IDYES indicates that the operation should be carried out . IDNO means that the operation should not be performed and IDCANCEL means that the shell should discontinue calling handlers (there can be more than one copy-hook handler).

## REGISTERING SHELL EXTENSIONS

All in-process servers must be entered into the Registry to work and shell extensions are no exception. Each extension that you support must register their class ID in the

```
HKEY_CLASSES_ROOT\Clsid
```

key in the registry. The Clsid key is a globally unique identifier (GUID). You generate GUID with the utility UUIDGEN. UUIDGEN uses your network id and a time stamp to generate the identifier. If you have a network card UUIDGEN can guarantee that the number generated will be unique throughout

**435**

the globe. If you do not have a network card then your GUID is only unique within your machine. Here's what UUIDGEN generated for me:

```
{d24f8f40-40b0-11ce-a074-524153480000}
```

Within the Clsid key, add an *InProcServer32* key that gives the location of your extension DLL. You either give the fully qualified path name to the DLL or make sure it resides on the path. Otherwise the shell won't be able to find it. The easiest way to register you entry is to create a .REG file. Here's an example of the CLSID and InProcServer32:

```
[HKEY_CLASSES_ROOT\CLSID\{d24f8f40-40b0-11ce-a074-524153480000}]
    @="Chap11 Shell Extension Sample"
[HKEY_CLASSES_ROOT\CLSID\{d24f8f40-40b0-11ce-a074-
524153480000}\InProcServer32]
    @="c:\chap11.dll"
      "ThreadingModel"="Apartment"
```

After you add the InProcServer32 key you must add keys for each of your handlers (see Listing 11–4 ). Notice that they all use the same GUID. Once you create your .REG file, you can merge it into the Registry in one of two ways: You can double click on its icon or run:

```
regedit yourfile.REG
```

to merge your entry into the database. The system is responsible for the default menu items that appear on the My Computer and Network Neighborhood icons. You can add your own menu items to these object by registering your context menu shell extension under the "Folder" key of HKEY_CLASSES_ROOT.

If everything goes great for you you're done. Otherwise this next section explains how to debug a shell extension.

**Listing 11–4** Chap11.reg

```
REGEDIT4


[HKEY_CLASSES_ROOT\CLSID\{d24f8f40-40b0-11ce-a074-524153480000}]
```

```
   @="Chap11 Shell Extension Sample"
[HKEY_CLASSES_ROOT\CLSID\{d24f8f40-40b0-11ce-a074-
524153480000}\InProcServer32]
   @="c:\chap11.dll"
     "ThreadingModel"="Apartment"


[HKEY_CLASSES_ROOT\.kjg]
   @="KJGFile"
[HKEY_CLASSES_ROOT\KJGFile]
   @="Chap11 Shell Extension file"
[HKEY_CLASSES_ROOT\KJGFile\shellex\IconHandler]
   @="{d24f8f40-40b0-11ce-a074-524153480000}"
[HKEY_CLASSES_ROOT\KJGFile\shellex\ContextMenuHandlers]
   @="KJGMenu"
[HKEY_CLASSES_ROOT\KJGFile\shellex\ContextMenuHandlers\KJGMenu]
   @="{d24f8f40-40b0-11ce-a074-524153480000}"
[HKEY_CLASSES_ROOT\KJGFile\shellex\PropertySheetHandlers]
   @="KJGPage"
[HKEY_CLASSES_ROOT\KJGFile\shellex\PropertySheetHandlers\KJGPage]
   @="{d24f8f40-40b0-11ce-a074-524153480000}"
[HKEY_CLASSES_ROOT\Folder\shellex\DragDropHandlers\KJGDropExt]
   @="{d24f8f40-40b0-11ce-a074-524153480000}"
[HKEY_CLASSES_ROOT\directory\shellex\CopyHookHandlers\KJGCopyHook]
   @="{d24f8f40-40b0-11ce-a074-524153480000}"
[HKEY_CLASSES_ROOT\*\shellex\CopyHookHandlers\KJGsCopyHook]
   @="{d24f8f40-40b0-11ce-a074-524153480000}"
```

# DEBUGGING SHELL EXTENSIONS

Like all DLLs, shell extensions require that you have an executable for your debug session. For your extension DLL, the executable that you need is the shell, explorer.exe. There is a bit of trickery that needs to take place first, though. Since the shell cannot be running when you start debugging you must first shut down the shell. How can you do this without shutting down Windows? When you click on Start...Shut Down... a dialog box is diplayed. While simutaneously holding down ALT-CTRL-SHIFT, click on the No button and the shell will terminate without terminating Windows. From there, choose

Go in Visual C++ to begin debugging your extension. Visual C++ will report back that EXPLORER.EXE does not contain debugging information, but you can safely ignore this message and begin debugging. If you're like me this will be an iterative approach of installing your shell extension, coding, installing, and so on. If so then you will find that you need to copy over your existing DLL with the freshly compiled DLL. To do this close the shell (with the ALT-CTRL-SHIFT trick) then copy your new DLL over the old one. If you just want to test immediately (no need to debug--I know I've got it this time) double-click on the desktop to bring up the task manager. The choose File...Run application... and type in explorer.exe and the shell (and your shell extension) will be loaded. Once you have your shell extension debugged you're ready to install.

## HOW TO SETUP OR UPGRADE A SHELL EXTENSION.

The bottom line is if your DLL file is in use by the system at the time of installation, there is no way you can update the file. Given that the user may (and will) be in a situation where your extension DLL is already loaded, you will need to ask them to reboot. There are two paths that you can take. First, when you are beginning your installation, check for the existance of your DLL file. If it exists, try to rename it to xxx.BAK. If the rename succeeds, you're home free (since the user will not be able to load your extension now, even if he does switch away from your install program). Now, procede with your installation as usual, and when you are done, simply delete MYDLL.BAK. If the user cancels the installation at any time, you can rename your DLL to it's original name so that any previous installations are still intact. However, if the first attempt to rename the file fails, than the DLL is probably already in use by the system. In this case, you must put something in the users AUTOEXEC.BAT file(or load= ) that copies your new DLL over the old one. This is far from an elegant solution, however. As I write this many developers are requesting a better solution from Microsoft so stay tuned. There may be a better solution when Windows 95 ships.

## SUMMARY

Originally, Microsoft was going to include a feature into the shell called the Name Space Browser (NSB) in Windows 95. NSBs were cool because they allowed you to further extend the shell by allowing applications to expose the hierarchical structure of objects through the shell. Unfortunately NSBs were dropped from Windows 95. Perhaps due to time contraints or because of stability problems. Maybe they will show up in a later version.

# THE EXPLORER

The default shell in Windows 95 is called the Explorer. The Explorer's goal is to make it easier to work with all kinds of resources. Therefore, it takes the place of the Program Manager, File Manager, Print Manager, Control Panel and Windows Setup. All system resources such as documents, programs, printers, utilities, and so on are now organized into a flexible hierarchy of folders. The Explorer makes big use of drag-and-drop. Drag and drop operations are supported for all system resources. This combined with long filename and Universal Naming Convention (UNC) path names (\\servername\share) means that browsing and locating stuff should be much easier. But, this also put the burden upon you to take advantage of UNC path names. Don't assume that drive letter is necessary. This way files that your application has open accross the network share can be easily accessed the next time the user reboots without forcing the user to reconnect to the same drive letter. For example, suppose that the user adds a CD-ROM drive. When the user reboots the CD-ROM drive becomes drive E:. But your application installed to what was previously drive E: and is now drive F:. Get the picture? If you use the common dialogs, you will automatically get long filename and UNC path name support. However you may want to go back into your code to make sure your buffers are long enough. Long files can now be 255 characters and UNC path names can be 260 characters.

## CHAPTER 12

# WINDOWS
# AND WIN32 SECURITY

Welcome to the world of C2 Security. This chapter explains the NT security model and shows how to exploit the security features of NT. It also gives you some tips so you can develop applications that meet the requirements for a B-level secure program. Notice that I said NT. Windows 95 does not support the Win32 security APIs—mainly due to the memory and file system requirements that I'll go into. Windows 95 does have some degree of security, however, it is mainly network security (the ability to share files, printers, much the same as Windows for WorkGroups).

The requirements for a C2 secure system are as follows:

## SECURITY LEVELS

- Division D Minimal Protection
  For any system that fails to meet the requirements of a higher class
- Division C Discretionary Protection

Class C1

Log-on control

Discretionary access control

Class C2

All of C1 plus

Users own objects

Users control access to the objects they own

Individual identification (log-ons)

Users are accountable for access-related actions—auditing

Memory initialized before use (memory is zeroed out, unless you are loadingfrom disk)

Auditing capabilities by system administrator

■■ Division B Mandatory Protection

Class B1

Labeled Security Protection

Class B2

Structured Protection

This chapter also describes how each of these requirements is implemented and how this affects the software developer.

# INDIVIDUAL IDENTIFICATION

Windows NT requires every user who accesses the system to have a user account in the user database. The system administrator creates, for each machine, the account with the User Manager program (located in the Administrative Tools Program Manager group). The users' first experience with the C2 security policy of Windows NT is when they log on to the system. Logging on fulfills the C2 requirement for individual identification. Every account in NT's user database is unique and contains a username, password, and group membership list (which indicates what groups the account belongs to). Other user-specific information, such as log-on hours (how long a user was logged on) and home directories, is also kept in this database. NT supports several built-in groups, including Administrators, Privileged Users, Guests, and Backup Operators, to make it easy to assign rights to users. The capabilities the user has on the system are determined by the rights assigned to a user and the group the user is a member of.

# SECURITY IDENTIFIERS

NT uses security identifiers (SIDs) to represent every account in the security database. A SID is a globally unique number. All account types (users, groups) use SIDs. The User Manager generates a SID for the new user program when the System Administrator creates the user. The following information is stored in a SID:

```
//////////////////////////////////////////////////////////////////
//                                                              //
//   Security Id    (SID)                                       //
//                                                              //
//////////////////////////////////////////////////////////////////
//
//
// Pictorially the structure of a SID is as follows:
//
//      1  1  1  1  1  1
//      5  4  3  2  1  0  9  8  7  6  5  4  3  2  1  0
//     +--------------------------------------------------------+
//     |   SubAuthorityCount      |Reserved1 (SBZ)|   Revision  |
//     +--------------------------------------------------------+
//     |                  IdentifierAuthority[0]                |
//     +--------------------------------------------------------+
//     |                  IdentifierAuthority[1]                |
//     +--------------------------------------------------------+
//     |                  IdentifierAuthority[2]                |
//     +--------------------------------------------------------+
//     |                                                        |
//     + - - - - - - - - SubAuthority[] - - - - - - - - - -+
//     |                                                        |
//     +--------------------------------------------------------+
//
// from winnt.h
```

This copy of the SID structure is from WINNT.H. However, you should consider a SID to be an "opaque structure." That is, don't try to manipulate the variables in the structure. Instead use the Win32 APIs to gather information or make changes. Think of a SID as resembling your birth certificate. Your birth certificate identifies you, tells where you were born, and identifies your parents. Your SID identifies you, tells where your account was created, and identifies the groups you are a member of.

The SDK documentation recommends a shorthand notation of S-R-I-S-S as a method of breaking a SID into the following parts:

- S means that the following number is a SID.
- R is for revision level.
- I is for identifier-authority value.
- S is the subauthority value.
- S for each additional sub-authority value.

If you look into the Registry with REGEDT32 you can find the SIDs that are associated with each log-on account. On my machine, which is named CPQ586, all of the accounts appear something like S-1-5–xx-xx-xx. S-1-5 is the notation for SECURITY_NT_AUTHORITY, and is known as a predefined identifier authority or "well-known SID." NT has several predefined identifier authorities, and, while the numbers they correspond to aren't important, you need to be familiar with them. An application can combine an identifier authority level with a 32-bit relative ID, called a RID, to create a SID that is meaningful on all installations. For example, S-1-1-0 (SECURITY_WORLD_SID_AUTHORITY and SECURITY_WORLD_RID) always identifies all users. We will see how to tie SIDs to processes and threads in a moment. The important thing to remember is that this scheme ensures that all SIDs are unique.

# ACCESS TOKENS

When a user logs on, the system creates a token, called an access token, that represents the user. The security model states that this access token is associated with every transaction that a process or thread makes while the user is logged on. If a SID is a birth certificate, an access token is akin to one of those electronic security badges many corporations have these days, the type that has your picture and an electronic stripe that identifies you to the card readers that are located throughout the building. Just as a security badge identifies you and grants you access to certain locations within a building, the access token identifies the user and defines what access the user has throughout the system. (For example, only authorized employees can gain entrance to the accounting department, and only authorized users can execute the Disk Manager program.)

When a thread needs access to an object (perhaps a file that needs to be deleted), the thread specifies the desired access using an access mask. NT compares the thread's token to the permissions in the object's security descriptor. If the user doesn't have the proper security, the call fails. The token is also used for auditing purposes. If auditing is turned on for file deletes, the System Administrator will have a record of you deleting the file. (A security database in the corporation records all the employees who gained access to the accounting department.)

Processes inherit the token of the user who started them, and threads run in the user context defined by that user token. Each access token contains the information given in Table 12–1:

**Table 12–1** Access Token information

| Access Token | Information |
|---|---|
| TokenUser | Holds the SID of the user that is currently logged on. |
| TokenGroups | Tells the number of groups TokenUser is a member of and contains an array of SIDs identifying the groups. |
| TokenPrivileges | Specifies the access rights that TokenUser has. Privileges are covered later in this chapter. |
| TokenOwner | Contains the SID of the owner of any objects created on behalf of TokenUser. TokenOwner comes in to play when a client is being impersonated. The TokenOwner SID must be one of the user or group SIDs already in the token. |
| TokenPrimaryGroup | Contains the SID that will be assigned as the primary group for objects created on behalf of TokenUser. |
| TokenDefaultDacl | Defines the default discretionary access control list to be assigned to any objects created by this token. |

**Table 12–1** (continued)

| Access Token | Information |
| --- | --- |
| TokenSource | Contains an 8-byte identifier and an LUID. An LUID is a locally unique identifier that is guaranteed to be unique on the system that generated it for the life of the session (that is, until you reboot or log off). When we look at privileges, you will see how LUIDs come into play. |
| TokenType | Indicates whether this token is being impersonated. |
| TokenImpersonationLevel | Specifies impersonation levels. |
| TokenStatistics | Contains information, including TokenType, ImpersonationLevel, and Privilege count. |

There are two APIs you can use, OpenProcessToken or OpenThreadToken, to get a handle to the token. Once you have a handle to the token you can make changes to it. The API function calls, OpenProcessToken and GetTokenInformation, provide an alternative method to finding the SID for a process. To avoid the chance of being denied access, call the Open with TOKEN_READ. In the GetTokenInformation call, specify TokenUser, not TokenOwner. TokenUser always gets the associated user, and the associated user doesn't always own the access token. The following sample code shows how to do this.

```
if (!OpenProcessToken(GetCurrentProcess(),
    TOKEN_ADJUST_PRIVILEGES | TOKEN_QUERY, &hToken))
```

# SECURABLE OBJECTS

C2 security requires that users control access to any objects they own. The security information associated with each object is known as a security descriptor. Any object, such as a file, printer, thread, or semaphore, that can have a security descriptor is known as a securable object. If you can attach a security descriptor, you can control the security of the object. When developing your application, you must make decisions about objects that you own. The type of restrictions you build into your objects determines what capabilities users have with respect to the objects in your application.

The following are all securable objects:

- Kernel objects
- File and file mapping objects
- User objects
- Private objects
- Registry objects
- Service objects

To give you an idea of how securable objects work, let's say I log on as CPQ586\KevinG and run an application that creates a file. CPQ586\KevinG now owns the file. That means that CPQ586\KevinG has discretion over the disposition of the file. Actually, it will be the thread (or any other thread that is also running) that makes Win32 API calls that has control. What your application does with the objects it owns will determine the user's capabilities on the system with respect to these objects. This is where the discretionary part comes in. It is up to your application (acting on behalf of CPQ586\KevinG) to decide who else can control this file object. If you like, you can arrange it so that only CPQ586\KevinG can read, write, and delete the file. You can also set it up so anyone logged on can have read, write, and delete access. If you do nothing that is, you create your object with no security descriptor (say, you pass a NULL as a parameter to the create function) it is as if you explicitly granted all access to everyone. This is different from creating an object with a NULL security descriptor. A NULL security descriptor implicitly denies access to everyone.

# CONTROLLING ACCESS PERMISSIONS

Access control lists (ACLs) control all access permissions. There are two types of ACLs:

- The first type is the discretionary ACL (DACL). DACLs specify the type of processes and the access to the object that each type of process is granted or denied.

■ The second type of ACL is the system ACL (SACL). SACLs control auditing. As I stated before, to qualify in a C2-level secure system the System Administrator must be able to audit security-related events. The audit related data is contained within the SACL. Whenever an auditable action occurs, the system records the access attempts in a security log. Use the Event Viewer (EVENTVWR.EXE) to view the security log.

Each security descriptor contains the name of the object's owner. The object's owner always has the ability to change permissions. Also in the security descriptor is the owner's primary group.

A security descriptor contains the following information:

Owner (Pointer to SID)

Group (Pointer to SID)

DACL (Pointer to ACL)

SACL (Pointer to ACL)

A typical security descriptor might look like this:

```
OBJECT:  File: C:\winword\chap12.doc
Owner:   Cpq586\KevinG
Group:   PowerUsers
Discretionary ACL:
        Grant: RW Cpq586\Editors
        Grant: RW RWD Cpq586\KevinG
        Grant: R Cpq586\Users
System ACL:
        Audit -- W -- Everyone.
```

As you can see, the object in this security descriptor is a file, in this case chap12.doc in the c:\winword directory. I am the owner and I logged on as Cpq586\KevinG. Cpq586 is a member of the Group PowerUsers. The security descriptor for C:\winword\chap12.doc has two ACLs associated with it: a DACL and a SACL. Inside each ACL is at least one access control entry (ACE). Each ACE uses an access mask to describe an account's access rights to an object. AccessMasks specify whether your thread can access the object. The DACL for c:\winword\chap12.doc has three ACEs:

- ▪▪ An ACE that gives permission to Cpq586\Editors to read and write chap12.doc. (The AccessMask has read access and write access turned on.)
- ▪▪ An ACE Cpq586\KevinG has given itself to enable read, write, and delete access.
- ▪▪ An ACE for the group Cpq586\Users that allows everyone in the group to read the document.

The second ACL is the SACL, which the administrator for Cpq586 will use for auditing. This SACL contains one ACE that audits everyone who writes to the file. If my editors make any changes and then try to deny it, I will catch them. (Goodman and Associates is a small company and I am also the system administrator.) In order to accomplish this feat, several things must take place. First, the file system must be NTFS. You cannot attach security descriptors to file objects without NTFS. Keep in mind that all other securable objects can have security descriptors regardless of whether NTFS is installed. In a moment, you will see SecureView, which is a sample program that displays SIDs and ACLs for all securable objects. The second thing that must take place to secure c:\winword\chap12.doc is to programmatically add the ACLs.

The code in Listing 12–1 shows how to add an ACL, but first let's look at the algorithm.

1. Allocate memory for a new security descriptor.
2. Retrieve a pointer to the security descriptor by calling GetFileSecurity.
3. Get a pointer to the discretionary ACL by calling GetSecurityDescriptorDACL.
4. Initialize a new ACL with InitializeACL.
5. Get a pointer to the SID by calling TokenQueryInformation for TokenUser.
6. Add the ACE to the ACL with AddAccessAllowedAce by using the pointer to the new SID and the new ACL.

7. Add the ACL to the copy of Security descriptor with SetSecurityDescriptorDACL.

8. Use SetFileSecurity to apply the descriptor to the file.

**Listing 12–1** ADDACE.CPP

```
BOOL AddanAce(void)
{
TCHAR ErrorText[80];
PSECURITY_DESCRIPTOR pSD;
DWORD cbSD = 2048;
LPSTR lpszDOCFile="c:\\winword\\chap5.doc";
DWORD cbNeeded;
PACL pACLPrevious, pACLNew;
BOOL fDaclPresent, fDefaulted;
DWORD cbACL = 1024;
PSID pSID;
DWORD cbSID = 1024;
SID_IDENTIFIER_AUTHORITY sidAuth = SECURITY_WORLD_SID_AUTHORITY;
LPSTR lpszAccount = "Administrator";
LPSTR lpszDomain;
DWORD cchDomainName = 80;

PSID_NAME_USE psnuType;
BOOL fResult;
CDC * dc;
CString s;

//
// Retrieve a pointer to the security descriptor
//

pSD = (PSECURITY_DESCRIPTOR) LocalAlloc(LPTR, cbSD);

s = "GetFileSecurity";
if (!GetFileSecurity(lpszDOCFile,
        DACL_SECURITY_INFORMATION,
        pSD,
```

```
        cbSD,
        &cbNeeded))
{
    MessageBox(NULL,"GetFileSecurity","ERROR",MB_OK);

    return FALSE;
}


s ="GetSecurityDescriptorDacl";
if (!GetSecurityDescriptorDacl(pSD,
        &fDaclPresent,
        &pACLPrevious,
        &fDefaulted))
{
    MessageBox(NULL,"GetSecurityDescriptorDacl","ERROR",MB_OK);
    wsprintf(ErrorText,"Last Error = %d",GetLastError());
    MessageBox(NULL,ErrorText,"GetDACL",MB_OK);
    return FALSE;
}


//
// Initialize new ACL.
//

pACLNew = (PACL) LocalAlloc(LPTR, cbACL);

if (!InitializeAcl(pACLNew, cbACL, ACL_REVISION2)) {
    MessageBox(NULL,"InitializeAcl","ERROR",MB_OK);
    return FALSE;
}

pSID = (PSID) LocalAlloc(LPTR, cbSID);
psnuType = (PSID_NAME_USE) LocalAlloc(LPTR, 1024);

lpszDomain = (LPSTR) LocalAlloc(LPTR, cchDomainName);

fResult = LookupAccountName((LPSTR) NULL,  // local name
        lpszAccount,
```

```
                pSID,
                &cbSID,
                lpszDomain,
                &cchDomainName,
                psnuType);

if (!fResult) {
    MessageBox(NULL,"LookupAccountName","ERROR",MB_OK);
    return FALSE;
}


//
// Allow READ but not WRITE access to the file.
//


if (!AddAccessAllowedAce(pACLNew,

        ACL_REVISION2,
        GENERIC_READ,
        pSID)) {
    MessageBox(NULL,"AddAccessAllowedAce","ERROR",MB_OK);
    return FALSE;
}

/* Add new ACL to copy of SD. */

if (!SetSecurityDescriptorDacl(pSD,
        TRUE,                          // fDaclPresent flag
        pACLNew,
        FALSE)) {                              // not a default DACL
    MessageBox(NULL,"SetSecurityDescriptorDacl","ERROR",MB_OK);
    wsprintf(ErrorText,"Last Error = %d",GetLastError());
    MessageBox(NULL,ErrorText,"SetDACL",MB_OK);

    return FALSE;
}

//
```

```
// Set the new security descriptor
// to the file.
//

if (!SetFileSecurity(lpszDOCFile,

        DACL_SECURITY_INFORMATION,
        pSD)) {
    MessageBox(NULL,"SetFileSecurity","ERROR",MB_OK);
    return FALSE;
}


FreeSid(pSID);

return TRUE;
}
```

If you want to change the security descriptor for an already-existing object, you must consider two situations. The first scenario is for an object that has no security descriptor (a NULL was passed to the security attributes parameter). For objects created without a security descriptor, you must first create a security descriptor with the InitializeSecurityDescriptor call. Create a new SID and call LookupAccountName to initialize the SID. Then, initialize a new ACL. Add your rights to the ACL by calling the AddAccessAllowedAce or AddAccessDeniedAce functions. Add your ACE to the ACL with the SetSecurityDescriptorDacl call. Finally, add the descriptor to the object by calling SetxxSecurity functions (using SetFileSecurity, SetKernelObjectSecurity, and so on).

The second situation occurs when the object in question already has a security descriptor and you want to add another ACE to the security descriptor's ACL. To do this you must retrieve the security descriptor by calling GetxxSecurity (where xx is File or KernelObject or UserObject). This gives you a pointer to the security descriptor. Once you have the security descriptor, call GetSecurityDescriptorDacl to get a handle to the discretionary ACL. With the pointer to the ACL, you can call AddAccessDeniedAce or AddAccessAllowedAce.

If you want to delete an ACE from the ACL, you must call GetAce to retrieve the index of the ACE in the ACL followed by DeleteAce to remove it from the ACL. However, when you create an object with a discretionary ACL, make sure to pass it into the Create API with a LPSECURITY_ATTRIBUTES cast. Don't accidentally pass in just a PSECURITY_DESCRIPTOR. This is an easy error to make, and you have to manually watch out for it. PSECURITY_DESCRIPTOR is typedef'd as PVOID so the compiler will not warn you of the mismatched types.

Another method would be to create c:\winword\chap12.doc with the proper security attributes instead of adding them later:

```
HANDLE CreateFile("c:\\winword\\chap12.doc",
                GENERIC_READ | GENERIC_WRITE,
                0,
                lpsa,    //pointer to security attributes
                CREATE_NEW,
                FILE_ATTRIBUTE_NORMAL,
                NULL)
```

Unfortunately, I am using a Win16 word processor that doesn't understand security and I had to manually add the ACLs. Almost every sample that ships with the SDK creates its object with a NULL security descriptor. You may be wondering what circumstances dictate adding security to your objects. Isn't the default that NT provides enough? Here is one idea. In the future, an NT word processor will allow you, as owner of your document, to assign rights. Remember in our example we had to do it manually. Just about any application that handles files is a candidate for additional security. For example, a fax server program could read the name from the fax header of incoming faxes and secure the file so only the proper owner could read it.

# SAMPLE APPLICATION: SECUREVIEW

The SecureView sample application displays security information for all of the processes in the system and all of the files on disk. To display information for a file, SecureView uses the CFileDialog common dialog box to choose a file. For processes, SecureView displays the Choose a Process dialog box shown in Figure 12–1. This dialog allows you to choose the process you are interested in.

When you select the file or process, SecureView opens it and retrieves its handle. SecureView then determines whether there is a valid security descriptor attached to the object. If the object has a valid security descriptor, SecureView displays the SID, DACL, and any attached ACES. The code in Listing 12–2 contains the OnProcess and the OnFile member functions to accomplish this.

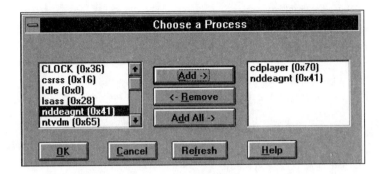

**Figure 12–1** The SecureView process list dialog box

## Listing 12–2

```
// Chap12.cpp : Defines the class behaviors for the application.
//

#include "stdafx.h"
#include "Chap12.h"
#include "Chap1dlg.h"

#ifdef _DEBUG
#undef THIS_FILE
static char BASED_CODE THIS_FILE[] = __FILE__;
#endif

/////////////////////////////////////////////////////////////////////////////
// CChap12App

BEGIN_MESSAGE_MAP(CChap12App, CWinApp)
    //{{AFX_MSG_MAP(CChap12App)
        // NOTE - the ClassWizard will add and remove mapping macros here.
        //    DO NOT EDIT what you see in these blocks of generated code!
    //}}AFX_MSG
```

```
        ON_COMMAND(ID_HELP, CWinApp::OnHelp)
END_MESSAGE_MAP()


/////////////////////////////////////////////////////////////////////////
// CChap12App construction

CChap12App::CChap12App()
{
    // TODO: add construction code here,
    // Place all significant initialization in InitInstance
}


/////////////////////////////////////////////////////////////////////////
// The one and only CChap12App object

CChap12App theApp;


/////////////////////////////////////////////////////////////////////////
// CChap12App initialization

BOOL CChap12App::InitInstance()
{
    // Standard initialization
    // If you are not using these features and wish to reduce the size
    //  of your final executable, you should remove from the following
    //  the specific initialization routines you do not need.

    Enable3dControls();
    LoadStdProfileSettings();  // Load standard INI file options (including MRU)

    CChap12Dlg dlg;
    m_pMainWnd = &dlg;
    int nResponse = dlg.DoModal();
    if (nResponse == IDOK)
    {
            // TODO: Place code here to handle when the dialog is
            //  dismissed with OK
```

```
        }
        else if (nResponse == IDCANCEL)
        {
                // TODO: Place code here to handle when the dialog is
                //  dismissed with Cancel
        }

        // Since the dialog has been closed, return FALSE so that we exit the
        //  application, rather than start the application's message pump.
        return FALSE;
}


// Chap1dlg.cpp : implementation file
//

#include "stdafx.h"
#include "Chap12.h"
#include "Chap1dlg.h"
#include "procdlg.h"

#ifdef _DEBUG
#undef THIS_FILE
static char BASED_CODE THIS_FILE[] = __FILE__;
#endif

/////////////////////////////////////////////////////////////////////////////
// CAboutDlg dialog used for App About

class CAboutDlg : public CDialog
{
public:
     CAboutDlg();

// Dialog Data
     //{{AFX_DATA(CAboutDlg)
     enum { IDD = IDD_ABOUTBOX };
```

```
        //}}AFX_DATA

    // Implementation
    protected:
        virtual void DoDataExchange(CDataExchange* pDX);      // DDX/DDV support
        //{{AFX_MSG(CAboutDlg)
        virtual BOOL OnInitDialog();
        //}}AFX_MSG
        DECLARE_MESSAGE_MAP()
    };


    CAboutDlg::CAboutDlg() : CDialog(CAboutDlg::IDD)
    {
        //{{AFX_DATA_INIT(CAboutDlg)
        //}}AFX_DATA_INIT
    }


    void CAboutDlg::DoDataExchange(CDataExchange* pDX)
    {
        CDialog::DoDataExchange(pDX);
        //{{AFX_DATA_MAP(CAboutDlg)
        //}}AFX_DATA_MAP
    }


    BEGIN_MESSAGE_MAP(CAboutDlg, CDialog)
        //{{AFX_MSG_MAP(CAboutDlg)
                // No message handlers
        //}}AFX_MSG_MAP
    END_MESSAGE_MAP()


    /////////////////////////////////////////////////////////////////////////
    // CAboutDlg message handlers

    BOOL CAboutDlg::OnInitDialog()
    {
        CDialog::OnInitDialog();
        CenterWindow();
```

```
        // TODO: Add extra about dlg initialization here

        return TRUE;  // return TRUE  unless you set the focus to a control
}


/////////////////////////////////////////////////////////////////////////
// CChap12Dlg dialog

CChap12Dlg::CChap12Dlg(CWnd* pParent /*=NULL*/)
        : CDialog(CChap12Dlg::IDD, pParent)
{
        //{{AFX_DATA_INIT(CChap12Dlg)
        m_strDomain = _T("");
        m_strObject = _T("");
        m_strOwner = _T("");
        m_strList = _T("");
        //}}AFX_DATA_INIT
        // Note that LoadIcon does not require a subsequent DestroyIcon in Win32
        m_hIcon = AfxGetApp()->LoadIcon(IDR_MAINFRAME);
}


void CChap12Dlg::DoDataExchange(CDataExchange* pDX)
{
        CDialog::DoDataExchange(pDX);
        //{{AFX_DATA_MAP(CChap12Dlg)
        DDX_Control(pDX, IDL_OBJECT, m_ctlObject);
        DDX_Text(pDX, IDC_DOMAINTEXT, m_strDomain);
        DDX_Text(pDX, IDC_OBJECTTEXT, m_strObject);
        DDX_Text(pDX, IDC_OWNERTEXT, m_strOwner);
        DDX_LBString(pDX, IDL_OBJECT, m_strList);
        //}}AFX_DATA_MAP
}


BEGIN_MESSAGE_MAP(CChap12Dlg, CDialog)
        //{{AFX_MSG_MAP(CChap12Dlg)
        ON_WM_SYSCOMMAND()
        ON_WM_PAINT()
```

```
        ON_WM_QUERYDRAGICON()
        ON_BN_CLICKED(IDC_PROCESS, OnProcess)
        ON_BN_CLICKED(IDC_FILE, OnFile)
        //}}AFX_MSG_MAP
    END_MESSAGE_MAP()


    /////////////////////////////////////////////////////////////////////////
    // CChap12Dlg message handlers

    BOOL CChap12Dlg::OnInitDialog()
    {
        CDialog::OnInitDialog();
        CenterWindow();

        // Add "About..." menu item to system menu.

        // IDM_ABOUTBOX must be in the system command range.
        ASSERT((IDM_ABOUTBOX & 0xFFF0) == IDM_ABOUTBOX);
        ASSERT(IDM_ABOUTBOX < 0xF000);

        CMenu* pSysMenu = GetSystemMenu(FALSE);
        CString strAboutMenu;
        strAboutMenu.LoadString(IDS_ABOUTBOX);
        if (!strAboutMenu.IsEmpty())
        {
            pSysMenu->AppendMenu(MF_SEPARATOR);
            pSysMenu->AppendMenu(MF_STRING, IDM_ABOUTBOX, strAboutMenu);
        }

        // TODO: Add extra initialization here

        return TRUE;  // return TRUE  unless you set the focus to a control
    }

    void CChap12Dlg::OnSysCommand(UINT nID, LPARAM lParam)
    {
        if ((nID & 0xFFF0) == IDM_ABOUTBOX)
        {
            CAboutDlg dlgAbout;
```

```
                dlgAbout.DoModal();
        }
        else
        {
                CDialog::OnSysCommand(nID, lParam);
        }
}


// If you add a minimize button to your dialog, you will need the code below
//  to draw the icon.  For MFC applications using the document/view model,
//  this is automatically done for you by the framework.

void CChap12Dlg::OnPaint()
{
        if (IsIconic())
        {
                CPaintDC dc(this); // device context for painting

                SendMessage(WM_ICONERASEBKGND, (WPARAM) dc.GetSafeHdc(), 0);

                // Center icon in client rectangle
                int cxIcon = GetSystemMetrics(SM_CXICON);
                int cyIcon = GetSystemMetrics(SM_CYICON);
                CRect rect;
                GetClientRect(&rect);
                int x = (rect.Width() - cxIcon + 1) / 2;
                int y = (rect.Height() - cyIcon + 1) / 2;

                // Draw the icon
                dc.DrawIcon(x, y, m_hIcon);
        }
        else
        {
                CDialog::OnPaint();
        }
}


// The system calls this to obtain the cursor to display while the user drags
//  the minimized window.
```

```
HCURSOR CChap12Dlg::OnQueryDragIcon()
{
     return (HCURSOR) m_hIcon;
}


void CChap12Dlg::OnProcess()
{
#define SD_BUF 1024
DWORD dwReferencedDomain=SD_BUF;
SID_NAME_USE snu;
HANDLE             hProcess;
PSECURITY_DESCRIPTOR psdProcessSD;
PSID               psidProcessOwnerSIDTemp;
TCHAR              szAccount [SD_BUF];
TCHAR              szReferencedDomain[SD_BUF];
UCHAR              ucBuf[SD_BUF];
DWORD              dwSDLength = 2048;
DWORD              dwAccount = SD_BUF;
DWORD              dwSDLengthNeeded=SD_BUF;
BOOL               bOwnerDefaulted;
TCHAR s[256];

  CProcessDlg SView;
  SView.DoModal();
  hProcess = GetCurrentProcess();
  m_strObject = SView.m_strProcess;
  psdProcessSD = (PSECURITY_DESCRIPTOR)&ucBuf;


  if (!GetKernelObjectSecurity(SView.m_hProcess,
        (SECURITY_INFORMATION)(DACL_SECURITY_INFORMATION),
        psdProcessSD,
        dwSDLength,
        (LPDWORD)&dwSDLengthNeeded))
    {
    wsprintf(s, "Last Error %ld",GetLastError());
    MessageBox(s,"GetKernelObjectSecurity");
    return;
```

```
    }
  int iTabs[2] = {140,140};
  m_ctlObject.ResetContent();
  m_ctlObject.SetTabStops(2,iTabs);



if (!IsValidSecurityDescriptor(psdProcessSD))
   {
   wsprintf(s,"Last Error = %d",GetLastError());
   MessageBox(s,"ValidSD");
   }
  BOOL fDaclPresent;
  PACL  pAcl;
if (!GetSecurityDescriptorOwner(psdProcessSD,
         (PSID *)&psidProcessOwnerSIDTemp,
         (LPBOOL)&bOwnerDefaulted))

   {
   wsprintf(s, "GetSecurityDescriptor Last Error %ld",GetLastError());
   MessageBox(s);
   return;
   }
   if (psidProcessOwnerSIDTemp==NULL)
      MessageBox("No SID");

  if (!GetSecurityDescriptorDacl(psdProcessSD,
         (LPBOOL)&fDaclPresent,
         (PACL *)&pAcl,
         (LPBOOL)&bOwnerDefaulted))

   {
   wsprintf(s, "GetSecurityDescriptorDacl Last Error %ld",GetLastError());
   MessageBox(s);
   return;
   }

  if (!fDaclPresent)
```

```
      return;

   ACL_SIZE_INFORMATION asiAclSize;
   DWORD               dwBufLength = sizeof(asiAclSize);
   ACCESS_ALLOWED_ACE  *paaAllowedAce;
   DWORD               dwAcl_i;


   if (!GetAclInformation(pAcl,
                       (LPVOID)&asiAclSize,
                       (DWORD)dwBufLength,
                       (ACL_INFORMATION_CLASS)AclSizeInformation))
     {
     MessageBox("GetAclInformation");
     return;
     }


   for (dwAcl_i = 0; dwAcl_i< asiAclSize.AceCount;  dwAcl_i++)
      {

      if (!GetAce(pAcl,
             dwAcl_i,
             (LPVOID *)&paaAllowedAce))
        {
        MessageBox("GetAce");
        return;
        }

     { // Find SID of ACE,

     #define                  SZ_DMN_NAME_BUF  1000
     #define                  SZ_ACCT_NAME_BUF  1000

   TCHAR szList[256];
   TCHAR szTemp[256];
      UCHAR      ucNameBuf      [SZ_ACCT_NAME_BUF];
      DWORD      dwNameLength  = SZ_ACCT_NAME_BUF;
```

```
UCHAR        ucDomainNmBuf  [SZ_DMN_NAME_BUF];
DWORD        dwDNameLength = SZ_DMN_NAME_BUF;
SID_NAME_USE peAcctNameUse;
DWORD        dwLastError   = NO_ERROR;


/***********************************************************************\
*
* This validity check is here for demonstration purposes.  It's not
*   likely a real app would need to check the validity of the SID
*   contained in the returned ACL.  The validity check APIs are more
*   intended to check validity after app code has manipulated the
*   structure and is about to hand it back to the system
*
\***********************************************************************/

if (!IsValidSid((PSID)&(paaAllowedAce->SidStart)))
{
  MessageBox("IsValidSid said bad SID!");
  return;
}

if (!LookupAccountSid
      ((LPTSTR)"",            // Look on local machine
      (PSID)&(paaAllowedAce->SidStart),
      (LPTSTR)&ucNameBuf,
      (LPDWORD)&dwNameLength,
      (LPTSTR)&ucDomainNmBuf,
      (LPDWORD)&dwDNameLength,
      (PSID_NAME_USE)&peAcctNameUse))
{
  dwLastError = GetLastError();
  if (ERROR_NONE_MAPPED != dwLastError)
    {
    MessageBox("LookupAccountSID");
    return;
    }
}
else
```

```
              {
            strcpy(szList,(LPTSTR)ucNameBuf);

      switch (paaAllowedAce->Header.AceType)
        {
      case  ACCESS_ALLOWED_ACE_TYPE:
            wsprintf(szTemp,"\t Allowed \t%x",paaAllowedAce->Mask);
            break;
      case  ACCESS_DENIED_ACE_TYPE:
            wsprintf(szTemp,"\t Denied \t%x",paaAllowedAce->Mask);
            break;
      case  SYSTEM_AUDIT_ACE_TYPE:
            wsprintf(szTemp,"\t System Audit \t%x",paaAllowedAce->Mask);
            break;
      case  SYSTEM_ALARM_ACE_TYPE :
            wsprintf(szTemp,"\t System Alarm \t%x",paaAllowedAce->Mask);
            break;
      default:
            MessageBox("Invalid AceType");
            return;


        };
        strcat(szList,szTemp);
        m_ctlObject.AddString(szList);


  }
  }
  }


if (!GetSecurityDescriptorOwner(psdProcessSD,
        (PSID *)&psidProcessOwnerSIDTemp,
        (LPBOOL)&bOwnerDefaulted))


    {
    wsprintf(s, "GetSecurityDescriptor Last Error %ld",GetLastError());
    MessageBox(s);
    return;
    }
```

```
        if (psidProcessOwnerSIDTemp==NULL)
           MessageBox("No SID xxx");

if (LookupAccountSid((LPTSTR)"",
                    psidProcessOwnerSIDTemp,
                    szAccount,
                    &dwAccount,
                    szReferencedDomain,
                    &dwReferencedDomain,
                    &snu))
    {
    wsprintf(s, "%s\r\n%s",szAccount,szReferencedDomain);
    MessageBox(s,"Process Owner");
    }
else
    if (GetLastError() != ERROR_NONE_MAPPED)
    {
    TCHAR s[256];
    wsprintf(s, "LookupAccountSid Last Error %ld",GetLastError());
    MessageBox(s);
    }


if (!GetSecurityDescriptorGroup(psdProcessSD,
        (PSID *)&psidProcessOwnerSIDTemp,
        (LPBOOL)&bOwnerDefaulted))

    {
    wsprintf(s, "GetSecurityDescriptorGroup Last Error %ld",GetLastError());
    MessageBox(s);
    return;
    }

if (LookupAccountSid("",
                    psidProcessOwnerSIDTemp,
                    szAccount,
                    &dwAccount,
                    szReferencedDomain,
```

```
                    (LPDWORD)&dwReferencedDomain,
                    (PSID_NAME_USE)&snu))
    {
    wsprintf(s, "%s\r\n%s",szAccount,szReferencedDomain);
    MessageBox(s,"Process Owner");
    }
else
   if (GetLastError() != ERROR_NONE_MAPPED)
     {
     TCHAR s[256];
     wsprintf(s, "LookupAcount Last Error %ld",GetLastError());
     MessageBox(s,"LookupAccountSid");
     }


}


void CChap12Dlg::OnFile()
{
     static char BASED_CODE szFileDialogFilter[] =
            "Text Files (*.txt)|*.txt|All Files (*.*)|*.*||";
static char BASED_CODE szFileDialogExt[] = "txt";

  #define SZ_SD_BUF 1000
  UCHAR ucBuf[SZ_SD_BUF];
  DWORD dwSDLength = SZ_SD_BUF;
  DWORD dwSDLengthNeeded;
  PSECURITY_DESCRIPTOR psdFileSD;
  PSID psidFileOwnerSID;
  TCHAR szList[256];
  TCHAR szTemp[256];
  CFileDialog fileDialog(TRUE, szFileDialogExt, NULL,
            OFN_HIDEREADONLY, szFileDialogFilter);

  if (fileDialog.DoModal() == IDOK)
    {
    m_strObject=fileDialog.GetPathName();

    }
```

```
psdFileSD = (PSECURITY_DESCRIPTOR)&ucBuf;
if (!GetFileSecurity(m_strObject,
        (SECURITY_INFORMATION)(OWNER_SECURITY_INFORMATION
                            | DACL_SECURITY_INFORMATION),
        psdFileSD,
        dwSDLength,
        (LPDWORD)&dwSDLengthNeeded))
{
MessageBox("GetFileSecurity");
return;
}
BOOL  bOwnerDefaulted;

if (!GetSecurityDescriptorOwner
        (psdFileSD,
         (PSID *)&psidFileOwnerSID,
         (LPBOOL)&bOwnerDefaulted))
  {
  MessageBox("GetSecurityDescriptorOwner");
  return;
  }

  DWORD       dwLastError   = NO_ERROR;
  #define                   SZ_ACCT_NAME_BUF 1000
  UCHAR       ucNameBuf     [SZ_ACCT_NAME_BUF];
  DWORD       dwNameLength  = SZ_ACCT_NAME_BUF;
  #define                   SZ_DMN_NAME_BUF  1000
  UCHAR       ucDomainNmBuf [SZ_DMN_NAME_BUF ];
  DWORD       dwDNameLength = SZ_DMN_NAME_BUF ;
  SID_NAME_USE peAcctNameUse;

  if (!LookupAccountSid
        ((LPTSTR)"",                 // Look on local machine
        psidFileOwnerSID,
        (LPTSTR)&ucNameBuf,
        (LPDWORD)&dwNameLength,
        (LPTSTR)&ucDomainNmBuf,
        (LPDWORD)&dwDNameLength,
```

```
                    (PSID_NAME_USE)&peAcctNameUse))
     {
     dwLastError = GetLastError();
     if (ERROR_NONE_MAPPED != dwLastError)
       {
       MessageBox("LookupAccountSID");
       return;
       }
     }
     else
     {
     m_strOwner = ucNameBuf; //SetDlgItemText(SViewOwnerText,(LPSTR)ucNameBuf);
     m_strDomain = ucDomainNmBuf;
                 //SetDlgItemText(SViewDomainText,(LPSTR)ucDomainNmBuf);
     }


//////////////////////////////////////////////////////////////////


     PACL                paclFile;
     BOOL                bHasACL;
     DWORD               dwAcl_i;

     ACL_SIZE_INFORMATION asiAclSize;
     DWORD               dwBufLength = sizeof(asiAclSize);
     ACCESS_ALLOWED_ACE  *paaAllowedAce;

     if (!GetSecurityDescriptorDacl(psdFileSD,
                                (LPBOOL)&bHasACL,
                                (PACL *)&paclFile,
                                (LPBOOL)&bOwnerDefaulted))
     {
        MessageBox("GetSecurityDescriptorDacl");
        return;
     }

     if (!bHasACL)  // No ACL to process so return
        return;
```

```
if (!GetAclInformation(paclFile,
                    (LPVOID)&asiAclSize,
                    (DWORD)dwBufLength,
                    (ACL_INFORMATION_CLASS)AclSizeInformation))
    {
    MessageBox("GetAclInformation");
    return;
    }
int iTabs[2] = {140,140};



m_ctlObject.ResetContent();
m_ctlObject.SetTabStops(2,iTabs);



for (dwAcl_i = 0; dwAcl_i< asiAclSize.AceCount;  dwAcl_i++)
    {

    if (!GetAce(paclFile,
            dwAcl_i,
            (LPVOID *)&paaAllowedAce))
        {
        MessageBox("GetAce");
        return;
        }

    { // Find SID of ACE,

        UCHAR       ucNameBuf      [SZ_ACCT_NAME_BUF];
        DWORD       dwNameLength  = SZ_ACCT_NAME_BUF;
        UCHAR       ucDomainNmBuf [SZ_DMN_NAME_BUF];
        DWORD       dwDNameLength = SZ_DMN_NAME_BUF;
        SID_NAME_USE peAcctNameUse;
        DWORD       dwLastError   = NO_ERROR;

        if (!LookupAccountSid
            ((LPTSTR)"",            // Look on local machine
```

```
                (PSID)&(paaAllowedAce->SidStart),
                (LPTSTR)&ucNameBuf,
                (LPDWORD)&dwNameLength,
                (LPTSTR)&ucDomainNmBuf,
                (LPDWORD)&dwDNameLength,
                (PSID_NAME_USE)&peAcctNameUse))
    {
      dwLastError = GetLastError();
      if (ERROR_NONE_MAPPED != dwLastError)
        {
        MessageBox("LookupAccountSID");
        return;
        }
    }
    else
      {
      strcpy(szList,(LPTSTR)ucNameBuf);

  switch (paaAllowedAce->Header.AceType)
    {
    case  ACCESS_ALLOWED_ACE_TYPE:
          wsprintf(szTemp,"\t Allowed \t%x",paaAllowedAce->Mask);
          break;
    case  ACCESS_DENIED_ACE_TYPE:
          wsprintf(szTemp,"\t Denied \t%x",paaAllowedAce->Mask);
          break;
    case  SYSTEM_AUDIT_ACE_TYPE:
          wsprintf(szTemp,"\t System Audit \t%x",paaAllowedAce->Mask);
          break;
    case  SYSTEM_ALARM_ACE_TYPE :
          wsprintf(szTemp,"\t System Alarm \t%x",paaAllowedAce->Mask);
          break;
    default:
          MessageBox("Invalid AceType");
          return;

      };
      strcat(szList,szTemp);
```

```
        m_ctlObject.AddString(szList);


        }
    }
  }
UpdateData(FALSE);


}


// procdlg.cpp : implementation file
//


#include "stdafx.h"
#include "Chap12.h"
#include "procdlg.h"
#include "registry.h"


#ifdef _DEBUG
#undef THIS_FILE
static char BASED_CODE THIS_FILE[] = __FILE__;
#endif


/////////////////////////////////////////////////////////////////////////////
// CProcessDlg dialog


CProcessDlg::CProcessDlg(CWnd* pParent /*=NULL*/)
    : CDialog(CProcessDlg::IDD, pParent)
{
    //{{AFX_DATA_INIT(CProcessDlg)
    m_strProcess = _T("");
    //}}AFX_DATA_INIT
}


void CProcessDlg::DoDataExchange(CDataExchange* pDX)
{
    CDialog::DoDataExchange(pDX);
```

```
        //{{AFX_DATA_MAP(CProcessDlg)
        DDX_Control(pDX, IDL_PROCESS, m_ctlProcess);
        DDX_LBString(pDX, IDL_PROCESS, m_strProcess);
        //}}AFX_DATA_MAP
}


BEGIN_MESSAGE_MAP(CProcessDlg, CDialog)
        //{{AFX_MSG_MAP(CProcessDlg)
        //}}AFX_MSG_MAP
END_MESSAGE_MAP()


#define   PROCESS 230
#define   PROCESSID 784


TCHAR chName[80];
TCHAR chList[80];


/////////////////////////////////////////////////////////////////////////////
// CProcessDlg message handlers

BOOL CProcessDlg::OnInitDialog()
{
        CDialog::OnInitDialog();

        CenterWindow();

        CPerfRegistry *pReg = new CPerfRegistry;

        pReg->FirstObject();

        if (pReg->FindObject(PROCESS))
                {
                pReg->FirstInstance();
                for (unsigned int i = 0; i < pReg->NumInstances(); i++)
```

```
                        {
                        if (pReg->FindCounter(PROCESSID))
                                {
                                LPDWORD lpdw = (LPDWORD)pReg->GetCounterData();
                                pReg->InstanceName(chName);
                                wsprintf(chList,"%s (0x%x)",chName,*lpdw);
                                m_ctlProcess.AddString(chList);


m_ctlProcess.SetItemData(m_ctlProcess.FindString(0,chList),*lpdw);
                                }
                        pReg->NextInstance();
                        }
                }
     delete pReg;

     return TRUE;  // return TRUE unless you set the focus to a control
                   // EXCEPTION: OCX Property Pages should return FALSE
}


void CProcessDlg::OnOK()
{
     UpdateData();
     m_dwProcessId =
                m_ctlProcess.GetItemData(m_ctlProcess.FindString(0,m_strProcess));
     m_hProcess=OpenProcess((STANDARD_RIGHTS_REQUIRED |
                PROCESS_QUERY_INFORMATION),FALSE,m_dwProcessId);
     if (!m_hProcess)
                {
                TCHAR TempBuf[1024];
                wsprintf(TempBuf,"OpenProcess failed. Last error = %d\nProcess Id =
0x%x",GetLastError(),m_dwProcessId);
        MessageBox(TempBuf);
                }
     else
                CDialog::OnOK();
}
// Chap12.h : main header file for the CHAP12 application
```

```
//

#ifndef __AFXWIN_H__
     #error include 'stdafx.h' before including this file for PCH
#endif

#include "resource.h"           // main symbols


/////////////////////////////////////////////////////////////////////////
// CChap12App:
// See Chap12.cpp for the implementation of this class
//

class CChap12App : public CWinApp
{
public:
     CChap12App();

// Overrides
     // ClassWizard generated virtual function overrides
     //{{AFX_VIRTUAL(CChap12App)
     public:
     virtual BOOL InitInstance();
     //}}AFX_VIRTUAL

// Implementation

     //{{AFX_MSG(CChap12App)
          // NOTE - the ClassWizard will add and remove member functions here.
          //    DO NOT EDIT what you see in these blocks of generated code !
     //}}AFX_MSG
     DECLARE_MESSAGE_MAP()
};



/////////////////////////////////////////////////////////////////////////
// Chap1dlg.h : header file
//
```

```
/////////////////////////////////////////////////////////////////////////
// CChap12Dlg dialog

class CChap12Dlg : public CDialog
{
// Construction
public:
    CChap12Dlg(CWnd* pParent = NULL);   // standard constructor

// Dialog Data
    //{{AFX_DATA(CChap12Dlg)
    enum { IDD = IDD_CHAP12_DIALOG };
    CListBox m_ctlObject;
    CString  m_strDomain;
    CString  m_strObject;
    CString  m_strOwner;
    CString  m_strList;
    //}}AFX_DATA


    // ClassWizard generated virtual function overrides
    //{{AFX_VIRTUAL(CChap12Dlg)
    protected:
    virtual void DoDataExchange(CDataExchange* pDX);      // DDX/DDV support
    //}}AFX_VIRTUAL


// Implementation
protected:
    HICON m_hIcon;

    // Generated message map functions
    //{{AFX_MSG(CChap12Dlg)
    virtual BOOL OnInitDialog();
    afx_msg void OnSysCommand(UINT nID, LPARAM lParam);
    afx_msg void OnPaint();
    afx_msg HCURSOR OnQueryDragIcon();
    afx_msg void OnProcess();
    afx_msg void OnFile();
    //}}AFX_MSG
```

```
        DECLARE_MESSAGE_MAP()
};
// procdlg.h : header file
//


/////////////////////////////////////////////////////////////////////////////
// CProcessDlg dialog

class CProcessDlg : public CDialog
{
// Construction
public:
        CProcessDlg(CWnd* pParent = NULL);    // standard constructor

// Dialog Data
        //{{AFX_DATA(CProcessDlg)
        enum { IDD = IDD_PROCESS };
        CListBox m_ctlProcess;
        CString  m_strProcess;
        DWORD    m_dwProcessId;
        HANDLE m_hProcess;
        //}}AFX_DATA


// Overrides
        // ClassWizard generated virtual function overrides
        //{{AFX_VIRTUAL(CProcessDlg)
        protected:
        virtual void DoDataExchange(CDataExchange* pDX);    // DDX/DDV support
        //}}AFX_VIRTUAL

// Implementation
protected:

        // Generated message map functions
        //{{AFX_MSG(CProcessDlg)
        virtual BOOL OnInitDialog();
        virtual void OnOK();
```

```
//}}}AFX_MSG
    DECLARE_MESSAGE_MAP()
};
```

# ENABLING PRIVILEGES

The concept of SIDs and user accounts allows NT to support multiple accounts on a single workstation (albeit one at a time). A typical installation may allow several users to log on to the system. Since this system may have services running, you do not want just anyone to be able to reboot the system. The ability to reboot is a system-wide resource, so it doesn't make sense to attach an Access Control List. Besides, what would you attach it to? To solve this problem, NT has the concept of privileges. Privileges are the rights granted to a user when the administrator sets up his or her account. NT has privileges for most system-wide resources. If you enable a particular privilege, you have permission to use or modify the resource. For example, the ability to reboot the system requires SE_SHUTDOWN_PRIVILEGE. On CPQ586 only, Administrators and PowerUsers have SE_SHUTDOWN_PRIVILEGE. However, even though Administrators and PowerUsers have SE_SHUTDOWN_PRIVILEGE, NT initially disables this feature for performance reasons. To enable a privilege you must call the AdjustTokenPrivileges function as shown in the following code:

```
LookupPrivilegeValue(NULL, TEXT("SeShutdownPrivilege"),
        &tkp.Privileges[0].Luid);
tkp.PrivilegeCount = 1;  // one privilege to set
tkp.Privileges[0].Attributes = SE_PRIVILEGE_ENABLED;

// Get shutdown privilege for this process.
//
if (!AdjustTokenPrivileges(hToken, FALSE, &tkp, 0,
        (PTOKEN_PRIVILEGES)NULL, 0))
```

Another privilege is the ability to claim ownership. The main reason for this privilege is to reclaim orphaned objects. (Perhaps the owner of the object left the company and the administrator deleted his or her user account.) The SDK provides sample code that finds all orphaned file objects and assigns them to

**479**

the user running the program (provided that the user has SE_TAKE_OWNERSHIP_NAME privilege). The SDK example is on the CD in the \mstools\samples\sidcln directory. In the case where only AXP\KevinG has delete access, a System Administrator with SeTakeOwnership privilege could take the file from CPQ586\KevinG (and change the security descriptors SID from CPQ586\KevinG to CPQ586\Administrator). At that point, access to the file is at the discretion of CPQ586\Administrator, just as if CPQ586\Administrator had created the file. Unlike other operating systems, CPQ586\Administrator can only give ownership to him- or herself. There is also no concept of a SuperUser in NT as there is in UNIX. The SuperUser in UNIX not only has the capability to take ownership of an object, but also has the ability to give ownership. In NT you can only take ownership, you can't give it to another user. Also, the SuperUser in UNIX can circumvent the audit trail. NT audits all actions, and there is no way for you to disable this feature. The other resources that require privileges are shown in Table 12–2.

Users who do not have privilege to shut down the system (or any other system resource that they try to access) receive an error message when they try to do so.

**Table 12–2** Privilege Resources in Windows NT

| System Resource | Privilege Required |
| --- | --- |
| Auditing | SE_AUDIT_NAME |
| Backup | SE_BACKUP_NAME |
| Creating paging files | SE_CREATE_PAGEFILE_NAME |
| Creating permanent objects | SE_CREATE_PERMANENT_NAME |
| Debugging | SE_DEBUG_NAME |
| Increasing the base priority of a process | SE_INC_BASE_PRIORITY_NAME |
| Increasing the quota of a process | SE_INCREASE_QUOTA_NAME |
| Loading device drivers | SE_LOAD_DRIVER_NAME |
| Locking physical memory | SE_LOCK_MEMORY_NAME |
| Profiling | SE_PROFILE_SINGLE_PROCESS |
| Rebooting from remote console | SE_REMOTE_SHUTDOWN_NAME |
| Restoring from backup | SE_RESTORE_NAME |
| Required for auditing | SE_SECURITY_NAME |

| | |
|---|---|
| Rebooting | SE_SHUTDOWN_NAME |
| Changing environment variables | SE_SYSTEM_ENVIRONMENT_NAME |
| System profiling | SE_SYSTEM_PROFILE_NAME |
| Changing TIME/DATE | SE_SYSTEMTIME_NAME |
| Taking ownership of an object | SE_TAKE_OWNERSHIP_NAME |
| Trusted computer base | SE_TCB_NAME |
| Receiving unsolicited input | SE_UNSOLICITED_INPUT_NAME |

# SAMPLE APPLICATION: EXITWINDOWS

The ExitWindows sample uses the Win32 Security APIs to show how to enable a privilege in NT. ExitWindows sits as an icon on the desktop and provides a quick way to log off, shut down the system, or reboot NT. To do this, ExitWindows takes over QueryOpen and calls the new ExitWindowsEx function. Use of the ExitWindowsEx parameters, EWX_REBOOT and EWX_SHUTDOWN, requires SeShutdownPrivilege. If the account you logged on to does not have SeShutdownPrivilege, you receive an error if you attempt to shut down or reboot. If the account you logged on with does have SeShutdownPrivilege, you must still explicitly enable the privilege before calling ExitWindowsEx. You call OpenProcessToken to get a handle to the access token followed by LookupPrivilegeValue to get the value for SE_SHUTDOWN_PRIVILEGE, which is a macro for _T("SeShutdownPrivilege"). The _T macro prepends an L in front of the string, making the string suitable for UNICODE, like so:

```
#define _T(quote) L##quote
```

UNICODE strings require two bytes per character, and the prepended L tells the compiler to create two bytes of storage per character.

LookupPrivilegeValue returns the privilege value in the form of an LUID. When you have the LUID and the access token, call AdjustTokenPrivileges with SE_SHUTDOWN_ENABLED. For all other privileges you should disable the privilege after using it (to improve performance). However, in ExitWindows you never return so you won't get the chance. Since ExitWindows has no user interface, it adds "About..." to the system menu. Choosing this option displays the dialog box in Figure 12–2. Listing 12–3 lists the source code.

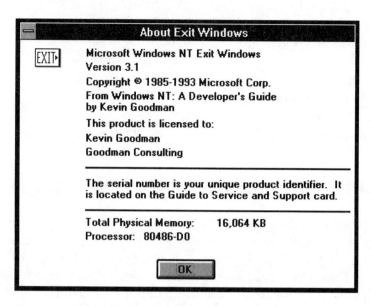

**Figure 12–2** ExitWindows About box

**Listing 12–3** The source for ExitWindows

```
// chap1dlg.cpp : implementation file
// Note: This sample is used in both Chapter 12 and 14

#include "stdafx.h"
#include "chap14.h"
#include "chap14dlg.h"

#ifdef _DEBUG
#undef THIS_FILE
static char BASED_CODE THIS_FILE[] = __FILE__;
#endif

/////////////////////////////////////////////////////////////////////////
// CAboutDlg dialog used for App About

class CAboutDlg : public CDialog
{
public:
```

```
        CAboutDlg();

// Dialog Data
        //{{AFX_DATA(CAboutDlg)
        enum { IDD = IDD_ABOUTBOX };
        //}}AFX_DATA


// Implementation
protected:
        virtual void DoDataExchange(CDataExchange* pDX);        // DDX/DDV support
        //{{AFX_MSG(CAboutDlg)
        virtual BOOL OnInitDialog();
        //}}AFX_MSG
        DECLARE_MESSAGE_MAP()
};

CAboutDlg::CAboutDlg() : CDialog(CAboutDlg::IDD)
{
        //{{AFX_DATA_INIT(CAboutDlg)
        //}}AFX_DATA_INIT
}

void CAboutDlg::DoDataExchange(CDataExchange* pDX)
{
        CDialog::DoDataExchange(pDX);
        //{{AFX_DATA_MAP(CAboutDlg)
        //}}AFX_DATA_MAP
}

BEGIN_MESSAGE_MAP(CAboutDlg, CDialog)
        //{{AFX_MSG_MAP(CAboutDlg)
                // No message handlers
        //}}AFX_MSG_MAP
END_MESSAGE_MAP()

/////////////////////////////////////////////////////////////////////////////
// CAboutDlg message handlers

BOOL CAboutDlg::OnInitDialog()
```

**483**

```
{


    CDialog::OnInitDialog();
    CenterWindow();

    // TODO: Add extra about dlg initialization here

 .

    return TRUE;  // return TRUE  unless you set the focus to a control
}


/////////////////////////////////////////////////////////////////////////////
// CChap14Dlg dialog

CChap14Dlg::CChap14Dlg(CWnd* pParent /*=NULL*/)
    : CDialog(CChap14Dlg::IDD, pParent)
{
    //{{AFX_DATA_INIT(CChap14Dlg)
    m_ctlStatus = 0;  //default to ShutDown
    //}}AFX_DATA_INIT
    // Note that LoadIcon does not require a subsequent DestroyIcon in Win32
    m_hIcon = AfxGetApp()->LoadIcon(IDR_MAINFRAME);
}


void CChap14Dlg::DoDataExchange(CDataExchange* pDX)
{
    CDialog::DoDataExchange(pDX);
    //{{AFX_DATA_MAP(CChap14Dlg)
    DDX_Radio(pDX, IDC_SHUTDOWN, m_ctlStatus);
    //}}AFX_DATA_MAP
}


BEGIN_MESSAGE_MAP(CChap14Dlg, CDialog)
    //{{AFX_MSG_MAP(CChap14Dlg)
    ON_WM_SYSCOMMAND()
    ON_WM_PAINT()
    ON_WM_QUERYDRAGICON()
    ON_BN_CLICKED(IDC_SHUTDOWN, OnDataChange)
```

```
        ON_BN_CLICKED(IDC_RESTART, OnDataChange)
        ON_BN_CLICKED(IDC_LOGOFF, OnDataChange)
        ON_WM_KILLFOCUS()
        //}}AFX_MSG_MAP
END_MESSAGE_MAP()


////////////////////////////////////////////////////////////////////////
// CChap14Dlg message handlers

BOOL CChap14Dlg::OnInitDialog()
{
        CDialog::OnInitDialog();
        CenterWindow();

        // Add "About..." menu item to system menu.

        // IDM_ABOUTBOX must be in the system command range.
        ASSERT((IDM_ABOUTBOX & 0xFFF0) == IDM_ABOUTBOX);
        ASSERT(IDM_ABOUTBOX < 0xF000);

        CMenu* pSysMenu = GetSystemMenu(FALSE);
        CString strAboutMenu;
        strAboutMenu.LoadString(IDS_ABOUTBOX);

        pSysMenu->AppendMenu(MF_SEPARATOR);
        pSysMenu->DeleteMenu(4,MF_BYPOSITION);
        pSysMenu->DeleteMenu(2,MF_BYPOSITION);
        pSysMenu->DeleteMenu(0,MF_BYPOSITION);
        if (IsWin32s())
                {
                pSysMenu->AppendMenu(MF_STRING |
                                                 MF_ENABLED,
                                                 IDM_RESTART,
                                                 "Restart Windows");


        pSysMenu->AppendMenu(MF_STRING |
                                         MF_ENABLED,
                                         IDM_REBOOT, "Reboot");
```

**485**

```
        }
        else
        {
                //
                // If the user has the SE_SHUTDOWN_PRIVILEGE append the menu items
                //

                if (GetPrivilege())
                        {
            pSysMenu->AppendMenu(MF_STRING |

                                                MF_ENABLED,
                                                IDM_SHUTDOWN, "Shutdown System");
                        pSysMenu->AppendMenu(MF_STRING |

                                                MF_ENABLED,
                                                IDM_REBOOT, "Reboot");
            }
        }
        pSysMenu->AppendMenu(MF_STRING |
                                MF_ENABLED,
                                IDM_LOGOFF,
                                IsWin32s() ?
                                    "Return to DOS...":"Logoff");

    pSysMenu->AppendMenu(MF_SEPARATOR);

    pSysMenu->AppendMenu(MF_STRING |
                            MF_ENABLED,
                            IDM_ABOUTBOX, strAboutMenu);


//
// Make Logoff the default
//
    pSysMenu->CheckMenuItem(IDM_LOGOFF, MF_CHECKED);
    return TRUE;  // return TRUE  unless you set the focus to a control
}


void CChap14Dlg::OnSysCommand(UINT nID, LPARAM lParam)
```

```
{
    if ((nID & 0xFFF0) == IDM_ABOUTBOX)
    {
        CAboutDlg dlgAbout;
        dlgAbout.DoModal();
    }
    else
    {
        CDialog::OnSysCommand(nID, lParam);
    }
}


// If you add a minimize button to your dialog, you will need the code below
//  to draw the icon.  For MFC applications using the document/view model,
//  this is automatically done for you by the framework.

void CChap14Dlg::OnPaint()
{
    if (IsIconic())
    {
        CPaintDC dc(this); // device context for painting

        SendMessage(WM_ICONERASEBKGND, (WPARAM) dc.GetSafeHdc(), 0);

        // Center icon in client rectangle
        int cxIcon = GetSystemMetrics(SM_CXICON);
        int cyIcon = GetSystemMetrics(SM_CYICON);
        CRect rect;
        GetClientRect(&rect);
        int x = (rect.Width() - cxIcon + 1) / 2;
        int y = (rect.Height() - cyIcon + 1) / 2;

        // Draw the icon
        dc.DrawIcon(x, y, m_hIcon);
    }
    else
    {
        CDialog::OnPaint();
```

```
        }
    }


    // The system calls this to obtain the cursor to display while the user drags
    //   the minimized window.
    HCURSOR CChap14Dlg::OnQueryDragIcon()
    {
        return (HCURSOR) m_hIcon;
    }




    BOOL
    CChap14Dlg::IsWin32s()
    {
     return  (GetVersion() & 0x80000000) ? TRUE: FALSE;
    }


    BOOL
    CChap14Dlg::GetPrivilege()
    {


    HANDLE hToken;
    TOKEN_PRIVILEGES tkp;
    //
    // SeShutdownPrivilege must be enabled
    //
       if (!OpenProcessToken(GetCurrentProcess(),
                            TOKEN_ADJUST_PRIVILEGES |
                            TOKEN_QUERY, &hToken))
         {
         return FALSE;
         }
    //
    // Get a LUID for SeShutdownPrivilege
    //
```

```
        LookupPrivilegeValue(NULL, TEXT("SeShutdownPrivilege"),
            &tkp.Privileges[0].Luid);

//
// PrivilegeCount enables more than one privilege to be set
// at a time.
//
    tkp.PrivilegeCount = 1;
    tkp.Privileges[0].Attributes = SE_PRIVILEGE_ENABLED;


//
// Some privileges are initially disable. So each process must adjust the
// privilege by calling AdjustTokenPrivilege
//
    if (!AdjustTokenPrivileges(hToken, FALSE, &tkp, 0,
                                (PTOKEN_PRIVILEGES)NULL, 0))

        return FALSE;
    return TRUE;
}



void CChap14Dlg::OnDataChange()
{



switch (m_ctlStatus)
{
        case 0:
        OnShutDown();
        break;
        case 1:
        OnReboot();
        break;

        case 2:
        OnLogOff();
        break;
```

```
    };

    }



void CChap14Dlg::OnShutDown()
{
//
//   Shutdown the system
//

     ExitWindowsEx( EWX_SHUTDOWN, 0 );
//      ExitWindowsEx( EWX_SHUTDOWN | EWX_FORCE, 0 );
}




void CChap14Dlg::OnReboot()
{

//
// Reboot
//
    if (IsWin32s())
      {
    ;//  ExitUT(EXIT_SRV_REBOOT);
      }
    else
      ExitWindowsEx(EWX_REBOOT | EWX_FORCE, 0);


}

void CChap14Dlg::OnLogOff()
{
//
```

```
// Logoff
//

    ExitWindowsEx( EWX_LOGOFF | EWX_FORCE, 0 );

}

void
CChap14Dlg::OnRestart()
{
//      ExitUT(EXIT_SRV_RESTART);
}




void CChap14Dlg::OnKillFocus(CWnd* pNewWnd)
{
    CDialog::OnKillFocus(pNewWnd);

    // TODO: Add your message handler code here

}

BOOL CChap14Dlg::Create(LPCTSTR lpszClassName, LPCTSTR lpszWindowName, DWORD
dwStyle, const RECT& rect, CWnd* pParentWnd, UINT nID, CCreateContext* pContext)
{

    return CWnd::Create(lpszClassName, lpszWindowName, dwStyle, rect, pParentWnd,
nID, pContext);
}
```

# HOW SECURITY AFFECTS APPLICATIONS

The existence of a user database means that somehow, somewhere, someone will have to administer it. Understanding the NT administration model should help you understand the overall concept of a secure system. Any application you develop may have potential users running in the following environments:

- ▚ A stand-alone NT workstation
- ▚ A peer-to-peer network
- ▚ A single-domain network NT BackOffice
- ▚ A multiple-domain network NT BackOffice

## SINGLE WORKSTATION

If someone purchases your product for use on a NT Workstation, the user who logs on as administrator controls the desktop. This doesn't necessarily mean the administrator is the only user to execute your application, since NT supports multiple users at different times on a single workstation. This means that many users of varying experience levels are potential users of your application on a single machine. Do not assume that just because someone with the privilege of acting as part of the operating system installed your application, the users running your application will have the same privileges. On the other hand, do not code to the lowest common denominator and become inflexible for sophisticated users. By finding the SID and determining the privilege level, you can determine at run time which level of security the user is running.

However, just because NT provides this database of users, you should resist the temptation to build added security into your application. For instance, do not add another user database and password list to your application to restrict its use to a subset of all users. In other operating systems this technique is quite common. In Windows and DOS you normally have passwords everywhere: one to log on to each domain (or File Server in NetWare) on the network, another to access e-mail, and yet another to get back into the system after the screen saver has kicked in. In NT, additional passwords would be redundant as well as unnecessary, and would probably prevent these products from selling into a C2-secure environment. Instead, in the documentation (or during setup), instruct the administrator to create groups with the required restrictions to preclude unprivileged users. Then use the Win32 security APIs to determine whether the current user qualifies to perform operations with your application.

## SINGLE- AND MULTIPLE-DOMAIN NETWORKS

Everything that applies to standalone workstations also applies to applications running on a network. In addition, multiple-domain networks provide the concept of trust. When users log on they specify a user name, password, and home domain. If the domain being accessed trusts the specified home domain, it asks the home domain to validate the user. For example, suppose you had two domains, Engineering and Marketing. As shown in Figure 12–3, Marketing trusts Engineering to authenticate Engineering\KevinG. Note that trust is unidirectional. Just because Marketing trusts Engineering, that doesn't mean that Engineering trusts Marketing (almost like real life!).

There are many benefits to this arrangement. Users have only one password to remember and update. Administrators have only one account to manage for any user.

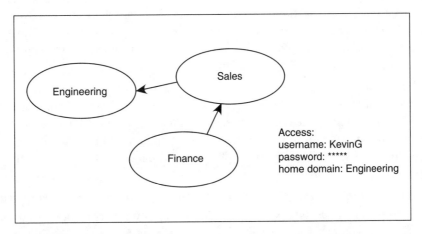

**Figure 12–3** Inter-domain trust. Note that trust is direct only. Finance>Sales>Engineering does not imply Finance>Engineering

# IMPERSONATION

In NT, users have security levels, not processes or threads. Therefore, the security abilities for a process or thread change when the current user logs off and another user logs on and runs the same application. If you are developing a client-server application, you have additional responsibilities. Since the client portion of your application may reside anywhere on the network, the server must verify the privilege level of the client. For example, suppose you have a typical client-server application in which the clients make requests to the server to access data in a file controlled by the server. As the process that makes the Win32 API calls to open, read, and write the file, the server must have open/read/write privileges on that file. What if the client making the request does not have the security clearance to do so? If the server provides the information from this file to the unprivileged client, that would be a breach in the C2-secure system. This certainly won't fly in a B2-secure system. B2 compliance means that no privileged process can supply information to an unprivileged one.

Fortunately, Win32 provides the concept of impersonation. Impersonation allows servers to access data on behalf of privileged clients by assuming the security level of the client. If a user on the network without the proper security clearance ran the client, then the server, impersonating the client and using the Win32 impersonation APIs, would not be granted access to the file. With impersonation, a thread takes on the security context of the client. The thread then receives the proper access validation.

Unfortunately, the first release of NT does not support all protocols. If you include security in your client/server application, you must choose between named pipes, DDE, and remote procedure calls (RPCs) over named pipes. If you are unfamiliar with these terms, you may want to read Chapter 7, "Remote Procedure Calls," and Chapter 9, "Memory Management," before trying to digest this next section.

You can attach security descriptors if you are using named pipes or RPCs running on the named pipe's protocol. You cannot do this over other transports or protocols. You can specify a DACL on the server end of the pipe when you create it. When the client connects to the server end of the pipe, NT authenticates the request as if the same client tried to open a file locally. That is, you can use DACLs to protect the server ends of pipes just as you can use DACLs to protect shared directories or files on an NTFS partition. The ImpersonateNamedPipeClient Win32 API temporarily switches the named pipe server code to run under the security context of the client, rather than that of the server. In most cases the security context of the server is more powerful than the client. When the server impersonates the client, it temporarily reduces its privileges/rights down to those of the client. The server thread performs the operations on behalf of the client, and if the client is not authorized to do the operations, the operations fail. For example, if the server calls a function on behalf of the client and the function returns ACCESS_DENIED, then the client does not have the required privilege level.

**494**

When your server application requires access to an object for itself, call NamedPipeRevertToSelf to revert back to security level of the server.

## SECURITY AND SCREEN SAVERS

Screen savers provide an interesting challenge for NT. Screen savers must be flexible enough to allow third parties to develop their own screen savers. You must fight for your right to flying toasters! Yet NT must be sure that screen savers obey the rules of a secure desktop. A well-behaved screen saver obscures the desktop from prying eyes, but an ill-behaved one may leave the desktop visible. NT works around this problem by having two desktops. The desktop most users are familiar with is actually the second desktop in the system. Program Manager and all of the consoles and windows run in this desktop. A program named WinLogon actually owns the first desktop. WinLogon owns the desktop when you log on and when the screen saver runs. You may have noticed this when you returned from the screen saver. No matter how many applications you have running, the first screen you see is an empty desktop. If the screen saver makes a mistake and shows the windows on the desktop when the workstation is locked, only the empty WinLogon desktop will be exposed.

## NT SECURITY ARCHITECTURE: THE BIG PICTURE

C2 certification covers identification and authentication, mandatory and discretionary access controls, and object reuse specifications. Despite the C2 certification that Microsoft is seeking from the National Computer Security Center, this security does not address matters that are beyond the control of an operating system. For example, it does not matter how much front-end security you place on a system (individual identification, access tokens, etc.). If someone has physical access to your CPU, they can remove the hard drive and with little difficulty read the data stored on the drive. The security facilities in Windows NT, such as NTFS, CtrlAltDel\Lock-Workstation, as well as the integrated password in the screen saver, make it more difficult for many potential intruders to intrude, but not impossible. The administration facilities that NT provides permit very large enterprises to manage the user accounts and passwords easily. This paves the way for many organizations to implement increased security. So don't let the fact that there is always a way for a determined intruder to trespass into any secure system bother you. Knowledge, combined with intent, can defeat any system.

Even though the security facilities in Windows NT won't defeat all potential intruders, they will make it a good deal harder than it has been in the past. NT is vastly superior to the security policies of all other currently shipping operating systems. If it comes down to your application versus a competitor's and only your application conforms to the NT security policies, your application will probably sell more copies.

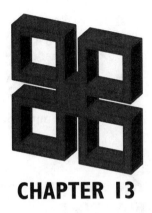

## CHAPTER 13

# THE GDI

Whenever a discussion arises about the limitation of 16-bit Windows, the subject inevitably turns to weaknesses in the Graphics Device Interface, known as GDI. GDI for 16-bit Windows does provide a useful device-independent drawing set for applications. It is a definite pleasure not to have to worry about supporting a particular printer or display directly in your application. However, because the original Windows debuted several years ago, output devices have become more and more sophisticated and 16-bit GDI is starting to show its age.

To remedy the situation, Microsoft has made several enhancements to the Win32 version of GDI. These enhancements can be broken down into several distinct categories, each of which is examined in this chapter. If you are a developer who found the 16-bit GDI lacking, you will see that the 32-bit GDI is significantly improved.

Specifically, this chapter provides the following:

- ∷ An overview of the Client-Server nature of NT's version of GDI, including a discussion of changes to GDI functions and how they differ from Windows 95

- ∷ A look at the various enhancements to GDI, lines, curves, paths, bitmaps, palettes, enhanced metafiles, and transforms.

- ∷ Tips for improving graphics drawing performance.

# AN OVERVIEW OF GDI'S CLIENT-SERVER NATURE

One of the most significant conceptual improvements of Windows over MS-DOS is its ability to separate an output device from the application. In MS-DOS, the application is responsible for programming all output devices (displays, printers, plotters, and so on). This means that many applications must frequently be updated to add support for new hardware. In Windows, applications aren't responsible for programming output devices. Instead, hardware manufacturers supply a driver, and applications create and maintain device contexts. Windows requires all hardware devices to support a minimum functionality. Applications can be assured that if they adhere to the minimum functionality subscribed by Windows, they will work on every desktop. If your application needs to access an output device with enhanced features (perhaps a raster plotter), then your application checks, at runtime, the output device's capabilities to determine if the enhanced support is present. At no time is a Windows application forced or even expected to fool directly with the hardware. In 16-bit Windows, this process is a pretty straightforward operation. Figure13–1 shows a flow chart describing data from an application to an output device in 16-bit Windows.

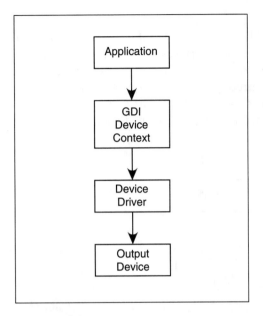

**Figure 13–1** Accessing an output device in 16-bit Windows

Now that all applications are separated into user-mode and kernel-mode pieces under Windows NT, calling a GDI function isn't as simple as it used to be. Figure 13–2 presents a conceptual overview of the Windows NT graphics device model. The change was necessary for two reasons:

- The secure nature of Windows NT requires that applications be separate from each other.
- Because all processes share the same output devices (like the display), it is necessary to secure the data going to these output devices. Otherwise, if screen data were stored in some globally available memory location, a intruder or renegade application could gain access to potentially

sensitive data. Therefore, any functions that alter an output device reside in the server-side of GDI instead of the Win32 client side DLL. (The next chapter delves deeper into security, but for now imagine someone executing a program on your machine—perhaps remotely— that captured the screen to a disk file every two minutes. In an unprotected system, it would be possible to screen-capture a sensitive document that you just happened to have up in your word processor.)

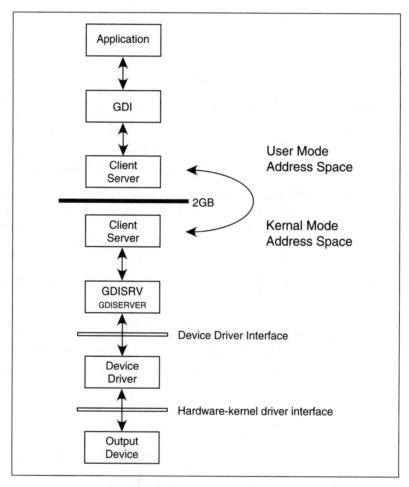

**Figure 13–2** Windows NT GDI Device Driver Mode

## CHANGES TO GDI API FUNCTIONS

Other changes were made the GDI functions as a result of the move to 32-bits. As you would expect, all Handles (hDCs, hMF, hBITMAPs, and so on) are now 32-bits. So are all limits and coordinates. Of course, all pointers are now 32-bit flat pointers. This is another area where, due the memory constraints Windows 95 differs. All coordinates in Windows 95 are still 16-bit.

The client-server nature of Windows NT GDI also causes some other subtle differences in API functions. For example, in Win16, the DeviceCapabilities function is provided by device drivers. To use the Win16 version of DeviceCapabilities, you must call LoadLibrary on the driver you wish to query. In Win32, DeviceCapabilities is provided as part of GDI32.DLL. Therefore, the LoadLibrary call is no longer necessary.

## DELETED GDI FUNCTIONS

In Windows 3.1, you can define your own resource type. To access your new type you call SetResourceHandler and pass in a callback to your hook resource function. Windows 3.1 then calls your callback every time any application calls LoadResource. Your callback function is free to manipulate the data in the resource before LoadResource returned. Win32 no longer supports calculated resources (as they are called in Windows 3.1) and the SetResourceHandler function has been deleted.

Two other resource functions were removed because of the different structure of the executable files. The functions AccessResource and AllocResource have also been deleted. The functionality provided by these APIs is no longer useful. As you will learn in Chapter 10, which contains information on memory mapped files, there is no benefit to allocating a block of memory at run-time for a piece of your EXE image, when the entire EXE image is already mapped into your virtual run-time address space, and will be paged in as needed.

## ENHANCEMENTS TO GDI

Besides the changes to GDI to migrate to 32-bits, some significant enhancements have been made. One big improvement over 16-bit Windows is the removal of the restriction that only five common device contexts are allowed in the system at a time. In Windows 3.1, unless the device context belongs to a window class, you must call ReleaseDC to release the context after drawing. Since only five contexts are available at any given time, failure to release your device context prevents other applications from accessing a device context. In Windows NT, you can have any number of DCs (they are limited only by available memory).

## Enhancements to lines

Many Windows 3.1 developers complain about the way lines are drawn in Windows 3.1. All versions of Windows (including NT) draw inclusive-exclusive lines. This means that the displayed line begins at the starting point and continues up to but does not include the ending point. For example, if you draw a line segment from x1, y1 to x2, y2, the displayed line does not include the endpoint (x2, y2). This in itself is not a problem, but the algorithm to determine which pixels to light in Windows 3.1 is an inefficient one. The algorithm is loosely based upon Bresanham's Algorithm for Computer Control of Digital Plotter, commonly known as Bresanham's. Bresanham's uses only integers to determine which pixel positions to light. Because Bresanham's rounds off to the nearest integer value, the actual line and the displayed line quite often differ. Rounding errors are most obvious at the endpoint. For example, if you draw two lines from x1, y1 to x2, y2 and x2, y2 to x3, y3 and there is a rounding error in the first line, the two lines won't connect. A pixel or two won't be lit when you think they should be.

The line drawing algorithm used by the Win32 GDI, known as Grid Intersection Quantization is based upon fractional end points. Grid Intersection Quantization has two rules:

⊞ When the geometric line crosses the grid, light the nearest pixel. Ties go up and left. When $dy/dx = 1$ exactly, ties go up and right.

⊞ Clipping in no way affects which pixel is chosen.

As a result, output in Windows NT more closely matches the calculated line. Which means that when you want to connect two lines they actually have a chance of connecting!

### Enhancements to curves

One of the more notable additions to GDI has to do with curves. Windows defines a curve by specifying a set of control points that indicate the shape of the curve. GDI uses the control points to set up mathematical equations to display curves. When a curve passes through its control points, it is said to be interpolating the control points. Consequently, if a curve approximates its control points it does not pass through them. In Windows, a curve that is interpolated is called a regular curve, and an irregular curve is a curve that is approximated.

A Bézier curve is a type of irregular curve named after Pierre Bézier, who developed the formula for the curve when he worked as an engineer for the Renault Corporation in France. Almost all of the sophisticated Windows 3.1 graphic packages support Bézier curves. However, they do it by supplying Bézier's algorithm to generate the curve. (Since it is no longer important for you to know the algorithm, I have excluded it. But it is available in any trigonometry text book.)

In Win32, Béziers are the fundamental drawing primitive for curves. In addition to curves, GDI also draws both ellipses and arcs using Béziers. To improve graphics throughput, GDI will pass Béziers off to any device driver that supports drawing Béziers. But if a particular driver does not support Béziers, then GDI will just draw the curve itself. To draw a Bézier curve, call the PolyBezier or PolyBezierTo functions:

```
BOOL
PolyBezier(HDC hdc,               // handle of device context
           CONST POINT * lppt;    // address of endpoints
                                  // and control points
           DWORD cPoints;         // count of endpoints and
                                  // control points
```

The second parameter, lppt, points to an array of POINT structures that contains the end points and control points for the curve. In theory, you can specify any number of control points for a Bézier curve, but Win32 allows you to specify just two control points. If you need to generate something more complex, you must piece together several Bézier sections. GDI draws the first Bézier from the current position to the third point (interpolating the first two points as control points). If this sounds like a drawback, it isn't. Not only is piecing together Bézier sections faster (because fewer complicated calculations have to be dealt with) it also gives you more control. However, you are responsible for maintaining continuity between sections. When all two curves do is connect at the end points, they have zero-order continuity. Since Bézier curves pass through endpoints, maintaining zero-order continuity is easy. Just make sure that the ending control point of the preceding section is the starting control point for the next section. You can do this two ways, with PolyBezier and PolyBezierTo.

The first way is to call PolyBezier with multiple control and end points. For each subsequent Bézier, supply exactly three more points in the array that lppt points to. The ending point of the previous Bézier will be used as the starting point for the next Bézier. This means that the value of the third parameter, cPoints, is equal to three times the number of curves you want to draw:

```
BOOL
PolyBezier(HDC hdc,
           CONST POINT * lppt,     // address of endpoints
                                   // and control points
           DWORD cCount);          // count of endpoints and
                                   // control points
```

The second way is to make repeated calls to PolyBezierTo. PolyBezierTo updates the current position so the starting control point will always be the previous curve's ending control point. PolyBezierTo takes the same parameters as PolyBezier.

```
PolyBezierTo (hdc, aPoint, 4);
```

However, as you can see from Figure13–3, the curves are not "smooth." That is, they don't flow evenly from one curve to the other. To make the curves smooth they must have first-order continuity. Curves have first-order continuity when they attach along tangent lines. First-order continuity requires that you choose control points so that the second control point and the ending position of the first curve are along the same straight line as the beginning and second control point of the second curve. Figure13–4 shows what this looks like. Figures13–5 and13–6 give more examples of Béziers.

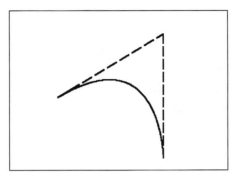

**Figure13–3** Bézier curve. Here the curves are not smooth

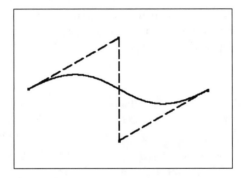

**Figure13–4** Bézier curve. This curve has first-order continuity

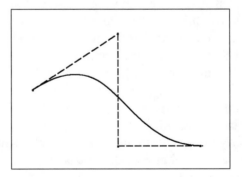

**Figure13–5** Another Bézier curve with first-order continuity

**505**

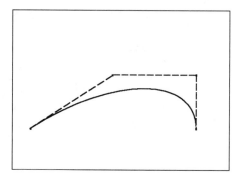

**Figure13–6** A Bézier curve with first-order continuity

**Note:** Win32 GDI curves also exclude the ending point the same as lines. The grid intersection quantization algorithm applies to curves as well.Enhancements to arcsAs I stated before, all arcs are now drawn using Béziers. A demonstration of this can be seen in Figure13–7 and in the new AngleArc function:

```
BOOL AngleArc(HDC hdc;      // handle of device context
              int X;        // x-coordinate of circle's center
              int Y;        // y-coordinate of circle's center
              DWORD dwRadius;      // circle's radius
              FLOAT eStartAngle;   // arc's start angle
              FLOAT eSweepAngle;   // arc's sweep angle
```

As its name implies, the AngleArc draws an angle and an arc. The first thing AngleArc does is draw a line from the current position to the beginning of the arc. It then draws the arc constructing an imaginary circle around the specified center point with the specified radius. Parameters two and three define the x and y coordinates of a circle's center. Parameter four, dwRadius, determines the radius of the circle. The starting point of the arc is determined by measuring counterclockwise from the x-axis of the circle by the number of degrees in the starting angle. Define the length of the arc by passing in a starting angle in parameter five, and you define the arc's sweep angle in parameter six. The starting angle is in degrees relative to the x-axis, and the sweep is in degrees relative to the starting angle.

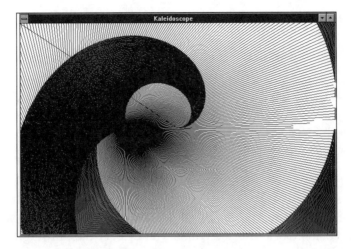

**Figure 13–7** Putting AngleArc in a loop reveals interesting results

Figure 13–8 and Listing 13–1 show typical uses for the AngleArc function. In this case, there are multiple arcs ranging from 10 to 360 degrees.

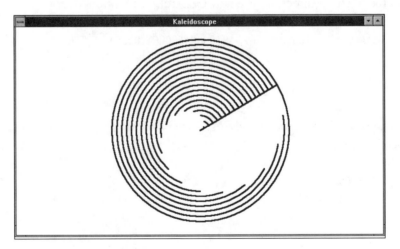

**Figure 13–8** AngleArc showing sweep

AngleArc is unlike the Arc function in that it updates the current position. If you want to draw a regular Arc and update the current position, use the new

ArcTo function. ArcTo has the same parameters as Arc, except it updates the current position.

**Listing13–1** AngleArc function

```
for (i = 0; i < 361; i +=20 )
{
    MoveToEx(hdc, cxClient /2, cyClient /2,  NULL);
    AngleArc(hdc,  cxClient/2, cyClient /2,i/2, (FLOAT)30,
            (FLOAT) i);
}
```

In Win16, the functions Arc, ArcTo, Chord, Ellipse, Pie, Rectangle, RoundRect are drawn counterclockwise. In Win32 you can set the drawing direction to either clockwise or counterclockwise with the new SetArcDirection.

```
SetArcDirection(hdc, AD_CLOCKWISE);
```

To get the previous direction, use new GetArcDirection function:

```
if (GetArcDirection(hdc) == AD_COUNTERCLOCKWISE)
 .
 .
 .
```

Combine MoveToEx, LineTo and PolyBezier and what do you get? The answer is PolyDraw.:

```
BOOL PolyDraw(HDC hdc,
        CONST POINT * lppt,        // address of array of
                                   // points
        CONST BYTE * lpbTypes,     // address of line and
                                   // curve identifiers
        int cCount;                // count of points
```

Using an array of points, PolyDraw draws any combination of line segments and Bézier splines. Use PolyDraw instead of consecutive calls to MoveToEx,

LineTo, and PolyBezierTo functions to draw figures. The one drawback to PolyDraw is that everything is drawn with the current pen.

The polygon boundary that determines control points for a Bézier curve is referred to a the convex hull. Figure13–9 shows an example of output using PolyDraw to display the convex hull of a Bézier curve. Listing13–2 shows the source to generate a Bézier and its convex hull using PolyDraw.

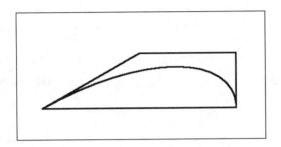

**Figure13–9** Convex hull for a Bezier using PolyDraw

**Listing13–2** Bézier Curve and Convex Hull Using PolyDrawstatic

```
BYTE lpbTypes[8] = {(BYTE)PT_MOVETO,
                        (BYTE)PT_BEZIERTO,
                        (BYTE)PT_BEZIERTO,
                        PT_LINETO,
                        PT_LINETO,
                        PT_LINETO, PT_LINETO};
char szErrMsg[80];
        SelectObject (hdc, GetStockObject (BLACK_PEN)) ;
        if (!PolyDraw (hdc, aPoint,lpbTypes, 8))
            {
        FormatMessage( FORMAT_MESSAGE_FROM_SYSTEM
                | FORMAT_MESSAGE_ALLOCATE_BUFFER,
                NULL, GetLastError(),
                MAKELANGID( LANG_NEUTRAL,
                        SUBLANG_NEUTRAL),
                szErrMsg, 0, NULL );
        MessageBox(NULL,szErrMsg,"GDI",MB_OK);
            }
```

As you can see, the array of points (aPoint) can get quite complex for one simple Bézier and its convex hull. This next section on Paths will show a more effective use of PolyDraw.

## ENHANCEMENTS TO PATHS

The Win32 GDI has a complete set of path calls. A path is a collection of lines, Béziers, and MoveToExs accumulated in fractional device coordinates. Paths are now fundamental to all drawing in Win32 GDI. Internally, GDI sends all drawing commands across the device driver interface as path objects.

To activate a path, you must call BeginPath with a valid device context:

```
BeginPath(hdc);
```

BeginPath creates what is known as a path bracket. The following list shows all the functions that are associated with paths:

AngleArc
Arc
ArcTo
Chord
CloseFigure
Ellipse
ExtTextOut
LineTo
MoveToEx
Pie
PolyBezier
PolyBezierTo
PolyDraw
Polygon
Polyline
PolylineTo

PolyPolygon

PolyPolyline

Rectangle

RoundRect

TextOut

Once you activate a path, all of the calls in the above list will be collected in an internal GDI buffer until you call EndPath.

EndPath is written like so:

```
EndPath(hdc);
```

After you call EndPath, the path is said to be "closed. " A closed path is different than a closed figure. Figures inside a path are closed by drawing a line from the current position to the first point of the figure. You explicitly close a figure by calling the CloseFigure function:

```
CloseFigure(hdc);
```

Once you have closed the path, there are several new Win32 functions available to make it easy for you to manage multiple shapes (consisting of lines and Béziers) efficiently. For example, this next section shows you how to draw, fill, and clip through these shapes.

## StrokePath

The function StrokePath displays the path using the current pen. The function call is simple, just pass in a valid hDC:

```
StrokePath(hDC);
```

Once "stroked", the path is no longer valid. That is to say that once you call StrokePath, GDI deletes the buffer associated with the path and any other calls expecting a valid path will fail. Just to test this, I coded a small example that used StrokePath and FillPath (described next) back to back. On theFillPath instruction I received a MessageBox with "Error R6018 unexpected heap error" displayed.

**511**

## FillPath

FillPath fills the path's interior by using the current brush and polygon-filling mode. There are two fill modes: alternate and winding. You can determine the fill mode yourself by calling SetPolyFillMode. If you need to retrieve or save off the current fill mode, call GetPolyFillMode.

If you did not call CloseFigure before calling FillPath, FillPath calls it for you:

```
FillPath(hDC);
```

## StrokeAndFillPath

The all-purpose StrokeAndFillPath does the job of CloseFigure, StrokePath, and FillPath all in one function call. With one exception: The filled region doesn't overlap the stroked region even if the pen is wide:

```
StrokeAndFillPath(hDC);
```

## GetPath and PolyDraw

One of the first drawing packages I ever used was LisaDraw on the now defunct Apple Lisa. LisaDraw had the ability to "group" several shapes into a single object. You could place several objects on top of each other and each object would retain its properties. Each object could be selected and manipulated individually. For example, LisaDraw had the features Bring-to-front and Send-to-back. These functions were similar to the ones that are in the SDK dialog manager. One way to mimic the behavior of LisaDraw in NT is to use paths and PolyDraw.

Remember when I said there was a more effective use of PolyDraw? Well, the true power of PolyDraw is demonstrated when you combine it with paths. By using the GetPath function you can effectively save off a path. GetPath retrieves the coordinates defining the path in a series of end points and control points. The parameters to GetPath are identical to the parameters to PolyDraw. Therefore, once you get the path you can re-create it using PolyDraw. Listing 13–3 gives an example.

**Listing 13–3** Save path buffer using GetPath and PolyDraw

```
// NOTE: This requires an active path
// Since you don't know the size of the
// buffers, first call GetPath with a zero
// in parameter 4. The size of the buffer
// needed is then the return value
int nSize = GetPath(hdc, NULL, NULL, 0);
LPPOINT lpPoints = new POINT [nSize];
LPBYTE lpTypes = new BYTE [nSize];
if (GetPath(hdc, lpPoints, lpTypes, nSize) == GDI_ERROR)
    {
        .
        .

        .
    }
else
    PolyDraw (hdc, lpPoints, lpTypes, nSize);
```

GetPath accumulates all of the shapes into one "object." To display the object you can use either StrokePath or PolyDraw. Here's the algorithm:

```
BeginPath
Create a drawing shape (Bezier, line, rectangle, text)
EndPath
GetPath
```

Here's where the interesting part comes in. If you want to add to your object, just begin another path, then PolyDraw the original object into it. Then continue adding shapes, like so:

```
BeginPath
PolyDraw original object into path
Create drawing shapes (Beziers, lines, rectangles, text, and so on)
EndPath
GetPath
```

Once you have the desired shapes, save off the buffer that GetPath returns. This is now your object. Repeat the process for as many objects as you wish. To implement Bring-to-front or Send-to-back, simply change the order of your PolyDraws (one for each object buffer). If you want an object brought to the front, PolyDraw its buffer last. Consequently, if you want an object in the back, PolyDraw its buffer first.

## PathToRegion

Paths can also be converted to regions with the PathToRegion call:

```
HRGN hRgn = PathToRegion(hdc)
```

Like other functions that manipulate paths, the hdc device context contains a closed path. Once you have a handle to a region, you can manipulate the region the same as any other region (FillRgn, OffsetRgn, and so on). Our Lisa-like drawing package uses OffsetRgn to move objects around and FillRgn to paint the interiors. Lisa-like also uses GetRgnBox to determine a paths frame. Once a path has a frame, Lisa-like can draw a rectangle around it to make set it apart from the other shapes. Listing 13–4 and Figure 13–10 show how.

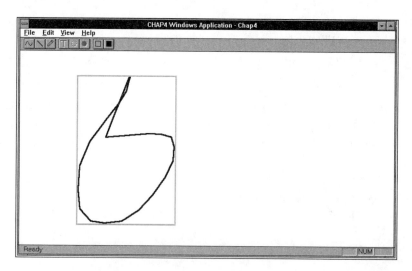

**Figure 13–10** Bounding rectangle for a path

**Listing 13–4** Bounding Rectangle for a Path

```
HRGN hRgn = PathToRegion(hDC);
if (!hRgn)     {     wsprintf(szErrMsg,"PathToRegion  %d",GetLastError());
                          MessageBox(NULL,szErrMsg,"GDI",MB_OK);
}RECT r;
if (!GetRgnBox(hRgn,&r))
{    wsprintf(szErrMsg,"GetRgnBox error %d",GetLastError());
MessageBox(NULL,szErrMsg,"GDI",MB_OK);
     }
SelectObject (hDC, CreatePen (PS_SOLID, 1,
           RGB(192,192,192)));MoveToEx(hDC, r.left, r.top, NULL);
LineTo(hDC, r.right, r.top);
LineTo(hDC,r.right, r.bottom);
LineTo(hDC,r.left, r.bottom);
LineTo(hDC,r.left, r.top);
```

If a wide pen is used, WidenPath expands the path by the width of the pen:

```
WidenPath(hdc);
```

This could be used in subsequent calls to PathToRegion for hit-testing:

```
hRgn = PathToRegion(hdc);
bSuccess = PtInRegion(hRgn, Pt.x, Pt.y);
DeleteObject(hRgn);
```

## BeginPath

If you don't save off your path it will remain valid for a particular display context until one of the following calls are made: StrokePath, FillPath, StrokeAndFillPath, PathToRegion or SelectClipPath or another BeginPath at which time the previous path will no longer be valid.

## SelectClipPath

SelectClipPath allows you to select the path as your clipping region. Use TrueType fonts within a path and you can create outlined characters, as in

Figure13–11. Combine this with SelectClipPath and you can shade the characters of your outlined text. Listing13–5 shows an example. The algorithm looks like this:

```
BeginPaint
MakePath
CreateFontIndirect
SelectFont
BeginPath
TextOut
EndPath
SelectClipPath
Fillrect
EndPaint
```

**Figure13–11** Outline characters

You can also shade the background if you desire by using SetBkMode set to OPAQUE. If you choose not to have a background for your outlined characters, you must also call SetBkMode and set the background to transparent, like so:

```
SetBkMode(hdc, TRANSPARENT);
```

**Listing 13–5** Outlined Text

```
// obtain the window's client rectangle
GetClientRect(hwnd, &r);
SetBkMode(hdc, TRANSPARENT);

// bracket begin a path
BeginPath(hdc);

TextOut(hdc, r.left, r.top, "Outline Characters", 4);

// bracket end a path
EndPath(hdc);

// derive a region from that path
SelectClipPath(hdc, RGN_AND);

FillRect(hdc, &r, GetStockObject(GRAY_BRUSH));
```

Unfortunately, GDI doesn't provide the ability to use something like SetROP2 to display and move standard application fonts. In other words, It would be neat for text to be displayed and moved the same way as lines and points, using SetROP2. However, using TrueType fonts, you can place the text in a path bracket. This will generate a GDI path for the text for you. From there, you can retrieve the path as an array of points using GetPath. Then you are able to draw text with the appropriate ROP. For non-TrueType fonts, you probably will have to treat them as bitmap to achieve the same effect.

## ENHANCEMENTS TO BITMAPS

Windows provides two types of bitmaps and there always seems to be a lot of confusion surrounding which format to use, the device-dependent format known as a DDB or the device independent format known as DIB. DDBs are device dependent because they depend upon the particular driver that created them. On the other hand, DIBs are device independent because they have header information, which each driver uses to properly translate bitmap information. In 16-bit Windows, many developers found it easier to dump

DDBs and do all their work with DIBs. However, with the introduction of the of the Client-Server GDI model in Win32, if your application manipulates or redraws bitmaps you should adhere to the following philosophy: If the bitmap is meant to be persistent—that is saved and retrieved from disk—or shared with other applications (via the clipboard), then you must store it as a DIB. Otherwise, you should use DDBs. This means that if you have a DIB on disk, you should read it in and then convert it to a DDB before displaying. DDBs are much faster than DIBs when you are using the Blt functions. This is because each bitmap is private to the client side of your application, and must be sent in a message to the server each time the screen is updated. Therefore, if you convert your DIBs to DDBs, then the device-independent-to-device-dependent conversion only takes place once, instead of each time you cross the client-server boundary.

## Converting a DIB to a DDB

Even though it appears to do so, CreateDIBitmap does not create a device-independent bitmap, but instead creates a device-dependent bitmap from a DIB. On CreateDiBitmap the palette is set to the given color table. The palette may be changed with RealizePalette:

```
HDC hdcBitmap; HBITMAP hBitmap; HBITMAP hBitmapOld;

void MyCreateBitmap (HWND hwnd) {
    BITMAPINFOHEADER bmi;
    HDC hdc;

// Initialize the BITMAPINFOHEADER to create the bitmap.
    bmi.biSize = sizeof (BITMAPINFOHEADER);
    bmi.biWidth = x; // Width of bitmap in pixels
    bmi.biHeight = y; // Height of bitmap in pixels
    bmi.biPlanes = GetDeviceCaps (hdc, PLANES);
    bmi.biBitCount = GetDeviceCaps (hdc, BITSPIXEL) *
                            GetDeviceCaps (hdc, PLANES);
    bmi.biCompression = BI_RGB;
    bmi.biSizeImage = 0;
    bmi.biXPelsPerMeter = 0;
    bmi.biYPelsPerMeter = 0;
    bmi.biClrUsed = 0;
```

**518**

```
    bmi.biClrImportant = 0;

// Get the DC for the Window
    hdc = GetDC (hwnd);

// Create a compatible DC
    hdcBitmap = CreateCompatibleDC (hdc);

// Release the DC to prevent resource problems.
    ReleaseDC (hwnd, hdc);

// Create a DIBitmap.
    hBitmap = CreateDIBitmap (hdcBitmap, &bmi, 0,
        NULL, NULL, DIB_RGB_COLORS);

// Select the bitmap into the memory DC
    hBitmapOld = SelectObject (hdcBitmap, hBitmap);

}/* end of MyCreateBitmap */
Converting DDBs to DIBs
To convert a DDB to DIB, use the GetDIBits function:
int
GetDIBits(HDC hdc,
        HBITMAP hbmp,
        UINT uStartScan,        // first scan line to set
                                // in destination bitmap
        UINT cScanLines;        // number of scan lines
                                // to copy
        LPVOID lpvBits,         // address of array for bitmap
                                // bits
        LPBITMAPINFO lpbi,      // address of structure with
                                // bitmap data
        UINT uUsage);           // RGB or palette index
```

GetDIBits doesn't work directly on a screen DC, so you must create a memory DC first, then use BitBlt to copy the screen image onto the memory DC. Once you have the screen image into a memory DC, you can use GetDIBits on the memory image:

```
hBitmap = CreateCompatibleBitmap (hdc, width, height);
hdcTmp = CreateCompatibleDC (hdc);
SelectObject (hdcTmp, hBitmap);
However, the order in which you call CreateCompatibleBitmap and
CreateCompatibleDC is important. For example, don't accidentally do this:
hdcTmp = CreateCompatibleDC (hdc);
hBitmap = CreateCompatibleBitmap (hdcTmp, width, height);
SelectObject (hdcTmp, hBitmap);
```

Because when the hdcTmp DC is created, Windows selects a stock monochrome bitmap into it, by default. CreateCompatibleBitmap then creates a bitmap, compatible with the hdc you passed in—that is, a monochrome bitmap. CreateCompatibleBitmap(hdc), rather than being compatible with the monochrome hdcTmp, creates a bitmap compatible with the screen.

If space is a major concern, you may only want to allocate enough memory required to hold the DIB in compressed mode. If you pass GetDIBits a NULL pointer for the fifth parameter, then the function places the necessary buffer size in the biSizeImage field. Be sure the BITMAPINFO structure has BI_RLE4/8 in the biCompression field when you call GetDIBits the first time.

## NEW BITBLT FUNCTIONS

Table13–1 lists each of the bitmap operation functions and shows what you can do with each of the calls. The Win32 API has two new functions to help you display your bitmaps, PlgBlt and MaskBlt.

**Table13–1** Features of the five standard "blit" calls

| Feature | ROP | mask | stretch | shear |
|---|---|---|---|---|
| PatBlt | x | | | |
| BitBlt | x | | | |
| StretchBlt | x | | x | |
| MaskBlt | x | x | | |
| PlgBlt | | x | x | x |

In the Win16 API, there is no straightforward way to create a single plane bitmap with a transparent background. This means that if you want to display a nonrectangular bitmap you must jump through hoops to make it look transparent. Win32 corrects this deficiency with the new MaskBlt function. MaskBlt lets you use any two arbitrary ROP3 codes and apply them on a pel-by-pel basis using a mask:

```
MaskBlt(hdcTrg,  // handle of target DC
        0,  // x coord, upper-left corner of target rectangle
        0,  // y coord, upper-left corner of target rectangle
        15,  // width of source and target rectangles
        15,  // height of source and target rectangles
        hdcSrc,  // handle of source DC
        0,  // x coord, upper-left corner of source rectangle
        0,  // y coord, upper-left corner of source rectangle
        hbmMask,  // handle of monochrome bit-mask
        0,  // x coord, upper-left corner of mask rectangle
        0,  // y coord, upper-left corner of mask rectangle
        0xAACC0020);  // raster-operation (ROP) code
```

```
static BYTE aBits [] = {0x51, 0x77, 0x10, 0x00,
                        0x57, 0x77, 0x50, 0x00,
                        0x13, 0x77, 0x50, 0x00,
                        0x57, 0x77, 0x50, 0x00,
                        0x51, 0x11, 0x10, 0x00};
HBITMAP hBitmap = CreateBitmap (20, 5, 1, 1, aBits);
HDC hdcMem, hdc;

hdc = BeginPaint (hWnd, &ps);
hdcMem = CreateCompatibleDC (hdc);
SelectObject (hdcMem, hBitmap);
BitBlt (hdc, x, y, 20, 5, hdcMem, 0, 0, SRCCOPY);
```

Use the PlgBlt (Parallelogram blt) to rotate or mirror. PlgBlt also has an optional mask parameter. Here are the parameters:

```
BOOL
PlgBlt(HDC hdcDest,     // handle of destination DC
       LPPOINT lpPoint, // vertices of destination parallelogram
       HDC hdcSrc,      // handle of source DC
       int nXSrc,       // x of upper left corner of source rect.
       int nYSrc,       // y of upper left corner of source rect.
       int nWidth,      // width of source rectangle
       int nHeight,     // height of source rectangle
       HBITMAP hbmMask, // handle of bitmask
       int xMask,       // x of upper left corner of bitmask rect.
       int yMask);      // y of upper left corner of bitmask rect.
```

Figure13–12 shows the output of a bitmap that has had its output altered by PlgBlt.

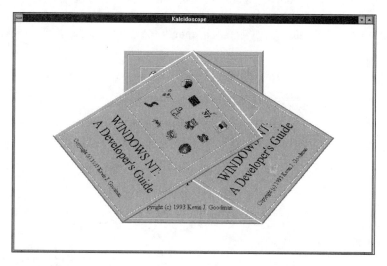

**Figure13–12** PlgBlt with various originating points

You may have noticed that PlgBlt does not take a DWORD ROP code as one of its parameters. If you want a ROP other than SRCCOPY, use BitBlt first, and then use PlgBlt. If during PlgBlt, your mouse cursor disappears, don't panic. This is not a bug in PlgBlt. For example, standard VGA displays seem to have this behavior. If the mouse cursor is implemented entirely at the GDI level, then GDI makes the cursor invisible while it is over the source, during blt operations. This is just an easier implementation than special casing the bits behind the mouse. However, some sophisticated graphics boards include hardware support for the mouse cursor. When GDI informs a driver for such a board that the blt transfer is beginning, the driver can ignore the notification to hide the cursor.

## HALFTONING

Halftoning is a technique first used in the newspaper industry to print gray-scale images. The idea is to produce an image by just varying intensities of a single color (in a newspaper's case, black ink). Monochrome printers have been using this technique for ages to print color images. Windows NT implements color halftoning to help you achieve the same effect for color images on displays. Use halftone for two reasons:

▪▪ When you want to display a bitmap that was created on a device with more bits per pel than the device you're running on.

▪▪ For performance reasons.

If halftoning sounds like dithering, that may be because they are similar. However, there is a subtle difference between halftoning and dithering. GDI (or the driver ) actually makes computations during halftoning to avoid the repetitious patterns that are associated with dithering. This makes halftoning more pleasing to the eye when viewing images and such.

To take advantage of halftoning, set the stretch mode parameter to HALFTONE when calling SetStretchBltMode, like so:

```
int SetStretchBltMode(hdc,HALFTONE;)
```

## ENHANCED METAFILES

Halftoning solves the problem of displaying bitmaps that were originally created on an incompatible display. However, displaying and looking the same are two different things. For example, if you have a bitmap that you created to fill an entire VGA screen, it will only cover about one quarter of a 1024x768 display. Not exactly what you would call device independence. Depending upon what you are displaying, this may be acceptable. However, if the bitmap is your company's logo (perhaps on a splash screen), then you want your name to display front and center on every display (with proper scaling and such). This is where metafiles come in. The idea behind metafiles is that they provide device independence for pictures. Metafiles make it easy to store graphics commands that create text or images (like LineTo and TextOut).

Table 13–2 lists all of the functions that can be stored into a metafile. By creating text or images with GDI commands and then placing the commands in a metafile, your application can re-create the text or images on other device contexts.

**Table 13–2** Functions that Metafiles Can Record

| AnimatePalette | OffsetViewportOrg | SetBkMode |
|---|---|---|
| Arc | OffsetWindowOrg | SetDIBitsToDevice |
| BitBlt | PatBlt | SetMapMode |
| Chord | Pie | SetMapperFlags |
| CreateBrushIndirect | Polygon | SetPixel |
| CreateDIBPatternBrush | Polyline | SetPolyFillMode |
| CreateFontIndirect | PolyPolygon | SetROP2 |
| CreatePatternBrush | RealizePalette | SetStretchBltMode |
| Ellipse | RestoreDC | SetTextColor |
| Escape | RoundRect | SetTextJustification |
| ExcludeClipRect | SaveDC | SetViewportExt |
| ExtTextOut | ScaleViewportExt | SetViewportOrg |
| FloodFill | ScaleWindowExt | SetWindowExt |
| IntersectClipRect | SelectClipRgn | SetWindowOrg |
| LineTo | SelectObject | StretchBlt |
| MoveToEx | SelectPalette | StretchDIBits |
| OffsetClipRgn | SetBkColor | TextOut |
| | SetMapMode | |
| | SetWindowExtEx | |
| | SetViewportExtEx | |
| | SetViewportOrgEx | |
| | PolyBezier | |
| | PolyBezierTo | |

**524**

Win16 also supports metafiles, but they aren't truly device independent. Win16 metafiles, which I'll start calling 16-bit metafiles, also do not support the new GDI paths and curves discussed in this chapter. To remedy this, Win32 provides a revamped 32-bit metafile format called the enhanced metafile format. Enhanced metafiles make it easier to provide device and configuration independence across platforms. Unfortunately, the CMetaFile class that ships with MFC 2.0 only supports 16-bit metafiles.

To create an enhance metafile call the new CreateEnhMetaFile function:

```
HDC
CreateEnhMetaFile(HDC hdcRef,              // handle of a reference DC
                  LPCTSTR lpFilename,      // filename string
                  CONST RECT * lpRect,
                  LPCTSTR lpDescription);  // description
```

Like 16-bit metafiles, CreateEnhMetaFile returns a handle to DC that you use to "record" into the enhanced metafile. Enhanced metafiles can be both disk-based and memory-based. To create a memory-based metafile, set the second parameter, lpFilename, to NULL. In Windows 3.1, it is necessary to have memory-based metafiles because disk-based metafiles are extremely slow to load and playback. However, as a consequence of this fact, it is a pain to convert 16-bit memory metafiles to 16-bit disk-based metafiles. Due to a new feature in Windows NT called memory-mapped files, the image of both disk-based and memory-based enhanced metafiles is identical. Although Chapters 9 and 10 delve into mapped files in greater detail, a mapped file is basically a file's contents mapped to a process's virtual address space. This means that you don't have to write a separate header, retrieve the metafile bits, and then write them out like you do for 16-bit metafiles. With memory-mapping, there's no longer a performance difference between memory-based and disk-based metafiles. With memory-mapped files you no longer need to call the CopyMetaFile (or in an enhanced metafile's case, CopyEnhMetaFile) function to get the metafile into memory to avoid slow disk accesses while you play back.

Once you have created the metafile, it is simple to start "recording." First, direct the GDI commands you want in the metafile to the device context returned by CreateEnhMetaFile. Once you have completed step one, close the metafile by calling the CloseMetaFile function:

```
HENHMETAFILE CloseEnhMetaFile(HDC hdc);
```

CloseEnhMetaFile returns a HENHMETAFILE, which you pass to other functions to display the image or text contained in the metafile. For example, to play back the entire metafile use the PlayMetaFile function:

```
BOOL
PlayEnhMetaFile(HDC hdc,              // handle of a device context
                HENHMETAFILE hemf,    // handle returned from
                                      // CloseEnhMetaFile
                CONST RECT * lpRect);
```

Internally, enhanced metafiles are stored as an array of records. The PlayEnhMetaFileRecord function displays the text or image stored in the given enhanced-format metafile record by calling GDI functions in the record:

```
BOOL
PlayEnhMetaFileRecord(HDC hdc,
                      LPHANDLETABLE lpHandletable,
                      CONST ENHMETARECORD * lpEnhMetaRecord,
                      UINT nHandles);
```

The structure that defines a metafile record is the variable-length ENHMETARECORD structure, defined in WINGDI.H:

```
typedef struct tagENHMETARECORD { /* enmr */
    DWORD iType;
    DWORD nSize;
    DWORD dParm[1];
} ENHMETARECORD;
```

The first ENHMETARECORD in an enhanced metafile is always the enhanced-metafile header, also from WINGDI.H:

```
typedef struct tagENHMETAHEADER { /* enmh */
    DWORD iType;
    DWORD nSize;
```

```
        RECTL rclBounds;
        RECTL rclFrame;
        DWORD dSignature;
        DWORD nVersion;
        DWORD nBytes;
        DWORD nRecords;
        WORD  nHandles;
        WORD  sReserved;
        DWORD nDescription;
        DWORD offDescription;
        DWORD nPalEntries;
        SIZEL szlDevice;
        SIZEL szlMillimeters;
    } ENHMETAHEADER;
```

The ENHMETAHEADER record is what enables enhanced metafiles to be truly device independent. It contains information concerning the dimensions of the picture frame in both device units and in .01 millimeter units. It also contains the resolution of the original device, called the reference device, in both pixels and millimeters. It also contains a pointer to an optional text description, which follows the header record.

If you choose to take advantage of the text description when creating your own enhanced metafile, use the new GDIComment function to do so.

```
    BOOL
    GdiComment(HDC hdc;
            UINT cbSize,            // size of text buffer
            CONST BYTE * lpData);   // pointer to buffer
```

## EDITING METAFILES

The one drawback to using metafiles is that they are slow in drawing. One way to speed up the performance of an enhanced metafile is to manually edit the metafile records. Use the EnumEnhMetaFile function to examine individual metafile records:

```
BOOL
EnumEnhMetaFile(HDC hdc,                        // DC handle
                HENHMETAFILE hemf;              // EMF handle
                ENHMFENUMPROC lpEnhMetaFunc;    // callback
                LPVOID lpData;                  // additional data
                CONST RECT * lpRect;            // bounding rect
```

The lpEnhMetaFunc points to your callback function. EnumEnhMetaFile enumerates each ENHMETARECORD and passes it to your callback. The iType variable of ENHMETARECORD contains the type of GDI function that the metafile record represents. In WINGDI.H there are #defines for each iType variable. For example, in a recent enhanced metafile I was editing, I found that almost every other record contained a call to SetROP2(R2_COPYPEN). After examining the other records, I decided to delete the extraneous SetROP2s.

## CHANGING PALETTES

An application that plays back a metafile must realize its palette manually before playback. You might think that if an enhanced metafile contains a record for "realizepalette," that playing the metafile back would automatically allow the metafile to realize whatever palettes it wants to along the way. However, it doesn't work that way. The metafile has to realize its palette, and so does the application that plays back the metafile. The reason is that it would be difficult to include metafiles in a document if they changed palettes in an unmanageable way. So, GDI requires that the application explicitly set up the palette before playing the enhanced metafiles. Therefore, whenever an enhanced metafile record realizes a palette during playback, the system forces the realization to occur as a background palette. If the containing document wants the metafile to show with its best colors, the containing document may choose to realize the same palette in advance in the foreground.

Once in memory, the application can use SetWinMetaFileBits to create an enhanced metafile and/or SetMetaFileBitsEx to create a Windows format metafile.

## IMPROVING GDI DRAWING PERFORMANCE

The Client-Server protection model will dominate most of the graphics performance issues that you have. It is time-consuming for a function to make the jump from the Client-side GDI to the Server side in the Win32 subsystem. Your goal in writing graphics programs is to avoid crossing the Client-Server boundary as much as possible. NT helps you where it can with techniques such as lazy realization and batching of calls on the Client-side. Some of the calls (including some that are not returning Boolean) have already been moved to the Client side.

Following are some suggestions for improving graphics throughput:

▪▪ In 16-bit Windows it is very common to create an object, select an object, use the object, select the former object, destroy the original object, and so on. The following sample illustrates what I mean:

```
SelectObject(hdc, GetStockObject(BLACK_PEN));
    .
    .
    .
SelectObject(hdc, CreatePen (PS_DASH, 1, RGB(192,192,192)));
    .
    .
    .
DeleteObject(SelectObject(hdc, GetStockObject(BLACK_PEN)));
    .
    .
    .
DeleteObject(SelectObject(hdc, CreatePen (PS_DOT, 1,
                               RGB(192,192,192))));
```

▪▪ When you create brushes, pens, or fonts in Win32, they aren't realized until actually needed. So the proper procedure is to create, create, create, and then select and use; select and use:

```
HPEN hPenDash = CreatePen (PS_DASH, 1, RGB(192,192,192));
HPEN hPenDot = CreatePen (PS_DOT, 1, RGB(192,192,192));
HGIDOBJ hBlackPen = GetStockObject(BLACK_PEN);

HGDIOBJ hOld = SelectObject(hdc, hBlackPen);
    .
```

```
       .
       .
SelectObject(hdc, hPenDash);
       .

       .

       .
SelectObject(hdc, hBlackPen);
       .

       .

       .
SelectObject(hdc,hPenDot);
       .

       .

       .
SelectObject(hdc, hOld);//can't delete selected object
DeleteObject(hPenDash);
DeleteObject(hPenDot);
```

■ For each DC, attempt to use the same attributes in a row as much as possible. For example, instead of red, black, gray, black, red, gray, use the following: gray, gray, gray, black, black, red, red. This avoids the cache lookup for all pens, fonts, colors, palettes, and brushes.

■ Use the Polyxxx functions as much as possible: PolyLineTo, PolyPolyLine, and PolyDraw are much faster than multiple MoveToExs, LineTos, and PolyBeziers.

■ Use OwnDC whenever possible. This avoids the need for GetDC and ReleaseDC.Can CreateWindow, GetOwnDC, and proceed.

■ Avoid GDI calls that return the previous current position if you don't need it. For instance, MoveToEx with the last parameter equal to NULL is faster than MoveToEx that requires the previous location.

■ Use one Win32 call instead of two. Whenever you can call a Win32 function that does the work of two functions, do so. For example, StrokeAndFillPath is faster than StrokePath and FillPath. Don't bother calling CloseFigure if you are planning on calling a function that closes a figure for you.

■ StetchBlt with the halftone mode set is usually faster than other blit functions.

Minimize device access whenever possible. For instance, if possible, draw on a memory DC instead of drawing directly to the screen DC. Only redraw the modified portions of a bitmap image instead of bitting the entire image. If your bitmap exceeds the client area only update the visible portions.

If you are also a Win16 developer, you may already be performing some of these optimizations. But, if you have five gazillion lines of code and you want it to be portable between Win32 and Win16, some of these techniques aren't viable. Especially if you plan on keeping more than five DCs cached in Win32. For situations like this, NT provides batching. As I stated in Chapter 1, to enhance performance, GDI32.DLL queues all GDI calls that return a BOOL. When your program reaches a certain number, known as the batch limit, the GDI calls are turned over to the Win32 subsystem for processing. When this happens just one message is sent to the server side, instead of a message for each function. The default batch limit is 10, but you can change it with the GDISetBatchLimit function. If you increase the batch limit too high, your output will become choppy. Note, however, that the following calls cause an immediate flush of the batch:

▪▪ All USER calls

▪▪ GDI calls that return a handle or a number

▪▪ Selecting bitmaps and regions flush

▪▪ SetWorldTransform and SetMapMode flush

▪▪ GDIFlush

However, selecting fonts, brushes, and pens does not cause a flush.

Batching is not always desirable because the screen does not update immediately when you make a GDI call. This is the result of not reaching the batch limit. If this behavior is unacceptable, either strategically place calls that will cause GDI to flush the batch or explicitly call

GDIFlush; GDIFlush flushes all of the calls so they execute immediately, instead of waiting for the batch limit. To turn batching off, call GdiSetBatchLimit with the batch limit set to one.

Another reason to disable batching is if you want to see error return values. When you call a GDI function that returns a BOOL and batching is enabled, the function returns TRUE to indicate it is in the batch. When the system flushes the current batch and executes the function for the second time, the return value is either TRUE or FALSE, depending on whether the function succeeds. This second return value is reported only if GdiFlush is used to flush the batch.

The third reason to disable batching is if you want to profile individual API calls. If you are trying to decide which GDI calls are optimal you must run them one at a time to profile them.

## GDI BATCHES ARE THREAD-SPECIFIC

The Client side GDI maintains, for each thread that you maintain, its own batch. The other aspect of GDI programming in a multithreaded environment is the sharing of GDI objects (such as DCs). GDI objects are different from other objects in Win32. For performance reasons you cannot name GDI objects, assign a security descriptor, or use the WaitforxxObjects APIs. Whether you are using MFC or not, you must take care to make sure that no two threads are accessing the same GDI object at the same time. A good rule of thumb is to treat GDI objects the same as other persistent objects. It is fine to use GDI objects in different DCs in separate threads, just not the same DC. If you are making GDI calls in a multiple thread with the same DC, serialize access to the GDI objects by using a mutex or a critical section. Before releasing ownership, ensure that the batch is flushed (using any method outlined above). If you don't do this, another thread can tromp on your DC.

## SUMMARY

Although GDI has been given a much needed face-lift, it is not perfect. For one thing, you have the potential to lose significant precision when using paths in Win32. When using the ISOTROPIC mapping mode, as well as world transforms, paths are stored in device coordinates, there is a large potential for loss of precision. As I stated earlier, there is no way to control the text display with ROP codes (short of drawing the text into a path and drawing the path using ROP code). Perhaps in a future release Microsoft could implement text drawing to use a pen and brush like the other GDI objects, instead of having a single API call to set the color.

**CHAPTER 14**

# WIN 32s

Win32s is the subset of the Win32 API that allows Win32 applications to execute directly on 16-bit Windows (such as Windows 3.1 or Windows for Workgroups). When running on 16-bit Windows, a Win32 application is a true 32-bit application. If you are currently programming for 16-bit Windows, the thought of jumping cold-turkey to 32-bit Windows may scare you. Or, let's say you already have a 32-bit application (say in UNIX or OS/2) and would like to tap the lucrative Windows 3.1 market, but find porting to 16-bits prohibitive. Maybe your dreadful marketing department doesn't believe there's a market yet for 32-bit Windows applications. Or perhaps you want to switch to 32-bits, but not all at once. If so, Win32s is your answer.

Win32s is also the term frequently used to describe the set of executables and drivers necessary to run Win32 programs on Windows 3.1, as in "Did you install Win32s yet?" These executables and drivers are an extension of the Windows 3.1 operating environment. The nice thing about Win32s is you don't have to do anything special to get your Win32 application to run. Once you have developed your application under NT, all you have to do is install the

Win32s binaries on Windows 3.1 and your Win32 application is ready to run. No additional compiler switches or linker commands are necessary. All Win32 programs compiled on an x86 machine are automatically Win32s programs.

As long as you install Win32s properly, all you have to do is run your program. It's important to note that all of the Win32 API functions are exported, but since Win32s is just a "subset" of Win32, some calls fail and *GetLastError* returns *ERROR_CALL_NOT_IMPLEMENTED*. Other functions return TRUE when in reality it doesn't mean anything. Instead of failing, some functions, such as *EnterCriticalSection*, return TRUE even though Win32s doesn't support Critical Sections. This is because, in a cooperative-multitasking operating system such as Windows 3.1, the application that is executing always controls the critical section. Like Windows 95, Win32s doesn't support UNICODE. However, both Windows 95 and Win32s support the functions to deal with UNICODE characters, *WideCharToMultiByte* and *MultiByteToWideChar*. This is for developers who want to create menus on the fly. The function *LoadMenuIndirect* requires wide character strings in the *MENUITEMTEMPLATE* structure.

```
typedef struct {     /* mit */
    WORD mtOption;
    WORD mtID;
    WCHAR mtString[1]; // UNICODE strings
} MENUITEMTEMPLATE;
```

Win32s does not support UNICODE because the underlying operating system (Windows 3.1) does not support UNICODE.

# HOW WIN32S WORKS

One normally doesn't develop an application specifically for Win32s. Win32s is a by-product of developing for Win32. Microsoft's strategy is to use Win32s as a stepping stone to NT. Win32s opens up the lucrative Win16 market to vendors who are porting their applications to Win32 from environments other than Windows (UNIX, for example). Many of these vendors have avoided the Win16 market because it has been too hard to port their 32-bit applications back "down" to 16-bits. Many UNIX developers feel that life is too short to deal with segmented memory. In addition, now that this 32-bit API is available for Windows 3.1 (one that is portable to NT and Windows 95), some Win16 developers may consider porting 3.1 code just to get it to work under Win32s. This chapter sorts out the myriad of options the Win32 developer has, and also explains how they work and how to take advantage of each of them.

Using a combination of EXEs, DLLs, and a virtual device driver, Win32s manages to "shoehorn" a 32-bit executable into the 16-bit operating system and gets it to "talk" to all of the 16-bit system DLLs (including USER.EXE, KERNEL.EXE, GDI.EXE, SHELL.DLL). In Win16, the way to create a process is via the *LoadModule* function. You may not have realized it, but functions such as *ShellExecute, WinExec,* and the protected mode Int 21h function 4B are all just wrappers around *LoadModule* (protected mode Int 21h 4B is actually intercepted by Windows and then passed to *LoadModule*). Since it shipped in April 1992, Windows 3.1 has been awaiting Win32s. The designers of Windows 3.1 added hooks to many functions to support Win32s, including *LoadModule. LoadModule* now contains code similar to this:

```
if ((hModule = LoadLibrary("W32SYS.DLL")) > 32)

    GetProcAddress(hModule, "ExecPE")
```

W32SYS.DLL is one of the DLLs that ships with Win32s. Without Win32s, Windows 3.1 cannot execute Win32 programs because they have an incompatible file format. This new format is the Portable Executable (PE) file. Now, if an attempt to execute a program fails due to *ERROR_BAD_FORMAT, LoadModule* makes a call to determine if the program that you are attempting to run has a PE file format. If the *IsPeFormat* function returns TRUE, *LoadModule* executes a PE loader program instead. This loader program, WIN32S.EXE, receives the name of the original Win32 program to run as a command-line parameter. So when you run FREECELL in Windows 3.1, the LoadModule function does the following:

1. Attempts to execute FREECELL.EXE and recognizes this program as a non-Windows 3.1 application.

2. Checks to see if the file format is the PE format.

3. Calls the *ExecPE* function.

4. Calls, thanks to the *ExecPE* function, WIN32S.EXE with FREECELL.EXE on the command line, as for example WIN32S.EXE C:\\WIN32APP\\FREECELL.EXE.

## WIN32S.EXE: CREATING A TASK DATABASE

Win32s.exe is a 16-bit Windows 3.1 program. During the load process of all Win16 programs, Windows creates a task database for each task. Win32s.exe, not Windows, is responsible for creating a task database for all Win32 programs. When you execute Win32s.exe, it parses its command line parameters and reads the executable file into memory. It then creates the task database and modifies the task queue for the application by calling the *BootTask* function in W32SYS.DLL. As long as a Win32s task is active, Win32s.exe stays in memory. For each additional Win32s application you execute, it is as if you executed "Win32s.exe {filename.exe}". It is important to note that if you call *LoadModule* directly, you cannot spawn a Win32s program unless you use the "Win32s.EXE {filename}" convention. Once in memory, Windows 3.1 thinks the Win32 process is another 3.1 task. The difference is that the Win32 task is running in 32-bit mode. Most of it, that is. Remember, your 32-bit application is now sitting on top of a 16-bit operating system.

## THUNKS FOR TRANSLATING BETWEEN 16- AND 32-BIT MODULES

Getting a 32-bit application to load is just half the battle. The other half involves taking advantage of 32-bit code while running on, and using, the services of a 16-bit operating system. Win32s uses *thunks* to implement this. A thunk is the name given to the translation that takes place between 16- and 32-bit modes. Table 14–1 lists all of the Win32s files and the 16-bit DLLs that each Win32s DLL is thunked to. Most of the thunking is transparent to you, however. Chapter 3, "Thunking," explains how to use the technique called Universal Thunks that enable you to create your own 32- to 16-bit thunking layer. This thunking layer enables your 32-bit program to call 16-bit DLLs.

The following thunk takes place when each Win32 API call is made:

1. Win32s translates pointers from linear to segmented

2. Win32s switches to a 16-bit stack

3. Win32s modifies parameters on the stack (truncating if necessary)

4. Win32s jumps from 32- to 16-bit code

5. Win32s creates an exception frame around the call to 16-bit code to handle errors (exceptions) in 16-bit code

## FILES THAT MAKE UP THE WIN32S SYSTEM

The files in Table 14–1 make up the Win32s system. Many of the files in the table have Win32 equivalents with the same name. This is one of the reasons why Win32s refuses to install when it detects it is running under Windows 95 or NT. Besides the obvious reason that if you have 32-bit Windows you don't need to install Win32s, overwriting the NT or Windows 95 version of KERNEL32.DLL with the Win32s version would be disastrous. Here is the algorithm used to determine which system is loaded. In a nutshell, find out if you're in NT. If not then if the major version is < 4, then you're on Win32s; otherwise, you're on Windows 95.

This sample shows how to check for the operating system; it works for both Win16 and Win32 applications. For Win32 processes, it can tell if the system is Windows NT, Win32s, or Windows 95. For Win16 processes, it distinguishes between Windows 95, Windows 3.1, and Windows on Windows NT (WOW).

```
#ifdef WIN32    // Win32 code here:

    // Windows NT — High bit is clear
    // Win32s     — High bit is set, version less than 4.00
    // Chicago    — High bit is set, version is 4.00

DWORD dwVersion = GetVersion();

if (dwVersion < 0x80000000)
   {
```

```
        // Windows NT.
        }
    else if (LOBYTE(LOWORD(dwVersion)) < 4)
        {
        // Win32s
        }
    else
        {
        // Chicago
        }

#else   // Win16 code here:

#ifndef WF_WINNT
#define WF_WINNT  0x4000     // New flag for GetWinFlags
#endif

    // Windows 3.1            — Version = 3.10
    // Windows on Windows NT  — Version = 3.10, WF_WINNT set
    // Windows 95               — Version = 3.95

    DWORD dwVersion = GetVersion();
    WORD  wWinVer   = LOWORD(dwVersion);

    // Swap high and low bytes before comparison
    wWinVer = wWinVer << 8 | wWinVer >> 8;

    if (wWinVer == 0x035F)
        {
        // Chicago
        }
    else if (wWinVer == 0x030A)
        {
        // Windows 3.1 or Windows on Windows NT (WOW)
        if (GetWinFlags() & WF_WINNT)
            {
            // Windows on Windows NT (WOW)
            }
```

```
        else
          {
          // Windows 3.1
          }
        }
  #endif
```

If you swap the high and low bytes of the Windows version, you'll find that GetVersion returns 0x030A (3.10) for Windows 3.1 and 0x035F (3.95) for Windows 95. Why return 3.95? Why not return 4.0? During the BETA period for Windows 95, Microsoft found that more existing applications run 3.95 than 4.00. Quite a few applications do not swap the high and low bytes of the Windows version before comparing with the expected Windows version. In other words they use an algorithm like this:

```
  if ( (LOWORD(GetVersion) >= 0x0A03)
        // Running on at least Windows 3.1  !! Wrong !!
```

This fails on Windows 95 if GetVersion returns 4.00 because 0x0004 is less than 0x0A03.

**Table 14-1** The "Parts" of Win32s

| File | Description |
| --- | --- |
| W32s.386 | A virtual device driver (VxD) that uses the PageAllocate VxD memory management services to allocate memory. W32s.386 does not use DPMI (DOS Protected Mode Interface) as many people believe. |
| Win32s.exe | The 32-bit loader for Win32s. WIN32S.EXE loads the 32-bit application into memory and creates a Windows 3.1 task. |
| KERNEL32.DLL USER32.DLL GDI32.DLL | These DLLs translate the 32-bit calls and map them to their 16-bit equivalents in KERNEL.EXE, USER.EXE, and GDI.EXE. During this translation, Win32s programs concur the most overhead. This also explains why Win32s have some of the same limitations as Windows 3.1 programs. For example, Win32s edit controls and list boxes are limited to 32KB and 64KB respectively, because that is a limitation of Windows 3.1. |
| lz32.dll | The 32-bit equivalent of lzexpand.dll. |

**539**

**Table 14–1** (continued)

| File | Description |
|------|-------------|
| olecli32.dll | The 32-bit equivalent of oleclient.dll. |
| olesvr32.dll | The 32-bit equivalent of oleserver.dll. |
| shell32.dll | The 32-bit equivalent of shell.dll. |
| advapi32.dll | This file is new in Win32 and has no corresponding Win16 file. It is included in Win32s strictly for compatibility reasons. The majority of the functions exported have to do with the Registry and security. |
| comdlg32.dll | The 32-bit equivalent of commdlg.dll. |
| crtdll.dll | This file has no equivalent in Windows 3.1. It contains C-runtime library functions. |
| ntdll.dll | This file has no equivalent in Windows 3.1. It contains NT-specific calls that Microsoft has not yet documented. |
| version.dll | The 32-bit equivalent of ver.dll. |
| w32sem87.dll | The 32-bit equivalent of win87em.dll. |
| w32skrnl.dll | A "helper" DLL for WIN32S.EXE. The *ExecPE* function is in this DLL. |
| winspool.drv | The 32-bit driver for printing that thunks to the 16-bit printer driver. |
| WIN32S16.DLL | A "helper" DLL that handles all of the translations from 32-bit flat memory to 16-bit segmented memory and vice versa. WIN32S16.DLL is the home of *UTSelectorOffsetToLinear* and *UTLinearToSelectorOffset*. |

Without Win32s, Windows 3.1 is unable to extract resources from a PE file. If a call such as *ExtractIcon* fails and Win32s is loaded, SHELL.DLL (where *ExtractIcon* resides) calls a function in one of the helper DLLs to load the resource. This is how Program Manager is capable of displaying a Win32 program's icon.

# DETERMINING WHEN WIN32S IS APPROPRIATE FOR AN APPLICATION

There are specific times when Win32s makes sense for an application:

■ When the Win32 application only uses the subset of API calls that are in Win32s

■ When the application has mathematical calculations that would benefit from 32-bits

■ When the application is memory-intensive

If you are currently shipping a Windows 3.1 application, the decision to support Win32s is the same as the decision to go to Win32.

Win32s is not right for every installation. There are many times when Win32s is not appropriate. The following sections explain when to use either Win16 or Win32 instead of developing an application to take advantage of Win32s.

## USING WIN16 INSTEAD OF WIN32S

Your application must be a Win16 application if your customers have or require support for the following:

■ *Standard Mode.* Since Win32s depends upon W32s.386, it requires the 386 Enhanced Mode of Windows 3.1. No 32-bit applications run in Standard Mode.

■ *Windows 3.0.* Believe it or not, some MIS shops out there are still using Windows 3.0. Win32s does not support Windows 3.0. It would be nice if Win32s was the final nail in the Windows 3.0 coffin, but don't count on it. One MIS manager told me that his three-person department was dutifully upgrading the entire corporation to 3.1 from 3.0. He estimated they could upgrade all 1700 machines in a year and a half!

■ *Floating point without a coprocessor.* Without a coprocessor, a Win32 application that makes heavy use of floating point operations executes slower under Win32s than an equivalent Win16 program. However, on machines that do contain a coprocessor, Win32s is faster than Win16 code running on the same machine. Also, due to the thunking layer, any Win32 application that is extremely kernel-intensive may run slower on Win32s than an equivalent 16-bit version. This is due to the constant thunking that takes place between KERNEL32.DLL and KERNEL.EXE

## USING WIN32 INSTEAD OF WIN32S

Your application will have to forego the Win32s environment if it requires the following:

■■ *Multiple threads.* If there is no way your application can survive without multiple threads or preemptive multitasking, Win32 only is the way to go.

■■ *NT-specific features.* If you are developing a Win32 application to specifically take advantage of features provided only in NT such as Security, OpenGL, 32-bit World coordinates, or NT and Windows 95 such as Console, Registry, RPC servers, and so on, then Win32s doesn't make sense for your application.

## COEXISTING WITH WIN16 APPLICATIONS

If you develop your application under 32-bit Windows and initially run it in Windows 95 or NT, it is easy to forget that the underlying operating system for a Win32s application is not *32-bit Windows.* Therefore, the following suggestions will help your Win32s application coexist with other Win16 applications and Windows 3.1:

*Remember to yield.* Windows 3.1 is non-preemptive. You must voluntarily give up your time slice or other applications will freeze (remember the Terminator from the Introduction.)

There is a limit of five cached DC's (same as in Windows 3.1). If you call GetDC , remember to call ReleaseDC before yielding. Also, don't delete pens or brushes when they are still selected. Like in Windows 3.1, this will orphan those objects and slowly eat up system resources. In Windows 95 or NT this can't happen because the DeleteObject call will fail if the object is still selected.

Like Windows 95, Windows 3.1 has a 16-bit coordinate system, therefore Win32s applications must stay in this range. This shouldn't be a big deal if you also plan to support Windows 95.

Applications the run on Windows 3.1 have a limit of 128 bytes for their command lines. This includes Win32s applications.

**542**

You cannot use EM_SETHANDLE and EM_GETHANDLE for Win32s applications. If you are not familiar with these messages they allow you to share memory handles between you application and an edit control. Since the underlying edit control of a Win32s application is 16-bits, there is no way to share data with your 32-bit memory

The Sleep is useless in Win32s. All it does is call Yield which will only yield if your application has no messages in its queue. If you need to remain dormant for a specific period of time try this:

Like Windows 95, a Win32s application that calls DeleteFile on an open file will succeed (it fails in NT).

*Don't depend upon specific memory locations.* One of the parameters to the *VirtualAlloc* function allows you to specify a virtual address. In NT, the virtual addresses of all user mode processes are in the lower 2GB of memory. WIN32s runs on top of the Windows 3.1 memory manager and virtual memory system and relies on Windows 3.1 for memory management. Windows 3.1 allocates memory where the resulting linear addresses can be either above or below the 2GB boundary. WIN32s simply asks Windows 3.1 for memory and WIN32s returns the address to your application. Win16 applications are ignorant of the linear address because Win16 applications reference memory via selectors. Therefore, the ability to specify an initial address from *VirtualAlloc* is not conducive to portable programs.

Use *SetHandleCount* to increase file handles. In Windows 3.1, a Win32 program has only 15 file handles free. Originally there are 20 minus stdin, out, err, prn, and aux. The *SetHandleCount* function sets the number of available file handles for the calling process. The range is from 20 to 255. When using *CreateFile* under NT, you are only limited by available memory, thus *SetHandleCount* is unnecessary.

Use SetMessageQueue to increase the default message queue. Windows 3.1 has a default message queue size of eight. In Windows 95 and NT, the queue grows dynamically.

*Determining a Win32s application from a Win16 program.* According to *Undocumented Windows,* offset 0x16 in a Windows 3.1 task database is a word containing the task flags. A *Win32s App* will have a value of 0x10 in this field. The following function, IsWin32sApp, accesses the undocumented task structure and returns the value at offset 0x16. Of course, this function is not portable to NT.

```
WORD WINAPI IsWin32sAPP(HANDLE hTask)
{
 ASSERT(IsTask(hTask));
 if ((*((WORD far *) MK_FP(hTask, 0x16))) == 0x10)
    return TRUE;
 else return FALSE;
}
```

## NOTIFYREGISTER AND WIN32S

*NotifyRegister* is a function exported from the Win16 TOOLHELP.DLL. *NotifyRegister* installs what is known as a "notification handler" that will call your callback based on certain events. One of these events is the starting of tasks (NFY_STARTTASK). Because Win32s requires the PE loader for Win32 executables, the results of *NotifyRegister* can get confusing. Instead of passing the name of the Win32 executable that is starting, *NotifyRegister* gives you the name of the PE loader, Win32s.exe.

Suppose you wanted to keep a record of all programs executed by Windows 3.1. The following code snippet shows how to modify a *NotifyRegister* callback to report Win32 executables correctly. This callback is 16-bit code that is meant to be incorporated into a Win16 program. I will show you ways to duplicate *NotifyRegister* functionality in Win32 next. This callback makes use of the Win16 API function, *GetCurrentPDB*. This is the method used to retrieve a Win16 executable's command line parameters. In Win32, this function is obsolete. To retrieve the command line in a Win32 program you would call *GetCommandLine:*

```
BOOL CALLBACK _export
NotifyHandler(WORD wID, DWORD dwData)
{
GLOBALENTRY ge;
MODULEENTRY me;
  if (wID == NFY_STARTTASK)
    {

    ge.dwSize=sizeof(ge);
```

**544**

```
    if (GlobalEntryHandle(&ge,HIWORD(dwData)) == 0)
        return 01;
    me.dwSize = sizeof(me);
    if (ModuleFindHandle(&me,ge.hOwner) == 0)
        return 01;


    if (_fstrstr((LPSTR)me.szExePath,"WIN32S.EXE") != NULL)
{
static char szApp[256];

//
// Get the command line from the Program Segment Prefix,
// same as you would in DOS. Then copy to the global gszAppName
//
    LPSP lpsp = (LPSP) MAKELP(GetCurrentPDB(), 0);
    lstrcpy((LPSTR)gszAppName,
            (LPSTR)lpsp->pspCommandTail+1);
    }
```

## AN ALTERNATIVE TO NOTIFYREGISTER FOR WIN32

Besides receiving the notification of starting tasks, one of the very useful functions of *NotifyRegister* is the notification of terminating tasks. Receiving notification of a terminating task allows you to simulate modal dialog boxes between two processes.

Let's say you have an application that allows the user to view a readme.txt file. In this case you spawn Notepad to view the text file. *NotifyRegister* is handy in this case because you can install a notification handler to let you know when the user terminates Notepad. This way you can temporarily disable your main window until the user finishes with Notepad, perhaps even calling *MessageBeep* if the user tries to activate you. The method to achieve this in Win32 is much less complex. Simply wait on the object (in this case the HINSTANCE returned by *WinExec*) to go away:

```
IF(ghInstChild = (HINSTANCE)WinExec("notepad.exe", SW_SHOW)) < 32 )
    WaitForSingleObject(ghInstChild, INFINITE);
```

**545**

# DEBUGGING WIN32S APPLICATIONS

Completely debug your Win32 application on NT before attempting to debug it as a Win32s application. After you are satisfied that you have debugged your application fully on NT, then you can move to Windows 3.1 and Win32s. It is imperative that you run the debug version of Windows 3.1. The debug version is only available in the Windows 3.1 SDK (or other products that include the SDK, such as the Profession Edition of Visual C++). Once you have installed the debug version of Windows 3.1, install the debug version of Win32s (it ships with the Win32 SDK and other products such as Visual C++ for NT). You can control the amount of information that Win32s emits via an entry in SYSTEM.INI, [386Enh] section, Win32sDebug, such as

```
[386Enh]
Win32sDebug=flags
```

where *flags* is a hex value determined by any combination of the following flags. (For example, Verbose would be Win32sDebug = 0x00000001.)

Verbose (0x00000001). Displays information about loading, unloading, and exceptions. This is what displayed when I executed ExitWindows:

```
ExecPE: C:\SRC\CHAP8\EXIT\EXITW.EXE
LELDR: Module linked with alignment != 4K (temporary support)
LELDR: Module linked with alignment != 4K (temporary support)
ExecPe: return code = 0
```

Break on fatal exceptions (Ox00000002). If you are debugging your application, this flag causes the debugger to break if an exception occurs.

Break on initialization code (0x00000004). If you are debugging, this flag causes the debugger to break right before DLLs initialize.

Display Win16 APIs (0x00000008). Displays all Win16 APIs as they are called. Here is a dump of the Win16 calls made by FREECELL.EXE (the first 20 or so):

```
GETLANGID
GETSYSTEMDIRECTORY
GETWINDOWSDIRECTORY
```

```
GETDRIVETYPE
GETLANGID
INITRESLOADER
CREATEPEHEADER
SETPFNDISPATCHCB
SETFLATSELECTORS
INITRESLOADER
CREATEPEHEADER
SETPFNUTENTRY
GETVERSION
CREATEIC
GETDEVICECAPS
CREATEPEN
CREATESOLIDBRUSH
DELETEDC
LOADICON
REGISTERCLASS
GETSYSTEMMETRICS
CREATEWINDOWEX
DEFWINDOWPROC
```

Break on SetError (0x00000010). Apparently, several of the flags are so the folks who wrote Win32s can debug Win32s itself. This is the only output I have noticed from setting this flag on:

```
SetError 182 in thread 0x807f9d38
```

Verbose Loader (0x00000020). Another flag useful to someone debugging Win32s. The verbose loader flag produced the following information when I executed FREECELL (this code has been edited for brevity):

```
LdrBoot: load krnl hdr at 0x807e1000
LdrBoot: load Object 0x11a00 bytes at 0x807e2000
THREAD: 4K Krnl Stack bottom at 80809000
LELDR: allocating 0x10000
LELDR: Module C:\WINNT\SYSTEM32\FREECELL.EXE [1] loaded at 0x8080d000
LELDR: obj  1 loaded @ 0x8080e000, 0x    5c00 bytes    FLoadLibRef:
looking for CARDS.dll
```

```
LELDR: allocating 0x2d000
LELDR: Module C:\WINNT\SYSTEM32\CARDS.dll [2] loaded at 0x8081d000
LELDR: obj  1 loaded @ 0x8081e000, 0x    c00 bytes
.text,flags=0x60000020
FLoadLibRef: looking for GDI32.dll
LELDR: allocating 0x8000
LELDR: Module C:\WINDOWS\SYSTEM\win32s\GDI32.dll [3] loaded at
0x8084a000
LELDR: obj  1 loaded @ 0x8084b000, 0x   2400 bytes
.text,flags=0x60000020
LELDR: allocating 0x1c000
LELDR: Module C:\WINDOWS\SYSTEM\win32s\KERNEL32.dll [4] loaded at
0x80852000
LELDR: obj  1 loaded @ 0x80853000, 0x   10e00 bytes
.text,flags=0x60000020
LELDR: allocating 0xd000
LELDR: Module C:\WINDOWS\SYSTEM\win32s\USER32.dll [5] loaded at
0x8086e000
LELDR: obj  1 loaded @ 0x8086f000, 0x   4400 bytes
.text,flags=0x60000020
FLoadLibRef: looking for NTDLL.dll
LELDR: allocating 0x5000
```

Display message (0x00000040) return codes. Use this flag when you want to see the values of messages before and after a thunk. The following was also generated from executing FREECELL. 0x0086 is the window message *WM_NCACTIVATE,* 0x0006 is *WM_ACTIVATE,* and 0x001c is *WM_ACTIVATE_APP.*

```
Msg 0x0086 returns 0x00000001
Msg 0x0086 returns 0x00000001 after xlat
Msg 0x0086 returns 0x00000001
Msg 0x0086 returns 0x00000001 after xlat
Msg 0x0086 returns 0x00000001 after xlat
Msg 0x0006 returns 0x00000000
Msg 0x0006 returns 0x00000000 after xlat
Msg 0x0006 returns 0x00000000
Msg 0x0006 returns 0x00000000 after xlat
Msg 0x0006 returns 0x00000000 after xlat
Msg 0x001c returns 0x00000000
```

```
Msg 0x001c returns 0x00000000 after xlat
Msg 0x001c returns 0x00000000
Msg 0x001c returns 0x00000000 after xlat
Msg 0x001c returns 0x00000000 after xlat
```

Display resource information (0x00000080). This flag displays a variety of information from the NE resource table. Again from FREECELL:

```
ulLanguageID: 409
RESAUX_resources: 10 integer types, 0 named types
Loading resource types (ID) 0x1
Loading resource (ID) 0x4  409, Picked English language.
Setting language 0x409
 - Offset: 0x1A0 - Size: 308
Loading resource types (ID) 0x2
Loading resource (named) 0x4EE  409, Picked English language.
Setting language 0x409
 - Offset: 0x1B8 - Size: 616
Loading resource (named) 0x504  409, Picked English language.
Setting language 0x409
 - Offset: 0x1D0 - Size: 616
```

Display SEH information (0x00000100). Choosing this flag causes Win32s to display information about structured exception handling (SEH). In the following output, Esp is the stack pointer.

```
EspFromTrap: User mode
EspToTrap: User mode
KiDispatchException: code=0xc0000006, PrevMode=1, First chance
EspFromTrap: User mode
EspFromTrap: User mode
EspToTrap: User mode
BackToUser: Flags=0x1000
EspFromTrap: User mode
EspFromTrap: User mode
EspToTrap: User mode
BackToUser: Flags=0x1000
EspFromTrap: User mode
```

This was generated from the following code:

```
try {
    RaiseException(0xc0000006,  /* exception code        */
                   0,           /* continuable exception */
                   0, NULL);    /* no arguments          */
}
finally {

    .
    .
}
```

Display paging information (0x00000200). Another flag useful only if your are debugging Win32s.

Warn about unimplemented functions (0x00000400). Set this flag when you want Win32s to warn you when your Win32 application calls a function outside the subset of calls supported by Win32s. The following message is displayed during the loading of ExitWindows:

```
W32S: Function OpenProcessToken not supported.
```

You also receive notice when an unimplemented window message is sent. For example, if a Win32 application sends a *EM_SCROLLCARET* message to an edit control, the following message appears:

```
UNIMPLEMENTED MESSAGE THUNK: 0x00b7
```

This flag will help if your application runs fine on NT, but fails inexplicably on Win32s. Perhaps you didn't realize that your application required a function outside of the subset.

Break after load completion (0x00002000). Use this flag to give your debugger control immediately after Win32s loads your application.

Trace into VMM in VxD (0x00004000). Enables you to trace into the Virtual Memory Manager while debugging.

Debugger Cohesion.(0x00010000). This flag allows a high-level debugger to coexist with the kernel debugger. If you want to use WDEB386 and WinDbgRm at the same time, you need to turn this switch on.

Disable demand paging (0x80000000). This flag causes all modules to be preloaded, making it easier to set breakpoints.

To view the debug information, you must have either a debugger running (CodeView for Win32s or WinDbgRm) or the Win16 utility, DEBUGWIN.EXE (not to be confused with the Win32 debugger, WinDbg.)

Pick your Win32sDebug flags carefully. If you select too many, you'll get more information than you ever cared to see, and if you pick too few, you'll miss important information and warnings.

Take special care with remote WinDbg because currently it does not support software flow control. Therefore, it is imperative that you have your hardware flow control set up properly. If you don't, you will have problems as the buffers overflow. Remote WinDbg requires 2 machines, the Win32s machine to run the App and WinDbgRm and a Windows NT machine to run WinDbg. Also, make sure that your cable is set up exactly as specified in the Win32s Programmer's Reference.

## DON'T SAY GOOD-BYE TO INT 21H JUST YET

Win32 applications do not directly use the interrupt services of DOS (that is, Int 21h functionality), so the Win32s VxD, W32s.386, has Win32 entries for each Int 21 and various other Int x(BIOS) calls. These Int x equivalents are mapped back to virtualized DOS. This means if you are using a debug package such as WinIce, you can set breakpoints on Int 21 to debug at the assembly language level.

## SUMMARY

If you program your application to the subset of the Win32 API that Win32s supports, you can create applications that run on Windows 3.1 and 32-bit Windows. The key to maintaining compatibility is to not have operating-system dependent code. You should use Win32s as a stepping stone so you can take advantage of both 32-bit Windows and Windows 3.1 with a single executable. In many cases a Win32s application will perform better than an equivalent Win16 application.

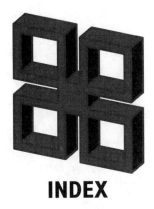

# INDEX

**553**

## USING THE CD-ROM:

The enclosed disk contains the souirce code for all the listings in this book.

### What you need:

Hardware:      A machine capable of running Windows 95 or Windows NT.

Software:      Windows 95 or Windows NT and Visual C++ 2.0 or later.

### To install the software do the following:

**On Windows NT:**

Run SETUP.EXE, located in the root drive of the CD-ROM.

**On Windows 95:**

Through the use of autoplay.inf, the setup program will automatically run when you mount the CD-ROM in the drive.